W9-DEW-057

A LOGIC
BOOK

A LOGIC BOOK

Second Edition

Robert M. Johnson

CASTLETON STATE COLLEGE

WADSWORTH PUBLISHING COMPANY
BELMONT, CALIFORNIA
A DIVISION OF WADSWORTH, INC.

Philosophy Editor: Kenneth King
Editorial Assistant: Cynthia Campbell
Production: Mary Douglas
Interior Designer: Adriane Bosworth
Print Buyer: Martha Branch
Copy Editor: Sheryl Rose
Cover Designer: Albert Burkhardt
Cover Painting: Bill Ramage, *The Fleming Piece,* detail, 1990. An installation of
    chalk and colored tape in the East Gallery of the Robert Hull Fleming Museum,
    University of Vermont in Burlington, Vermont.
Signing Representative: Susan Goerss
Compositor: G&S Typesetters, Inc.

© 1992 by Wadsworth, Inc. All rights reserved. No part of this book may be
reproduced, stored in a retrieval system, or transcribed, in any form or by any
means, without the prior written permission of the publisher, Wadsworth
Publishing Company, Belmont, California 94002.

This book is printed on acid-free paper that meets Environmental Protection
Agency standards for recycled paper.

1 2 3 4 5 6 7 8 9 10—95 94 93 92

Library of Congress Cataloging-in-Publication Data
Johnson, Robert M.
    A logic book / Robert M. Johnson. — 2nd ed.
        p.   cm.
    Includes bibliographical references and index.
    ISBN 0-534-16500-1 : $15.00
    1. Logic.   I. Title.
BC71.J48   1992
160—dc20   91-4078
                                              CIP

To Rebecca

Contents

Categorical Logic Part II   75

CHAPTER 10
Evaluating Extended Arguments   280

Preface

A Logic Book is an introductory text for a first course in logic. It is also suitable as a supplementary text for courses in critical thinking or rhetoric or as an introduction for the reader who seeks a clear and concise survey of logic. This book presupposes no previous training in logic but goes to great pains to make logic understandable and, most importantly, useful. If there is a single motivation for the writing of this book, it is that students will make that discovery, so gratifying to teachers, that the study of logic is both intriguing and worthwhile.

As teachers of logic know, introductory textbooks in logic vary little in subject matter. The majority cover the same material. They differ from one another, when they do, in subtle though perhaps very important fine points of logic, in depth of treatment, in reading level, and teaching approach.

In terms of subject matter, *A Logic Book* is traditional. It covers categorical logic, truth-functional or sentential logic, formal deduction, inductive logic, informal fallacies, and the treatment of extended arguments. In terms of depth, reading level, and pedagogic approach, *A Logic Book* is designed for a typical one-semester (fifteen week), lower-level introductory course. It is written in clear, straightforward language and employs a number of "user friendly" features.

- Each chapter opens with a brief summary of the major concepts or skills presented. New terms and concepts are printed in italic type.

- Each chapter includes an abundance of examples, explanatory charts and diagrams, and sample problems.

- Each chapter is divided into sections with exercise sets.

- Exercises range in difficulty from simple problems designed solely to help students acquire the relevant skills to more complex examples from magazines, newspapers, and literature that will give students practice in the everyday application of the concepts.

- Solutions to selected exercises in the back of the book enable students to study on their own.

- Review questions at the end of each chapter focus attention on central concepts and encourage students to explain them in their own words.

The New Edition

Professors using this new edition of *A Logic Book* will find two basic changes. First, two new chapters are added. Chapter 8 on inductive logic provides explanations and criteria for evaluating inductive generalizations, causal arguments by means of Mill's methods, and inductive arguments from analogy. Chapter 10, the culmination of the book, provides a procedure, with explanations and numerous samples, for evaluating extended arguments.

Second, the book has a new organization:

Chapter 1	Logic, Inference, and Argument
Chapter 2	Deductive Validity
Chapters 3 and 4	Categorical Logic
Chapters 5 and 6	Truth-Functional Logic
Chapter 7	Formal Deduction
Chapter 8	Inductive Logic
Chapter 9	Informal Fallacies
Chapter 10	Evaluating Extended Arguments

Chapters 1 and 2 form the basis of this text and should be read first. They have been pared down to move the reader quickly into a study of formal techniques. In particular, Chapter 1 introduces the student to the important concept of inferential support and, in terms of that, the distinction between deductively valid and inductively strong support. That distinction marks what can be understood as a division between Chapters 3 through 7 on formal techniques for determining deductive validity and Chapters 8 and 9 on inductive strength and informal fallacies.

As with the first edition, the chapters on truth-functional logic and formal deduction do not presuppose a knowledge of categorical logic. It is possible then that professors will choose to omit some or all of categorical logic. Furthermore, professors may move directly to Chapter 8 on inductive logic after a study of Chapters 1 and 2. However, some treatment of formal techniques for determining validity—as provided in either the chapters on categorical or truth-functional logic—and inductive logic is recommended for the chapters on informal fallacies and extended arguments.

Logic teachers will notice some minor deviation from the usual syllabus in the chapters on categorical logic. Omitted are discussions of the distribution of terms, the mood and figure of the syllogism, and the rules of the syllogism. The emphasis instead is on translating into categorical form and using the operations, the traditional square of opposition, and Venn diagrams to evaluate arguments. These are the most portable and practical tools of categorical logic. The choice of topics was guided by one question: What is essential for a one-term course in logic? I answered that question on the basis of extensive experience teaching logic and a conviction that every student of logic should have some idea of both categorical and truth-functional logic.

A final note to teachers. The book preserves the standard language and conventions of logic except in one case. In the sections on truth-functional logic, conjunction is symbolized by a plus sign (+) rather than the more commonly used period (.). I have found the plus sign easier to read on students' papers and on the blackboard.

Many thanks to all those people whose comments were so helpful with the first edition. And particular thanks to those who took the time to let me know what worked well and what needed improvement in the preparation of this second edition: Raymond Frey, Centenary College; Michael McMahon, College of the Canyons; Paul Shepard, El Camino College; Ted Stolze, California State Polytechnic University, Pomona; F. J. O'Toole, California Polytechnic State University, San Luis Obispo; and my good friend Wendell Stephenson, Lewis and Clark College.

Some people I cannot thank enough: my students who over the years taught me that teaching logic is a joy; Castleton State College for her enthusiastic support; Ken King of Wadsworth and Mary Douglas for the pleasure of working with them again; my parents, Myles and Adelaide; Sherry and Brian; Aunt Panda; and specifically Lauren, Karen, and Rebecca for making it their project too.

Robert M. Johnson

CHAPTER ONE
Logic, Inference, and Argument

The purpose of this chapter is to define logic and certain of its basic concepts: statement, inference, and argument. *Logic* is the study of the principles of correct reasoning. A *statement* is any sentence that may be true or false. *Inference* is a movement in thinking in which it is believed that one statement follows from another. An *argument* is a group of statements, one of which is claimed to follow from the others.

1.1 Logic Defined

Logic can be defined as the study of the principles of correct reasoning. Its purpose is to develop a science of reasoning involving the fundamental concepts of *argument, inference, truth, falsity, validity,* and *invalidity,* among others. Logic is enormously important in all areas of human knowledge. It clarifies our thinking and helps us evaluate the reasoning behind the systems of belief and theories that we encounter in life. Logic helps us to understand what our beliefs mean, how to express them clearly, and how they may be supported.

Logic, then, is about reasoning, and reasoning is a kind of thinking. It is a kind of thinking in which we try to solve a problem, make a decision, or determine what is true. It is thinking with a purpose, as opposed to daydreaming or speculating. We may define reasoning as *thinking that aims at a conclusion*. We reason countless times a day. (How often we reason is a matter of dispute, but some philosophers and psychologists believe that we reason subconsciously nearly every waking minute.) It is at least true that we reason so frequently and so naturally that we are often not aware of the logical principles underlying our reasoning. Hence, we make errors and believe or choose what we should not. One advantage of studying logic is the increased awareness of our own reasoning that we gain. Another advantage is, of course, that it enables us to avoid the errors of reasoning that others make or may try to foist upon us.

Reasoning is studied not just in logic but in psychology as well. However, the two disciplines are different in important ways. Psychologists studying reasoning are concerned with how people do in fact reason. They observe people, either individually or in groups, and seek to describe patterns of thinking. Logicians, on the other hand, are concerned not with how people *do* reason but with the principles of reasoning, independent of any individual or group. Logic, unlike psychology, is not dependent upon observations of what people do in fact do. Its purpose is largely to formulate the principles of correct reasoning and to distinguish good from bad reasoning.

Here is an illustration of some simple logical principles that underlie the thinking you should be having while reading this. Logic was defined as the study of reasoning, and reasoning was defined as thinking that aims at a conclusion. Your sense of logic should already tell you that logic must therefore be the study of thinking that aims at a conclusion. Logic is defined in terms of reasoning, and reasoning in terms of thinking. Therefore, logic may also be defined in terms of thinking. The principle at work here is called *transitivity*. Formally, transitivity may be expressed in the following schema: 'If A is B and B is C, then A is C'. Transitivity is one example of a principle of logic.

As a second example, notice that reasoning is defined as a kind of thinking. The definition asserts, in other words, that all reasoning is thinking. Suppose we switch the terms 'reasoning' and 'thinking' to form the new statement 'all thinking is reasoning'. (Switching the terms is called *conversion* and results in a new statement called the *converse*.) Does the statement 'all reasoning is thinking' imply the converse, 'all thinking is reasoning'? We can establish that it does not, simply by using logic.

Suppose we graphically represent the statement 'all reasoning is thinking'. Let a circle be drawn to represent all thinking. Then let another circle representing reasoning be placed so as to show what the statement asserts about their relation. Since the statement asserts that *all* reasoning is thinking, the circle representing reasoning should be placed fully inside the circle representing thinking. But the statement does not assert that reasoning is the same as thinking. Thus, the "reasoning" circle will not be coextensive with the "thinking" circle; it will be a smaller circle inside, as shown here.

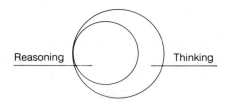

Reasoning   Thinking

The diagram shows what the statement implies. The area outside the "reasoning" circle represents types of thinking that are not reasoning, such as daydreaming.

The above example illustrates the logical principle that any statement of the form 'all A is B' does not imply its converse, 'all B is A'. Make up some examples to test this principle for yourself.

1.2 Statements

A basic element in reasoning is the statement. A *statement* is any sentence or part of a sentence that may be true or false. That is, a statement is an assertion that something is the case or that something is not the case; this assertion may be true or false. For example, these are statements:

Example 1   *Logic is the study of the principles of correct reasoning.*

Example 2   *At least twelve different species of hummingbirds can be found in the United States.*

Example 3   *Being a president is like riding a tiger. (Harry S Truman, Memoirs)*

Example 4   *Charles Dickens wrote* Romeo and Juliet.

Example 5   *That's my book.*

Every statement has a *truth-value;* that is, it has the property of being true or false. In the examples above, the first two are true, the third is arguably true, the fourth is false, and the truth-value of the fifth depends on the context in which it occurs.

Now consider the following examples.

Example 6   *Will you help me?*

Example 7   *Sit down and behave!*

Example 8   *Ouch!*

Example 9   *Let's take the earlier history course.*

Are they true or false? Are they assertions that something is or is not the case? Certainly not. Think how odd it is to say "it is true that Ouch!" or "the speaker asserts that Will you help me? is the case." However, the sentences are not meaningless; we may learn something from them. For instance, usually people who say "Ouch!" are feeling pain and people who make requests, as in examples 6 and 9, want something. So a natural way of thinking about such examples is to distinguish between the words or sentences themselves and what we may infer from them. Thus, while "Ouch!" is not a statement, we can reasonably infer a statement from it, for example, "I feel pain." Similarly, while "Isn't it time you fed the dog?" is not a statement, we can infer the statement "It's time you fed the dog." *In general we can say that questions, exclamations, commands, requests, and the like are not statements but may be the occasion for inferring statements.*

To analyze sentences as suggested above is to go beyond the mere written or spoken words. Analyzing is one example of a very important practice in logic, the practice of paraphrasing, interpreting, or drawing inferences from what we are given. (For more on this, see Chapter 10, section 10.3.) It is making use of information and beliefs we have about human situations and what people usually mean by their words. It is also introducing our interpretation of a person's words, and *to interpret is to risk interpreting incorrectly.* So, as a general practice, it is always wise to use the person's own words as much as possible *and to apply the most plausible interpretation to them.* This is one of the features of doing logic well, one of the virtues of the good logician: to give the other person the benefit of the doubt. In logic we call it the Principle of Charity.

> Principle of charity: *When in doubt, apply the most plausible interpretation.*

You will have occasion to apply the principle of charity in many of the exercises throughout this book. It is worth pausing to consider why one should be charitable with one's opponent. Isn't the purpose of studying logic to help us win arguments? No. We study logic to learn to reason well, not to win at all costs. There are at least two good reasons in support of charity in the use of logic. First, *failure to show charity in logic is a waste of time.* Interpreting a person's words or reasoning unfavorably simply means that the more plausible interpretation is not being addressed. Sooner or later, you will face the issue again.

Second, *failure to show charity is unethical.* It is morally objectionable to take advantage of an opponent's lack of skill in reasoning or communicating. Unfortunately, we all know people who do exactly that, and it is probable that your study of logic will enable you to join them, if you choose. But it is an ill-gotten victory that comes by way of "logic-chopping" bullying or deception. Thus, reasoning well is not just reasoning astutely or efficiently; it is reasoning with fairness and good will.

Thus far we have seen that statements are sentences that have truth-value. We have seen also that we must be aware of the distinction between sentences that are statements and sentences that are not but from which we may infer a statement.

To sharpen our thinking about statements let's consider more complex examples and notice some points, some of which will be more fully developed in later chapters.

First, only part of a grammatically complex sentence may be a statement. In the examples below, notice that it is the underlined part of the sentence that makes a statement.

Example 10   Listen carefully; <u>I heard a noise</u>.

Example 11   Don't be rude but <u>you should be assertive</u>.

Example 12   <u>The choice is clear</u>; make yours at the voting booth.

Second, a sentence may contain more than one assertion, thus more than one statement.

Example 13   Research is a requirement for tenure but most professors would prefer to concentrate solely on teaching.

Example 14   Officials denied reports of a gas leak and encouraged workers to return to the plant.

Examples 13 and 14 are what we can call *compound statements* in that they contain simpler statements. Those examples each consist of two statements and assert that both are the case.

On the other hand, a sentence containing more than one statement may assert that one *or* the other is the case. Consider these examples:

Example 15   Your pain may be caused by inflammation of the surrounding tissue or by the displaced cartilage.

Example 16   The forecast is for overnight fog or patchy clouds.

Third, a sentence containing more than one statement may assert a relationship between the two, that one bears on the other in some way.

Example 17   Max doesn't trust Smith because Smith lied to him.

Example 18   Raising questions helps us clarify our beliefs in that questions force us to reflect.

Example 19   American youth do not appreciate the seriousness of war because they have forgotten the trauma of Vietnam.

Each of those examples is a complex consisting of three assertions. For instance, example 17 asserts that (1) Max doesn't trust Smith, that (2) Smith lied to Max, and that (3) statement (1) is so because of (2). Thus, a complex statement may assert or deny that two or more things are the case, and that one's being so bears on the other.

Consider now a special type of statement called the *conditional*.

Example 20   *If Smith lied to Max, then Max doesn't trust him.*

Example 21   *If America's young people forget Vietnam, then they will not appreciate the seriousness of war.*

These examples express conditional statements. Each asserts that something is the case *on the condition that* something else is the case. Example 20, for instance, does not assert that Smith lied. Neither does it assert that Max does not trust him. Rather it asserts that Max doesn't trust Smith *if* Smith lied to him.

We can summarize what we have seen about statements in the following points:

1. A statement is any sentence or part of a sentence that may be true or false.
2. A statement asserts that something is or is not the case.
3. A statement may contain two or more simpler statements.
4. A statement may assert that something is (or is not) the case *because* something else is (or is not) the case.
5. A conditional statement asserts that something is (or is not) the case *if* something else is (or is not) the case.

Exercise 1.2   Identifying Statements.   Read the sentences and determine which are statements. Draw a line under the sentences or sentence parts that express statements. Make a special note of those you believe to be conditional statements.

1. If you require a broker only to place, buy and sell orders, you can save on commissions by using a discount broker. (J. K. Lasser, *Smart Money Management*)
2. Don't criticize imaginative writing until you fully appreciate what the author has tried to make you experience. (Mortimer Adler, *How to Read A Book*)
3. Deep in the heart of the mountains of Guerrero lies the picturesque village of Olinala. (Chloe Sayer, *The Crafts of Mexico*)
4. It is absurd to divide people into good and bad. People are either charming or tedious. (Oscar Wilde, *Lady Windermere's Fan*)
5. Lead me from the unreal to the real! (The Upanishads)

6. East is east; and west is west . . .

7. The Simiadae then branched off into two great stems, the New World and Old World monkeys; and from the latter at a remote period, man, the wonder and glory of the universe, proceeded. (Charles Darwin, *The Descent of Man*)

8. A man is rich in proportion to the number of things which he can afford to let alone. (Henry David Thoreau, *Walden*)

9. There are two cardinal sins from which all the others spring: impatience and laziness. (Franz Kafka, *Reflections*)

10. O True Believers, take your necessary precautions against your enemies, and either go forth to war in separate parties or go forth all together in a body. (the Koran)

11. Fight for the religion of God. (the Koran)

12. If I am mad then I'm not mad, and if I'm not mad then I'm mad.

13. Let us eat and drink; for tomorrow we shall die. (Isaiah 22:13)

14. No freeman shall be taken, or imprisoned, or outlawed, or exiled, or in any way harmed . . . (the Magna Carta, Clause 39)

15. At two hours after midnight appeared the land, at a distance of two leagues. (Christopher Columbus, *Journal 1492*)

16. The foxes have holes, and the birds of the air have nests; but the Son of man hath not where to lay his head. (Matthew 8:20)

17. Your eyes shall be opened, and ye shall be as gods, knowing good and evil. (Genesis 3:5)

18. The one means that wins the easiest victory over reason: terror and force. (Adolf Hitler, *Mein Kampf*)

19. Rose is a rose is a rose is a rose. (Gertrude Stein, *Sacred Emily*)

20. Let every nation know, whether it wishes us well or ill, that we shall pay any price, bear any burden, meet any hardship, support any friend, oppose any foe to assure the survival and the success of liberty. (John F. Kennedy, 1961 Inaugural Address)

21. Neither a borrower nor a lender be; for loan oft loses both itself and friend . . . (Shakespeare, *Hamlet*)

22. I want to be alone. (Attributed to Greta Garbo)

23. Nice guys finish last. (Attributed to Leo Durocher)

24. Nonviolence is the answer to the crucial political and moral questions of our time. (Martin Luther King, Jr., Nobel Prize address)

25. Macbeth does murder sleep! the innocent sleep, sleep that knits up the ravel'd sleave of care . . . (Shakespeare, *Macbeth*)

26. Candy
   Is dandy
   But liquor
   Is quicker.
   (Ogden Nash, *Many Long Years Ago*)

1.3 Inference

Earlier we encountered the idea of making an inference, as in the case of inferring that a person feels pain from his or her saying "Ouch!" Let us look more closely at the concept of inference.

Making an inference is something people do when they reason that one thing follows from another. For example, seeing shoe prints on the kitchen floor, you infer that someone failed to wipe his or her shoes. What does it mean to infer that "someone didn't wipe" from "there are muddy shoe prints"? It means that you take the sight of the shoeprints *as a reason for* believing that someone didn't wipe. The two statements are not accidentally related as you see the matter. Rather they are logically or, to be precise, *inferentially* related. To make an inference, then, is to reason that one thing is so because of another.

Having said this we can now say that examples 17 through 19 above express inferences. They illustrate that compound statements may assert that one thing's being the case is a reason for another's being the case.

For practice recognizing inferences, look at the examples below. Some are inferences, some are not. Try to identify those examples that express an inference.

Example 22	*The birds are flying south. Winter must be coming on.*
Example 23	*Iris is standing by her dish meowing. She's probably hungry.*
Example 24	*She graduated summa cum laude. She must have studied hard in college.*
Example 25	*If a society has no common moral code, there is little respect for law and order.*
Example 26	*The lights are out and their car is gone. I suspect they aren't at home.*
Example 27	*Raisins are dried grapes. Prunes are dried plums.*
Example 28	*These are some of the symptoms of neurosis: strong guilt feelings, irrational fears, insomnia, and inability to make decisions.*
Example 29	*She goes by the title "Ms." Watkins. I can't infer from that that she is married.*
Example 30	*She's a Leo. She'll be an excellent therapist.*

Example 31   *Brian is an avid bird-watcher. In*
fact, they call him "Big Bird." He's
identified over 450 different species
of birds.

All the examples above contain inferences except 25, 27, 28, and 31. Those examples describe their subjects but do not express a logical movement from one statement to another. In the other examples the speaker asserts an inferential connection between the statements. Again, whenever one idea or statement seems to lead us to another, we make an inference. This concept is essential to the related concept of an argument.

1.4 Argument Defined

Astronomy is the study of the stars. Biology is the study of living things. *Logic is the study of arguments.* Arguments are the subject matter of logic because they are specific instances of reasoning. In logic we study the types of arguments, the meanings or logical implications of arguments, and, most importantly, the criteria for distinguishing good arguments from bad. Ultimately we want to decide which arguments about life we should accept and which we should reject.

In logic arguments have nothing to do with quarrels or fights. Rather, an argument is one distinct piece of reasoning in which a point is expressed and reasons are offered for that point. In that sense whenever someone tries to persuade you to believe something and offers reasons for the belief, that person is giving an argument. Politicians give you reasons why you should vote for them. Salespersons try to convince you to buy their product. Friends offer advice about what you should do. All of these are occasions for arguments. Let us define the term 'argument' precisely.

Argument: *A group of statements, one of which is claimed to follow from the others.*

From this definition notice, first, that an argument consists of at least two statements, one that is claimed to follow, called the *conclusion,* and at least one other, called the *premise,* that is claimed to support the conclusion. More commonly, arguments consist of two or more premises. Second, every argument involves at least one inference—that is, the inference from the premises to the conclusion. Third, arguments involve a claim that one statement follows from the others; that is, arguments purport to show that something is true. We qualify the definition this way because if 'argument' is defined as 'a group of statements, one of which *does follow* from the others', then the only arguments would be good arguments. But obviously not all arguments are good. Thus, the definition must reflect the fact that although all arguments claim that a statement follows from others, only some arguments successfully establish their claim.

Exposing the Argument   To expose an argument is to pick out the conclusion and the premise or premises. This can be difficult, so you have to read the argument carefully and think about what the words mean. With experience your sensitivity to the language and your skill at recognizing the logic of words will improve. Here are some tips at exposing arguments. *Usually it is easier to pick out the conclusion first.* To do so, read the argument and ask yourself, "What does the speaker want to persuade me to believe? What is the main point?" That should help you to identify the conclusion. To identify the premises, ask, "What reasons does the speaker give to persuade me?" Thus, to expose an argument you look for the speaker's main point and his or her reasons.

There are clues one can use to pick out the conclusion and premises of an argument. Certain words in our language may be used to signal conclusions or premises, such as the following:

> *therefore, thus, hence, it follows that, it must be that,*
> *we may conclude that, we may infer that, implies that,*
> *entails that, consequently, so*

Notice how any one of the above *conclusion clues* could fill the blank in this argument:

> *All humans are mortal, Socrates is a human,*
> _____ *Socrates is mortal.*

On the other hand, premises may be signaled by words such as these:

> *since, because, for, for the reason that, in that, due to*
> *the fact that, given that, may be concluded from*

Try each of the above *premise clues* in the blank below.

> *Socrates is mortal,* _____ *all humans are*
> *mortal and Socrates is a human.*

Be aware of the words that typically introduce conclusions and premises, and use them as clues to exposing the argument.

Argument Form   When we examine an argument in logic we can see it more clearly if we write it out in *argument form*. In this format, the premises are listed first, followed by a solid line separating them from the conclusion, listed at the bottom. Each statement is numbered. The form is as follows:

Premise	1. ....
Premise	2. ....
	.
	.
Premise	n ....
Conclusion	n + 1 ....

So, for example, the argument 'All humans are mortal. Socrates is a human; therefore, Socrates is mortal' is written in argument form as follows:

Example 32

1. *All humans are mortal.*

2. *Socrates is a human.*

___

3. *Therefore, Socrates is mortal.*

Here is a more challenging argument as it might appear in print.

Example 33

God does not exist because if he did, there would be no suffering and evil in the world; but obviously suffering and evil do exist. Thus, there is no God.

Exposed and written in argument form, it appears as:

1. *If God existed there would be no suffering and evil in the world.*

2. *But obviously suffering and evil do exist.*

___

3. *Thus, there is no God.*

Whether or not you accept that argument, writing it out in argument form clearly exposes its reasoning. It attempts to persuade you to conclude that there is no God, and it offers as reasons in support of that conclusion the two statements listed as premises. Besides clarifying the argument, writing it in argument form prepares it for evaluation.

___

Exercise 1.4   Recognizing Arguments.   Read the exercises carefully and determine which express arguments and which do not. Expose those that express arguments by writing them out in argument form and numbering the premises and conclusions.

1. Every literature major must take a course in Shakespeare. John has taken the Shakespeare course; therefore, he must be a literature major.

2. All the finalists were flown to Houston. From there they went to Galveston for the banquet and presentation of awards. Jay was a finalist, so he must have gone to Galveston.

3. Events in the Middle East are very discouraging for U.S. interests. Anti-American sentiments, it has been reported, have never been so strong.

4. Any professional can outplay any amateur. Jones is a professional, but he cannot outplay Meyers. It follows that Meyers is not an amateur.

5. If the president dies in office, then the first lady becomes the new president. Since Barbara Bush is the first lady, she will take over if President Bush dies in office.

6. For reasons we don't quite understand, artists are frequently neurotic individuals. The incidence of artistic creativity in conjunction with neurosis is so remarkably high that it is probable that neurosis is a symptom of artistic creativity.

7. If the creationists are right, then the universe was created and has a beginning in time. Now, whatever has a beginning must also have an end. Therefore, if the creationists are right, the universe must have an end as well.

8. Some fruits are sweet. Honey is sweet; so it must be a fruit.

9. A person can't be a marine and a sailor both. Since Max is a sailor, it must be that he is not a marine.

10. If the fever continues into tomorrow, give me a call and I'll drop by on my way home. Now don't hesitate to call.

11. There is freedom in the sense of being able to move as one pleases, freedom in the sense of being able to do and speak as one pleases, and freedom in the sense of being able to think for oneself. This last type makes the others possible. Consequently, it is our most important freedom.

12. Because there has been such an increase in costs and because the potential hazards have not been eliminated, the only sensible thing to do is to defeat the proposal for a nuclear plant in our county.

13. The Mennonites are members of a Protestant sect that originated in Zurich, Switzerland, in about 1525 under the direction of Menno Simons. They first came to the United States in 1663 and are currently found in small communities throughout the Midwest and parts of the East.

14. It is better not to marry for love. Marriage is supposed to last a lifetime, but love never does. And once love is gone you'll need some lasting reason for the marriage. It is therefore better not to marry for love.

15. Computers do not have feelings for the reasons that only living things can have feelings and computers are not living things.

16. You cannot teach people to love something. Philosophy is the love of wisdom; hence, you cannot teach philosophy.

17. You cannot hold a person liable for something he or she did not know about. But you have not shown that your client did not know about the faulty wir-

ing in the house he sold. We can conclude then that your client cannot be excused for damages.

18. We have a duty to protect citizens from crime. Punishment protects society by deterring criminals. Thus, we have a duty to punish criminals.

19. House builders work awfully hard. The workday is often more than eight hours long; there's heavy lifting to do, the possibility of injury, and cranky supervisors; and the weather doesn't always cooperate.

20. Beat an egg and add cornstarch. Heat milk and sugar in saucepan; gradually add egg mixture. Stir until thick. Add vanilla. Top with graham cracker crumbs and chill. Serves six.

21. The mind directly perceives only ideas. Material objects are not ideas. These facts entail that the mind does not directly perceive material objects.

22. Every time a public official opens his mouth someone or some group claims to be offended. People are getting much too sensitive to public statements.

23. Kids should not be put behind bars with adults. Being in jail is frightening enough for kids, but locking them up with adults is inviting tragedy.

24. Dollar for dollar the new Victory is the best car on the road. If you want comfort and economy, make the Victory your family car.

25. Since mice are just smallish rats, it would seem to follow that housecats are just smallish tigers.

26. Every month with thirty-one days except July and December is followed by a month with fewer days. Since August follows July, August does not have fewer than thirty-one days.

27. Why fear death? If there is no afterlife, then at the moment of death we are nothing. If there *is* an afterlife, then at the moment of death we are born into a new life.

28. At last, someone with good sense! You can tell people with good sense by the way they spend their money—on things that last. And you buy to last!

29. The most common large woodpecker in our area is the Red-headed Woodpecker. What I saw was a large woodpecker, so, even though I did not see its head, it probably was a Red-headed Woodpecker.

30. In the event of a tornado the sirens blast, the police drive their cars through the neighborhoods giving warning, and everyone is urged to seek shelter immediately.

1.5 Diagraming Arguments

Another way to expose an argument is to diagram it. A brief introduction will be helpful for now. In Chapter 10 we will see that this method proves to be more versatile than writing out an argument in argument form.

To diagram an argument, first read it through and number each statement in sequence. For example,

Example 34   ① *Webb was promoted to vice-president; therefore,* ② *she will move to Pittsburgh.*

Then draw an arrow from the statement number of the premise to the number for the conclusion as follows.

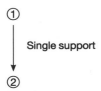

Single support

The diagram shows that statement ① is the only support offered for the conclusion, statement ②.

Example 35   ① *If Webb is promoted to vice-president, then she will move to Pittsburgh.* ② *She's bound to be promoted.* ③ *So, she will be moving to Pittsburgh.*

This argument offers two premises for concluding that ③ 'She will be moving to Pittsburgh'. Notice that statement ① is a conditional asserting that *if* she is promoted, *then* she will move. It does not assert that she *is* promoted; neither does it assert that she will move. Rather, as a conditional, it counts as one complex statement. Second, notice that the premises operate together in support of the conclusion. Premise ① does not provide a reason for ③ without being joined with ②. We will call this kind of support *joint support* and indicate their dependence with the sign '+'.

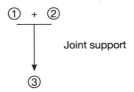

Joint support

On the other hand, consider the structure of this argument.

Example 36   ① *Cats make good pets because* ② *they are affectionate.* ③ *They are clean.* ④ *They are entertaining and* ⑤ *they do well in apartments.*

The conclusion is statement ①. Notice that four distinct premises are offered in support. Further, notice that the premises do not need one another to provide support. We will call this *independent support*.

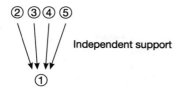

Independent support

How can we tell whether premises offer joint or independent support? Let's say that a premise provides *independent support if it does not need another premise or is not needed by another premise to support the conclusion*. Otherwise it provides joint support along with another premise.

Now consider a structure in which an argument has, in effect, two conclusions. For example,

Example 37   ① *Cats make good pets because* ②
they are affectionate. ③ *They are
clean.* ④ *They are entertaining and*
⑤ *they do well in apartments. So,*
⑥ *if you want a good pet, you
should get a cat.*

Premises ② through ⑤ support the conclusion ① that cats make good pets. From that conclusion it is further concluded that ⑥ if you want a good pet, you should get a cat.

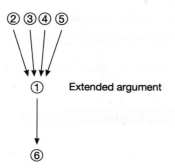

Extended argument

We will call this an *extended argument* because it contains an argument within an argument. Here is another example.

Example 38   ① *Cats make good pets and* ② *cats make good anatomical subjects. Therefore,* ③ *some good pets make good anatomical subjects. Since* ④ *good anatomical subjects are in high demand in medical schools, it follows* ⑤ *that some good pets are in high demand in medical schools.*

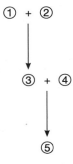

Here we see that premises ① and ② support ③. Statement ③ is then combined with ④ to support the conclusion ⑤.

To summarize this brief introduction to diagramming, recall these points:

1. On your first pass through an argument, number the statements sequentially.
2. Write down the number of the conclusion first.
3. Above the conclusion number write the statement numbers that support it.
4. Indicate independent support by drawing an arrow from each independent premise to the conclusion.
5. Indicate joint support by linking premises with a + and an arrow to the conclusion.
6. An arrow indicates that an inference is being drawn from a statement or statements to a conclusion. Two or more arrows indicate an extended argument.

Exercise 1.5   Diagraming Arguments.   Diagram the following arguments and identify any of the particular structures we have studied: single support, joint support, independent support, or extended argument.

1. All humans are mortal. Socrates is a human. Therefore, Socrates is mortal.

2. There is no reason for fearing death because if there is no afterlife, then at the moment of death we are nothing. Or if there is an afterlife, at the moment of death we are born into new life.

3. House builders work awfully hard. The workday is often more than eight hours long; there's heavy lifting to do, the possibility of injury, and cranky supervisors; and the weather doesn't always cooperate.

4. If interest rates continue to rise, then loans will be harder to obtain. If loans are harder to obtain, then sales will fall. And if sales fall, there will be a production slowdown. Therefore, if interest rates continue to rise, there will be a production slowdown.

5. Since history is a required subject, you should take the course now.

6. Research is a requirement for tenure and is generally more lucrative and often more exciting than teaching. As a result, research has gradually displaced teaching as the principal concern of many faculty members. (Don Wycliff, *New York Times*)

7. Parents are principally responsible for the education and upbringing of their children and are, therefore, the most qualified persons to select the formal schooling for their children. (Letter to the editor)

8. Under the GI Bill we enabled over 9 million people to go to college. Now that the GI Bill is gone, a college education is out of the reach of most young people.

9. The United States spends nearly $2,000 per year per capita on health care. Yet the indicators of national health show that we are getting less for our dollars than countries that spend less per capita. This is the reason why we need to thoroughly reexamine our health care system in the U.S.

10. There is no system of health care delivery in the United States. The word 'system' implies organization and uniformity. What we have is a disorganized and varied complex of competing parties: the federal government, state gov- ‧ ernments, Medicaid, Medicare, HMOs, various insurers, private organizations, and so on.

11. If people want good roads, then they must pay for them. That is the reason why you should support increased highway taxes.

12. In an infinite universe, every point can be regarded as the center, because every point has an infinite number of stars on each side of it. (Stephen Hawking, *A Brief History of Time*)

13. Whenever a solid is heated, its color changes from red to orange, yellow, and then bluish white. Since this change is the same for all solids, it seems that it could be explained without having to know much about the actual structure of any particular solid. Furthermore, it seems reasonable to conclude that there could be a unified theory of radiant energy.

14. Big-time college athletics has nothing to do with education; it is entertainment pure and simple. In our society people who entertain are paid for it. It is about time we began paying college athletes for the entertainment they provide and stop fooling them and ourselves by calling it education.

15. In general the child from a large family makes a better team player. Such a child develops better interpersonal skills because he or she learns to cooperate with others, to share responsibilities, and to see things from the other's viewpoint.

1.6 Good Arguments

We have defined an argument as a group of statements, one of which is claimed to follow, or to put it differently, is *inferred* from the others. In this section we will survey the complex notion of a *good argument*. Identifying good arguments is one of the most important objectives of logic and is, in large part, what the rest of this book is about.

We know that some arguments are good and some are bad but how do we tell the difference? As a beginning, notice that whenever a person offers an argument he or she is implicitly stating that the premises are good reasons for inferring the conclusion. In other words, two claims are presupposed in every argument: (1) that the conclusion *does* follow from the premises and (2) that the premises are true. It is easy to see that if either one of these claims is not the case, the argument has failed. For instance, if a premise is false, as in the example below,

Example 39

1. Cats are invertebrates.
2. Invertebrates are cuddly.

3. Therefore, cats are cuddly.

then the premise has no support to pass to the conclusion. On the other hand, if the conclusion does not follow, then whether or not the premises are true, they do not support the conclusion drawn. For example,

Example 40

1. Physicists are good at mathematics.
2. Engineers are good at mathematics.

3. Therefore, physicists are engineers.

Thus, an argument can be bad for one of two reasons: the conclusion does not follow from the premises or at least one premise is false. A good argument, on the other hand, is one in which the conclusion does follow and the premises are true. Both conditions must be the case for an argument to be good, we will say.

GOOD ARGUMENT =   *(1) the conclusion fol-*
lows from the
premises; and
(2) the premises are
true.

Defining the concept of a good argument in this way enables us to see what concerns us most in logic: the relationship expressed in condition (1), the inference from premises to conclusion. What does it mean to say that "the conclusion follows from the premises"? In logic this means one of two things: either the conclusion follows *necessarily* or the conclusion follows *probably*. This gives us two different notions of a good inference. The first we will call *deductive validity* and the second we will call *inductive strength*. Each of these important concepts is explained thoroughly in later chapters but let's get a sense of their difference. Consider these two arguments:

Example 41

1. *All snakes are poisonous.*
2. *The cobra is a snake.*

_____

3. *Therefore, the cobra is poisonous.*

Example 42

1. *Most snakes are poisonous.*
2. *The cobra is a snake.*

_____

3. *Therefore, the cobra is poisonous.*

Given the premises in example 41, the conclusion *must* follow. That is, if all snakes are poisonous and the cobra is a snake, then it must be that the cobra is poisonous. Here the conclusion is said to follow with deductive validity. In example 42, however, given the premises, the conclusion does not *have* to follow; it could be false. Yet, given that most snakes are poisonous and the cobra is a snake, there is good reason to infer that the cobra also is poisonous. Here the conclusion is *probably* true, given the premises, and the argument is said then to be *inductively strong*.

Compare the above two examples with a third and we see an additional point about inference.

Example 43

1. *Few snakes are poisonous.*
2. *The cobra is a snake.*

_____

3. *The cobra is poisonous.*

The conclusion in example 43 does not *necessarily* follow; furthermore, it does not follow *probably*. Example 43 provides less support for the conclusion than does example 42 since, given that few snakes are poisonous, it is even less likely that the cobra is poisonous. Example 43 is said to be *inductively weak*.

Looking at all three examples and focusing just on the relationships of support, we can see that they compare differently on the *degree* of support each offers the conclusion. If we think of inferential support as a descending scale of strength from the strongest to the weakest, we can see that these three examples rest at different places on that scale ranging from logical certainty—as is the case with deductive validity—through degrees of inductive strength to inductive weakness.

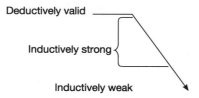

Deductively valid

Inductively strong

Inductively weak

We are now in a position to be more precise in our account of a good argument and to appreciate some of the complexity of that concept. A good argument, we said, is one in which the premises are true and the conclusion follows from them. We have seen, however, that arguments vary in the degree of support they provide for their conclusion. In a good argument the conclusion may follow from the premises with deductive validity or with some degree of inductive strength. Thus, our more complete definition of a good argument is:

GOOD ARGUMENT =   *(1) the conclusion fol-*
lows from the prem-
ises either with
deductive validity
or a degree of in-
ductive strength;
and
(2) the premises are
true.

Conversely, an argument may be bad for either of two reasons: (1) it is neither deductively valid nor inductively strong or (2) at least one premise is false.

The points in this section can be summarized as follows.

1. A good argument is one in which (1) the conclusion follows from the premises and (2) the premises are true.

2. Since the conclusion may follow from the premises with deductive validity or with a degree of inductive strength, it follows that:

3. A *good argument* is one in which (1) the conclusion follows from the premises either with deductive validity or with inductive strength and (2) the premises are true.

4. A conclusion follows with *deductive validity* if, given the premises, the conclusion follows necessarily.

5. Otherwise, a conclusion follows with *inductive strength* if, given the premises, the conclusion follows probably. The degree of support premises lend to an inductive conclusion varies from little or none to very strong.

Summary

This chapter has covered some of the most important basic concepts in logic. We defined logic as the study of the principles of correct reasoning. When reasoning is made explicit we have what we called an argument. We defined *argument* as a group of statements one of which is claimed to follow from the others. *Statements* we defined as sentences that have truth-value. In the context of an argument the statement that is claimed to follow is called the *conclusion* and the statement or statements that provide support are called *premises*. The relationship between premises and conclusion is called inferential; that is, drawing a conclusion from premises is making an *inference*. We then surveyed the concept of a good argument and saw that good arguments must have both true premises and a strong inference. That inferential support may be one of deductive validity or some degree of inductive strength.

Assessing the degree of support premises pass to a conclusion is a central objective of logic. Thus, in the chapters to follow we will concentrate on systematic techniques for determining inferential support. Chapters 3 through 7 focus on two logical systems and their techniques for determining deductive validity. In Chapter 8 we will explore methods for assessing inductive strength. In Chapter 9 we will look at failures in good reasoning called informal fallacies. Finally, Chapter 10 outlines an overall strategy for analyzing arguments and applying the techniques we have learned.

Review Questions Chapter 1

1. What is logic? What is its purpose?
2. What is reasoning?
3. How do logic and psychology differ in their treatment of reasoning?
4. What is a statement?

5. Define the term 'argument' and explain the parts of an argument.

6. What exactly does a conditional statement assert?

7. What features must a good argument have?

8. What is an inference?

9. What is the principle of charity? Why is it recommended in the practice of logic?

10. From what we have seen so far, what differences do you notice between deductive validity and inductive strength?

True or False?

1. Every argument has a conclusion and two premises.

2. To say that a statement has a truth-value means that it is a true statement.

3. Arguments may build on one another such that one argument may be inside another.

4. If an argument is deductively valid, then it is a good argument.

5. In diagraming arguments, if a premise can stand alone in support of the conclusion, then we call it an independent premise.

6. According to the principle of charity, it is always best to let your opponent win the argument.

7. An argument is a group of statements one of which follows from the others.

8. Speaking of arguments generally, the inference from premises to conclusion can vary in degrees from those that are deductively valid to those that are inductively weak.

CHAPTER TWO
Deductive Validity

In this chapter we will examine the concept of
deductive validity, two methods for testing validity,
and the relation between validity and truth.

In Chapter 1 we defined a good argument as one in which two conditions must
be met: (1) the conclusion follows from the premises either with deductive validity
or inductive strength and (2) the premises are true. These two conditions are logically separable. The first has to do solely with the logical connection, the inference,
from premises to conclusion. The second has to do with the actual truth of the
premises. An argument may meet one condition but not the other. Such an argument cannot be a good one by our definition. By focusing on deductive validity—
the most rigorous sense in which the conclusion follows from the premises—we can
see how conditions (1) and (2) are separable. Thus, the purpose of this chapter is to
examine deductive validity and its relationship to truth. We will define deductive
validity, illustrate it, and become acquainted with two nontheoretical methods for
testing validity.

2.1 Deductive Validity Defined

*An argument is deductively valid if and only if, given the premises, the conclusion necessarily
follows.*

In a valid deductive argument the connection between the premises and the conclusion is such that if you assume the premises are true, then it must be that the conclusion is true. The conclusion cannot be false, given the premises. That is what is meant by saying that the conclusion *necessarily* follows from the premises. For example,

Example 1a

1. Max is taller than Fred.
2. Fred is taller than Stella.

_____

3a. Therefore, Max is taller than Stella.

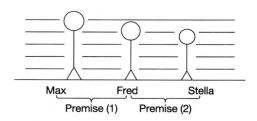

Given that Max is taller than Fred and Fred is taller than Stella, *it must be* that Max is taller than Stella. Indeed, *it could not fail to follow,* given those premises. To see how the premises logically force you to accept the conclusion, notice what happens if you assume the premises are true yet deny the conclusion, as in this modification of example 1:

Example 1b

1. Max is taller than Fred.
2. Fred is taller than Stella.

_____

3b. Max is not taller than Stella.

Example 1b is logical nonsense. In fact, it contains a contradiction. For if premises (1) and (2) are true, then (3b) must be false. Or if (1) and (3b) are true, then (2) must be false, and so on. Thus, example 1b is logically impossible. A valid argument will yield a logical contradiction if you assert the premises and deny the conclusion.

On the other hand, an *invalid* argument does not logically compel acceptance of the conclusion. For example,

Example 2

1. If Max is a Frenchman, then he speaks French.
2. Max speaks French.

_____

3. Therefore, Max is a Frenchman.

Given premises (1) and (2), the conclusion does not have to be true. In this example it is easy to assume the premises are true yet deny that Max is a Frenchman. For example, assume it is true that *if* he were a Frenchman he'd speak French. Assume also that he *does* speak French, having studied it in school, perhaps. But he happens not to be a Frenchman. No contradiction results. Why is this? Notice that premise (1) states that *if* he's a Frenchman he'll speak French. It does not state that *only* Frenchmen speak French. The logical difference between those words makes the difference in this case between an invalid and a valid argument.

2.2 The Counterexample Method

In examples 1 and 2 we were testing for validity by trying to suppose the premises true and the conclusion false. To do so is to try to construct a counterexample to the argument. *A counterexample is a conceivable case in which the premises are assumed true and the conclusion false.* If there is such a case, then the argument is deductively invalid. If there is not, then it is valid. This gives us a simple though unreliable method for recognizing validity. It is unreliable as a general procedure because it depends on how clever we are in imagining an appropriate counterexample. Failing to think of a case may mean we haven't tried hard enough, not that the argument is thereby shown valid.

Let's use the counterexample method with the following examples. Try to imagine an example in which the premises are true yet the conclusion false.

Example 3

1. If you study, you will pass the test.

2. You do not study.

---

3. Therefore, you do not pass the test.

Is it conceivable that if you study, you will pass, and you do not study, yet you *do pass* the test? Surely we can imagine this. Here is a counterexample: You got a copy of the test questions in advance and passed not by studying but by copying the answers. So, in this case we have imagined it is true of you that if you'd studied you would have passed and you didn't study yet false that you did not pass. Thus, our counterexample shows that example 3 is invalid.

Example 4

1. No one is both a sailor and a marine.

2. Alice is a sailor.

---

3. Therefore, Alice is not at the same time a marine.

Is there an imaginable case in which it is true that no one is both a sailor and a marine, Alice is a sailor, and Alice is simultaneously a marine? We are trying to imagine the inconceivable: that no one is both a sailor and a marine, and Alice is both. There can be no such case. The argument is valid.

Here is another example.

Example 5

1. *If something is dangerous, then people should avoid it.*

2. *People should avoid hang gliding.*

---

3. *Therefore, hang gliding is dangerous.*

Premises (1) and (2) do not force us to accept that hang gliding is dangerous (in spite of the fact that we know it is). Let us suppose that (1) and (2) are true yet (3) is false. That would be the case if, for example, the dangerous should be avoided and hang gliding should be avoided, but hang gliding should be avoided because it's too expensive. In this counterexample we see that it does not follow that hang gliding is dangerous.

The counterexample method tests for validity by having us try to construct a conceivable example that runs counter to the argument. If a counterexample is possible, then it shows that the premises may be true and the conclusion false. Such an argument fails to meet the definition of validity.

Exercise 2.2   Valid or Invalid?   Use the counterexample method to test the following arguments for validity. If you think an argument is valid, explain why there can be no conceivable case in which the premises are true and the conclusion false. If you think an argument is invalid describe the counterexample.

1. Every chemistry major must take one year of organic chemistry. Max took one year of organic chem, so he must be a chemistry major.

2. All life requires water. There is no water on the planet Venus. Therefore, no life is possible on Venus.

3. There are 367 students in my history class. Therefore, at least two of them have birthdays on the same day of the year.

4. Only movie stars live in Hollywood. Robert Redford is a movie star. Therefore, he lives in Hollywood.

5. All movie stars live in Hollywood. Robert Redford is a movie star. Therefore, he lives in Hollywood.

6. All movie stars live in Hollywood. Robert Redford lives in Hollywood. Therefore, he is a movie star.

7. A sound argument is one that is valid and has all true premises. Argument (2) above has all true premises; therefore, it is valid.

8. The human mind has no weight, no shape, and no size. The human brain has weight, shape, and size. Two or more things are identical only if they have all the same properties. Therefore, the mind and the brain are not identical.

9. The right to life, which every person possesses, does not give one the right to whatever one needs in order to live. So, even though a person dying of, say, kidney disease has a right to life, that person does not thereby have a right to use another's kidneys.

10. Drinking coffee stunts your growth. Max's growth is stunted. Therefore, Max drinks coffee.

11. Society has a right to protect itself and to secure what is necessary for its continued existence from both external and internal threats. A common moral view is essential for society's continued existence. Yet a common moral view is threatened internally by so-called harmless acts of personal morality such as gambling, public nudity, the use of marijuana, prostitution, and homosexuality. Since these constitute a threat, society has a right lawfully to prohibit such acts of personal morality.

12. The only legitimate moral justification for establishing laws restricting personal conduct is to prevent harm among people. Gambling, public nudity, the use of marijuana, prostitution, and homosexuality, to name a few, are practices that could be regulated so as to eliminate all harm. Therefore, there is no moral justification for current laws restricting those practices.

13. The superior forms of art are those that capture reality and display it for us. Film is one art form that most successfully captures reality and displays it; thus, film is a superior art form.

14. Every life belongs to God as the creator of all things. The act of suicide is an act of destroying a life that, therefore, belongs to God.

15. Regarding the great extinction of animal life at the end of the Permian period 225 million years ago, Stephen Jay Gould writes: We can be sure that a removal of half the families requires the death of a much greater percentage of species. A family is not gone until all its species die, and many families contain tens or hundreds of species.

16. We can never prove absolutely, but we can falsify. A set of ideas that cannot, in principle, be falsified is not science. "Scientific creationism" is a self-contradictory, nonsense phrase precisely because it [scientific creationism] cannot be falsified. (Stephen Jay Gould, "Evolution as Fact and Theory")

17. Artist Richard Serra defending his artwork *Tilted Arc* before a hearing deciding whether to remove the work: I don't make portable objects. My works become part of and are built into the structure of the site, and they often restructure, both conceptually and perceptually, the organization of the site.

    When the government invited me to propose a sculpture for the plaza, it asked for a permanent, site-specific sculpture. As the phrase implies, a site-specific sculpture is one that is conceived and created in relation to the particular conditions of a specific site, and only to those conditions. To remove *Tilted Arc,* therefore, would be to destroy it. (General Services Administration hearing, March 1985)

18. As I write this, in November 1971, people are dying in East Bengal from lack of food, shelter, and medical care. The suffering and death that are occurring

there now are not inevitable, not unavoidable in any fatalistic sense of the term. It is not beyond the capacity of the richer nations to give enough assistance to reduce any further suffering to very small proportions.

I begin with the assumption that suffering and death from lack of food, shelter, and medical care are bad. My next point is this: if it is in our power to prevent something bad from happening, without thereby sacrificing anything of comparable moral importance, we ought morally to do it.

[Therefore, we have a moral duty to give enough assistance to reduce further suffering.] (Peter Singer, "Famine, Affluence, and Morality")

2.3 Validity and Logical Form

Let us introduce another method for recognizing deductive validity called *the method of substitution by logical form* or, for convenience, the substitution method. This method employs two powerful rules:

Rule 1 Any argument with a valid logical form is a valid argument.

Rule 2 Any argument with an invalid logical form is an invalid argument.

Let us begin by illustrating logical form. Consider the following example.

Example 6

1. All cows are ruminating animals.
2. All ruminating animals are docile.

_____

3. All cows are docile.

Now compare example 6 with the example below.

Example 7

1. All A are B
2. All B are C

_____

3. Therefore, all A are C

Letting the letters 'A', 'B', and 'C' stand for 'cows', 'ruminating animals', and 'docile' respectively, we see that example 7 is the underlying form of example 6. We will call example 7 the *logical form* of 6 and we can say that example 6 is a *substitution instance* of that form.

Example 6	**Example 7**
1. All cows are ruminating animals.	1. All A are B
2. All ruminating animals are docile.	2. All B are C
3. All cows are docile.	3. All A are C

Example 7 happens to be a well-recognized example of a valid logical form called "Barbara" (a mnemonic device by which medieval logicians could remember the forms of the statements and their exact order in an argument). Since example 7 is a valid logical form and since example 6 is a substitution instance of 7, example 6 is a valid argument. To put it differently, example 6 is an argument with a valid logical form; therefore, it is valid by rule 1 above.

1. All A are B	VALID LOGICAL FORM
2. All B are C	BARBARA
3. Therefore, all A are C	

Just as example 6 is an exact substitution of the form Barbara, so other arguments may also have that valid logical form. They, too, will be valid under rule 1 which states that any argument with a valid logical form is a valid argument.

Let's consider other examples and introduce several other valid logical forms.

	VALID LOGICAL FORM
Example 8	DISJUNCTIVE SYLLOGISM
1. Max wears glasses or contact lenses.	1. A or B
2. Max does not wear glasses.	2. Not A
3. Max wears contact lenses.	3. B

The *disjunctive syllogism* is a valid logical form according to which, if we are given that A *or* B is the case, and that A is *not* the case, then it must follow that B is the case. Since example 8 has that form, it is a valid argument. Disjunctive syllogism derives its name from the fact that it consists of three statements (hence, "syllogism"): an 'or' statement called a disjunction, the denial of one part of the disjunction, and an inference to the other part. It can be demonstrated, as we will see in Chapter 7, that the logical form below

1. A or B
2. Not B

3. Not A

is also an instance of disjunctive syllogism: a disjunction, the denial of one part, and the inference to the other.

Here is a third valid logical form.

	VALID LOGICAL FORM
Example 9	MODUS PONENS
1. If it rains, then your car is wet.	1. If A then B
2. It rains.	2. A
3. Your car is wet.	3. B

Briefly consider the form of *modus ponens*. Given that if A then B, and that A obtains, it must follow that B obtains. Notice that example 9 is of the form *modus ponens*. Therefore, it is a valid argument.

A fourth valid logical form is *modus tollens*.

	VALID LOGICAL FORM
Example 10	MODUS TOLLENS
1. If it rains, then your car is wet.	1. If A then B
2. Your car is not wet.	2. Not B
3. It does not rain.	3. Not A

We can intuitively convince ourselves of the validity of *modus tollens* by considering what it asserts: (1) states that if A occurs, then B occurs; (2) states that B does not occur. It must follow then that A does not occur, since if (3) were false, then by (1), (2) would be false. Thus, given (1) and (2), (3) must follow. Since *modus tollens* is a valid form and since example 10 is one of its instances, example 10 is a valid argument.

Let's consider three *invalid* logical forms. First, the fallacy of denying the antecedent, illustrated in this example.

	FALLACY OF
Example 11	DENYING THE ANTECEDENT
1. If you study, then you pass.	1. If A then B
2. You do not study.	2. Not A
3. You do not pass.	3. Not B

As the name suggests, the fallacy of denying the antecedent involves a premise, here premise (2), that denies the *antecedent,* or first part, of a conditional statement, here premise (1). The conclusion (3) does not necessarily follow, since both (1) and (2) may be true yet (3) false as we saw when we examined example 3.

A second invalid logical form involving the conditional is the fallacy of affirming the consequent:

	FALLACY OF AFFIRMING THE CONSEQUENT
Example 12	
1. If you study, then you pass.	*1. If A then B*
2. You pass.	*2. B*
3. You study.	*3. A*

Here the *consequent,* the second part of the conditional, is asserted, as in premise (2); the argument concludes that (3), the antecedent of the conditional must follow. But this argument form is invalid, since, for example, it does not follow that you studied from the facts that if you study, you pass, and you did pass. Again, in our discussion of example 3 we saw that a counterexample is conceivable: namely, that you pass by means other than studying, yet it may still be true of you that if you study, you will pass.

A third and final invalid logical form is the fallacy of undistributed middle, illustrated below.

	FALLACY OF UNDISTRIBUTED MIDDLE
Example 13	
1. All ants are insects.	*1. All A are B*
2. All beetles are insects.	*2. All C are B*
3. All beetles are ants.	*3. All C are A*

Notice that the term B in the form (and its counterpart 'insects' in the example) is the term common to the other two terms, A and C. Yet being common to A and C doesn't entail that A and C are related as the conclusion (3) asserts. The problem is that neither premise attributes being an A or being a C to all B's. In the example, neither premise attributes being an ant or being a beetle to all insects. In technical language, the middle term, B, is not *distributed over* at least one of the other terms. Hence the name fallacy of undistributed middle.

VALID LOGICAL FORMS

BARBARA	DISJUNCTIVE SYLLOGISM
1. All A are B	*1. A or B*
2. All B are C	*2. Not A*
3. All A are C	*3. B*

MODUS PONENS	MODUS TOLLENS
1. *If A then B*	1. *If A then B*
2. *A*	2. *Not B*
———————————	———————————
3. *B*	3. *Not A*

INVALID LOGICAL FORMS

FALLACY OF DENYING THE ANTECEDENT	FALLACY OF AFFIRMING THE CONSEQUENT
1. *If A then B*	1. *If A then B*
2. *Not A*	2. *B*
———————————	———————————
3. *Not B*	3. *A*

FALLACY OF
UNDISTRIBUTED MIDDLE

1. *All A are B*
2. *All C are B*
———————————
3. *All C are A*

We have reviewed four valid forms of arguments and three invalid forms. We have illustrated how an argument may be understood as having a form and, thus, how two or more arguments may be said to have the same form. We have also illustrated these two important rules about validity: (1) a substitution instance of a valid logical form is a valid argument; and (2) a substitution instance of an invalid logical form is an invalid argument. Perhaps the most important point to emerge from this discussion is that validity is a matter of the logical form or structure of an argument, not a matter of its content. This review also raises important questions. How do we determine the form of an argument? What counts as form and what counts as content? How do we know that valid forms are indeed valid? Are there ways to prove validity and invalidity? These are questions answered by a study of the two logical systems we will take up. We will see that there are techniques for supplying the form of an argument and procedures for proving validity and invalidity.

Exercise 2.3　Validity and Logical Form.　Use the substitution method to identify validity or invalidity in the arguments below. State which logical form the argument exhibits and whether it is a valid or invalid argument.

1. If Webb is promoted, then Walters is transferred. Webb is promoted; therefore, Walters is transferred.

2. There will be either sunshine or rain. It will not rain; therefore, there will be sunshine.

3. Every fire official came to the conference and, since all who came to the conference enjoyed the dinner, all the fire officials enjoyed the dinner.

4. If she doesn't have a fever, then she doesn't have the flu. She doesn't have a fever. So she doesn't have the flu.

5. All logicians have good manners and all physicians have good manners. Therefore, all logicians are physicians.

6. All Chinook winds have the föhn effect and the föhn effect can raise air temperatures by as much as 40° F. So all Chinook winds are capable of raising the temperature as much as 40° F.

7. There is no need for surgery because if there is a tumor then there is need for surgery but there is no tumor.

8. If her argument is good, then all her premises are true. But it's not the case that all her premises are true; thus, her argument is not good.

9. If Shakespeare's works are histories, then they are not science fiction. Shakespeare's works are histories; therefore, they are not science fiction.

10. If Shakespeare's works are histories, then they are not science fiction. They are science fiction. Therefore, they are not histories.

11. If there is a tumor, then there is need for surgery. There is need for surgery; therefore, there is a tumor.

12. Either the emergence of democracy is a cause for hope or environmental problems will overshadow any promise of a bright future. Since environmental problems will not overshadow any promise of a bright future, it follows that the emergence of democracy is a cause for hope.

13. If it is possible to keep people alive indefinitely, then we face serious questions about the purpose and quality of such life. Therefore, since it is not possible to keep people alive indefinitely, we do not have to face those serious questions.

14. Every pediatrician is an M.D. and so is every podiatrist. Hence every pediatrician is a podiatrist.

15. If all elementary and secondary schools across the country are reexamining their educational objectives, then major educational reform will be a national goal. Since such reexamination is the case, so is the national goal of educational reform.

2.4 Truth and Validity

That an argument is deductively valid does *not* mean that it is a good argument. A good *deductive* argument, you recall, must possess validity *and* true premises, and validity guarantees neither true premises nor true conclusion. Let's go over five important points about validity, truth, and good arguments.

1. *A valid argument may have one or more false premises.*

Example 13

1. *Smoking makes you stronger.*

2. *Being stronger makes you happier.*

---

3. *Therefore, smoking makes you happier.*

As example 13 illustrates, false premises do not mean an invalid argument.

2. *An invalid argument may consist of statements all of which are true*

### Example 14	### Example 15
1. *5 is greater than 3*	1. *Mozart was a musician.*
2. *4 is greater than 3*	2. *Composers are musicians.*
	---
3. *Thus, 5 is greater than 4*	3. *Mozart was a composer.*

As these two examples show, true premises and conclusion do not make an argument valid. Each example conforms to the fallacy of undistributed middle.

3. *If the conclusion of a valid argument is false, then at least one premise is false.*

Example 16

1. *The only justification for a military invasion of another country is self-defense.*
2. *It is self-defense only if a nation faces imminent danger at its borders.*
3. *The United States was not threatened by imminent danger at its borders before or during the military invasion of Grenada.*

---

4. *Therefore, the United States was not acting in self-defense in the military invasion of Grenada.*

---

5. *Therefore, the United States was not justified in the military invasion of Grenada.*

Example 16 is a valid argument; it exemplifies the valid logical form *modus tollens.* Many would argue that the conclusion of this valid argument, statement (5), is false. We were justified in invading Grenada, they say. Therefore, since the argument is valid and (5) is denied, it follows that at least one premise must be denied. This illustrates a useful strategy in criticism: If you see that an argument is valid and yet you deny the conclusion, then at least one premise must be denied. Locating such a premise and showing that it is false is, of course, to show that the argument is not a good one.

4. *If the premises of a valid argument are true, then the conclusion is true.* Given that you know an argument is valid and you know the premises are true, then you must conclude that the conclusion is true. As we have seen above, to deny the conclusion entails asserting either that the argument is not valid or that at least one premise is not true.

5. *An argument may be valid yet not a good argument.* Argument 13 above is valid yet not good since it contains at least one false premise. Do not think that an argument is good and should be accepted merely because it is valid. Validity is only part of the concept of a good argument.

There is perhaps no more important point in logic than the point we have been discussing here from different angles. *Validity has to do with the logical connection between premises and conclusion, not with the actual truth or falsity of the premises.* So do not confuse what you may know about the *actual* truth or falsity of the premises with asking whether a particular argument is or is not valid. To determine validity, always assume the premises are true and ask, "Must the conclusion follow?"

Summary

In this chapter we have examined the concept of deductive validity. We have briefly considered two approaches to recognizing validity: the counterexample method and the substitution method. The latter method introduced ideas we will develop further: the logical form of an argument, valid and invalid logical forms, and the need for a procedure to prove validity. We examined as well the point that validity is independent of the truth of statements. Next we will study two systems of logic, categorical logic and truth–functional logic. Each system provides, among other things, a precise framework for supplying a logical form to arguments and examining them for deductive validity.

Review Questions Chapter 2

1. What is a counterexample to an argument?
2. What is a valid deductive argument?
3. What is a good deductive argument?
4. Make up examples illustrating each of the following logical forms: *modus ponens*, Barbara, disjunctive syllogism, *modus tollens*.

5. Make up examples illustrating each of these forms: the fallacy of affirming the consequent, the fallacy of denying the antecedent, the fallacy of un-distributed middle.

6. Explain why an argument must have at least one false premise if it is valid and the conclusion is false.

7. Explain why all true premises do not make an argument valid.

8. Explain in your own words why the form called the fallacy of denying the antecedent is invalid.

True or False?

1. A valid argument can have premises that are false.

2. If an argument is valid and you believe the conclusion is false, then you must conclude that at least one premise is false.

3. If the conclusion of an argument does not necessarily follow from the premises, then it must be an inductive argument.

4. Deductive validity is only part and not a necessary part of a good argument.

5. A statement may be valid or invalid depending on who judges it.

6. An argument in the form *modus tollens* is a valid argument.

7. If you assume the premises are true and get a contradiction when you deny the conclusion, then the argument must be valid.

8. Two arguments can have the same logical form yet one is valid and the other invalid.

9. A good deductive argument must be valid but it could have false premises.

10. If a counterexample to an argument is inconceivable, the argument is deductively invalid.

CHAPTER THREE
Categorical Logic
Part I

In this chapter we begin our survey of categorical logic. We discuss the *categorical forms,* the use of *Venn diagrams,* and the process of drawing inferences by means of the *square of opposition.* We also examine how the traditional *operations* are performed on the categorical forms.

3.1 Introduction

The Practical Use of Logical Systems   Imagine that you are a farmer living in the previous century. You would want to know the condition of the soil on your farmland, as all farmers do. You might not know about soil acidity and alkalinity, but you would probably have your own terms, handed down through the generations, for describing and evaluating the soil. You would check the soil by looking at it, smelling it, tasting it, squeezing it between your fingers, and seeing how well it held water. Using your senses and applying what you'd learned from your ancestors, you would reach a judgment about the quality of the soil. Such a method works fairly well, but it is not accurate or wholly reliable, and it might vary from person to person. Today, farmers have their own soil testing kits, developed by chemists specializing in soil composition, with which they can evaluate the condition of their soil. The analysis is accurate, objective, and certain.

Prior to learning a system of logic, the thinker is in much the same position as the old-time farmers relying on their senses and experience. For instance, in the previous chapter you were relying on your intuition to tell whether an argument was valid. You really had no way yet of checking your judgment other than by appealing to what seemed to "make sense." Suppose you and a friend disagree about the validity of an argument. You know the argument cannot be both valid and invalid, but how do you tell who is correct? It would be useful at such a time to have a "testing kit" for evaluating arguments. With an accurate test not only could you determine which judgment is correct, but you could do so with certainty and objectivity. This is precisely what the system of categorical logic is designed to do. *In general, the purpose of a system of logic is to provide an objective procedure for (1) clarifying language, (2) revealing its logical structure, (3) defining the concepts of logic, and (4) evaluating arguments for their validity.* An objective procedure is desirable because it is easy to apply, it gives the same results no matter who uses it, and it is free of the human errors associated with intuitions. So, in short, a system of logic provides methods of testing our reasoning.

Categorical logic originated with the Greek philosopher Aristotle (384–322 BC). Thus, much of what we will learn in this survey is over two thousand years old. From fragments of their writings we know that philosophers living as early as 700 BC had an understanding of good argument and used reasoning to draw abstract conclusions, but Aristotle was the first person to develop a logical system. His comprehensive theory includes precise definitions, principles of reasoning, a system for exposing arguments, and rules for evaluating reasoning. Most of our common notions of reasoning—inference, argument, affirmation, denial, contradiction, tautology, validity, and so on—were deliberately and systematically studied and refined by Aristotle. Categorical logic is not the whole of Aristotle's work in logic, but it is one of his most important contributions and provides an excellent example of a deductive system.

Before we begin this survey of categorical logic let us briefly preview what will be covered. Categorical logic is a system for analyzing deductive arguments, or what Aristotle called *syllogisms*. (A syllogism, as we see in Chapter 4, is a precisely defined format for expressing certain deductive arguments.) One of the requirements of categorical logic is that statements be in a certain form, called categorical form. These statements are *categorical statements,* and they assert a relationship between one group of things and another. In this chapter we learn about categorical statements and how they are logically related to each other. In the next chapter we learn how to translate many ordinary sentences into categorical statements. We then apply our knowledge of the relations among categorical statements to the task of evaluating arguments expressed in categorical form. We use a nineteenth-century technique called Venn diagraming to represent statements and arguments graphically. In these chapters you learn a systematic way of translating sentences and arguments into a form that makes them clear and easy to evaluate. The technique of Venn diagraming gives you a graphic way of showing the implications of statements and the validity or invalidity of arguments.

3.2 Categories and Reasoning

Categorical logic is a deductive logical system. It makes certain important basic assumptions about deductive reasoning, which we discuss in this section.

(1) *Categories are classes or groups of things.* The words and phrases we use in our language to refer to or name categories will be called *terms.* Here are some examples of terms that name categories:

red things	*humans*	*metals*
silverfish	*living things*	*nonmetals*
guitar players	*soft things*	*senators*
biting insects	*people who are athletic*	

The membership of a category or class is relative to our interests and needs. We could conceivably categorize or "break things up into categories" any way we wished, but such categorizing might not be useful or sensible. Look around your room and categorize things into 'all wooden things', 'all living things', or 'all things requiring oxygen'. As you can see, many things are members of more than one group. You, for instance, belong to the classes of living things, things requiring oxygen, fleshy things, thinking things, and so on. You are not a member of the class of wooden things. (Are you classifiable into any of these categories: Democrats, athletes, chess players, chocolate lovers, science fiction buffs, rednecks, stamp collectors, card sharks, sun worshippers, or car owners?) Describing yourself may be thought of as a matter of finding the categories that correctly apply to you. (Is there a list of categories that applies to you and you alone for all eternity? That is, do you possess a unique classification?)

The notions of categories and categorizing extend beyond logic and involve a number of thought-provoking philosophical questions. For instance, are there any limits to the ways we can classify reality? Some argue that there are no limits; others argue that there are, at the very least, those limits imposed by the character of reality itself. Is thought possible without categorizing? Could we think if we did not have the ability to think in terms of groups of things? Many philosophers believe that the concept of the category is so fundamental to thinking that without it we could not have developed science, probably could not have learned to communicate beyond grunts and groans, and would very likely not experience the world and ourselves as we do. Aristotle's great genius is evident in his recognition of the immense importance of the notion of the category.

(2) *Statements in categorical logic assert a relationship between one category and another.* Whenever we form a statement, we pick out something and we think something about it. Suppose you are thinking right now that these desks are hard. What you have picked out to think about is 'these desks'; the subject of your statement is 'these desks'. Every statement must have a subject. What you are thinking about these desks is that they 'are hard'; this second part of the statement is called the predicate. Your statement 'these desks are hard' can be seen as asserting a relationship between the *subject category,* named by the words 'these desks', and the *predicate category,* named

by the words 'hard things'. In effect, you are saying that these desks belong to the category of hard things.

Example 1

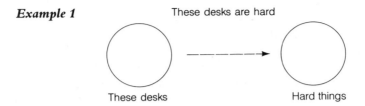

These desks are hard

These desks   Hard things

It is almost as though you were rounding up all the desks you are thinking about and moving them into a pigeonhole in your mind labeled 'hard things'. Think of statements as assertions about such relationships of groups of things.

Aristotle's system is based on the idea that almost all statements can be expressed in terms of categories and the assertion of a relationship between categories. Here are some examples of how ordinary statements can be understood as making assertions about categories.

	ORDINARY STATEMENT	CATEGORICAL INTERPRETATION
Example 2	Some dogs bark.	At least one member of the class of dogs is a member of the class of things that bark.
Example 3	All spiders have eight legs.	All members of the class of spiders are members of the class of things having eight legs.
Example 4	No bankers favor the withholding of interest on savings accounts.	No members of the class of bankers are members of the class of persons favoring withholding interest on savings accounts.
Example 5	The Syrians deported Yassar Arafat.	All things identical to the government of Syria are members of the class of things deporting Yassar Arafat.

Such categorical interpretations as these may strike you as unnecessarily wordy, but the advantages of treating statements as assertions about categories will become clear to you soon. In chapter 4 we learn how to translate ordinary statements into categorical form, which, you will see, need not be as wordy as the examples above.

(3) *All reasoning in categorical logic is reasoning about categories.* This is merely an application to arguments of what we have seen about statements. Here is a simple example of an argument:

Example 6

1. *Artists are humans.*

2. *Humans are mortal.*

---

3. *Therefore, artists are mortal.*

We may analyze this reasoning as follows: Premise (1) asserts that all artists belong to the category of humans. Premise (2) asserts that all humans belong to the category of mortal things. Now, since all artists are part of the group of humans, and all humans are part of the group of mortal things, it must follow that (3) all artists are part of the group of mortal things as well. We see that the conclusion of the argument follows from the relationships expressed in the premises. The example above relates categories in this pattern:

> *All A's are B's.*
> *All B's are C's.*
>
> ---
>
> *Therefore, All A's are C's.*

Looking over the form or pattern of this argument, we can see that other possible arguments exemplify that form also. For example, these arguments both have the same form as the example above:

Example 7

1. *All Soviet agents are communists.*

2. *All communists are Marxists.*

---

3. *Therefore, all Soviet agents are Marxists.*

Example 8

1. *All mothers are Democrats.*

2. *All Democrats are liberals.*

---

3. *Therefore, all mothers are liberals.*

The arguments may not have true premises, but they all have the same form. This fact means that if the form above is a valid argument form—and it happens that it is—then so are all arguments having that form. This appeal to valid forms enormously simplifies the business of checking for validity, for *if an argument conforms to a valid argument form, then it is a valid argument.* We will be using Venn diagrams to help us discover valid argument forms.

3.3 The Four Categorical Forms

Every statement asserts a relationship between categories. Given a statement with 'artists' as its subject and 'humans' as its predicate, categorical logic specifies four basic forms that such a statement can take. In other words, there are four relationships between those two categories, as exemplified in these statements:

All artists *are* humans.

No artists *are* humans.

Some artists *are* humans.

Some artists *are not* humans.

Either all artists belong to the group of humans, none do, some do, or some do not. We can represent the form of those statements by letting the letter S stand for the subject and the letter P stand for the predicate.

EXAMPLES	THE FOUR CATEGORICAL FORMS
All artists are humans	*All S are P*
No artists are humans	*No S are P*
Some artists are humans	*Some S are P*
Some artists are not humans	*Some S are not P*

Every statement in categorical logic can be represented according to one of these four forms, which comprise the core of categorical logic. We will be studying these forms very carefully, so for convenience we will name them as follows:

CATEGORICAL FORM NAME	CATEGORICAL FORM
A	*All S are P*
E	*No S are P*
I	*Some S are P*
O	*Some S are not P*

Now let's look at how each form will be understood, that is, what it is logically asserting.

Form A: 'All S are P' asserts that the predicate *is affirmed of all members* of S, the subject category.

Form E: 'No S are P' asserts that the predicate *is denied of all members* of S.

Form I: 'Some S are P' asserts that *there is at least one member* of S and the predicate *is affirmed of it*.

Form O: 'Some S are not P' asserts that *there is at least one member* of S and the predicate *is denied of it*.

Notice that forms A and E are about all members of the subject group. Form A says that they are *all* P's; form E says that *none* of them are P's. Because they are statements about all of the subject group they are called *universal*. Universality is their logical *quantity*. Logical quantity has to do with how much of the subject class is referred to in the statement. Forms I and O, on the other hand, are not about all members of the subject class, nor can one tell from the statement form how many S's are referred to. But there must be at least one S for the statement form to be true. Logically speaking, we must understand the statement forms as referring to at least one member of the S group. There may, of course, be more S's that are or are not P's, but we cannot conclude that without further information. Thus, the statement form 'Some S are P' asserts that *there is at least one S* and it is a P; whereas, 'Some S are not P' asserts that *there is at least one S* and it is not a P. These two forms are said to be *particular* in *quantity* because they refer to at least one S.

Now notice that both forms A and I are affirmative. They assert that the predicate *does* belong to the subject; they are said to be *affirmative* in *quality*. The quality of a statement refers to its affirmation or denial of the predicate of the subject class. Forms E and I both deny that the predicate belongs to the subject, so they are said to be *negative* in *quality*.

To summarize at this point, we can say that the four categorical forms named A, E, I, and O are the core of categorical logic. In this system almost all statements and therefore almost all arguments can be expressed in terms of these forms. The four forms may be distinguished by quantity and quality. Quantity refers to how much of the subject group is referred to: either all or some. Quality refers to whether the predicate is affirmed or denied of the subject. Thus, regarding quantity, A and E are universal, whereas I and O are particular. Regarding quality, A and I are affirmative, whereas E and O are negative. All that we have learned thus far can be seen represented in the diagram shown in Figure 3.1.

Figure 3.1

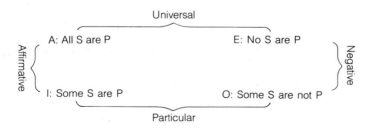

Exercise 3.3A Categorical Forms.   For each of the statements listed below, (1) identify the subject and the predicate; (2) identify the categorical form, A, E, I, or O; (3) determine its quality; and (4) determine its quantity.

1. All astronomers are trained in mathematics.
2. Some Dachshunds are dogs with back problems.
3. All past presidents are invited to a luncheon on Friday.
4. No students are protesters.
5. Some traffic monitors are not well-trained people.
6. Some dermatologists are bald.
7. All football fans are fanatics.
8. No careless drivers are licensed drivers in Idaho.
9. Some members of the Kiwanis Club are active supporters of the right-to-life movement.
10. Some photographers who develop their own film are not professionals.

Exercise 3.3B Change the Quality.   For each statement listed below, change the quality to its opposite. For example, the affirmative A-form statement 'All humans are mortals' would change to the negative E-form statement 'No humans are mortals'. Be sure not to change the quantity.

1. All piranhas are vicious fish.
2. No small land birds are nonmigratory birds.
3. Some sailboats are equipped with outboard motors.
4. Some passengers on the airplane are traveling to Los Angeles.
5. All good investments are tax-free investments.
6. Some logicians are not musically inclined.
7. All bartenders are licensed in this state.
8. No Red-headed Woodpeckers are here during the winter.
9. Some wheelwrights are still in business.
10. Some pastors are not Methodists.

Exercise 3.3C Change the Quantity.   If a statement is universal, change its quantity to particular. If it is particular, change it to universal. Do not change the quality at the same time.

1. All happy people are happy in the same way.
2. All unhappy people are unhappy in their own solitary way.
3. No specimens from the site are ready for examination.
4. Some sun worshippers are not permitted on the beach.
5. Some vicious fish are piranhas.
6. Some logicians are not musically inclined.
7. No bartenders are licensed in this state.
8. All philosophers are frustrated actors.
9. Some chess players are not grand masters.
10. No popular vocalists are poor.

3.4 Venn Diagrams

The *Venn diagram,* developed by the logician John Venn (1834–1923), is a very useful tool for representing graphically the logical meaning of a statement. It provides a simple method for testing inferences and arguments for their validity, among other things. The Venn diagram will be our main tool in this survey of categorical logic. We will use it to represent statements in this chapter and arguments in the next chapter.

The Venn diagram uses circles to represent categories. To begin with a very simple diagram, let us suppose the circle below stands for the category 'meat eaters'.

Example 9

Meat eaters

The area within the circle represents meat eaters, and the area outside the circle stands for everything that is not a meat eater. With this one circle we have thus represented pictorially a "logical" distinction between meat eaters and non–meat eaters.

Now by using an X (or any symbol) to stand for the existence of something, we can represent logically different statements. An X within the circle represents the statement 'something is a meat eater'. An X outside the circle represents 'something is not a meat eater'.

Example 10

Something is a meat eater

Something is not a meat eater

By using shading as illustrated in the diagram below we can show that an area has nothing in it. Thus, this diagram represents the statement 'nothing is a meat eater' or 'there are no meat eaters'. The shading marks close off an area and indicate that nothing exists there.

Example 11

Nothing is a meat eater

On the other hand, we can say that all things are meat eaters by crossing out the area outside the circle, as shown below:

Example 12

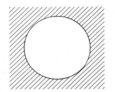

Everything is a meat eater
(or there are no non–meat eaters)

Diagraming with Two Categories

Now let us use the Venn diagram technique to represent categorical statements. To do this we need two circles, one for each of the categories of a statement. The circles overlap so the diagram can represent all possible relationships between the two categories. The diagram therefore has four distinct "logical" areas, as shown below. Suppose we use the categories 'people' and 'athletes'.

Example 13

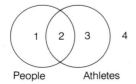

People   Athletes

Notice the meanings of the four areas. Area (1) would represent members of the category people who are not athletes. Area (2) would represent things that are both people and athletes. Something in that area would be a person and an athlete. Area (3) would represent things that are athletes but not people. And the area outside both circles, area (4), would represent things that are neither people nor athletes. (Where, for instance, would you place President Bush? Where would you place "Magic" Johnson, ET, and your logic book?)

To diagram categorical statements, we let one circle represent the subject category and the other the predicate category. Then by using either an X or the shading marks we can show what the relationship is. Let us consider each categorical statement form.

The A–form says that 'All S are P'. We first draw two overlapping circles. We let the left-hand circle represent the subject category and the right-hand circle represent the predicate category. We label them S and P respectively. Now we want to show that *all* S's are members of the P circle. We do this by closing out that area where no S's should be:

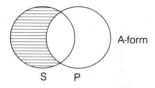

A-form

Think of it this way. In the A–form statement, 'All S are P', you are talking about S's, so you want to show in your diagram how *they* are related to P's. Thus, you must put shading inside area (1) to indicate that there are no S's there. Doing so "locates" all the S's inside area (2), the area representing things that are S's and also P's.

The E–form says that 'No S are P'; thus, you want the diagram to indicate that S's are completely separated from P's. By shading in area (2) you indicate that that area contains nothing. Thus, there are no S's that are P's. All S's are represented as being in area (1), as the diagram for the E–form shows:

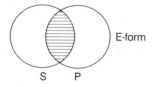

E-form

The I–form says that 'Some S are P'. The O–form says that 'Some S are not P'. The symbol X is traditionally used to represent the meaning 'some' or 'at least one'. To depict the I– and O–forms, you simply place the X in the proper place, as shown below:

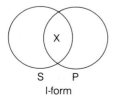

I-form

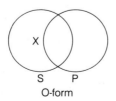

O-form

Remember that with a 'some' statement (that is, I or O), you must put the X in the appropriate place. In the statement 'Some S are P' you see that you are talking about S's, so you must place an X somewhere *within* the S circle; for only an X within the S circle can represent 'Some S's'. Then you see that it must also be placed inside the P circle. Below are some examples of ordinary categorical statements and the Venn diagrams representing them.

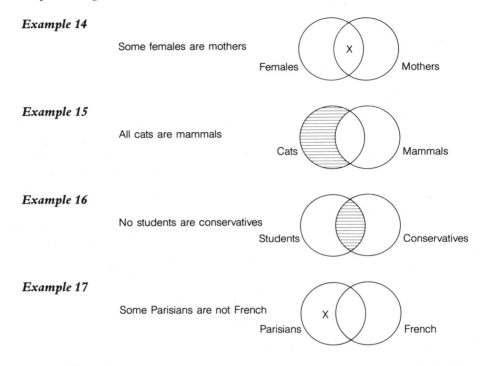

Example 14

Some females are mothers

Females   Mothers

Example 15

All cats are mammals

Cats   Mammals

Example 16

No students are conservatives

Students   Conservatives

Example 17

Some Parisians are not French

Parisians   French

Now try your hand at "reading" some Venn diagrams. What do you think the following diagrams depict?

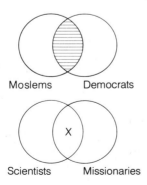

Moslems   Democrats

Scientists   Missionaries

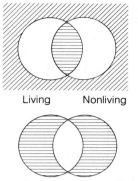

Living   Nonliving

Things that have shape   Things that have size

The first diagram says that no Moslems are Democrats. It also says that no Democrats are Moslems. The second diagram says that some scientists are missionaries. It also says that some missionaries are scientists. The third one tells us that everything is living or nonliving but not both. And the fourth one indicates that everything that has shape also has size and vice versa.

Exercise 3.4A   Drawing Venn Diagrams.   For each statement, identify the form, the quality, and the quantity and then draw a Venn diagram.

1. No Eucalyptus trees are natives of California.
2. All scientists are humanitarians.
3. All machines are the products of intelligent beings.
4. Some animals are not predators.
5. Some followers of "Reaganomics" are people whom we can respect.
6. No doctors who are not trained in neurophysiology are brain surgeons.
7. No person wants to be harmed.
8. Some sailcats do not reproduce.
9. All logicians love Venn diagrams.
10. Some students are registered voters.
11. No male vocalists are sopranos at the Met.
12. Some Western historians are historians who oppose the Marxist interpretation of the American Revolution.
13. All members of the student council must maintain a 3.0 grade point average.
14. Some of the professors I have had are excellent teachers.
15. No computers are capable of thought.
16. All dogs must have their day.

17. All animal lovers will appreciate the efforts of the Humane Society.

18. (a) No things are free. (b) Nothing is free.

19. Some teas contain caffeine.

20. Some psychologists are not Freudians.

Exercise 3.4B Reading Venn Diagrams.   Write the categorical statements represented by the following Venn diagrams.

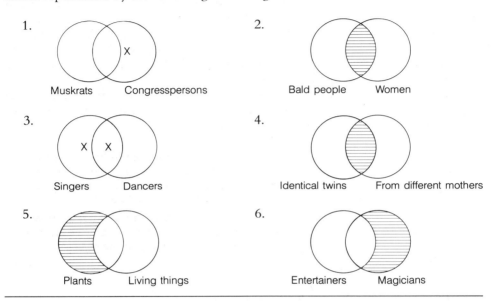

1.

Muskrats   Congresspersons

2.

Bald people   Women

3.

Singers   Dancers

4.

Identical twins   From different mothers

5.

Plants   Living things

6.

Entertainers   Magicians

3.5 The Square of Opposition: Traditional and Modern

What logical relations exist among the four categorical forms? If we know, for example, that some statement of the form 'All S are P' is true, what, if anything, can we infer about the truth or falsity of the other categorical statements? Interestingly enough, the answer depends on whether we make what is called an *existential assumption,* that is, whether we assume there are S's in existence or whether we do not. In this section we develop two versions of the *square of opposition,* a classical method of representing the logical relations among the four categorical forms. We first examine Aristotle's version, called the *traditional square of opposition,* and then the modern ver–

sion. The traditional square of opposition is based on the existential assumption that members of the subject class do exist. The modern version of the square of opposition does not make an existential assumption.

The Traditional Square of Opposition

According to the traditional version of the square of opposition, the statement "All Martians are intelligent" implies that there are Martians in existence. Similarly, the statement "No Martians are intelligent" also implies that there are Martians. In other words, the traditional version is based upon the *existential assumption* that members of the subject class (in this example, Martians) do exist. Now in order to make the existential assumption explicit, we will place a special X in the diagrams for forms A and O. In the four Venn diagrams shown in Figure 3.2, the X indicates our assumption that members of the subject class exist.

What logical relations hold among these four forms? The description of the logical relations among the four categorical forms is represented in the square of opposition. Let's develop it systematically.

1. *If A is true, then I is true.* If it is true that all Martians are intelligent, then it must be true that some Martians are intelligent. The Venn diagrams show this, for the I-diagram is "contained within" the A-diagram. In short, 'All Martians are intelligent' implies 'Some Martians are intelligent'.

2. *If E is true, then O is true.* If it is true that no Martians are intelligent, then it must be true that some Martians are not intelligent. The O-diagram is contained within the E-diagram. 'No Martians are intelligent' implies 'Some Martians are not intelligent'.

Figure 3.2   The Four Forms with Existential Assumption

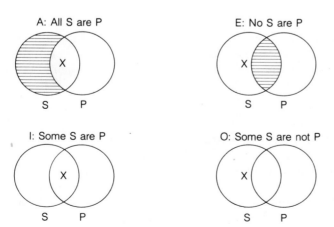

3. *A and E cannot both be true.* Start with either one as true. If it is true that all Martians are intelligent, for example, then it must be false that no Martians are intelligent. The A-diagram indicates that all Martians are in area (2), whereas the E-diagram indicates that no Martians are in area (2). Thus, if A is true, then E must be false, and if E is true, then A must be false. A and E are called *contraries,* which means that they cannot both be true but they can both be false. They can both be false, for example, if it turns out that some Martians are intelligent and some Martians are not intelligent. Consider the two statements 'All logicians are men' and 'No logicians are men'. Both can be and are false. But they cannot both be true, for the truth of one rules out the truth of the other.

4. *I and O cannot both be false.* Start with either one as false. If it is false that some Martians are intelligent, then it must be true that some Martians are not intelligent. If I is false, O is true; if O is false, then I is true. Martians must either be intelligent or not intelligent. If 'Some Martians are intelligent' is false, then it follows that 'Some Martians are not intelligent' is true. The same conclusion holds if we begin with the O-form as false. I and O are called *subcontraries* because they cannot both be false, but they can both be true. They can both be true if, for instance, it turns out that some Martians are intelligent and some are not.

5. *A and O are contradictories, and E and I are contradictories. Contradictories* have exact opposite truth-values. If A is true, then O is false, and vice versa. If I is true, then E is false, and vice versa. Consider what each pair asserts. A asserts, for example, that all Martians are intelligent, and O asserts that some Martians are not intelligent. They are exact opposites. The same applies for I and E. In Figure 3.2 the Venn diagrams diagonally opposite each other are contradictories. Thus, whatever truth-value E has, I has the opposite; and whatever A has, O has the opposite.

6. *If I is false, then A is false. If O is false, then E is false.* If it is not true that some Martians are intelligent, then it cannot be true that all Martians are intelligent: If I is false, then A is false. If it is not true that some Martians are not intelligent, then it cannot be true that no Martians are intelligent: If O is false, then E is false.

Now we can graphically represent the traditional square of opposition depicting the logical relations in detail (see Figure 3.3). Note the relationships of the contraries and the subcontraries, and also note the contradictories. Then notice how each universal form is related to its particular form.

The Modern Square of Opposition

The modern version of the square of opposition does not assert that any members of the subject class exist. When we state that 'All Martians are intelligent' we are not asserting that any Martians exist, nor are we asserting that they don't exist. We are making no commitment one way or the other about their existence. It is useful to

Figure 3.3 Traditional Square of Opposition

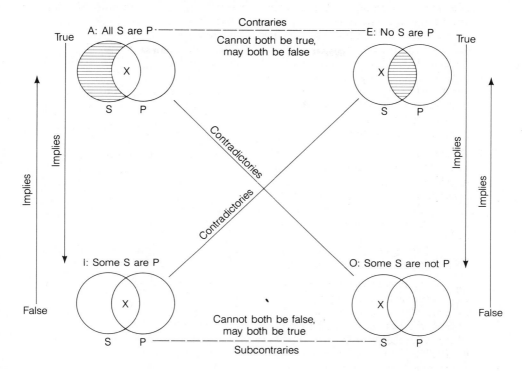

Summary

1. A implies I. I does not imply A.
2. E implies O. O does not imply E.

"Truth goes down"

3. A and E are contraries.

"Cannot both be true, may both be false"

4. I and O are subcontraries.

"Cannot both be false, may both be true"

5. A and O are contradictories.
   I and E are contradictories.

"They have exact opposite truth value"

6. The falsity of I implies the falsity of A.
   The falsity of O implies the falsity of E.

"Falsehood goes up"

---

avoid an existential assumption when we are talking about things whose existence we are unsure of, or whose existence is speculative or hypothetical. We might want to examine arguments and inferences about Martians, for example, without presupposing their existence, and we would like the logical implications of our statements to reflect that fact. Let us now develop the modern version of the square of opposition, showing the logical relations among the four categorical forms without an existential assumption. Note that we do not place an X in the diagrams for A and E, because we are not making an existential assumption.

1. *A and O are contradictories. E and I are contradictories.* 'All Martians are intelligent' asserts just what 'Some Martians are not intelligent' denies. If A is true, then O is false, and vice versa. Similarly, if A is false—if it is not true that all Martians are intelligent—then it is true that some Martians are not intelligent. The E- and I-forms are related in exactly the same way. If it is true that no Martians are intelligent, then it is false that some Martians are intelligent, and vice versa. The modern version preserves the relationships of the contradictories, as the diagrams of the pairs on the diagonals in Figure 3.4 show.

2. *A and E are not contraries.* It would seem that 'All Martians are intelligent' and 'No Martians are intelligent' cannot both be true, but this is not so. If there are no Martians, then both statements are true. If there are no Martians, then there are no Martians who are not intelligent and no Martians who are intelligent. Thus, if you know that A is true, you cannot infer that E is false.

3. *I and O are not subcontraries.* I and O may both be true, but I and O may also both be false, which means that in the modern version they are not subcontraries. I says that there is at least one Martian and that Martian is intelligent, and O says that there is at least one Martian and that Martian is not intelligent. If there are no Martians at all, then each statement is false.

4. *A does not imply I; E does not imply O.* We saw in the traditional version that A implies I and E implies O, but this is not so in the modern version. If there are no Martians at all, then I is false, for I claims that there is at least one Martian and that Martian is intelligent. Yet it still may be true that all Martians are intelligent. Likewise, if there are no Martians, then O is false, yet it still may be true that no Martians are intelligent. An example should help you see this. We know that 'All mermaids have tails' is true, yet it is false that 'Some mermaids have tails'; that is, it is false that there is at least one mermaid and she has a tail. Thus, A does not imply I, and E does not imply O. What makes this so, as you can see, is that A and E do not carry an existential commitment. But I and O do, for each asserts that 'there is at least one S'. And of course if there are no S's, then I and O are false because of that assertion.

5. *The falsity of I does not imply the falsity of A; the falsity of O does not imply the falsity of E.* Just as above, if there are no Martians, then both I and O are false. However, that does not make A or E false. Thus, the falsity of I does not imply that A is false, and likewise for O and E.

We can see from this examination that the only inference preserved in the modern version of the square is the inference between the contradictories, as shown in Figure 3.4. It is evident that the existential assumption makes an important logical difference in the relationships among the four categorical forms.

Figure 3.4   The Modern Square of Opposition

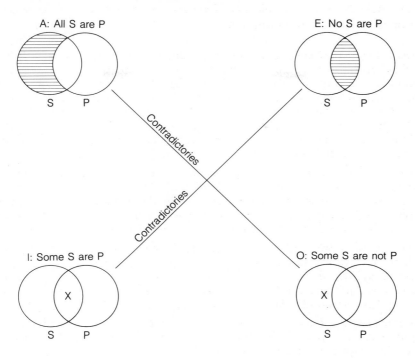

3.6 Inferences on the Traditional Square

By using Venn diagrams and the square of opposition we can evaluate common inferences made between any two of the four categorical forms. For example, if someone asserts that all snakes are poisonous and then concludes that it is false that some snakes are not poisonous, we can see from the Venn diagram and the square that this inference is valid. Let us work through several examples of such evaluations. In these exercises we are working with the traditional square and are therefore adopting the existential assumption that members of the subject category do exist. Remember that the Venn diagrams for the A- and E-forms reflect that assumption with an X in the circle representing the subject category.

Example 18

Some mushrooms are poisonous. Therefore it is false that no mushrooms are poisonous.

To determine whether this is a valid inference, we first identify the categorical forms. We have an inference from '*some mushrooms are poisonous*' to 'it is false that *no mushrooms are poisonous*', that is, from the truth of an I to the falsity of an E. We now look at the square and the diagrams of the relevant forms (refer to Figure 3.3). What can we tell about the relationship between the I and the E?

In the Venn diagram of the I-form statement we see an X in that area representing mushrooms that are poisonous. In the diagram of the E-form statement we observe that same logical area to be empty. The Venn diagrams show us that if I is true, then E is false. Recall also that I and E are contradictories and thus have opposite truth-values. We conclude, therefore, that it is a valid inference from the truth of I to the falsehood of E.

Example 19

No Buddhists are Catholics. Therefore, some Buddhists are not Catholics.

Is this inference—from E to O—a valid one?

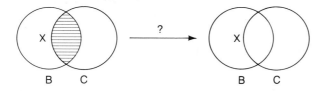

The diagrams show that O is implied by E; thus, it is a valid inference.

Example 20

Some senators are not communists. Therefore, some senators are communists.

Is this a valid inference? From the fact that some are not does it follow that some are?

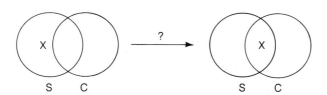

We see that this inference from O to I is not valid. Given that some senators are not communists, we do not have to conclude that some *are*. Some may be communists, but perhaps none are.

The inference from O to I is a very common mistake. Remember that I does not imply O and O does not imply I. If we know that some marines are tough, for example, we cannot conclude from that alone that some marines are not tough. All we know from the premise is that some are. It may turn out that *all* are, in which case the O statement would not be true. Thus, strictly speaking, it is invalid to reason from the truth of I to O and, as we saw, from the truth of O to I. Now, in everyday conversation the context may provide more information than is provided by statements of the form 'Some S are P' or 'Some S are not P'. From other things a speaker says we may be able to conclude that, for example, some marines are not tough. If a researcher reports, "I have examined all marines, and I can now say that *some* marines are tough," we can probably conclude that some marines are not tough. However, we are not entitled to that inference from the categorical statement alone; we can infer it only if there are additional unstated premises. For example, if all marines were examined we could expect the speaker to say that all rather than some were found to be tough if that is what the examination revealed.

Example 21

Given that a statement of the A–form is true,
what, if anything, can you conclude about the
following statement forms: (a) the I–form? (b) the
O–form? (c) the E–form?

Answers: If A is true, then (a) I is true; (b) O is false; and (c) E is false.

Example 22

Given that the I–form is true, what, if anything,
can you infer about (a) the A–form? (b) the O–
form? (c) the E–form?

Answers: If I is true, then (a) no inference can be made about A; (b) no inference can be made about O; and (c) E is false.

Example 23

Given that the O–form is false, what, if anything,
can you infer about (a) the A–form? (b) the E–
form? (c) the I–form?

Answers: If O is false, then (a) A is true; (b) E is false; and (c) I is true.

Example 24

Given that the E–form is false, what, if anything,
can you infer about (a) the A–form? (b) the I–
form? (c) the O–form?

Answers: If E is false, then (a) no inference can be made about A; (b) I is true; (c) no inference can be made about O.

For the following group of examples, determine whether the arguments are valid or invalid, using Venn diagrams. Then check your answers with those given below.

Example 25   It is false that no mechanics are on duty today; therefore, some are on duty today.

Example 26   Some lawyers are politicians; therefore, some lawyers are not politicians.

Example 27   All the people at the fair are from out of town; therefore, it is false that none are from out of town.

Example 28   It is not true that some political parties are revolutionary; therefore, none are.

Answers

Example 25

Example 26

Example 27

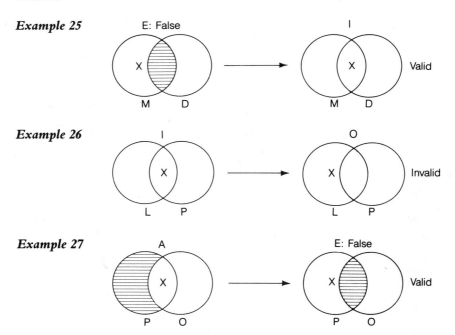

Example 28

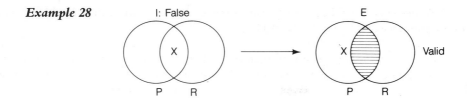

The logical relations shown in the square of opposition probably seem like common sense to you. The square of opposition is really just a convenient tool for organizing the kind of inferences you make every day. More than this, however, the diagrams in the square provide you with a simple method for demonstrating those logical relations and the inferences they allow you to make.

Exercise 3.6A Inferences on the Traditional Square of Opposition. Use the Venn diagrams and the square to determine whether the following arguments are valid or invalid. Remember to include the existential assumption in your diagrams. Show your work as illustrated in examples 25–28.

1. Is Smith's inference valid?
   Brown: Some players are not playing by the rules.
   Smith: I guess it follows from what you say that not all are playing by the rules.

2. Is Myles's inference valid?
   Adelaide: It's not true that all people like logic.
   Myles: Then no one likes logic.

3. There is at least one senator who voted for the tax cut. Therefore, it cannot be that no one voted for it.

4. It is false that all great chess players are foreigners. So none are foreigners.

5. No modern sculptors are better than Henry Moore. So it's false that some are better than Moore.

6. Some art historians are employed. It follows therefore that some art historians are not employed.

7. It is false that some philanthropists are not wealthy benefactors because all philanthropists are wealthy benefactors.

8. Is Wendell's inference valid?
   Annie: All logicians are cold and heartless.
   Wendell: Therefore, it can't be true that none are.

9. Is Maxine's inference valid?
   Betty: Some men are only interested in sex.
   Maxine: So you mean that not all men are interested in sex.

10. It's not true that every religion includes a belief in immortality; so some religions do not include such a belief.

Exercise 3.6B   More Inferences.   Use Venn diagrams and the traditional square to answer the following questions. Show your work as illustrated in examples 25–28.

1. Given that the E-form is true, what, if anything, can you infer about (a) the A-form? (b) the I-form? (c) the O-form?

2. Given that the I-form is true, what, if anything, can you infer about (a) the A-form? (b) the O-form? (c) the E-form?

3. If some bats are deaf, then what, if anything, can you infer about the claim that all bats are deaf?

4. If it's not true that all snakes are poisonous, then what about the claim that no snakes are poisonous?

5. If some people are not afraid of heights, then what can you infer about the claim that some people are afraid of heights?

6. Some humans are mortal. What can you infer about the claim that all humans are mortal?

7. Some humans are mortal. What can you infer about the claim that some humans are not mortal?

8. All houseplants need sunlight and water. What can you infer about the claim that it's false that some houseplants do not need sunlight and water?

9. If it's false that some Latin Americans do not speak Spanish, then what can you infer about the claim that all Latin Americans speak Spanish?

10. No great novelists are also great pianists. What can you infer about the claim that some great novelists are not great pianists?

Exercise 3.6C   Inferences on the Modern Square of Opposition.   Use Venn diagrams and the modern square to determine whether the following inferences are valid. Recall that on the modern square you do not assume the existence of members of the subject category. Show your work.

1. All mermaids are lovely creatures; therefore, some mermaids are lovely creatures.

2. Some Cheshire cats are big smilers, so it's false that no Cheshire cats are big smilers.

3. No spirits are material; therefore, it's false that all spirits are material.

4. Some subatomic particles are not theoretical entities; therefore, it's true that some *are* theoretical entities.

5. All serious music lovers are people who read music because it's false that some serious music lovers are not people who read music.

6. It's not true that some uranium mines are hazardous, so it must be that some are not hazardous.

7. It's false that all precocious children are gifted because it's false that some precocious children are gifted.

8. No atheists are Christians; therefore, some atheists are not Christians.

9. All golden mountains are fictitious, so it follows that some golden mountains are fictitious.

10. Since no intelligent television comedies are successful, it follows that 'some intelligent television comedies are successful' is false.

3.7 The Operations

Operations are defined procedures for manipulating statements. With the four types of categorical statements described above we can perform three important operations: *conversion, obversion,* and *contraposition.* These operations yield several valid inferences and in some cases provide different ways of saying the same thing while preserving logical meaning. Hence, they indicate certain ways of logically extending our knowledge.

An important concept in the study of the operations is that of logical equivalence. In logic we say that two statements are *logically equivalent* if and only if they necessarily have the same truth conditions. That is, if one statement is true (or false), then necessarily the other statement is true (or false). We mean the same thing in daily life when we say that two sentences "have the same meaning" or "are just two different ways of saying the same thing." Logically equivalent statements are typically interchangeable. When two statements are logically equivalent we can validly infer from the truth (or falsity) of one to the truth (or falsity) of the other. We can recognize logically equivalent statements by the fact that their Venn diagrams are identical.

In this section we will learn (1) how to perform each operation, (2) how to diagram the resulting statement, and (3) how to tell whether the resulting statement is logically equivalent to the original. Finally, (4) we will learn how to evaluate inferences made between a statement and its converse, obverse, and contrapositive. *Valid inferences made from the operations do not require an existential assumption.* That is, we do not need to assume that members of the subject category exist in order to assess these inferences. Let's begin with conversion and see how it applies to each of the four forms.

Conversion: Switch Subject and Predicate Terms

To perform this operation, we simply switch the subject and predicate of the statement. The resulting statement is called the *converse.* Here are the four forms and their converses:

STATEMENT FORM		CONVERSE
A: All S are P	*becomes*	All P are S
E: No S are P	*becomes*	No P are S
I: Some S are P	*becomes*	Some P are S
O: Some S are not P	*becomes*	Some P are not S

Here are some examples:

	STATEMENT	CONVERSE
Example 29	*All tomatoes are vegetables*	*All vegetables are tomatoes*
Example 30	*No snails are pretty*	*No pretty things are snails*
Example 31	*Some records are hits*	*Some hits are records*
Example 32	*Some dogs are not attackers*	*Some attackers are not dogs*

Venn diagrams provide a convenient way to determine the logical relation between a statement and its converse. Done correctly, they show us whether the statement resulting from an operation is logically equivalent to the original statement. When you are diagraming a statement formed from an operation it is very important to *label the circles exactly as they are labeled in the diagram of the original statement*. Even though the positions of subject and predicate may change, the circles must be labeled the same if you are to see the effect of the operation on the original statement. Notice how the statements are labeled in the illustration of the A-form below.

Example 33

A: All artists are painters

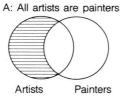

Artists   Painters

CONVERSE
All painters are artists

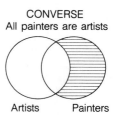

Artists   Painters

The diagram of the A-form and its converse are different; in fact they are mirror images of one another. This indicates that the A-form statement and its converse do not mean the same thing, or rather that converting an A-form statement does not produce just another way of saying the same thing. *The A and its converse are not logically equivalent.* Thus, no valid inference should be made from the A to its converse. For example, given that 'All artists are painters', it does not follow that 'All painters are artists'. From 'All biologists are scientists' you cannot validly infer that 'All scientists are biologists'. In sum, *the truth (or falsity) of the A does not imply the truth (or falsity) of its converse.*

Let us consider the E-form and its converse.

Example 34

E: No artists are painters

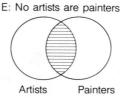

Artists   Painters

CONVERSE
No painters are artists

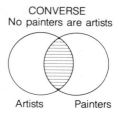

Artists   Painters

The diagrams are identical, so the converse of an E-form statement is logically equivalent to the original. Common sense also tells us that if no artists are painters, then no painters are artists. *We can validly infer from the truth (or falsity) of the E-form to the truth (or falsity) of its converse.* The diagrams indicate this by showing that the statements carry the same information.

Now consider the I-form.

Example 35

Some artists are painters

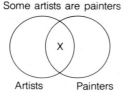

Artists   Painters

CONVERSE
Some painters are artists

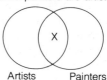

Artists   Painters

The diagrams are the same, indicating that the statements 'Some artists are painters' and 'Some painters are artists' are logically equivalent. If we know that one is true (or false), we can infer that the other is true (or false). *The I-form and its converse are logically equivalent, and therefore valid inferences can be made between them.*

Consider the O-form.

Example 36

Some artists are not painters

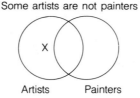

Artists   Painters

CONVERSE
Some painters are not artists

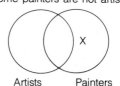

Artists   Painters

The O-form statement is not the same as its converse. Hence, you cannot infer that some painters are not artists from the fact that some artists are not painters. Suppose you know that some vegetables are not tomatoes. The converse, 'some tomatoes are not vegetables', surely does not follow. *The O and its converse are not equivalent, and therefore inferences cannot be validly made between them.*

In sum, conversion switches the subject and predicate. Statements of forms A and O are not logically equivalent to their converses, and statements of forms E and I *are* logically equivalent to their converses.

Obversion (1) Change the Quality;
(2) Negate the Predicate

We form the *obverse* of a statement in two steps. First we change the quality, from affirmative to negative or from negative to affirmative. Changing the quality of 'Some cats are runners' yields 'Some cats are not runners'. Changing the quality of 'All cats are runners' yields 'No cats are runners'. We change the quality of a statement by "moving horizontally across the square." The second step is to negate the predicate, which we do by adding the prefix *non* to it. Negating the terms 'mice', 'hermits', and 'combatants' yields 'nonmice', 'nonhermits', and 'noncombatants'. Here are some examples of this two-step procedure for forming the obverse:

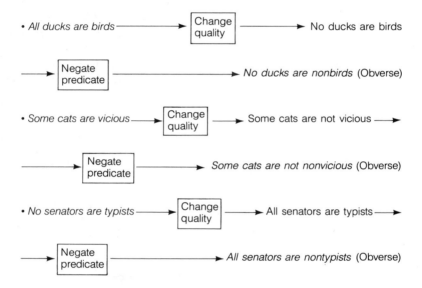

The four forms and their obverses are as follows:

STATEMENT FORM		OBVERSE
A: All S are P	*becomes*	No S are nonP
E: No S are P	*becomes*	All S are nonP
I: Some S are P	*becomes*	Some S are not nonP
O: Some S are not P	*becomes*	Some S are nonP

What logical relations do you expect between the four forms and their obverses? If you know that all ducks are birds, can you infer that no ducks are nonbirds? If some cats are vicious, does it follow that some cats are not nonvicious? Diagraming the forms reveals that all four of them are logically equivalent to their obverses.

Hence, valid inferences can be made between each form and its obverse. Here is the A-form and its obverse:

Example 37

A: All ducks are birds

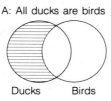

Ducks   Birds

OBVERSE
No ducks are nonbirds

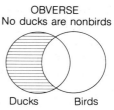

Ducks   Birds

To draw the diagram of the obverse of this statement, we must indicate something about its subject, ducks, with the circle representing ducks. We are saying that no ducks are nonbirds, and nonbirds would be anywhere *outside* the birds circle in this diagram, that is, either area 1 or area 4. We therefore cross out that area within the ducks circle that is outside the birds circle. The shading in area 1 show that there are no ducks that are nonbirds. Notice that the resulting diagram is identical to the original, indicating that the inference is valid. If all ducks are birds, it validly follows that no ducks are nonbirds.

Consider the E-form.

Example 38

E: No ducks are birds

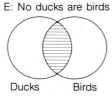

Ducks   Birds

OBVERSE
All ducks are nonbirds

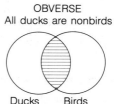

Ducks   Birds

The obverse of E states that all ducks are nonbirds. To depict this statement we want to show that all ducks are only in that part of the ducks circle in which they are nonbirds, that is, the area outside the birds circle, area 1. We therefore empty out area 2, and we obtain a diagram identical to the original.

Now consider the I-form and its obverse.

Example 39

I: Some ducks are birds

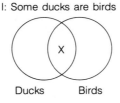

Ducks   Birds

OBVERSE
Some ducks are not nonbirds

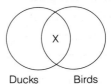

Ducks   Birds

To say that some ducks are *not nonbirds* is the same as saying that some ducks are *not* outside the birds circle; they are inside it. We can see that the phrase 'not nonP' really amounts to the phrase 'P'.

Now look at the O-form and its obverse.

Example 40

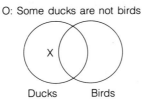

O: Some ducks are not birds

Ducks   Birds

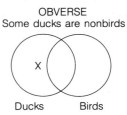

OBVERSE
Some ducks are nonbirds

Ducks   Birds

The two diagrams are the same because the phrase 'are nonbirds' is logically equivalent to the phrase 'are not birds'. If ducks are nonbirds, then they are represented *outside* the birds circle.

In sum, *every categorical statement is equivalent to its obverse. Obversion always yields a logically equivalent statement.*

Contraposition (1) Switch Subject and Predicate; (2) Negate Both

We also form the *contrapositive* of a statement in two steps. First we switch the subject and predicate terms of the statement. Then we negate each term by adding *non*. The four forms and their contrapositives are as follows:

STATEMENT FORM		CONTRAPOSITIVE
A: All S are P	*becomes*	All nonP are nonS
E: No S are P	*becomes*	No nonP are nonS
I: Some S are P	*becomes*	Some nonP are nonS
O: Some S are not P	*becomes*	Some nonP are not nonS

The A-form and its contrapositive are diagramed as follows:

Example 41

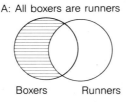

A: All boxers are runners

Boxers   Runners

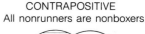

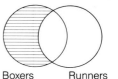

CONTRAPOSITIVE
All nonrunners are nonboxers

Boxers   Runners

As always, the circles must be labeled just as they were in the original statement. In the contrapositive the new subject of the statement is 'nonrunners', and these are represented as being *anywhere outside* the runners circle. The predicate states that they are all nonboxers; that is, that they are all *outside* the boxers circle. Hence, we want to show that everything outside the runners circle is also outside the boxers circle.

Thus, the area where there are nonrunners who are boxers is crossed out to show that all nonrunners are nonboxers. Try going through this with an example of your own. We see that *the A-form and its contrapositive are logically equivalent, and therefore we can validly infer from one to the other.*

Let us look at the contrapositive of the E-form.

Example 42

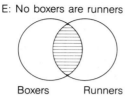

E: No boxers are runners

Boxers   Runners

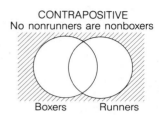

CONTRAPOSITIVE

No nonrunners are nonboxers

Boxers   Runners

The contrapositive of the E-form is an interesting one to diagram. The subject of the statement 'No nonrunners are nonboxers' is nonrunners, which is everything outside the runners circle. About nonrunners we are saying that none of them are non-boxers, that is, that none of them are outside the boxers circle. No things outside the runners circle are outside the boxers circle. Thus, we shade area 4, the area outside both circles. The two diagrams are not the same, indicating that *the E-form and its contrapositive are not equivalent.*

The I-form and its contrapositive are as follows:

Example 43

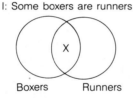

I: Some boxers are runners

Boxers   Runners

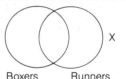

CONTRAPOSITIVE

Some nonrunners are nonboxers

Boxers   Runners

The contrapositive of the I in our example states that some nonrunners are non-boxers. We must place an X representing nonrunners somewhere *outside* the runners circle. That leaves only two places: area 1, where nonrunners and boxers are, or area 4, where nonrunners and nonboxers are. Clearly, the X should go in area 4, thus showing that there are some nonrunners who are also nonboxers. The diagram is not identical to the original, indicating that *the I-form and its contrapositive are not equivalent.*

Consider now the contrapositive of the O-form.

Example 44

O: Some boxers are not runners

Boxers   Runners

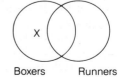

CONTRAPOSITIVE

Some nonrunners are not nonboxers

Boxers   Runners

Table 3.1   The Operations: Equivalences

CONVERSION: switch subject and predicate terms

A: All S are P	$\not\equiv$	All P are S
E: No S are P	$\equiv$	No P are S
I: Some S are P	$\equiv$	Some P are S
O: Some S are not P	$\not\equiv$	Some P are not S

OBVERSION: (1) change the quality, (2) negate the predicate

A: All S are P	$\equiv$	No S are nonP
E: No S are P	$\equiv$	All S are nonP
I: Some S are P	$\equiv$	Some S are not nonP
O: Some S are not P	$\equiv$	Some S are nonP

CONTRAPOSITION: (1) switch subject and predicate, (2) negate both

A: All S are P	$\equiv$	All nonP are nonS
E: No S are P	$\not\equiv$	No nonP are nonS
I: Some S are P	$\not\equiv$	Some nonP are nonS
O: Some S are not P	$\equiv$	Some nonP are not nonS

Notice in Table 3.1 that obversion yields equivalences on all forms. Conversion yields equivalences only on E and I. Contraposition yields equivalences on the other two forms, A and O—a surprising symmetry. A summary of the diagrams of the operations is provided in Figure 3.5.

The contrapositive states that some nonrunners are not nonboxers. We can understand this as saying that some things outside the runners circle are not outside the boxers circle; they are inside the boxers circle. Thus, an X representing nonrunners must be placed outside the runners circle and inside the boxers circle, in area 1. The resulting diagram is identical to the original, showing that *the O form is logically equivalent to its contrapositive.*

Table 3.1 summarizes the operations and shows which yield logically equivalent statements. The symbol '$\equiv$' indicates logical equivalence. The symbol '$\not\equiv$' indicates no logical equivalence. Valid inferences can be made between logically equivalent pairs.

Notice in Table 3.1 that obversion yields equivalences on all forms. Conversion yields equivalences only on E and I. Contraposition yields equivalences on the other two forms, A and O—a surprising symmetry. A summary of the diagrams of the operations is provided in Figure 3.5.

Negating Terms: A Special Note

Two of the operations we discussed above involve negating terms, which is done by adding the prefix *non* to the term. Frequently, the resulting negated term is awkward and would not be encountered in ordinary speech. For some terms, our

Figure 3.5 Diagrams of the Operations

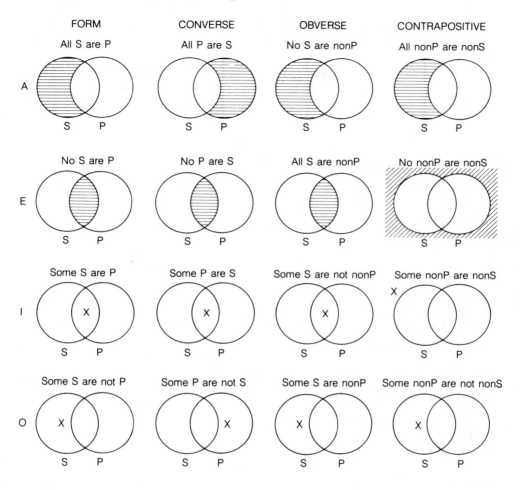

	FORM	CONVERSE	OBVERSE	CONTRAPOSITIVE
A	All S are P	All P are S	No S are nonP	All nonP are nonS
E	No S are P	No P are S	All S are nonP	No nonP are nonS
I	Some S are P	Some P are S	Some S are not nonP	Some nonP are nonS
O	Some S are not P	Some P are not S	Some S are nonP	Some nonP are not nonS

language contains a more familiar negated form, as, for example, 'unresponsive', 'undependable', 'unfriendly', 'immortal'. However, some negations are not merely negations of a term; they constitute an altogether different predicate. For example, the term 'unhappy' is not really the negation of 'happy'. The statements 'Max is nonhappy' and 'Max is unhappy' do not say the same thing, for Max may be *nonhappy* yet *not unhappy*. You would not be correct in inferring from 'Max is nonhappy' that Max is therefore unhappy, because the former does not mean the same as the latter. The logically proper negation of 'happy' is 'nonhappy' in spite of its odd sound. Likewise, the proper negation of 'living' is 'nonliving' rather than 'dead', since saying that something is dead is saying more than that it is nonliving. Rocks are nonliving but not dead.

To determine whether an ordinary language term constitutes a proper negation, you must ask yourself whether it is synonymous with the logically negated predicate formed by adding *non*. You must be sensitive to the language to do this; there is no hard-and-fast rule to follow.

A further point about negating terms is that we sometimes encounter what we call a *double negation*—for example, 'Some protesters are non-nonmilitants'. As a Venn diagram will show, this statement is equivalent to 'Some protesters are militants'. The doubled negatives cancel one another out. In logic the *rule of double negation* states that *'non-nonP'* is logically equivalent to *'P'*. Thus, double negations may be eliminated.

Examples of Inferences with the Operations

Now let's consider how the operations may yield valid inferences. In the following examples we will determine what operation or operations are being performed and whether the inferences made are valid or invalid.

Example 45

Some capitalists are not materialists. Therefore, some capitalists are nonmaterialists.

To determine what operation is involved, ask yourself what changes have been made from the original statement to the resulting statement. We see that the quality has changed and the predicate has been negated, indicating obversion. Venn diagrams of the premises and conclusion are identical; thus, the inference is valid.

Example 46

No welders are union members. Therefore, no non-union members are nonwelders.

In this example the subject and predicate have switched places, and each has been negated, indicating contraposition. The diagrams reveal that the inference is invalid.

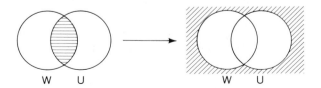

Example 47

*Some people are cooperative; therefore, some people
are not uncooperative.*

The quality has changed, and the predicate has been negated, indicating obversion.
The diagrams show that it is a valid inference.

Example 48

*Some nonviolent people are not dangerous. Therefore,
some nondangerous people are not violent.*

The subject and predicate terms have changed places, and both terms have been
negated. The subject term 'nonviolent people' appears in the predicate position,
changed to 'violent people', and the predicate term is similarly changed, indicating
contraposition. The diagrams below show that the inference is valid.

Example 49

*Some aggressive people are comedians. Therefore,
some comedians are not nonaggressive people.*

Look closely at this example. The subject and predicate terms have changed places,
but the quality has changed, too. Since no single operation has such results, this argument may employ more than one operation. Examining it we see that the terms
have switched places, the quality has changed, and the term 'aggressive people' has
been negated. The operation of obversion must be involved, since it is the only one
that changes the quality of a statement; obversion also accounts for the negation of
the term 'aggressive people'. To account for the switching of the terms, we consider
conversion and contraposition, and we eliminate contraposition because it negates
both terms. Thus, the conclusion results from the operation of conversion and then
obversion. Writing this all out and drawing the diagrams makes it quite clear.

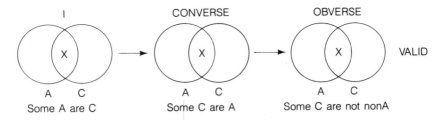

I	CONVERSE	OBVERSE
A C	A C	A C
Some A are C	Some C are A	Some C are not nonA

And since each of these operations yields a logically equivalent statement, it follows that the inference is valid.

Exercise 3.7A   Operations.   For each statement perform the operation indicated in parentheses, and then draw Venn diagrams for both the original and the resulting statement.

1. All scientists are researchers.
   (Converse) _____

2. Some capitalists are not materialists.
   (Obverse) _____

3. No artists are wealthy.
   (Contrapositive) _____

4. No filmmakers are independent artists.
   (Contrapositive) _____

5. All trees are plants.
   (Obverse) _____

6. Some mutts are mixed breeds.
   (Converse) _____

7. Some buyers are market managers.
   (Contrapositive) _____

8. Some cats type fifty words per minute.
   (Converse) _____

9. No gypsies are loiterers.
   (Obverse) _____

10. No planets in our solar system other than Earth are suitable for life.
    (Obverse) _____

11. Some citrus growers are not nonunion supporters.
    (Obverse) _____

12. No educated people are nongraduates.
    (Obverse) _____

13. Some retired servicepeople are nonbeneficiaries.

   (Converse) _____

14. All third-world countries are presently nonindustrialized.

   (Contrapositive) _____

15. Some sociopaths are not nonmoral people.

   (Obverse) _____

Exercise 3.7B   Valid or Invalid?   Use Venn diagrams to determine whether the inference is valid in each of the following statements. Identify the operation or operations involved. Show your work as illustrated in the example section above.

1. No patriots are traitors. Therefore, all patriots are nontraitors.

2. Some sales are not refundable sales. Therefore, some refundable sales are not sales.

3. All revolutionaries are radicals. So no revolutionaries are nonradicals.

4. Some noncombatants are not neutrals. Hence, some nonneutrals are not combatants.

5. Some people are not friendly, so some people are unfriendly.

6. All members of the faculty are recognized geniuses, because no members of the faculty are unrecognized geniuses.

7. Some metals are liquids. Therefore, some liquids are not nonmetals.

8. All Moslems are non-Buddhists, because no Moslems are Buddhists.

9. No senators are infants. Therefore, no noninfants are nonsenators.

10. All souls are immortal. Thus, no souls are mortal.

Review Questions Chapter 3

1. What is the purpose of a logical system? Explain in your own words why a mechanical and objective procedure is desirable.

2. What are categories?

3. In your opinion, is it conceivable that we could categorize reality in any way whatsoever? If not, what limitations are there?

4. What are the four categorical forms? What is meant by 'quantity' and 'quality'? Compare the four forms in terms of quantity and quality.

5. Explain what Venn diagrams are and what purpose they serve.

6. What is an existential assumption? Do you think that in everyday conversations we usually assume the existence of the things we talk about, or not? Explain your answer.

7. Briefly explain how the two versions of the square of opposition differ.

8. Which forms are the contraries? Explain what that means.

9. Which forms are the subcontraries? Explain what that means.

10. Which forms are the contradictories? Explain what that means.

11. Explain how each of these operations is performed: (a) conversion; (b) obversion; (c) contraposition.

12. What things can be learned from the operations?

13. What is the law of double negation? What does it permit one to do?

14. What is logical equivalence? How can you tell that two or more statements are logically equivalent by using Venn diagrams? What is useful about knowing that two or more statements are logically equivalent?

15. Which of the categorical forms yield logical equivalences when converted? When obverted? When contraposed?

True or False?

1. 'Some chemists are good mathematicians' is the contradictory of 'No chemists are good mathematicians'.

2. If two statements are logically equivalent, then they·have the same truth conditions.

3. Every categorical statement is equivalent to its converse.

4. The A–form statement is particular, affirmative.

5. If two statements are contraries, then they can both be true, but they cannot both be false.

6. If you obvert 'No human beings are immortal', you get 'All human beings are mortal'.

7. A statement of the form 'Some S are P' asserts that there is at least one S and it is a P. Thus, it asserts the existence of at least one S, and if there are no S's, then it is a false statement.

8. If A is true, then E is false only if you assume the existence of members of the subject category.

9. If one of the subcontraries is true, then the other must be false.

10. Inferences made between a statement and its converse, obverse, or contrapositive are valid only if one is making an existential assumption.

CHAPTER FOUR
Categorical Logic
Part II

In this chapter we apply the principles of categorical logic to the evaluation of deductive arguments. We learn how to translate sentences in ordinary language into proper categorical form and how to write arguments in the form we call the *categorical syllogism*. Finally, we learn to use Venn diagrams to evaluate syllogisms and chains of syllogisms called *sorites*.

4.1 Translating into Categorical Form

Everyday language does not usually come already expressed in categorical form. People do not restrict their speech to the four categorical forms. Therefore, to apply the system of categorical logic, we frequently have to translate ordinary language statements into proper categorical statements. Some guidelines are helpful for translating the more difficult constructions we encounter in ordinary language, but the basic idea of the process is not very difficult to grasp: First we identify the *categories* that are the subject and predicate of the statement, and then we determine how much of the subject is being referred to—all, none, or some. Translating a statement clarifies its meaning and reveals its precise logical sense by showing clearly what relationship between categories is being asserted and whether the assertion is an affirmation or a denial. Then the logical implications of the statement are more apparent to us.

To be in categorical form, a statement must, strictly speaking, have three features:

1. A standard quantifier: 'all', 'no', or 'some'
2. A copula: 'are' (or 'are not' in the case of the O-form)
3. Subject and predicate terms that refer to categories

These requirements make explicit what we saw in Chapter 3: Categorical statements must have a standard quantifier, 'all', 'no', or 'some'; they must have a linking verb, called the *copula,* either 'are' or (in the case of the O-form statement) 'are not'; and their subject and predicate terms should be *group terms,* that is, terms referring to categories or groups of things.

A statement in categorical form can be schematized as follows:

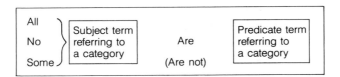

The sentences below are not in categorical form:

Not all magicians use mirrors.

The cat swallowed the bird.

There's a rusty car in the ditch.

No men are allowed.

Jane kissed Tom.

Only chemists are excluded.

Everyone except the graduating seniors is dismissed.

But each of these sentences can be translated into proper categorical form, and we turn now to a discussion of guidelines for such translations.

4.2 Translating Guide

1. Supplying Group Terms   Many words or phrases in ordinary language do not explicitly refer to a group or category. For example, in 'Some roses are red' the predicate term 'red' does not name a group of things. But we can easily supply it.

The sentence says, in effect, that some roses belong to the category of red things. We can therefore rewrite it as 'Some roses are red things' or '. . . red flowers', if we are sure it refers only to flowers. When we supply group terms we rewrite the subject or predicate terms so they name groups of things. In the following examples the words or phrases supplied to achieve proper categorical form are underlined.

Example 1	All bachelors are unmarried.	---	All bachelors are unmarried <u>males</u>.
Example 2	Some letter carriers are tired.	---	Some letter carriers are tired <u>persons</u>.
Example 3	No dancers are ready for the performance.	---	No dancers are <u>persons who are</u> ready for the performance.
Example 4	Some of the platoon are infantrymen.	---	Some <u>members</u> of the platoon are infantrymen.

2. Supplying a Copula   Translating sentences using verbs other than 'are' and 'are not' usually requires placing the original verb "inside" the predicate phrase. In the following examples notice how the verbs are translated, especially verbs in the past tense. The phrases supplied are underlined.

Example 5	No seagulls like pelicans.	---	No seagulls are <u>birds that</u> like pelicans.
Example 6	Some dogs would rather bite than bark.	---	Some dogs are <u>dogs that</u> would rather bite than bark.
Example 7	All dieters eat vegetables.	---	All dieters are <u>persons who</u> eat vegetables.
Example 8	Some players were not present.	---	Some players are <u>persons who</u> were not present.

3. Proper Names and Singular Expressions   Proper names are names of persons, countries, brands of products, and so on. Singular expressions are expressions that refer to a particular person or thing, such as 'this house', 'that car', or 'the man in the trenchcoat'. Both proper names and singular expressions refer to particular things rather than to groups of things. Here are some examples:

Socrates is a man.

This firefighter is due for a raise.

Venezuela is an oil-rich country.

John kissed Mary.

Today is my birthday.

This type of sentence presents a special problem in categorical logic because it is not a statement about a *group* of things. You might be tempted to translate 'Socrates is a man', for example, as 'All Socrates are men' (or, even worse, 'Some Socrates are men'). That not only sounds odd but suggests that 'Socrates' names a group of things (in this case, a group of men), and surely it does not. How then do we handle statements about individuals in a system designed for statements about groups? The solution is wordy but clever. We introduce a group that necessarily has only one member in it. The term 'persons identical to Socrates' names a group, but it is a group that can have only one member in it, since only one thing in existence is identical to Socrates, namely, Socrates himself. (This special expression 'identical to' is understood to mean *'one and the same as'*. It does not mean 'another one the same as', as in the sentence 'Your car is identical to my car'.) The examples given above can be translated into categorical statements using this special expression as follows:

Example 9	*Socrates is a man.*	---	*All persons identical to Socrates are men.*
Example 10	*This firefighter is due for a raise.*	---	*All persons identical to this firefighter are persons due for a raise.*
Example 11	*Venezuela is an oil-rich country.*	---	*All countries identical to Venezuela are oil-rich countries.*
Example 12	*John kissed Mary.*	---	*All persons identical to John are persons who kissed Mary.*
Example 13	*Today is my birthday.*	---	*All days identical to today are days identical to my birthday.*

4. Supplying Quantifiers   In some cases the quantifier of a statement is left unstated. You must determine how much of the subject is being referred to and whether it is meant to affirm or deny the predicate of the subject. Consider these examples:

Example 14	Roses are red.	---	<u>All</u> roses are red flowers.
Example 15	The ox is a strong beast.	---	<u>All</u> oxen are strong beasts.
Example 16	Emeralds are not cheap.	---	<u>No</u> emeralds are cheap things.
Example 17	The soul is not immortal.	---	<u>No</u> souls are immortal souls.

Some uses of the articles 'a' and 'the' are ambiguous. In some sentences they may be used to refer to all members of a class—as in 'The whale is an enormous mammal'—and in others they refer to a single individual—as in 'The whale is on the beach'. When the article is ambiguous ask yourself, In this sentence are we talking about all members of the subject class, some of them, or a single individual? Read the following examples carefully and notice how the same phrase may refer to a group in one context and to an individual in another.

Example 18	The police officer is our friend.	---	<u>All</u> police officers are our friends.
Example 19	The police officer is at the door.	---	<u>All</u> persons identical to this police officer are persons at the door.
Example 20	Police officers are our friends.	---	<u>All</u> police officers are our friends.
Example 21	Police officers are at our door.	---	<u>Some</u> police officers are persons at our door.
Example 22	An apricot is not a vegetable.	---	<u>No</u> apricots are vegetables.
Example 23	A fish is on the line.	---	<u>All</u> things identical to this fish are things on the line.

5. Other Quantifiers and Quantifying Expressions   Our language contains many other quantifiers besides 'all', 'no', and 'some'; some important ones are 'few', 'many', and 'most'. There is a standard way to translate sentences using these and other, similar quantifiers. Sentences using 'few', 'many', 'most', and so on, clearly refer to some rather than all of the subject class, but they also carry more information than the 'some' categorical statements. For example, 'Few people came to the game' implies that some came to the game *and* some did not. Unlike the I- and O-form statements, these sentences carry the implication that some are something and some are not. If you are able to say that 'few people came', then you imply those two categorical assertions. Thus, to translate such sentences, we rewrite them as *two categorical statements,* as these examples illustrate:

Example 24	Few people came to the game.	---	<u>Some</u> people <u>are</u> people who came to the game. <u>Some</u> people <u>are not</u> people who came to the game.
Example 25	Most cattle are breeders.	---	<u>Some</u> cattle <u>are</u> breeders. <u>Some</u> cattle <u>are not</u> breeders.
Example 26	Many voters are registered.	---	<u>Some</u> voters <u>are</u> registered voters. <u>Some</u> voters <u>are not</u> registered voters.

To diagram a sentence that has been translated into two categorical statements, you draw the two interlocking circles as usual, label them according to the two categories involved, and then simply diagram each statement, combining the information from both into one diagram. For example, consider the diagram for example 26 above, 'Some voters are registered voters. Some voters are not registered voters':

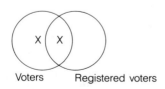

Voters   Registered voters

Notice that when you translate the quantifiers 'most', 'few', and 'many' into two categorical statements, forms I and O, you lose the distinction among them. There is no difference in the way they are treated. You could not infer from the translations themselves that the number of people who came to the game was *few*. Thus, some precision is lost in this method of translation.

Another quantifying expression in our language is 'all . . . are not', which almost always means 'none are', as indicated in these examples:

Example 27   *All toads are*   --- *No toads are*
                 not frogs.   *frogs.*

Example 28   *All Picassos*   --- *No Picassos*
                 are not cheap.   *are cheap*
                                       things.

However, the phrase 'all . . . are not' is occasionally used to give emphasis to a denial of an A-form statement ('All S are P'). For example, if someone says, 'All citizens are eligible to become president', you might deny this by saying, 'All citizens are *not* eligible to become president'. You would not be saying that no citizens are eligible; you would be saying that the statement 'All citizens are eligible to become president' is false. Your statement would be translated, 'Some citizens are not persons eligible to become president'. Examine the examples below and compare them to each other.

Example 29   *All recruits are* --- <u>No</u> *recruits are*
                 not on leave.   *persons on*
                                        leave.

Example 30   *All recruits are* --- *Some recruits*
                 <u>not</u> *on leave.*   *are <u>not</u> persons*
                                        on leave.

The second statement gives emphasis to a denial of an A-form statement. The first usage is the more likely, but you will have to consider the context to decide which is the better translation.

The phrase 'not all . . . are' is the denial of the A-form statement. 'Not all humans are mortals' means that it is not true that all humans are mortals. It is translated as 'Some humans are not mortals'.

Example 31   *Not all Demo-* --- *Some Demo-*
                 crats are   *crats are not*
                 voters.   *voters.*

6. Adverbs of Place and Time   Occasionally you will want to translate a statement in such a way that it refers to a time or place. Use the word 'places' in both the subject and predicate terms to translate adverbs of place like the following:

where
wherever
everywhere
somewhere
nowhere

Here are some examples:

Example 32   *Checkered squirrels are found nowhere.* --- *No places are places where checkered squirrels are found.*

Example 33   *Somewhere I lost my wallet.* --- *Some places are places where I lost my wallet.*

Example 34   *Wherever she goes, he goes.* --- *All places where she goes are places where he goes.*

Use the word 'times' in both the subject and predicate to translate adverbs of time like these:

always

never

when

whenever

sometimes

every time

Some examples of this method follow:

Example 35   *The team never loses.* --- *No times are times the team loses.*

Example 36   *When they sing we laugh.* --- *All times they sing are times we laugh.*

Example 37   *Sometimes it rains.* --- *Some times are times it rains.*

Example 38   *Every time I begin to work the phone rings.* --- *All times I begin to work are times the phone rings.*

7. Conditionals   'If . . . then', 'only if', and 'if and only if' are some of the more important phrases in our language that express conditionals. A conditional statement asserts that something is the case if a certain condition is met. For example,

'If it rains, then the streets will be wet' asserts that the streets will be wet given the condition that it rains. To translate statements expressing conditionals, you use either the A-form or the E-form, depending upon whether the statement is best rendered as affirmative or negative. Here are some examples of 'if . . . then' and 'only if' statements:

Example 39 If a man is a bachelor, then he is unmarried. --- _All_ bachelors are unmarried men.

Example 40 If it rains, then the streets will be wet. --- _All_ times it rains are times the streets will be wet.

Example 41 If this bird eats seeds, then it is not a flycatcher. --- _No_ birds that eat seeds are flycatchers.

Example 42 A man is a bachelor only if he is unmarried. --- _All_ bachelors are unmarried men.

Example 43 Your house is safe only if it is locked tightly. --- _All_ safe houses are houses that are locked tightly.

The phrase 'if and only if' is a "two-way" conditional; that is, it asserts an 'if . . . then' relationship in both directions. For example, 'A man is a bachelor if and only if he is an unmarried male' asserts that _if_ a man is a bachelor, then he is an unmarried male, _and if_ a man is an unmarried male, then he is a bachelor. 'If and only if' asserts that each is a condition of the other or, in other words, if either one is true, then the other is also true. Notice in the examples that these "double conditionals" must be translated using two categorical statements.

Example 44 A man is a bachelor if and only if he is unmarried. --- _All_ bachelors are unmarried men. All unmarried men are bachelors.

Example 45 It's a sound argument if and only if it is a good argument. --- _All_ sound arguments are good arguments. All good arguments are sound arguments.

To diagram the two categorical statements required to translate an 'if and only if' sentence, you combine the information from both statements into one diagram, thus representing exactly what the original sentence asserts. For example, the categorical statements 'All bachelors are unmarried men. All unmarried men are bachelors' would be diagramed as follows:

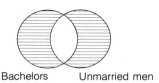

Bachelors   Unmarried men

8. Logical Groups 'Only', 'the only', 'all and only', and 'all except' are words and phrases in our language that are used to group things together or to separate things logically. To translate these words, you must consider carefully just what they do logically. The following guidelines show how the major logical grouping words work.

(a) 'Only' and 'none but' The words 'only' and 'none but' are frequently misunderstood. What does the statement 'Only humans use reason' really mean? Does it mean that *all* humans use reason? No, for you can sensibly say, 'Only humans use reason, but not all of them do'. What it does mean is that all things that use reason are humans. The statement form 'Only X are Y' really means 'All Y are X'. Similarly, the statement 'None but the coaches have keys' says that all who have keys are coaches, but it does not say that *all* coaches have keys. As a general rule, the phrase immediately following 'only' or 'none but' is the *predicate* of the categorical statement, not the subject. Here are some examples:

Example 46	Only dogs bark.	---	All <u>things that</u> <u>bark</u> are dogs.
Example 47	Only citizens can vote.	---	All <u>persons</u> who <u>can vote</u> are citizens.
Example 48	None but logicians love logic.	---	All <u>persons</u> who <u>love logic</u> are logicians.

(b) 'The only' This phrase operates differently than 'only'. If we say, 'The only owl here is the Barred Owl', we mean not that all Barred Owls are here but that all owls here are Barred Owls. As a general rule, the phrase immediately following 'the only' is the *subject* of the categorical statement. Consider these examples:

Example 49	The only people with keys are the coaches.	---	All <u>people</u> <u>with keys</u> are the coaches.

| **Example 50** | The seniors are the only students allowed to leave. | --- | All <u>students</u> <u>allowed</u> to leave are seniors. |

(c) 'All and only'   'All and only logicians love logic' states that all logicians love logic *and* all who love logic are logicians. The phrase 'all and only' is a combination of 'All S are P' and 'Only S are P'. Therefore, it must be translated into two categorical statements, as shown below:

| **Example 51** | All and only logicians love logic. | --- | All logicians are lovers of logic. All lovers of logic are logicians. |

| **Example 52** | All and only predators are meat eaters. | --- | All predators are meat eaters. All meat eaters are predators. |

Since the complete translation of 'all and only' statements requires two categorical statements, their diagrams resemble those of 'if and only if' statements. Here is a diagram representing the translation of example 51, 'All and only logicians love logic'.

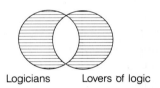

Logicians   Lovers of logic

(d) 'All except'   Statements using the phrase 'all except' are also translated with two categorical statements. A statement of the form 'All except X are Y' is asserting two things: 'All nonX are Y' and 'No X are Y', as in these examples:

| **Example 53** | All except the musicians are salaried. | --- | All <u>nonmusicians</u> are salaried persons. No <u>musicians</u> are salaried persons. |

| **Example 54** | All except the judges must leave the room. | --- | All _nonjudges_ are people who must leave the room. No judges are people who must leave the room. |

Follow this formula for treating sentences with 'all except':

All except X are Y $\equiv$ All nonX are Y
　　　　　　　　　　No X are Y

To diagram the translations of 'all except' sentences, you again need two circles for the two categories. Be careful to diagram the statement about 'nonX's' correctly. Here is the diagram of example 53, 'All nonmusicians are salaried persons. No musicians are salaried persons':

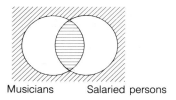

Musicians　　　Salaried persons

(e) '*All . . . except*'　A variation on 'All except X are Y' is the form 'All Z except X are Y'—for example, 'All seniors except the transfers are routine graduates'. This statement has three categories—seniors, transfers, and routine graduates—and it asserts two things: 'All nontransfer seniors are routine graduates' and 'No transfers are routine graduates'. Follow this formula when you translate 'all . . . except' sentences

All Z except X are Y $\equiv$ All nonX Z's are Y
　　　　　　　　　　　No X are Y

The diagram of this type of sentence *requires three circles,* because the statements involve three categories. (A detailed explanation of diagraming with three categories is given in section 4.4.) First draw three circles as shown below and label them. Then diagram each statement.

| **Example 55** | All seniors except the transfers are routine graduates. | --- | All _nontransfer seniors_ are routine graduates. No transfers are routine graduates. |

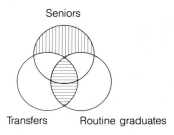

Seniors

Transfers   Routine graduates

Exercise 4.2A   Translating.   Translate the following sentences into proper categorical form.

1. Some phones are off the hook.
2. The firefighter is a civil servant.
3. It always rains whenever we have a picnic.
4. Tolstoy is the most important of all the Russian novelists.
5. Most historians are good writers.
6. If a patient has good skin color, then it can't be jaundice the patient has.
7. Only the young go to war.
8. All and only sound arguments are good arguments.
9. All faculty are not permitted to cancel classes.
10. Few people stayed to clean up.
11. Logic develops only the mind.
12. Only the wealthy go to France.
13. Where there's smoke there's fire.
14. Not all people are happy with their jobs.
15. Aristotle developed the doctrine of the golden mean.
16. A person is not morally responsible for acts that he or she cannot control.
17. Every major African religion contains the idea of a supreme god.
18. There's never a police officer around when you need one.
19. If consumer spending increases, then interest rates will decline.
20. Tonight is a special night.
21. Everyone needs regular exercise.
22. Where the drink goes in, there the wit goes out. (George Herbert)
23. The whole of science is nothing more than a refinement of everyday thinking. (Albert Einstein)
24. The mass of men lead lives of quiet desperation. (Henry David Thoreau)
25. Religion is an illusion. (Sigmund Freud)

Exercise 4.2B Translating. Translate the following sentences into proper categorical form. Then draw Venn diagrams representing them.

1. All and only sound arguments are good arguments.
2. All except freshmen must take the make-up exams.
3. Few singers are successful.
4. Only the doctors are permitted in the pathology lab.
5. A person is a medical doctor if and only if he or she has earned an M.D. degree.
6. The only isolated virus is the BK12 virus.
7. All North American geese except the Emperor Goose are regular visitors to Missouri.
8. None but the good die young.
9. You can order a drink here only if you are twenty-one.
10. Wherever we go we look for good, authentic Mexican food.

4.3 The Categorical Syllogism

The major argument form in categorical logic is the syllogism. A *categorical syllogism* is a deductive argument having the following three features:

1. There are three categorical statements: two premises and a conclusion.
2. There are exactly three different terms or category names.
3. Each term occurs exactly twice in the argument.

Here is an example of a categorical syllogism:

Example 56

   1. All successful businesspersons are good writers.

   2. All good writers are college graduates.

   3. Therefore, all successful businesspersons are college graduates.

Notice how the example meets the three requirements of the syllogism form: Each statement is in proper categorical form, there are three terms, and each term occurs exactly twice. Expressed in this form the argument is very clear. A great advantage of the syllogism form is that it enables us easily to use Venn diagrams to determine an argument's validity.

4.4 Testing Validity with Venn Diagrams

Using Venn diagrams to check validity requires that you learn only two new procedures: using three circles in diagraming and using the symbol '——', called the *bar*.

We have to use three circles in diagraming because we need one circle for each of the three terms in the syllogism. Begin by drawing three interlocking circles as shown below.

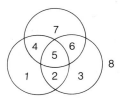

The circles must interlock to create exactly eight areas. This provides for every possible combination of relationships among the three categories. We will work with example 56:

1. *All successful businesspersons are good writers.*

2. *All good writers are college graduates.*

   ———————————————————————

3. *Therefore, all successful businesspersons are college graduates.*

To label the circles, let the *subject of the conclusion* be represented by the bottom–left circle, the *predicate of the conclusion* by the bottom–right circle, and the *remaining category name* by the top circle. (This format ensures that your diagrams are oriented the same as everyone else's. It does not affect the results of the testing technique.) Thus, the circles are labeled as follows:

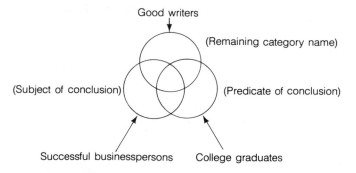

Good writers

(Remaining category name)

(Subject of conclusion)

(Predicate of conclusion)

Successful businesspersons   College graduates

The procedure for checking validity consists of two steps:

1. Diagram the premises.
   (a) If a premise is a universal statement, diagram it first.
   (b) Make explicit in your diagram any necessary existential assumptions (more on this later).

   Do not diagram the conclusion!

2. Check to see if the resulting diagram depicts the conclusion.
   (a) If it does, the argument is *valid.*
   (b) If it does not, the argument is *invalid.*

Let's go through this procedure with our example. First we diagram the premises. If an argument has a universal premise, it simplifies matters to diagram it first. (In our example both premises are universals, so we can diagram either one first.) We diagram the first premise just as though we were dealing with only two circles. We must represent what the premise says completely, so we fill in the entire area, extending the shading into the third circle. The first premise—'All successful businesspersons are good writers'—is depicted correctly in the diagram on the left below and incorrectly in the one on the right.

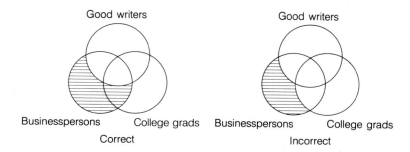

The diagram on the right leaves open the possibility that successful businesspersons are not good writers and so does not properly represent the premise.

After diagraming the first premise, we diagram the remaining one—'All good writers are college graduates'—using the circles just as though there were only two of them.

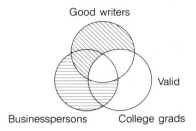

Good writers

Valid

Businesspersons   College grads

Proceeding to the second step, we examine the resulting diagram to see if it depicts the conclusion. If the conclusion is already represented in the diagram the argument is valid, for the premises taken together contain the information that the conclusion asserts. We can see that the conclusion 'All successful businesspersons are college graduates' is depicted in the diagram above. Thus, the argument is valid.

Let us consider another example:

Example 57

1. *All viceroys are kingsmen.*

2. *No dukes are viceroys.*

3. *Therefore, no dukes are kingsmen.*

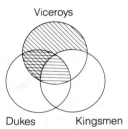

Viceroys

Dukes   Kingsmen

The Venn diagram *does not* show that no dukes are kingsmen. The diagram leaves open the possibility that there are dukes who are kingsmen. Thus, the conclusion does not validly follow, and the argument is invalid.

Consider a third example:

Example 58

1. *No congresspersons are novelists.*

2. *Some lawyers are congresspersons.*

3. *Therefore, some lawyers are not novelists.*

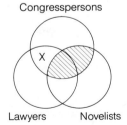

Congresspersons

Lawyers   Novelists

The Venn diagram has an X in the area representing some lawyers who are not novelists. Thus, it does correctly depict the conclusion, indicating that the argument is valid.

The Bar

The next example introduces a new device, the bar, symbolized '__'.

Example 59

1. *All hunters are conservationists.*
2. *Some conservationists are not protesters.*

---

3. *Therefore, some hunters are not protesters.*

The diagram below shows the first premise represented. As we diagram the second premise we see that there are two places where, it seems, we could place the X representing the second premise, 'Some conservationists are not protesters'.

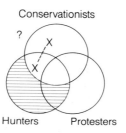

Conservationists

Hunters   Protesters

We want to show that some conservationists are not protesters, but by placing the X in area 7 we are also "saying" that those conservationists are *not* hunters. On the other hand, if we place the X in area 4 we are saying that those conservationists *are* hunters. Either way we would be symbolizing more than what the premise says and, hence, misrepresenting the premise. The only way to represent precisely what the premise says *and no more* is to indicate that those conservationists who are not protesters could be in either area. To do so, we use a bar running across the two areas where the X might be considered to be. The bar is understood to mean that the X could be in either area and that the premise alone does not specify which. Completing the diagram we see that the conclusion is not represented, for the diagram does not reveal that there is at least one hunter who is not a protester. The diagram shows that there could be hunters who are not protesters—the possibility indicated by the bar extending into the hunter circle—but not that there *must* be some hunters who are not protesters. Thus, this argument is invalid.

> The bar: *The bar is always and only used when a premise does not specify in which of two areas the X should be placed. The bar indicates that some (that is, at least one) members of the subject category are "in" one of the two areas into which it extends.*

Here is another example requiring a bar:

Example 60

1. *Some animals are trainable animals.*
2. *Some animals are vicious animals.*

---

3. *Therefore, some vicious animals are trainable animals.*

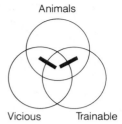

You can see that the argument fails to establish its conclusion. An argument whose diagram shows two bars will always be invalid. Make up some examples of your own to illustrate this point.

Making an Existential Assumption

The validity of some arguments can be demonstrated using Venn diagrams *only if* an existential assumption is made, that is, only if a premise is interpreted according to the traditional version (see section 3.5 above). Others, such as those valid arguments illustrated above, can be shown to be valid with or without an existential assumption. *Arguments whose validity depends upon an existential assumption are arguments whose premises are both universal statements and whose conclusion is a particular statement.* Consider this argument:

Example 61

1. *No computers are thinkers.*
2. *All humans are thinkers.*

---

3. *Therefore, some humans are not computers.*

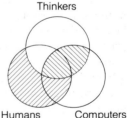

If we diagramed this argument without making an existential assumption, there would be no X in the completed diagram indicating that some humans are not computers, and it would therefore be an invalid argument. However, if we assume that members of the category of humans do exist, then we can place an X in the humans circle to express that assumption. (Recall that an existential assumption is permitted with the universal statements A or E and that we indicate it by placing an X within the circle representing the subject category.)

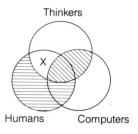

Thinkers

Humans   Computers

We can now see that the argument is valid. To generalize, we can say that if an argument with universal premises and a particular conclusion is valid, then we must make the existential assumption to show its validity with the Venn diagram method.

Exercise 4.4A   Diagraming with Three Circles.   The statements below are not arguments but exercises in constructing Venn diagrams with three circles. Practice diagraming the pair of statements as though they were the premises of an argument.

1. No members of the all-star team are professionals. All athletes with high salaries are professionals.
2. Some Indians are Hindus. All Hindus believe in Brahman.
3. No valid syllogisms are arguments with four premises. No valid syllogisms are unprovable by Venn diagrams.
4. All government bonds are good investments. Some good investments are not commodities.
5. All reptiles are cold-blooded creatures. Some cold-blooded creatures are good pets.
6. All whales are mammals. Some mammals are not carnivores.
7. Some chess players are grand masters. No grand masters are good checkers players.
8. All corporate executives are members of the board. All members of the board are civic leaders.
9. No Palestinians are elected officials. Some Palestinians are freedom fighters.
10. Some fast-food diners are purveyors of unsavory food. All fast-food diners are money-making operations.

Exercise 4.4B   Reading Venn Diagrams.   Read the diagrams and answer the questions below.

1. Does A show that no Buddhists are Moslems?
2. Does A show that some mystics are not Buddhists?

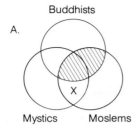

A.

Buddhists

Mystics   Moslems

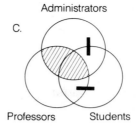

C.

Administrators

Professors   Students

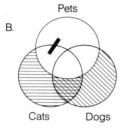

B.

Pets

Cats   Dogs

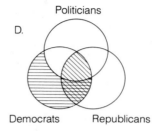

D.

Politicians

Democrats   Republicans

3. Does B show that some pets are not dogs?
4. Does B show that no cats are dogs?
5. Are all dogs pets according to B?
6. According to C could there be some professors who are students?
7. Does C show that some administrators are students?
8. According to D are there Democrats who are politicians?
9. Does D show that there are Republicans who are politicians?
10. Is it true according to D that no Republicans are Democrats?

Exercise 4.4C   Testing Validity with Venn Diagrams.   Use Venn diagrams to determine whether the following arguments are valid or invalid. Some arguments may be valid only if you make an existential assumption. Show your work.

1. All dancers are vegetarians. No dentists are dancers. Hence, no dentists are vegetarians.
2. No soldiers are comedians. Some Americans are soldiers; therefore, some Americans are not comedians.
3. No conservationists are advocates of nuclear energy. All farmers are conservationists. So no farmers are advocates of nuclear energy.
4. All spiders are things having eight legs. All Black Widows are spiders; therefore, all Black Widows are things having eight legs.
5. All books are books worth reading. Some books are novels. Therefore, some novels are books worth reading.

6. No pelicans are predators. All pelicans are birds. Therefore, no birds are predators.

7. Some females are not women. All mothers are females. So, some mothers are not women.

8. Some books are books worth reading. Some novels are books. Hence, some novels are books worth reading.

9. All Egyptians are North Africans. No Egyptians are Asians. Therefore, some North Africans are not Asians.

10. All New Mexico chilis are the hottest chilis. All the hottest chilis are chilis with the most vitamin C. Therefore, some chilis with the most vitamin C are New Mexico chilis.

11. Some emotions are sensations caused by thought. Some sensations caused by thought are neurotic states. Therefore, some emotions are neurotic states.

12. All anthropologists are gentlemen. Some politicians are gentlemen. So some politicians are anthropologists.

13. All cameramen are photographers. Some photographers are not artists. Therefore, some cameramen are not artists.

14. All modern recordings are things made of vinyl. Some recordings are not things made of vinyl. Therefore, some recordings are not modern recordings.

15. Some Japanese watches are digital watches. No analog watches are digital watches. Therefore, some analog watches are not Japanese watches.

4.5 Special Cases for the Syllogism

Almost all deductive arguments need some revision before they fit into the proper syllogistic form required for Venn diagraming. Recall that proper syllogistic form has three features: (1) the argument must have three categorical statements—two premises and a conclusion; (2) there must be exactly three terms or category names; and (3) each term must occur exactly twice in the argument. There are several ways of analyzing arguments that are not already in syllogistic form: (1) using the operations to reduce the number of terms; (2) diagraming arguments with three terms but also three premises; and (3) constructing *sorites,* or chains of syllogisms, by breaking up arguments with more than three terms and premises. Such arguments can be rewritten so that they fit into syllogistic form or at least so that the three-circle technique of Venn diagraming can be applied to them. Let us consider each of these methods in turn.

1. Using the Operations to Reduce Terms   In the last chapter we saw how applying some of the operations to some of the categorical forms produces logically equivalent statements. The operations can be used to simplify arguments with too many terms if one or more terms occur in both an affirmative and a negative form. Consider this example:

Example 62

1. *Some senators are noncommunists.*

2. *All communists are nonliberals.*

3. *Therefore, some liberals are not senators.*

Strictly speaking, this argument has two terms too many: 'senators', 'noncommunists', 'communists', 'nonliberals', and 'liberals'. We can check such an argument with Venn diagrams without revision, for Venn diagraming is sufficient to represent terms and their negations, but usually diagraming is simplified if we can *reduce the number of terms* to just three. In the example above, two of the terms occur in both affirmative and negative forms: 'communists' and 'noncommunists' and 'liberals' and 'nonliberals'. Arguments with such paired terms can almost always be rewritten with fewer terms. However, *a premise can be replaced only with a logically equivalent statement*. Thus, only an operation that results in a logically equivalent expression is permitted. We can use obversion to rewrite our example as follows:

1'. *Some senators are not communists.* (1 by obversion)

2'. *No communists are liberals.* (2 by obversion)

3. *Some liberals are not senators.*

The new premises are logically equivalent to the old ones because, as you recall, obversion always yields a statement that is logically equivalent to the original. The rewritten argument is in proper syllogistic form and can be diagramed more easily.

Here is another example:

Example 63

1. *All combatants are nonneutrals.*

2. *All volunteer advisors are neutrals.*

3. *Therefore, all volunteer advisors are noncombatants.*

The categories are 'combatants', 'noncombatants', 'nonneutrals', 'neutrals', and 'volunteer advisors'. There are at least two ways to reduce the number of terms in this argument. We could use obversion on statements (1) and (3) as follows:

1'. No combatants are neutrals. (1 by obversion)

2. All volunteer advisors are neutrals.

3'. Therefore, no volunteer advisors are combatants. (3 by obversion)

The argument can now be diagramed easily. However, an even simpler approach is to use contraposition on statement (1). Contraposition switches the subject and predicate terms in the first premise and negates both, producing this result:

1'. All neutrals are noncombatants. (1 by contraposition)

No other changes are needed because the argument now contains only three categories. Diagraming the argument will reveal whether it is valid or invalid.

In sum, if an argument contains too many terms because one or more occur in both an affirmative and a negative form, the number of terms can probably be reduced to three by substituting logically equivalent statements obtained by using the operations.

2. Diagraming Arguments with Three Terms but Also Three Premises   We saw earlier that it required *two* categorical statements to express some statements in categorical form. Such a translation may give us an argument with three premises—which is, strictly speaking, not in syllogistic form—yet still with only three terms, that is, three categories. As long as the argument contains only three terms the Venn diagram technique can be used. We simply have to diagram three premises rather than the usual two. Here is an example:

Example 64

1. Many African art objects are religious objects.

2. Religious objects are beautiful.

---

3. Thus, some African art objects are beautiful.

To translate the first premise into categorical form, we rewrite it using two categorical statements, as follows:

1. Some African art objects are religious objects.

2. Some African art objects are not religious objects.

3. All religious objects are things that are beautiful.

---

4. Thus, some African art objects are things that are beautiful.

The argument is still not in proper syllogistic form, but since only three categories are involved, we can use the three-circle Venn diagram to determine whether it is valid.

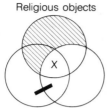

Religious objects

African art objects   Things that are beautiful

Here is another example.

Example 65

1. *All except the surveyors are government employees.*

2. *All government employees have retirement plans.*

3. *Therefore, no surveyors have retirement plans.*

Rewriting the statements as categorical statements yields this:

1. *All nonsurveyors are government employees.*

2. *No surveyors are government employees.*

3. *All government employees are persons with retirement plans.*

4. *Therefore, no surveyors are persons with retirement plans.*

The argument could be diagramed now without further revision. (And you should try to do so to appreciate how reducing the terms to three simplifies matters.) However, by using the operations—both conversion and obversion on statements (2) and (4)—we can reduce the number of different terms to three.

1. *All nonsurveyors are government employees.*

2'. *All government employees are nonsurveyors.* (2 by conversion and then obversion)

3. *All government employees are persons with retirement plans.*

4'. *Therefore, all persons with retirement plans are nonsurveyors.* (4 by conversion and then obversion)

3. Constructing Sorites   Many arguments have more than two premises. Techniques like those described above may be used to reduce the number of terms, but another approach is to break up the argument into smaller arguments, each of which is a syllogism. A chain of such syllogisms is called a *sorites* (pronounced "sō–RĪ-tēz"). The rationale behind breaking up an argument—that is, constructing a sorites—is that the original argument is valid if each syllogism it contains is valid. If any syllogism in the chain is invalid, then so is the original argument. To construct a sorites, follow these four rules:

RULES FOR THE SORITES

1. Each statement must be in categorical form.
2. Each term must occur twice.
3. The first premise must contain the subject or predicate term of the conclusion.
4. Each premise (except the first) must have a term in common with the premise preceding it.

Consider this example of an argument form:

Example 66

All A are B.
All B are C.
All C are D.
_____

Thus, all A are D.

First we see whether the argument meets the four requirements for the sorites. Each statement is in categorical form; each term occurs twice; the first premise contains a term that also occurs in the conclusion; and each premise except the first has a term in common with the one above it. Thus it does meet the requirements. If an argument cannot be brought into proper sorites form, then it cannot be evaluated as a chain of syllogisms.

Once the argument is in proper sorites form, then the procedure for evaluating the sorites is as follows:

Step (1) Construct a Venn diagram using the first two premises.

Step (2) Determine from that diagram what conclusion, if any, can be validly deduced.

Step (3) Take that intermediate conclusion together with the next premise and construct another Venn diagram.

Repeat Steps (2) and (3) Repeat until the conclusion of the original argument is reached or no valid conclusion can be deduced.

Let's go over the procedure slowly using the example on the previous page.

Step (1) Diagram the first two premises:

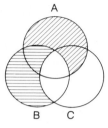

All A are B.
All B are C.

Thus, all A are C.

Step (2) The diagram allows you to draw the intermediate conclusion that 'All A are C'.

Step (3) Take the intermediate conclusion together with the next premise and construct another Venn diagram.

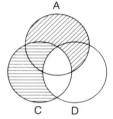

All A are C.
All C are D.

Thus, all A are D.

Repeat Step (2) The diagram allows you to draw the conclusion that 'All A are D', which is the conclusion of the sorites. Each syllogism in the chain is valid; thus, the whole sorites or chain of syllogisms is valid.

Now consider another example of an argument form:

Example 67

No T are Q.
All S are T.
No Q are R.

_____

Thus, No S are R.

Notice that this argument does not conform to the rules for proper sorites form— the first premise does not contain a term in common with the conclusion. However, the second premise does, so the argument can be rearranged as follows:

All S are T.

No T are Q.

No Q are R.

Thus, No S are R.

Step (1) Construct a Venn diagram with the first two premises.

All S are T.

No T are Q.

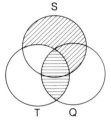

Thus, no S are Q.

Step (2) You can draw the intermediate conclusion that 'No S are Q'.

Step (3) Take the intermediate conclusion and construct a diagram with it and the next premise, which in this case is 'No Q are R'.

No S are Q.

No Q are R.

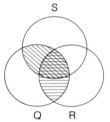

Repeat Step (2) The diagram shows that the conclusion of the sorites does not follow. Thus, this argument is invalid.

Here is another example:

Example 68

All Methodists are Protestants.

No Jews are Protestants.

All Hassidim are Jews.

All Catholics are Hassidim.

Thus, no Methodists are Catholics.

Does the argument conform to the four rules? It does. Proceed then to *Step (1)*.

All Methodists are Protestants.
No Jews are Protestants.

Thus, no Methodists are Jews.

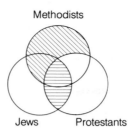

Step (2) The diagram shows that 'No Methodists are Jews'. That serves as a premise for the next syllogism.

Step (3)

No Methodists are Jews.
All Hassidim are Jews.

Thus, no Methodists are Hassidim.

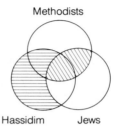

Repeat Step (2) The diagram shows that 'No Methodists are Hassidim'. Continue.

Repeat Step (3)

No Methodists are Hassidim.
All Catholics are Hassidim.

Thus, no Methodists are Catholics.

Repeat Step (2) The diagram shows that the conclusion to the sorites, 'No Methodists are Catholics', can be deduced. Thus, the original argument is valid.

Let us now consider a more complicated argument:

Example 69

Something is an art form only if it involves creativity and imagination. Photography is a mechanical process

*of exposing film to light. Mechanical processes involve
no creativity and imagination. Therefore, photography
is not an art form.*

First, the argument must be rewritten using categorical statements:

All art forms are things involving C and I.

*All things identical to photography are mechanical
processes.*

No mechanical processes are things involving C and I.

Thus, no things identical to photography are art forms.

This argument does not conform to the four rules for the sorites because, as the premises are arranged, it is not the case that each premise (except the first) has a term in common with its predecessor. However, proper form can be achieved by switching the second and third premises. Now follow the procedure for evaluating the sorites.

Step (1)

All art forms are things involving C and I.
No mechanical processes are things involving C and I.

Thus, no mechanical processes are art forms.

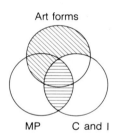

Step (2) The diagram shows that 'No mechanical processes are art forms'.

Step (3)

No mechanical processes are art forms.
*All things identical to photography are mechanical
processes.*

Thus, no things identical to photography are art forms.

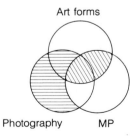

Repeat Step (2) The diagram shows that the conclusion 'No things identical to photography are art forms' can be validly inferred. Thus, the argument is valid.

Constructing sorites is a very useful method for evaluating arguments. Your own inventiveness becomes important as you explore ways to put arguments into syllogistic form. Ultimately, the basic task is to express the argument in such a way that you can check it easily with the three-circle diagraming technique.

Exercise 4.5A Valid or Invalid?   Determine whether the following arguments are valid by using Venn diagrams. Translate sentences into categorical form if necessary, and rewrite arguments in proper syllogism form where possible.

1. Few bankers voted for the new tax structure. All voters for the new tax structure were capitalists. Therefore, some bankers are not capitalists.

2. All except the candidates for officer training school were requested to submit records of their medical history. Cadet Murdoch must be a candidate because he was not requested to submit his medical record.

3. If a forecaster can predict the heat wave, then he or she is a good weather reporter. Someone is a good weather reporter only if he or she is trained in meteorology. Every forecaster who can predict the heat wave must, therefore, be trained in meteorology.

4. All cats except Manx cats have long tails. Iris is not a Manx cat; therefore, she has a long tail.

5. Only things capable of meaningful speech are capable of thought. Humans are capable of meaningful speech, so they must be capable of thought.

6. If you are strong you'll make it to the top. And Max is strong. So he'll make it to the top.

7. All poisonous snakes are things to avoid. But some snakes are nonpoisonous. Therefore, some snakes are not things to avoid.

8. No Californians are Easterners. Some Easterners are not unfriendly. Therefore, friendly people are non-Californians.

9. All and only Iranians are Persians. No Iraqis are Persians. Therefore, no Iranians are Iraqis.

10. Most experts on the ecology are of the opinion that the use of pesticides in farming is ecologically dangerous. Since those who are of that opinion are disliked by the major chemical manufacturers, it follows that some experts on the ecology are disliked by the major chemical manufacturers.

Exercise 4.5B Sorites.   Are the following arguments valid or invalid? Some of the arguments will have to be constructed as sorites before they can be evaluated. Be sure that all statements are in categorical form and that all arguments are in proper form as sorites before attempting to check them using Venn diagrams. Show your work.

1. *All X are Y.*
   All Y are Z.
   All Z are T.

   Thus, all X are T.

2. *All S are R.*
   No T are R.
   All O are T.

   Thus, no S are O.

3. *No A are non-D.*
   Some A are B.
   All B are C.

   Thus, some C are D.

4. *No F are G.*
   No G are H.
   No H are I.

   Thus, no F are I.

5. *Some humans are mortals.*
   Some mortals are Romans.
   Some Romans are Italians.

   Therefore, some Italians are mortals.

6. *All Texans are ranchers.*
   No ranchers are nonsheepherders.
   All sheepherders are wool gatherers.

   So, no Texans are wool gatherers.

7. *All sailors are recruits.*
   No volunteers are recruits.
   All officers are volunteers.
   All veterans are officers.

   Therefore, no sailors are veterans.

8. *All Bengal tigers are carnivores.*

   All noncarnivores are nonvicious animals.

   All vicious animals are dangerous animals.

   Thus, all Bengal tigers are dangerous animals.

9. *All computer programmers are proficient in BASIC.*

   No people proficient in BASIC are computer illiterate.

   No people who are computer illiterate are mathematicians.

   Thus, no computer programmers are nonmathematicians.

10. *No letter carriers are civil servants.*

    Some letter carriers are unemployed.

    All unemployed people are job seekers.

    Therefore, some job seekers are not civil servants.

11. *All carpenters are artisans.*

    All artisans are woodworkers.

    Some carpenters are journeymen.

    So, some journeymen are woodworkers.

12. *All those looking for the Elegant Trogon are bird-watchers.*

    All amateur ornithologists are those who are looking for the Elegant Trogon.

    No people with bird books are nonamateur ornithologists.

    If a person has a large bulge in his or her back pocket, then he or she has a bird book.

    Only those with large bulges in their back pockets are holding binoculars.

    Therefore, only bird-watchers are holding binoculars.

Summary

This chapter and the previous chapter have focused on the evaluation of both simple and complex deductive arguments according to the principles of categorical logic. We examined the four categorical forms of statements, and we saw how they can be represented in Venn diagrams as well as how they are logically related on the traditional and the modern squares of opposition. We then learned how categorical statements can be manipulated according to the operations of conversion, obversion, and contraposition. In certain instances these operations yield logically equivalent statements and, therefore, valid inferences. Using the operations we can rewrite statements within arguments to simplify the arguments and facilitate the Venn diagraming technique. We can follow certain guidelines to translate most sentences in ordinary language into categorical form.

This chapter has focused on the logical analysis of deductive arguments in syllogistic form. We applied the Venn diagraming technique to the evaluation of syllogisms, and we examined methods of analyzing arguments that are not in syllogistic form, most notably the method of constructing "chain arguments," called sorites.

You now have a good grasp of the basic concepts and techniques of categorical logic, certainly enough to apply its principles to many of the arguments you encounter in daily life. Equally important, you now understand what a deductive logical system is and how inferences may be demonstrated to be valid.

Review Questions Chapter 4

1. What features must a statement have in order to be in proper categorical form?

2. Which phrases in ordinary language require two categorical statements for proper translation?

3. What are proper names and singular expressions? Why do they present a special problem for categorical logic?

4. What is a conditional? List some of the phrases that assert a conditional.

5. What is a syllogism? What features must an argument have to be in proper syllogistic form?

6. What is the bar? What does it mean, and under what conditions is it used?

7. What type of argument requires an existential assumption in order to be valid?

8. What is a sorites? Under what conditions is a sorites invalid?

True or False?

1. Syllogisms can have two, three, or four premises.
2. 'Only A's are B's' is translated as 'All A's are B's'.
3. The phrase 'if and only if' is really two conditionals.
4. It makes no logical difference whether a statement begins with the phrase 'only' or 'the only'.
5. All syllogisms can be evaluated using Venn diagrams.
6. Some uses of conversion, obversion, and contraposition do not result in logically equivalent statements.
7. Longer arguments cannot be broken down without distorting their meaning.
8. Given a three-circle Venn diagram, if an I or an O statement does not specify in which of two areas the X is to be placed, then you may place the X in either area.

CHAPTER FIVE
Truth-Functional Logic
Part I

Truth-functional logic analyzes statements and arguments in terms of the truth or falsity of their component parts. In this chapter we learn the fundamentals of truth-functional logic: the symbols and their use in symbolizing statements, the *truth-functions* of the *logical operators,* and the *truth table* as a method for displaying the truth-values of compound statements. These fundamentals prepare us for the use of truth-functional techniques in evaluating arguments.

5.1 Introduction

The origins of truth-functional logic can be traced to certain ancient Greek philosophers, in particular the Megarians (approximately 400–300 BC) and the Stoics (approximately 330–200 BC). The most thorough formulation of truth-functional logic—and the modern symbolization theory we use here—is primarily the work of a group of major philosophers that includes Bertrand Russell (1872–1970), Alfred North Whitehead (1861–1947), and Charles Sanders Peirce (1839–1914). Truth-functional logic, also called propositional logic, takes its name from the notion of truth-functionality, the idea that the truth of a statement is a function of the truth-values of its component parts. This central notion will become clear soon.

Truth-functional logic differs from categorical logic in several important respects. First, it is not a logical system based on categories or classes. As we learned, an argument written according to the principles of categorical logic expresses a logical relationship among classes and is analyzed and evaluated in terms of class relationships. In truth-functional logic, statements, not categories, are considered basic; arguments are analyzed and evaluated in terms of the logical relationships between the truth-values of statements. Secondly, Venn diagrams are not used in truth-functional logic. Instead, symbolization and mechanical techniques such as truth tables are used to reveal the form of a statement or argument. Thirdly, truth-functional logic is completely formal; that is, statements and arguments are translated from ordinary language into a symbolic form that reveals their logical structure. To some extent you will find this more mechanical system easier to use than categorical logic. For our purposes, however, neither system is more reliable than the other. Applied correctly, both categorical logic and truth-functional logic accurately evaluate many common deductive arguments for validity.

5.2 Statements: Simple and Compound

The elements of truth-functional logic are statements. A statement is any sentence that may be true or false. A distinction is made between simple and compound statements, as follows:

Simple statement: *Any statement that cannot be further analyzed into one or more statements.*

Compound statement: *Any statement that can be analyzed into one or more statements.*

'The camera dropped' is an example of a simple statement. If we break this statement down further into its component parts, 'the camera' and 'dropped', we no longer have a statement, something that may be true or false. On the other hand, the statement 'The camera dropped and Francis paid for it' can be broken down into components that are themselves statements, namely, 'The camera dropped' and 'Francis paid for it'. The statement 'It is not snowing' is also capable of being broken down into one or more statements: 'It is snowing'. Thus, 'It is not snowing' is a compound statement. A statement is simple not because it is short but because it cannot be analyzed into component statements. Simple statements are the "building blocks" of compound statements. Examine the examples below and decide whether they are simple or compound.

Example 1	*George wins.*
Example 2	*Most people are usually hesitant to buy a car from a dealer who uses flashy gimmicks.*
Example 3	*The onions and the carrots are ready for picking.*
Example 4	*It is good to be alive and better to be healthy.*
Example 5	*The Asante of Ghana are noted for their skillfully carved statues.*
Example 6	*Men, women, and children over the age of twelve must pay full admission price.*
Example 7	*If the pain increases, then you may take two aspirins.*
Example 8	*All officers must report to the board room for a meeting.*

The simple statements are examples 1, 2, 5, and 8. The compounds are examples 3, 4, 6, and 7. Notice that simple statements can be as short as example 1, 'George wins' or as long as 2, 'Most people are usually hesitant to buy a car from a dealer who uses flashy gimmicks'. Notice also that statements like 3, 4, and 6 are compounds because logically they consist of several statements joined together. For example, 6 is a compound of the statements 'men must pay full admission price', 'women must pay full admission price', and 'children over the age of twelve must pay full admission price'. Obviously, forming compounds may facilitate communication, but this convenience may result in complexity.

5.3 The Logical Operators

Compound statements are formed from simple statements using *logical operators*. Five important logical operators are typically used in truth-functional logic. (It is possible to use truth-functional logic with fewer than five by reducing some to others.) The five operators we will use in this account of truth-functional logic are *'not'*, *'and'*, *'or'*, *'if. . . then'*, and *'if and only if'*. Notice that each compound statement in the list above contains one of these logical operators. Here are some other examples of compounds formed from simple statements by using operators:

Example 9	*It is* not *wise to ignore experience.*
Example 10	*The crops are harvested,* and *the farmers are clearing the fields.*

Example 11   *Eliot will take Barbara to the dance,* or *John will.*

Example 12   If *more water goes over the dam,* then *the valley below will be flooded.*

Example 13   *It is a valid argument* if and only if *the conclusion necessarily follows from the premises.*

The five operators represent five logically different ways of forming compound statements. What follows is a brief survey of the operators and the functions they establish.

'Not' and Negation   The operator 'not' serves to *negate* a statement. For example, the statement 'George wins' is negated in the compound statement 'George *does not* win'. Furthermore, a negation may itself be negated, as in 'It is *not* true that George does not win'. Our language has a variety of expressions that serve the function of negation, that is, of expressing the operator 'not', including 'it is not true that . . .', 'it is not the case that . . .', '. . . is not so', and so on. Since every statement is either true or false, if a statement is true, then its negation is false; and if a statement is false, then its negation is true.

'And' and Conjunction   The operator 'and' forms compounds called *conjunctions* (from the word 'conjoin'). In the following examples of conjunction notice the different expressions that have the same function as 'and'.

Example 14

It is past noon, and *the men are still working.*

It is past noon, but *the men are still working.*

It is past noon, yet *the men are still working.*

It is past noon; the men are still working.

It is past noon; nevertheless *the men are still working.*

Suppose we let P stand for 'It is past noon' and M for 'the men are still working'. Each example above then asserts that both P and M are true. The assertion of both simple statements is, in effect, the logical meaning of the operator 'and' serving to conjoin two statements. However, not every occurrence of the word 'and' establishes a conjunction. For example, Gandhi's remark 'Nonviolence and truth are inseparable' is not a compound even though it contains the word 'and'. It cannot be broken down into two simple statements; it is itself a simple statement. In this example, 'and' serves to connect the subjects, not two statements. (The same is true of the statement 'Water is nothing but hydrogen and oxygen'.)

'Or' and Disjunction   The operator 'or' forms compounds called *disjunctions*. A disjunction asserts of the statements it connects, called *disjuncts,* that *at least one disjunct is true*. It is consistent with this assertion that all disjuncts are true; however, a person who asserts a disjunction is making the minimal claim that *at least one* of the statements of the disjunction is true. The operator 'or' in truth-functional logic is called the *inclusive* 'or' because it includes the possibility that all disjuncts are true. For example, 'You may have mustard or relish on your hot dog' allows that you may have one or the other *or both*. On the other hand, the word 'or' in our language is sometimes used *exclusively,* that is, such that it excludes the possibility that more than one of the disjuncts may be true at the same time. For example, 'The baby may be a girl or a boy' would normally be taken to imply that the baby cannot be both. The exclusive sense of 'or' is 'one or the other but not both'. There is a special way of translating the exclusive 'or' (discussed in detail in section 5.6, paragraph 3, below), but when the context does not clearly indicate this meaning we will use the inclusive 'or'. Thus, the disjunctive form 'p or q' (where p and q stand for statements) is understood to mean that 'p is true or q is true or both'.

'If . . . then' and the Conditional   As we saw earlier, a conditional asserts that something is the case given a certain condition. For example, 'If it rains, then the streets will be wet' asserts that the streets will be wet given the condition that it rains. The word or phrase following the 'if' is the condition and is called the *antecedent*. The word or phrase following the 'then' is called the *consequent*. There are different ways of expressing a conditional, as these examples illustrate:

Example 15

If *it rains,* then *the streets will be wet.*

If *it rains, the streets will be wet.*

The streets will be wet on the condition that *it rains.*

The streets will be wet if *it rains.*

It rains only if *the streets are wet.*

Each example above is equivalent to 'If it rains, then the streets will be wet'. (When we examine some special cases of translating ordinary language into symbols we will review other expressions with the same function as 'if . . . then'.)

'If and only If' and the Biconditional   We met the phrase 'if and only if' in categorical logic. Here it is called the biconditional, for, as the name implies, it comprises two conditionals. Thus, 'It is a valid argument if and only if the conclusion necessarily follows from the premises' asserts that 'if it is a valid argument, then the conclusion necessarily follows from the premises, *and* if the conclusion necessarily follows from the premises, then it is a valid argument'. The biconditional can be expressed in the formula 'if *p* is true, then *q* is true, and if *q* is true, then *p* is true', where *p* and *q* stand for statements.

Using p and q to represent statements, we can summarize the five common logical operators and their functions as follows:

not p	Negation—asserts that p is not true
p and q	Conjunction—asserts that both p and q are true
p or q	Disjunction—asserts that one or the other or both are true
if p then q	Conditional—asserts that if p is true then q is also true
p if and only if q	Biconditional—asserts that if p is true then q is true, and if q is true then p is true

The aim of truth-functional logic is to translate statements and the deductive arguments they compose using one or more of these five logical operators. Many instances of deductive reasoning can be analyzed in terms of these five functions. Let's turn now to the symbolization of statements and operators.

5.4 The Symbols and Their Uses

In truth-functional logic there are symbols for each of the five logical operators, symbols for statements, and the symbols known as parentheses and brackets. They are shown in Table 5.1.

Table 5.1   Symbols Used in Truth-Functional Logic

SYMBOL	INTERPRETATION	NAME OF THE SYMBOL
—	not	bar or "not sign"
+	and	"and sign"
v	or	wedge
⊃	if . . . then	horseshoe
≡	if and only if	triple bar
p,q,r,s, . . .	Small letters stand for statements in general and are useful for referring to types of statements.	
A,B,C,D, . . .	Capital letters stand for simple statements, e.g., 'G' for 'George wins'.	
(. . .)	Parentheses separate or group compounds within compounds or indicate the scope of the bar.	
[. . .]	Brackets group statements that are already within parentheses.	

Symbolic Translation

We can symbolize nearly any statement with the symbols listed in Table 5.1. We symbolize a statement to reveal its form and to prepare it for further analysis, a process that is particularly important for statements occurring in arguments. The procedure for symbolizing a statement consists of three steps:

1. *Identify the simple statement or statements.* You do this by determining that a statement cannot be further broken down into one or more simple statements.

2. *Choose capital letters to symbolize the simple statements.* The choice of capital letters is arbitrary, but it is helpful to choose a letter that reminds you of the statement. A good practice is to choose the first letter of the most significant word of the statement. *Note: Once a capital letter has been chosen for a simple statement it must be used for every occurrence of that statement, and it cannot be used for a different statement in the same context.*

3. *For compound statements, supply the appropriate symbol for the logical operator.* (In section 5.6 we see how to translate various phrases other than the standard five logical operators.)

Let's examine some easy examples of symbolizing.

Example 16

It is not true that evil spirits exist.

In this example we have the compound statement 'Not evil spirits exist'. The simple statement is 'evil spirits exist'. It is natural to let the letter E stand for that simple statement, giving us

It is not true that evil spirits exist. $= -E$

Example 17

It is good to be alive and better to be healthy.

The simple statements are 'It is good to be alive' and 'it is better to be healthy'. Letting G stand for the first and B for the second we have

It is good to be alive and better to be healthy. $= G + B$

Example 18

Eliot bowls with Barb or June.

The simple statements are 'Eliot bowls with Barb' and 'Eliot bowls with June', which can be represented by B and J, respectively.

Eliot bowls with Barb or June. $= B \vee J$

Example 19

If more water goes over the dam, then the valley will be flooded.

The antecedent is 'more water goes over the dam', and the consequent is 'the valley will be flooded'. The two statements may be symbolized by W and V, respectively. The horseshoe symbol '⊃' goes between the antecedent and the consequent as follows:

$$\text{\textit{If more water goes over the dam, then}} \\ \text{\textit{the valley will be flooded.}} \quad = \quad W \supset V$$

Example 20

Statement P is a compound if and only if statement P contains at least one logical operator.

The simple statements are 'Statement P is a compound', which can be symbolized by S, and 'statement P contains at least one logical operator', which can be symbolized by C.

$$\text{\textit{Statement P is a compound if and only}} \\ \text{\textit{if statement P contains at least one}} \quad = \quad S \equiv C \\ \text{\textit{logical operator.}}$$

Here are some other examples of symbolized statements.

Example 21	*If Rome falls, then the empire is lost.*	$= \quad R \supset E$
Example 22	*The Civil War was not lost by lack of courage.*	$= \quad -C$
Example 23	*Coffee, sugar, and oil are the chief exports of Venezuela.*	$= \quad C + S + O$
Example 24	*If it does not crystallize, then it is not a salt.*	$= \quad -C \supset -S$
Example 25	*Myles is a medical doctor if and only if he has earned an M.D. degree.*	$= \quad M \equiv E$
Example 26	*You must take chemistry or physics.*	$= \quad C \vee P$

Exercise 5.4   Symbolic Translation.   Translate the following statements using the capital letters provided as translation cues. Name the type of compound statement—negation, conjunction, and so on—for those that are compounds.

1. If it is raining, then the forecast is correct. (R,C)

2. Congress enacts laws, and the judicial branch enforces them. (C,J)

3. If Japanese industrialists borrow heavily from American banks, then the interest rates will climb even higher. (J,I)

4. Melba left the car, and Roy cleaned the fish. (M,R)

5. Artists are not crazy about logic. (A)

6. Either breakfast is ready, or I'm not staying. (B,I)

7. Pizza and beer are not recommended for people with ulcers. (P,B)

8. If the soul is not immortal, then we do not live forever. (S,W)

9. There were three people involved in the accident, and no one was injured. (T,O)

10. Smoking is harmful if and only if the Surgeon General is correct in his warning. (S,C)

11. The Pawnee and Arapahoe once occupied what is now Nebraska. (P,A)

12. There are 640 species of birds that occur in North America. (B)

13. A person is morally responsible for his or her actions if and only if the person performed them voluntarily. (M,V)

14. If the signatures are the same, the will is genuine. (S,W)

15. The library is not closed, or the study hall is open. (L,S)

5.5 Grouping and the Scope of Operators

Parentheses and brackets are symbols that *group statements together and indicate the scope of operators.* They are necessary in more complex statements to indicate which parts of a compound are governed by a logical operator. For example, suppose a menu reads, 'eggs and hashbrowns or pancakes'. The words 'and' and 'or' connect the other words to indicate a choice you may make, but what exactly is the choice? Is it that you may choose eggs and hashbrowns or you may choose pancakes? Or is it that you may choose eggs and either hashbrowns or pancakes? Parentheses can make the phrase unambiguous, meaning either '(Eggs and hashbrowns) *or* pancakes' or

'Eggs *and* (hashbrowns or pancakes)'. Notice that the first version is a *disjunction,* an 'or' compound; by placing the words 'eggs and hashbrowns' together within parentheses we indicate that it is one of the disjuncts of the larger statement. The second version is a *conjunction,* an 'and' compound; the parentheses group together, the words 'hashbrowns or pancakes', indicating that that group is one of the conjuncts. Without parentheses the logical form of the example is ambiguous. Thus, parentheses serve to clarify logical form and indicate which operator "holds together" the entire compound. The statement form 'P or Q and S' is unacceptable as it stands. We resolve the ambiguity by adding parentheses, making it either 'P or (Q and S)', which is a disjunction, or '(P or Q) and S', which is a conjunction. As you can see, a statement is classified as a conjunction, a disjunction, a conditional, and so on, according to the logical operator that binds the entire statement. Here are some other examples illustrating the scope of operators:

Example 27

Max does not run, or Smith resigns. $\quad = \quad -M \lor S$

Example 28

It's not the case that Max runs or Smith $\quad = \quad -(M \lor S)$
resigns.

In example 27 the '$-$' governs only M, whereas in example 28 it governs the compound '(M $\lor$ S)'. The first example is a disjunction; the second is a negation. Consider these examples:

Example 29

If Max does not run, then Smith $\quad = \quad -M \supset S$
resigns.

Example 30

It's not the case that if Max runs then $\quad = \quad -(M \supset S)$
Smith resigns.

Example 29 is a conditional; the antecedent alone is negated. Example 30 is a negation—a negation *of* a conditional.

Symbolizing with Parentheses and Brackets

Parentheses are used to group simple statements within a compound. Brackets are used to group compound statements within a larger compound. Let's compare the use of parentheses and brackets by carefully symbolizing a complex sentence.

Example 31

*If the president vetoes the bill, or if Congress balks and
the people protest, then the chances of passing this
year's new tax amendment are not good.*

The first steps in translation are identifying the simple statements and assigning capital letters to them. We underline each simple statement and write its symbol above it.

         V   *C*

If the president vetoes the bill, or if Congress balks and

    P   *G*

*the people protest, then the chances of passing this
year's new tax amendment are not good.*

Now we write out the compound in skeleton form using those symbols and the operators:

    If V or if C and P then not G.

Before we supply symbols for the operators, it may help to supply parentheses and brackets. It is immediately clear that the compound 'C and P' should be grouped together:

    If V or if (C and P) then not G.

The consequent of this statement is 'not G', and the antecedent is the disjunction 'If V or if (C and P)'. (The second 'if' within the statement clarifies for us that the antecedent, the condition that must be met, is that either the president vetoes the bill or both Congress balks and the people protest.) Thus, the compound 'If V or if (C and P)' must be grouped together, and since it already contains a grouped compound, brackets are used as follows:

    [If V or if (C and P)] then not G.

Now the symbols for the operators can be supplied, producing the following symbolic translation:

    [V ∨ (C + P)] ⊃ −G

Now we can see clearly that this is a conditional statement, because the horseshoe sign binds the entire compound.

Here are two more examples. Try to symbolize them and identify what type of compound each is. Check your results with the answers below.

Example 32

*It's not true that if Max runs then Bill swims and
Cheryl bowls.*

Example 33

*It's not true that if Max runs and Bill swims then
Cheryl bowls, and it's not true that Max runs or Bill
swims.*

Example 32 is a negation and can be symbolized as $-[M \supset (B + C)]$. Example 33 is a conjunction and can be symbolized as $-[(M + B) \supset C] + -(M \vee B)$.

Exercise 5.5   Translating and Grouping.   Translate the following statements into symbolic form and identify the type of compound. Not all the statements require parentheses or brackets.

1. It's not true that if you have money then you are happy. (M,H)
2. Not a soul made a sound, and not an eye was dry. (S,E)
3. The test was not very hard, or I studied well. (T,I)
4. If you live in the Southwest and don't water your lawn, it will die. (Y,W,D)
5. If John plays quarterback, then Tod gets fullback position, and Randy is on the bench. (J,T,R)
6. If Sven plays quarterback, then either Marsh or Steve is replaced. (Q,M,S)
7. The baritones and the altos are in the choir but not the sopranos. (B,A,S)
8. If the lines go down, then the transformer will blow. (L,T)
9. If the lines go down, then the transformer blows and the power goes out. (L,T,P)
10. If the lines go down and the transformer blows, then the power goes out. (L,T,P)
11. If the lines go down or the transformer blows, then the power goes out. (L,T,P)
12. Either the lines go down or if the transformer blows, then the power goes out. (L,T,P)
13. The power goes out if the lines go down or the transformer blows. (L,T,P)
14. It's not true that either the lines go down or if the transformer blows, then the power goes out. (L,T,P)
15. Either all the tickets are sold or if the council retained their share, then there are no seats available. (T,C,S)
16. If all the tickets are sold and the council retained their share, then either there are no seats available or we miscounted. (T,C,S,M)

17. If it's not true that if you are a Parisian, you're a Frenchman, then it's not true that if you are a Berliner, you're a German. (P,F,B,G)

18. It's false that the construction will continue and the men will go back to work if and only if the banker releases the funds or the purchaser closes escrow. (C,M,B,P)

19. The birds will migrate if either the temperature drops and the days get shorter or the insects move south. (B,T,D,I)

20. Each taxpayer or an authorized tax preparer must file an income tax report and complete a statement of earnings. (T,C,A,S)

5.6 Special Cases for Translation

Truth-functional logic analyzes deductive reasoning in terms of the five logical operators 'not', 'and', 'or', 'if . . . then', and 'if and only if'. Ordinary language contains a variety of other phrases that can express the same ideas. We have already noted some different expressions of negation and conjunction. Consider now the sentences below, each of which expresses the same statement and is symbolized in the same way:

Example 34

Wilson will not run for office.	=	$-W$
It's not true that Wilson will run for office.	=	$-W$
It's not the case that Wilson will run for office.	=	$-W$
It's false that Wilson will run for office.	=	$-W$

In this section we consider how some of the more troublesome phrases in ordinary language can be symbolized using the five operators. We look first at variations on constructions of conjunction and disjunction and then at variations on the conditional. Using the symbols p, q, and r to stand for any statements, we will give a formula for translating constructions from ordinary language into symbolic form.

Variations on the Conjunction and Disjunction

1. 'Neither p nor q'; 'both p and q are not'; and variants   The sentence 'Neither Wilson nor Smith runs' is an example of the construction 'neither *p* nor *q*'. It asserts that Wilson does not run and Smith does not run. The construction 'neither *p* nor *q*' therefore asserts 'not *p* and not *q*'. The same is true for the constructions 'not either *p* or *q*' and 'both *p* and *q* are not'. Consider these examples and ask yourself whether they do not all say the same thing:

Example 35

Neither Wilson nor Smith runs.

It's not the case that either Wilson or Smith runs.

Both Wilson and Smith do not run.

It's not the case that Wilson runs, and it's not the case that Smith runs.

Each of these statements can be translated as '−(W ∨ S)' or as '−W + −S', for, as we see later, those two translations are equivalent. Thus, the formulas for these constructions are as follows:

$$
\begin{array}{ccc}
\text{\textit{neither} p \textit{nor} q} & & \\
\text{\textit{not either} p \textit{or} q} & = & -(p \lor q) \\
\text{\textit{both} p \textit{and} q \textit{are not}} & & \text{\textit{or}} \\
\text{\textit{not} p \textit{and not} q} & & -p + -q
\end{array}
$$

2. 'Not both p and q'; 'not p or not q'   Consider these examples:

Example 36

It's not the case that both Wilson and Smith run.

It's not the case that Wilson runs, or it's not the case that Smith runs.

Wilson does not run, or Smith does not run.

Each sentence makes the same assertion: it's not the case that both Wilson and Smith run. That assertion permits that one or the other runs or that neither runs; it rules out the possibility that both run. The constructions illustrated by the examples above are translated as follows:

$$
\begin{array}{ccc}
\text{\textit{not both} p \textit{and} q} & & -(p + q) \\
\text{\textit{it's not the case that} p, \textit{or it's not the}} & = & \text{\textit{or}} \\
\text{\textit{case that} q} & & \\
\text{\textit{not} p \textit{or not} q} & & -p \lor -q
\end{array}
$$

Notice that the two constructions 'not both p and q', discussed in this section, and 'both p and q are not', discussed in section 1 above, are not logically equivalent. The first denies that both p and q are true together. The second denies p and denies q. Consider the difference between these two statements and their different translations:

Example 37

It's not the case that both Wilson and Smith run.	$=$	$-(W + S)$
Both Wilson and Smith do not run.	$=$	$-W + -S$

As you can see from their translations, the first is a negation, with the '$-$' sign governing the compound '$(W + S)$'. The second is a conjunction, with the '$+$' sign governing the entire compound. (As the formulas above indicate, each of these translations has an equivalent, and you may use either one. But be careful not to confuse the two equivalent translations for 'not both', and so on, with the equivalent translations for 'both . . . are not', and so on.)

3. *'Either* p *or* q *but not both'; the exclusive 'or'*   A commonly misunderstood construction is 'either p or q but not both'. For example, the statement 'Either Wilson runs or Smith runs but not both' appears to be a disjunction—'Wilson runs or Smith runs'—symbolized as W v S. However, it is not a disjunction and translating it as one misrepresents the logical content of the statement. A disjunction—that is, a statement using 'or' in the inclusive sense—says, in effect, 'one or the other *or both*'. But the sentence above clearly states, 'one or the other *but not both*'. This is the *exclusive sense of 'or'*, which is translated according to this formula:

$$p \text{ } or \text{ } q \text{ } but \text{ } not \text{ } both \text{ } = \text{ } (p \lor q) + -(p + q)$$

Written schematically, the example above asserts

(Wilson runs or Smith runs) and not both (Wilson runs and Smith runs).

It is translated as $(W \lor S) + -(W + S)$.

Consider another example: 'The baby will be a boy or a girl'. On the surface it appears to be a simple disjunction, and strictly speaking, it would not be incorrect to translate it that way. However, it would more naturally be taken to imply that the baby cannot be both a boy and a girl; that is, the statement would mean, 'The baby will be a boy or a girl and not both'. Thus, a more precise rendering of the statement employs the exclusive 'or' and would be translated as follows:

Example 38

The baby will be a boy or a girl.	$=$	$(B \lor G) + -(B + G)$

Variations on the Conditional

We have already seen several different equivalent phrases that express conditionals, including the following:

$$\begin{array}{c}\text{if p, } then \text{ q} \\ if \text{ p, q} \\ \text{p } only\ if \text{ q } = \text{ p} \supset \text{q} \\ \text{q } on\ the\ condition\ that \text{ p} \\ \text{q } if \text{ p}\end{array}$$

Notice that the last two constructions—'on the condition that' and '. . . if . . .'—place the antecedent and consequent in reverse order as compared with 'if . . . then' and the others.

There are other common expressions that also express conditionals. We will look at three groups: (1) necessary and sufficient conditions; (2) the pair consisting of the constructions '*p* unless *q*' and '*p* or else *q*'; and (3) the pair consisting of 'implies' and 'is implied by'.

1. Necessary and sufficient conditions   A sufficient condition is the antecedent of a conditional; a necessary condition is the consequent. Thus, in the statement 'If Marsha is a mother, then Marsha is a female', Marsha's being a mother is a sufficient condition for her being a female, whereas Marsha's being a female is a necessary condition for her being a mother.

The concepts of necessary and sufficient conditions permit us to describe the logical relationship between the two characteristics of being a mother and being a female:

Example 39

Being a mother is a sufficient condition but not a
necessary condition for *being a female*.

This means that if something is a mother then it is a female, but it is not true that if something is a female then it is a mother. We can describe the relationship in the converse as well:

Example 40

Being a female is a necessary condition but not a
sufficient condition for *being a mother*.

(How would the relationship between being red and having color be described in terms of necessary and sufficient conditions?)

There are also cases in which two characteristics are both necessary and sufficient for one another, as in this example:

Example 41

Being a bachelor is a necessary and a sufficient condition for *being an unmarried man*.

Finally, there are relationships in which several things are jointly necessary or
jointly sufficient for another, as in these examples:

Example 42

*Being a mother of a mother or a father and being a
female is* jointly necessary and sufficient for *being a
grandmother*.

Example 43

Being two-legged and featherless is jointly necessary
but not sufficient for *being a human*.

Sentences using the words 'necessary condition' or 'sufficient condition' are
easily translated symbolically. Whatever is described as the sufficient condition is represented by the antecedent, and whatever is described as the necessary condition is
represented by the consequent.

$$p \textit{ is a sufficient condition for } q \;=\; p \supset q$$
$$p \textit{ is a necessary condition for } q \;=\; q \supset p$$
$$p \textit{ is a necessary and sufficient condition for } q \;=\; p \equiv q$$

2. 'p or else q'; 'p unless q'   These two constructions may both be translated using
the disjunction symbol 'v'. That is, the truth-functional interpretation of these constructions is to treat them as disjunctions. Such an interpretation may not be immediately obvious. Let's consider the construction '*p* or else *q*' more closely, as in this
example:

Example 44

*The Iraqis leave Kuwait or else the United States
attacks them.*

Assuming a speaker asserts that statement, what circumstances would affirm the
statement? What circumstances would falsify the statement?

	IRAQIS LEAVE	OR ELSE	U.S. ATTACKS
case 1	true	TRUE	false
case 2	false	TRUE	true
case 3	true	TRUE	true
case 4	false	FALSE	false

Case 1 describes that situation in which it is true that the Iraqis leave and that the U.S. does not attack. Were this the case, then the assertion of the compound "The Iraqis leave or else the United States attacks" would be true.

Case 2 describes that situation in which the Iraqis do not leave and the U.S. attacks. Were this the case, the compound is true.

Case 3 describes that situation in which the Iraqis leave and the U.S. attacks. Why is the compound statement true in that case? The simple answer is that it is true because the situation does not falsify it. To assert that the Iraqis leave or else the U.S. attacks is *not* to assert that if the Iraqis leave, then the U.S. does not attack. On the contrary, it is to assert no more than that if the Iraqis do not leave, then the U.S. attacks. It asserts, in other words, *at least one condition* in which the U.S. attacks, namely, the Iraqis do not leave. It is consistent with that assertion—that is, it does not falsify it—that the U.S. attacks even though the Iraqis leave.

Case 4 describes precisely that situation that does falsify the assertion. Having asserted that the Iraqis leave or else the U.S. attacks, then if the Iraqis do not leave and the United States does not attack, the assertion is false. Notice that this is the case in which neither simple statement is true.

By considering those circumstances that would affirm or falsify the assertion that "The Iraqis leave Kuwait or else the United States attacks them," we see that the compound is true just in case either one or both of the simple statements is true. It is false just in case both simple statements are false. This conforms to the truth-functional definition of the disjunction: true in case at least one part is true, otherwise false. Thus, the symbolic interpretation of 'or else' is as a disjunction.

$$p \text{ } or \text{ } else \text{ } q \quad = \quad p \lor q$$

The construction 'p unless q' expresses the same relationship between p and q as does 'p or else q', but the statements are in reverse order. Consider this example:

Example 45

The United States attacks unless the Iraqis leave Kuwait.

	U.S. ATTACKS	UNLESS	IRAQIS LEAVE
case 1	true	TRUE	false
case 2	false	TRUE	true
case 3	true	TRUE	true
case 4	false	FALSE	false

Again, it seems clear that the compound is true in cases 1 and 2 and false in case 4. Case 3 describes the situation in which the U.S. attacks and the Iraqis leave Kuwait. Recognizing that the assertion "The U.S. attacks unless the Iraqis leave Kuwait" means no more than that the U.S. attacks *if* the Iraqis do *not* leave Kuwait, we see that the assertion is true even in that case in which the U.S. attacks and the Iraqis leave.

Thus, both constructions 'p or else q' and 'p unless q' may be translated as 'p ∨ q'.

p *or else* q

$$= \ p \vee q$$

p *unless* q

3. *'Implies'; 'is implied by'* The construction 'p implies q' is normally taken to assert that the statement represented by q follows from that represented by p. On the other hand, 'p is implied by q' is understood to assert that the statement represented by p follows from that represented by q. Thus, these expressions are translated as follows:

$$p \ implies \ q \ = \ p \supset q$$
$$p \ is \ implied \ by \ q \ = \ q \supset p$$

Table 5.2 summarizes the formulas for translating the various special constructions we have examined. You should have no difficulty symbolizing a statement if

Table 5.2 Special Cases for Translation

CONSTRUCTION	TRANSLATION
neither p nor q not either p or q both p and q are not not p and not q	−(p ∨ q) or −p + −q
not both p and q not p or not q	−(p + q) or −p ∨ −q
p or q but not both	(p ∨ q) + −(p + q)
if p then q if p, q p only if q p is a sufficient condition for q p implies q	p ⊃ q
p if q p is a necessary condition for q p is implied by q	q ⊃ p
p or else q p unless q	p ∨ q

you look at the formula carefully and follow the changes exactly. Let's examine a few examples.

Example 46

You are not my friend, or else you would help me.

Schematically, this statement may be represented as 'not friend or else help me'. It often helps to "strip away" some of the nonlogical words of the statement to see its structure. Write the schema underneath the formula for 'or else' and follow the changes exactly.

$$\text{p } \textit{or else} \text{ q } = \text{ p } \vee \text{ q}$$
not friend or else help me

The formula requires that simple statements remain the same and 'or else' is changed to '$\vee$'. Thus, the symbolic translation is as follows:

You are not my friend, or else you would help me $= -F \vee H$

Example 47

He cannot be a lawyer and a doctor both.

Schematically, this statement asserts 'not both lawyer and doctor'. The construction is 'not both *p* and *q*', for which the formula is

$$\textit{not both} \text{ p } \textit{and} \text{ q } = -(\text{p} + \text{q})$$
$$\textit{not both lawyer and doctor} = -(L + D)$$

The formula indicates that the two statements following 'not both' are conjoined inside parentheses and then the whole conjunction is negated.

Exercise 5.6   More Symbolic Translations.   Translate the following statements into symbolic form. Use the translation cues provided.

1. You cannot be a sailor and a marine both. (S,M)
2. If you are a sailor, then you are not a marine, and if you are a marine, then you are not a sailor. (S,M)
3. There is a decline in crime only if there is a decrease in poverty. (C,D)
4. Macbeth can be killed only if Burnam Wood comes to Dunsinane and he is attacked by someone who is not born of a woman. (M,B,A)
5. If you send your child to a private school, you can deduct half the cost of tuition from your income tax. (S,D)

6. Each taxpayer must file an income tax report, or else the taxpayer will be penalized. (T,P)

7. You will help me, or else you are not my friend. (H,F)

8. Unless the heat wave ends, the corn crops will be ruined. (H,C)

9. The heat wave must end, or else the crops will be ruined. (H,C)

10. It is false that having money is a sufficient condition for being happy and living contentedly. (M,H,L)

11. Congress will ignore the president's request for increased military spending if the president refuses to approve more aid to education. (C,P)

12. Military pressure should be used in Central America if and only if it is coupled with serious efforts to negotiate a peace settlement. (M,S)

13. Neither the chemists nor the physicists were expecting the awards. (C,P)

14. That 91 percent of all Americans have married implies that marriage is still an important institution in our culture. (A,M)

15. (a) Either you are male or female but not both. (b) You cannot be both male and female. (M,F)

16. The pullout of the Israelis is a necessary condition for the withdrawal of the Syrians from the Bekaa Valley. (P,W)

17. "If you look closely at our quality and judge for yourself, you'll understand that at Ford Motor Company quality is not just an abstract idea, it's very, very real." (Ford advertisement) (L,J,U)

18. Honduras is the poorest country in Central America but not the ripest for revolution. (H,R)

19. Neither the Chinese nor the Russians have been willing to engage in a cultural exchange. (C,R)

20. Either you're with us or you're against us. (W,A)

21. Both *Desire in the Dust* and *The Redrock Canyon* are not worth reading. (D,R)

22. If the airline pilots settle their dispute with the managers, then we'll see a resumption of service unless some other obstacle arises. (A,R,O)

23. The whole biomedical scientific community is in trouble if the Secretary does not resist pressure from demonstrators and insist upon the protection of scientific research. (B,S,I)

24. Even if there are no new sources of funding, the problem of poor-quality elementary education must be addressed, or else we face a national disaster. (S,P,F)

25. In profession of his love for her he carved her name on the tree trunk, and neither she nor her young sister ever suspected it was he. (H,S,Y)

26. (a) Smoking is harmful. (b) Smoking is not harmful. (c) It's not the case that smoking is not harmful. (S)

27. That the congressional subcommittee leaders gathered in Los Angeles over the weekend is a necessary condition of the facts that the speaker selects the site of the yearly meeting and this speaker chose L.A. (C,S,T)

28. It's not the case that both the Blue Jay and the Scrub Jay reside in Iowa. (B,S)

29. That the number of English majors is increasing implies that the new courses in literature and creative writing form an attractive program. (N,C)

30. More educators, more administrators, and more students are turning to philosophy to provide them with the skills of reasoning. (E,A,S)

5.7 The Truth-Functions

In this section we examine closely the logical operations expressed by the five logical operators. Consider the following examples:

Example 48	*Dallas is* not *the capital of Texas.*
Example 49	*Dallas is the capital of Texas,* and *Texas is a state.*
Example 50	*Dallas is the capital of Texas,* or *Texas is a state.*
Example 51	If *Dallas is the capital of Texas,* then *Texas is a state.*
Example 52	*Dallas is the capital of Texas* if and only if *Texas is a state.*

In these sentences the different operators produce logically different types of statements, making the truth-value of each compound distinctly different. A conjunction, for instance, asserts that 'this *and* this' are true; therefore, the conjunction itself is true only if both of its parts are true. A disjunction asserts that 'this *or* this' is true, which means that the disjunction itself is true if at least one of its parts is true. Each of the logical operators forms a compound with distinct conditions for its truth-value. Those conditions define the *truth-function* represented by the operator. The *truth* of the compound is a *function of* the truth or falsity of its component parts. Now let's examine each of the operations.

1. Negation To negate a statement is to form a new statement whose truth-value is the opposite of that of the original. A negation is true if what it negates is false and false if what it negates is true. For example, 'Dallas is not the capital of Texas' is true if 'Dallas is the capital of Texas' is false. A statement and its negation have opposite truth-values. If a statement *p* is true, then its negation is false, and if *p* is false, then its negation is true.

We can conveniently see the truth-function represented by an operator by constructing a *truth table*. A truth table shows the possible truth-values of a statement, that is, the conditions under which the statement is true or false. Given a statement *p* and its negation, we ask first how many possible truth-values there are for *p*. Obviously, there are only two: true (T) and false (F). Given what we know about the truth-function of negation, we can represent the truth-values of the negation of *p* in a truth table that looks like this:

p	−*p*
T	F
F	T

Negation: *The truth-value of the negation is the opposite of the truth-value of the statement.*

When *p* is true −*p* is false, and vice versa. The table shows the truth-function represented by negation.

2. Conjunction   The statement 'Dallas is the capital of Texas, and Texas is a state' is true if and only if it is true that both Dallas is the capital of Texas *and* Texas is a state. In other words, the conjunction is true if and only if *all* of its parts are true, as indicated by the word 'and'. The truth table displaying the truth-function of conjunction represents two statements, *p* and *q,* so it must show each of four possible combinations of truth-values for those two statements, as below:

p	*q*
T	T
F	T
T	F
F	F

This table shows each possible combination of truth-values for *any* two statements: both are true, both are false, or one is true and the other false. Now we can show the truth value of the compound formed with the symbol '+'.

p	+	*q*
T	T	T
F	F	T
T	F	F
F	F	F

Conjunction: *True only if all parts are true; otherwise false.*

The column of T's and F's under the '+' sign indicates the truth-value of the compound when *p* is T, *q* is T, and so on. The table makes it easy to see that the conjunction is true in only one case: when *all* parts are true. It is false in every case in which one or more of its parts are false.

3. Disjunction   The truth-function given by disjunction—that is, by 'or'—is obviously different. 'Or' means one or the other element of the compound is true or both of them are true. The disjunction is true if at least one element is true.

p	v	q
T	T	T
F	T	T
T	T	F
F	F	F

Disjunction: *True if at least one part is true; false if both are false.*

4. The Conditional The conditional asserts that if *p* is true then *q* is true. Consider the conditional statement 'If Dallas is the capital of Texas, then Texas is a state'. Under what conditions is that conditional true? Obviously, if the antecedent 'Dallas is the capital of Texas' is true and 'Texas is a state' is true, then the conditional itself is true, for that is precisely what the conditional asserts. It is also obvious that if the antecedent is true and the consequent is false, then the conditional is false, for that is exactly the opposite of what the conditional asserts. Thus far, the conditional is true when both antecedent and consequent are true and false when the antecedent is true and the consequent false.

What is the value of the conditional when the antecedent is false? If Dallas is *not* the capital of Texas, is the conditional false? No, it is not. Remember that the conditional asserts a hypothetical situation: it says *if* the antecedent is true then the consequent follows. The conditional is not shown false because as a matter of fact the antecedent is not true. The conditional is, therefore, regarded as true whenever the antecedent is false. The complete truth-function of the conditional is displayed in the following table:

p	⊃	q
T	T	T
F	T	T
T	F	F
F	T	F

Conditional: *True in all cases except those in which* p *is true and* q *is false.*

5. The Biconditional The truth-function represented by the biconditional is similar in a certain respect to that of the conditional. As explained above, the conditional is false whenever the antecedent is true and the consequent is false. The biconditional is really two conditionals joined together ('if *p* then *q*' and 'if *q* then *p*'). Whenever one statement of a biconditional is true and the other false, one of the conditionals composing it will be false, and therefore the biconditional will be false. The biconditional is true when the truth-values of its components are the same and false when they are not the same.

p	≡	q
T	T	T
F	F	T
T	F	F
F	T	F

Biconditional: *True only when truth-values are the same.*

The truth-functions given by the five logical operators can be summarized as follows:

OPERATION	SYMBOLIZATION	TRUTH–FUNCTION
Negation	$-p$	True when p is false; false when p is true
Conjunction	$p + q$	True only when all parts are true; false if one or more are false
Disjunction	$p \vee q$	True when at least one part is true; false only if all parts are false
Conditional	$p \supset q$	True in all cases except those in which p is true and q is false
Biconditional	$p \equiv q$	True whenever all parts have same truth-value; false if there are different truth-values

5.8 Constructing Truth Tables

The purpose of the truth table is to display in a completely systematic and mechanical way the truth-values of statements (and, as we will see later, the validity of arguments). We have already seen how the tables can display the truth-functions given by the logical operators. But we can also apply the truth table method to any statement to reveal the conditions under which it is true or false. There are five steps for constructing truth tables in the easiest and most foolproof way.

Step (1) Determine the number of rows needed. The horizontal lines of T's and F's are called *rows* and the vertical lines of T's and F's are called *columns*. The table must be constructed so that every possible combination of T's and F's is displayed in an organized way. If only one simple statement is involved, then, of course, there are only two possible truth values, T and F, and the number of rows in the table is two, as shown below:

$$p \qquad \textit{One simple statement: two rows}$$

1   T
2   F

If there are two simple statements, then there are four possible combinations: both are true, both are false, the first is true and the second false, and the first is false and the second true. Thus, there must be four rows of T's and F's, as follows:

	p	q	Two simple statements: *four rows*
1	T	T	
2	F	T	
3	T	F	
4	F	F	

For three simple statements, eight rows are needed.

	p	q	r	Three simple statements: *eight rows*
1	T	T	T	
2	F	T	T	
3	T	F	T	
4	F	F	T	
5	T	T	F	
6	F	T	F	
7	T	F	F	
8	F	F	F	

We can put this pattern in a formula:

$$\text{Number of rows} = 2^{\text{ number of simple statements}}$$

The number of rows equals 2 taken to the power of the number of simple statements. Or you can simply remember that each additional simple statement doubles the number of rows needed.

1 simple statement	=	2 rows
2 simple statements	=	4 rows
3 simple statements	=	8 rows
4 simple statements	=	16 rows

Step (2) Fill in T's and F's for each simple statement. To make sure you capture every possible combination of T's and F's, follow this simple procedure:

1. Begin with the leftmost simple statement and alternate the T's and F's.
2. Double the T's and F's for the next *different* simple statement.
3. For the next different statement double the number of T's from the previous column, then double the F's. Do this until each column is completed for each new simple statement.

If a simple statement occurs more than once in a compound it receives exactly the same values for each occurrence. No matter how many simple statements you are dealing with, you always follow the same procedure: alternate T's and F's for the first column, then double the number of T's in the previous column and then the number of F's. Here is a sample table for four simple statements:

	p	q	r	s
1	T	T	T	T
2	F	T	T	T
3	T	F	T	T
4	F	F	T	T
5	T	T	F	T
6	F	T	F	T
7	T	F	F	T
8	F	F	F	T
9	T	T	T	F
10	F	T	T	F
11	T	F	T	F
12	F	F	T	F
13	T	T	F	F
14	F	T	F	F
15	T	F	F	F
16	F	F	F	F
	a	b	c	d

Column (a) alternates T's and F's. Column (b) doubles T's and F's. Column (c) doubles the number of T's of the previous column, then doubles the F's. The procedure continues for any number of simple statements.

Step (3) Supply the truth-values of all negations of simple statements. Go through the compound you are displaying and check for any negations of simple statements. Fill in the column of T's and F's for such negations as illustrated below:

p	v	−r
T		FT
F		FT
T		TF
F		TF

The column immediately underneath the '−' represents the truth values for −r based on the original values of r. The negation of any compounds is always done afterwards. Before continuing be sure that the truth-values for all negations of simple statements have been filled in.

Step (4) Supply the truth-values for compounds inside parentheses. If there are any compounds inside parentheses, you must fill in their truth-values before continuing. The guiding rule is *always work from the inside outward*. Notice in the example below how the compounds inside parentheses are completed before the operators outside parentheses can be done.

(p	⊃	s)	+	−	(r	∨	−	s)
1	T	T	T			T	T	F	T
2	F	T	T			T	T	F	T
3	T	F	F			T	T	T	F
4	F	T	F			T	T	T	F
5	T	T	T			F	F	F	T
6	F	T	T			F	F	F	T
7	T	F	F			F	T	T	F
8	F	T	F			F	T	T	F
	a	b	c	d	e	f	g	h	i

Column (b) represents the truth-values for the compound $p \supset s$. Column (h) shows the truth-values for the negation of s. And column (g) shows the truth-values for the compound $r \vee -s$.

Step (5) Supply the truth-values for the outer operators. Once you have filled in the truth-values for all negated simple statements and for compounds within parentheses, you are ready to write the truth-values for the operators outside the parentheses. A negation of a compound must be treated before operators between compounds. Thus, fill in the truth-values for any negated compounds next. Then compute the truth-values for the remaining operators outside parentheses. The truth-values for the final operator will be the truth-values of the entire statement as a whole. Here is our sample completed.

(p	⊃	s)	+	−	(r	∨	−	s)
1	T	T	T	F	F	T	T	F	T
2	F	T	T	F	F	T	T	F	T
3	T	F	F	F	F	T	T	T	F
4	F	T	F	F	F	T	T	T	F
5	T	T	T	T	T	F	F	F	T
6	F	T	T	T	T	F	F	F	T
7	T	F	F	F	F	F	T	T	F
8	F	T	F	F	F	F	T	T	F
	a	b	c	d	e	f	g	h	i

Notice that column (e), the negation of $r \vee -s$, is determined from the values of $r \vee -s$ in column (g). Notice also that the truth-values of the final operator, the '+' sign, are determined by the values of column (b) and column (e). We can circle the column under the final operator to show that it represents the truth-values for the entire compound. Thus, we can see clearly for what values of the simple statements the entire compound $(p \supset s) + -(r \vee -s)$ is true or false. Its truth-value is a function of the truth-values of its component parts.

SUMMARY OF STEPS

Step (1) Determine the number of rows required.

Step (2) Fill in T's and F's for each simple statement by first alternating T's and F's, then doubling the number of T's from the previous column and then doubling the F's. Give the same values to each occurrence of the same sign for a simple statement.

Step (3) Fill in the truth-values for all negations of *simple* statements.

Step (4) Fill in the truth-values for all compounds *inside* parentheses.

Step (5) Fill in the truth-values for all operators outside parentheses, completing negations of compounds first.

Exercise 5.8A   Truth Tables for the Operators.   Construct truth tables for the five logical operators.

1. Negation $-p$ 2. Conjunction $p + q$
3. Disjunction $p \vee q$ 4. Conditional $p \supset q$
5. Biconditional $p \equiv q$

Exercise 5.8B   The Truth-values of Compounds.   Construct truth tables for the following compounds. Put a circle around the column that displays the truth-values for the whole compound.

1. $R + -S$ 2. $P \vee (Q + R)$ 3. $P \vee (Q \supset R)$
4. $-P \supset Q$ 5. $Q \supset (P + Q)$ 6. $P \supset Q$
7. $-(P + R)$ 8. $-P + -Q$ 9. $-(P \vee Q)$
10. $P \vee (Q \vee R)$ 11. $R \equiv (S \supset T)$ 12. $-[S \equiv (P + -Q)]$

Exercise 5.8C   Translating and Truth Tables.   Translate the following statements into symbolic form and then construct truth tables to show their truth-values. Circle the column that displays the truth-values for the compound.

1. If it snows, then it does not rain. (S,R)

2. Either it rains or it snows but not both. (R,S)

3. If the temperature is not above freezing and it snows, then either the maintenance crews will salt the roads or classes will be canceled. (T,S,M,C)

4. If classes are canceled, then the temperature is not above freezing and it is snowing. (C,T,S)

5. If the Israelis leave Lebanon, then the Lebanese government must keep the Syrians out unaided. (I,L)

6. Max and Mildred live in the south, and Max practices medicine. (X,M,P)

7. Abraham Lincoln was born after George Washington, and if Thomas Jefferson was president before Lincoln, then Lincoln was born after Jefferson, too. (L,J,B)

8. Citizens of the United States have the right to vote if and only if the Bill of Rights is not abandoned. (R,B)

9. It is not the case that England is governed by Spain or Germany. (S,G)

10. Ben Franklin invented the television, George Washington was born in Turkey, and the president of the United States is a former heavyweight prize fighter. (F,W,P)

11. An object is a material object if and only if it occupies space and has mass. (O,S,M)

12. The lines are down, the electricity is out, and there is no heat, if reports from the police department are true. (L,E,H,R)

13. All things are either solid or not solid but not both. (S)

14. It is not the case that believers in God and believers in Krishna are both right about their beliefs. (G,K)

15. Most scientists are supporters of nuclear research only if it is not used for warfare and weaponry. (S,N,W)

16. If the human fetus is a person, then it has a right to life and killing it is morally wrong. (P,R,K)

17. If I do get home before dark, then either I will have to leave early or I must drive over seventy miles per hour. (I,L,D)

18. If you are not a student at the college, then you are either an administrator, a staff member, or a faculty member. (S,A,M,F)

19. Hawks eat rabbits and mice, or if there is no live food, they will eat carrion. (R,M,L,C)

20. If this paper is made of wood pulp, then it is either oak or maple. (P,O,M)

21. Capital punishment neither deters crime nor protects citizens. (C,P)

22. If Max is a Marxist and Smith is a socialist, then Wilson is a Democrat. (M,S,W)

23. Unless the mandatory industrial smokestack regulations are enforced and the exhaust emission control devices are legally required on all automobiles, the decrease of dangerous hydrocarbons in the atmosphere will not be evident within the next five to seven years. (M,E,D)

24. For the first time in four years the *Contras* will be strong enough to pose a serious threat to the Sandinista government of Nicaragua only if their numbers continue to swell, they receive support from the campesinos, and the $27 million allocated by the U.S. Congress is used for equipment. (C,N,R,E)

25. If a partner in a limited partnership invests $10,000, or 10 percent of the partnership's total investment, and the venture loses $700,000, the partner will be able to write off $70,000 but will be liable for only $10,000. (P,T,V,W,L)

Exercise 5.8D   Interpreting Symbolic Statements.   Using the interpretations of the symbols given below, translate the following symbolic statements into ordinary language.

S   =   It snows.

R   =   It rains.

P   =   There is precipitation.

T   =   The temperature is above freezing.

C   =   Classes must be canceled.

M   =   Maintenance crews are salting the roads.

1. S ∨ R
2. P ⊃ (S ∨ R)
3. (T + P) ⊃ R
4. (−T + P) ⊃ (−R + S)
5. (R + −T) ⊃ M
6. −T ⊃ [S ⊃ (−M ⊃ C)]
7. M ∨ (T ⊃ C)
8. S ≡ (P + −T)

Review Questions Chapter 5

1. Define 'truth-function'.
2. Define 'simple statement' and 'compound statement'.
3. What are the logical operators?
4. Under what conditions is the conjunction true?
5. Under what conditions is the disjunction true?
6. Under what conditions is the conditional true? Explain why the conditional is true even when the antecedent is false.
7. Under what conditions is the biconditional true?
8. What is the difference in meaning between $-(p + q)$ and $-p + -q$?
9. What is the difference in meaning between $-p \supset q$ and $-(p \supset q)$?
10. What are the different ways of expressing the 'if . . . then' in our language?
11. When you are determining the truth-values of a compound statement using a truth table, in what order do you determine the following: (a) T's and F's

for compounds inside parentheses; (b) T's and F's for negated simple statements; (c) T's and F's for negated compounds; (d) T's and F's for operators outside the parentheses?

12. What is the purpose of constructing a truth table with a precise number of rows and a systematic procedure for filling in T's and F's?

True or False?

1. The statement 'If the president dies in office, then the first lady becomes president' is false if the president does not die in office.

2. Simple statements are symbolized by capital letters.

3. The scope of an operator may be bound by parentheses and brackets.

4. Supposing a compound to be false, by using a truth table you can determine the truth-values of the component parts responsible for its falsity.

5. If some statement p is a necessary condition for a statement q, then it follows that q implies p.

6. The statement 'It shines unless it's cloudy' is logically different from the statement 'It shines or else it's cloudy'.

7. The logical operator 'or' is interpreted in truth-functional logic as the inclusive 'or'.

8. If p is a necessary and sufficient condition of q, then p is true if and only if q is true.

9. A conjunction is false only on the condition that all its parts are false.

10. The exclusive 'or' is symbolized as $(p \vee q) + -(p + q)$.

CHAPTER SIX
Truth-Functional Logic
Part II

In this chapter we learn the *truth table method* for
determining validity, the method of the *indirect
truth table* for determining validity, and the
use of truth tables to identify tautologies, self-
contradictions, and equivalences.

As we saw in the previous chapter, the truth table gives us a completely mechanical and systematic way of displaying the truth-values of statements. There are,
however, far more important uses of the truth table. In this chapter we use truth
tables to evaluate deductive arguments for validity, to identify the logical types of
statements, and to ascertain logical relations between two statements. By using truth
tables, in other words, we can demonstrate that an argument is or is not valid, that
a statement is a contingent statement, tautology, or self-contradiction, and that two
or more statements are contradictories, equivalences, or in neither relation. We also
learn how to use a shortcut version of the truth table called the indirect truth table.

6.1 Truth Tables for Evaluating Arguments

The truth table method for evaluating arguments consists of three steps:

Step (1) Translate the statements of the argument into symbolic form.

Step (2) Construct a truth table for the whole argument.

Step (3) Look for a row in which the truth-values of the premises are T and the truth-value of the conclusion is F. If there is such a row, the argument is invalid. If there is not such a row, the argument is valid.

The theory behind this method is easy to understand. First, as you recall, a deductive argument is valid if and only if on the assumption that the premises are true, it must also be the case that the conclusion is true. Secondly, as we have seen, the truth table displays all possible truth-values of a statement. Applied to an argument a truth table can show us when the premises are true or false and when the conclusion is true or false. Each row of the truth table shows a possible assignment of truth-values for the premises and conclusion. If in any one row the premises are all true and the conclusion is false, then we know the possibility exists that the premises are true and the conclusion false; hence, we know that the argument is *not* valid. Let's use the following invalid argument to examine the truth table method:

Example 1

If it rains, then my car is wet. But it does not rain.
Therefore, my car is not wet.

Step (1) Translate the argument into symbolic form.

If it rains, then my car is wet.	$R \supset W$
It does not rain.	$-R$
Therefore, my car is not wet.	$\therefore -W$

The three dots '∴' introducing the conclusion is a symbol for *'therefore'*. From now on we will use this symbol to signal the conclusion of an argument.

Step (2) Construct a truth table for the whole argument. Writing a truth table for an argument is virtually the same as writing a truth table for a compound statement. Arrange the premises and conclusion on one line, as though it were one compound statement, and then follow the steps outlined in the previous chapter for assigning truth-values. Remember always to assign the same values to each occurrence of a simple statement even though it appears in different compounds.

In the example below, the symbolized argument is written on one line with the three dots separating the premises from the conclusion. The initial T's and F's are written following the rule of alternating and then doubling for each different simple statement. Again, each occurrence of the same simple statement receives the same values. Next, the truth-values for the operators are entered, and the truth-values for each compound are entered. When you are finished, you should have for each statement in the argument a column representing its truth-values.

```
R ⊃ W        − R      ∴ − W

T [T] T      [F] T      [F] T
F (T) T      (T) F      (F) T     ← Premises true, conclusion false
T [F] F      [F] T      [T] F
F [T] F      [T] F      [T] F
```

Boxed columns show the truth-values of the premises and the conclusion, and the circled T's and F show that the argument is invalid.

Step (3) Look for a row in which the premises are all T and the conclusion is F. If there is such a row, the argument is invalid. If not, it is valid. The second row of the table has a T for each premise and an F for the conclusion. It is helpful to circle the values of such a row, for it shows that there is a case in which the premises are true yet the conclusion is false. When the truth table shows us the possibility of true premises and a false conclusion, as in our example, the argument is *invalid*. The presence of even one row with true premises and a false conclusion is enough to show that the whole argument is invalid.

Here is another example.

Example 2

If it rains, then my car is wet. $R \supset W$

My car is not wet. $- W$
_____   _____

Therefore, it does not rain. $\therefore - R$

The truth table is as follows:

```
R ⊃ W        − W      ∴ − R

T [T] T      [F] T      [F] T
F [T] T      [F] T      [T] F
T [F] F      [T] F      [F] T
F [T] F      [T] F      [T] F
```

Look across each row and you will see that there is *no* row in which the premises are T and the conclusion F. The fact that in no case are the premises true and the conclusion false means that it is not possible for the premises to be true yet the conclusion false. Therefore, the argument is proven to be valid.

Consider another example:

Example 3

You have to return the money unless it was not a loan.
If it was a gift, then it was not a loan. Therefore, if
you don't have to return the money, it was a gift.

You have to return the money or it was not a loan.	$R \vee -L$
If it was a gift, then it was not a loan.	$G \supset -L$
Therefore, if you don't have to return the money, it was a gift.	$\therefore -R \supset G$

R	v	−	L	G	⊃	−	L	−	R	⊃	G
T	T	F	T	T	F	F	T	F	T	T	T
F	F	F	T	T	F	F	T	T	T	T	T
T	T	T	F	T	T	T	F	F	T	T	T
F	T	T	F	T	T	T	F	T	T	T	T
T	T	F	T	F	T	F	T	F	T	T	F
F	F	F	T	F	T	F	T	T	F	F	F
T	T	T	F	F	T	T	F	F	T	T	F
F	(T)	T	F	F	(T)	T	F	T	(F)	F	←

The table shows that in the very last row the premises are T but the conclusion is F. Therefore, the argument is invalid.

Exercise 6.1   The Truth Table Method.   Use truth tables to evaluate the following arguments for validity. Circle the truth-values of the row that shows an argument invalid.

1. If people know what is right, they will do it. But people do not know what is right; therefore, they do not do it. (K,D)

2. God cannot be both loving and jealous. He is loving; therefore, he is not jealous. (L,J)

3. God cannot be both good and evil. He is not evil; therefore, he is good. (G,E)

4. Citizens of the United States have the right to vote if and only if the United States is not a monarchy. It is not a monarchy; therefore, citizens of the United States do have the right to vote. (R,M)

5. If the acid crystallizes, then either the solution was too weak or we made a mistake. We did not make a mistake. Therefore, if it crystallizes, then the solution was too weak. (C,S,M)

6. Ted cannot be both a tenor and an alto. He must be an alto, since he is not a tenor. (T, A)

7. If Sweden is in North Africa, then either Egyptians are blue-eyed or Swedes are dark and handsome. Sweden is not in North Africa; therefore, Egyptians are not blue-eyed. (S, E, D, H)

8. Neither the French nor the Belgians want to leave the Sudan. If the French do not want to leave the Sudan, then the Namibians will elect a new president. Therefore, the Namibians will elect a new president. (F, B, N)

9. The programmers will strike if management reduces their benefits. If the programmers strike, then services will suffer. But the programmers will not strike; thus, management will not reduce benefits, and services will not suffer. (P, M, S)

10. If there were no ownership or private property, then there would be no such thing as theft. Therefore, there is ownership and private property, or there is no theft. (O, P, T)

11. No thing can be moved if there is a void. (Aristotle) It is not the case that no thing can be moved. Therefore, there is no void. (M, V)

12. The whole numbers are either odd or even. If they are even, then they are not odd. Therefore, if they are odd, then they are not even. (O, E)

13. If he loves her, he will marry her. So, if he does not love her, he will not marry her. (L, M)

14. George is tired, or Fred is happy. George is not tired. Therefore, Fred is happy. (G, F)

15. If the moon can be settled, then Mars can be settled. If Mars can be settled, then Jupiter can too. Therefore, if the moon can be settled, then Jupiter can be settled. (S, M, J)

16. The facts that Wynton Marsalis plays classical and jazz trumpet imply that he is a better musician than Miles Davis. But Davis writes his own music, and if that is so then Marsalis is not a better musician. Therefore, Marsalis is not a better musician. (C, J, B, D)

17. "If Peewee Herman starred in *The Breakfast Club,* then I'm a cross-eyed pole-cat. Well, I'm not a cross-eyed polecat, so . . . you figure it out." (P, C)

18. God is in me or is not at all. (Wallace Stevens) Since it is false that he is not, it follows that he is in me. (G, H)

19. If a man has a talent and cannot use it, he has failed. If he has a talent and learns somehow to use the whole of it, he has gloriously succeeded and won a satisfaction and a triumph few men ever know. (Thomas Wolfe) He has not won a triumph few men ever know. Therefore, either he does not have a talent or he has not learned to use the whole of it. (T, U, F, L, G, W, K)

20. Unless we are to be the last generation of humans on the face of this earth, we must put an end to war. Thus, "mankind must put an end to war, or war will put an end to mankind." (John F. Kennedy) (L, M, W)

21. $-(A \lor B) \supset D$ $C + -D$ $\therefore A \lor B$

22. $L \supset (N + M)$ $-M \lor -L$ $\therefore -N$

23. $-(P + Q)$ P $\therefore -Q$

24. $S \equiv (S + R)$ $\therefore -S \lor R$

25. $T \supset W$ $-W$ $\therefore -T$

6.2 Indirect Truth Tables

Although the truth table method for determining validity is foolproof if followed correctly, it can be tedious and cumbersome, particularly for arguments with several simple statements. There is, however, a shortcut version, called the *indirect truth table method*. Rather than listing all possible assignments of truth-values, the indirect method shows quickly whether that crucial row in fact exists in which the premises are true and the conclusion false. We begin by hypothesizing (that is, assuming for the sake of argument) that there *is* such a crucial row in which the premises are T and the conclusion is F. *We assume, in effect, that the argument is invalid. We then attempt to apply that assumption consistently by completing truth-values for the simple statements*. If truth-values can be consistently assigned to all simple statements, then our hypothesis was correct: there is at least one case in which the premises are true and the conclusion false. The argument is, therefore, *invalid*. If, on the other hand, a consistent assignment of truth-values cannot be made, then the argument cannot have true premises and a false conclusion. Therefore, it is valid. Let us see how this works with an example.

Example 4

If it rains, then my car is wet.	$R \supset W$
It does not rain.	$-R$

| Therefore, my car is not wet. | $\therefore -W$ |

Step (1) Assign the value F to the conclusion and T to each premise. That represents our assumption that the argument is invalid, which we will try to prove.

$$\begin{array}{ccc} T & T & F \\ R \supset W & -R & \therefore -W \end{array}$$

Step (2) Try to complete the assignment of values to simple statements. Now we will see whether we can complete the assignment of truth values to simple statements. Notice what values you have to begin with: the compound $R \supset W$ is T, the compound $-R$ is T, and the compound $-W$ is F. Can you infer from those truth-values what the values of any simple statements are? Since $-W$ is F, it follows that W must be T. And since −R is T, it follows that R must be F. So we can make the following assignments:

$$
\begin{array}{ccc}
\text{T} & \text{T} & \text{F} \\
\text{R} \supset \text{W} & -\text{R} & \therefore -\text{W} \\
| \quad | & | & | \\
\text{F} \quad \text{T} & \text{F} & \text{T}
\end{array}
$$

As you can see, there is no problem in assigning values to the statements. The method shows that there *is* a row in which the premises are all T's yet the conclusion is F; thus, this argument is shown to be *invalid*.

Consider this example:

Example 5

Hot air rises and cold air falls.	*H + C*
If hot air rises, then the ground will be cooler than the ceiling.	*H ⊃ G*
————————————————	————
Thus, the ground is cooler than the ceiling.	∴ *G*

First, assign F to the conclusion and T's to the premises.

$$
\begin{array}{ccc}
\text{T} & \text{T} & \text{F} \\
\text{H + C} & \text{H} \supset \text{G} & \therefore \text{G}
\end{array}
$$

Try to complete the assignment of truth-values. G is false, so we can place an F under the G in H ⊃ G. The conjunction H + C is true, so each of its simple statements must be true, allowing us to place T's under H and C. The H in H ⊃ G must therefore also be T. But now a problem arises.

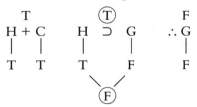

Notice that we have an inconsistency. According to our hypothesis, H ⊃ G is supposed to be T. But if H is T and G is F, then H ⊃ G must be F, which is *inconsistent with the hypothesis*. If we change H to F, then the conjunction H + C becomes F. We find that we cannot make a consistent assignment of values to this argument on the assumption that it is *not* valid. Since the hypothesis that the argument is invalid fails, it must be that the argument is *valid*.

Not all arguments are as easily evaluated as these examples. In some cases, the indirect truth table requires several attempts at assigning values. The first assignment of T's to premises and F to the conclusion may not give you much to go on. You have to try different possible assignments. Here is an example:

Example 6

T	T	F
P ∨ Q	P ⊃ Q	∴ P + Q

How should you begin? There is no initial assignment of truth-values to simple statements that must be made on the hypothesis that the argument is invalid. That P ∨ Q is T does not indicate what truth-values P and Q have; neither does P ⊃ Q. And that P + Q is F does not indicate what values P and Q have. Looking at the conclusion, we can see three possibilities that would account for a false conclusion: both P and Q are F, one is F and the other T. We may have to consider several possible sets of assignments to determine whether this argument can have true premises and a false conclusion, as we are assuming. Therefore, where we begin is arbitrary. Let's start with the conclusion and suppose that both P and Q are F for our first trial. We will then make the following assignments:

Trial (1)

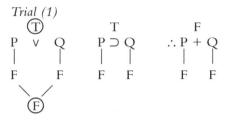

On the first trial—assigning F to P and Q in the conclusion—we see that an inconsistency results in the first premise. However, we cannot conclude that the argument is valid because we were not forced to that assignment. That is, we cannot say yet that *there is no consistent assignment of values possible* for this argument on the assumption that it is invalid. We must, therefore, make other attempts. Let's try assigning T to P and F to Q in the conclusion.

Trial (2)

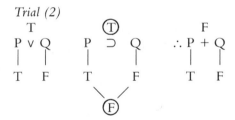

In trial (2) we encounter an inconsistency in the second premise. Again, we cannot yet conclude that no consistent assignment is possible. We must consider the last possibility, assigning F to P and T to Q in the conclusion.

Trial (3)

T	T	F
P ∨ Q	P ⊃ Q	∴ P + Q
F T	F T	F T

In this assignment no inconsistency is encountered. Therefore, this third trial shows that a consistent assignment of truth-values is possible on the hypothesis that the argument is invalid. After three attempts we have shown that the argument is *invalid*.

Example 6 illustrates the important point that the purpose of the indirect truth table method is to determine whether a consistent set of truth-values can be assigned to the simple statements on the assumption that the argument has true premises and a false conclusion. The fact that a trial assignment results in an inconsistency does not show that the argument is valid. Our aim is to show whether a consistent set is possible. The key question to ask in using the indirect truth table method is:

> Indirect truth table method: *Is there a consistent assignment of truth-values on the assumption that the premises are all true and the conclusion false?*

As the examples above illustrate, a consistent assignment may occur on the initial assigning of values. However, the method may require two or more trial assignments before either a consistent assignment has been reached or all possible assignments have been exhausted.

Exercise 6.2   Indirect Truth Table Method.   Use the indirect truth table method to determine whether the following arguments are valid. Circle the inconsistency you find for those arguments that are shown to be valid.

1. Winters are cold and summers are hot. Therefore, summers are hot or the moon is made of green cheese. (W,S,M)

2. Russell was either a realist or an empiricist. If he was a realist, then he was not an idealist. Therefore, Russell was not an empiricist. (R,E,I)

3. If there is a God, then he is good. If we disappear into nothingness at death, then death is not good. If God is good and God creates death, then death is good. Therefore, if we disappear into nothingness at death, there is no God. (G,H,N,D,C)

4. If he loves her, he will marry her. Therefore, if he does not love her, he will not marry her. (L,M)

5. If the moon can be settled, then Mars can be settled. If Mars can be settled, then Jupiter can be settled too. Thus, if the moon can be settled, then Jupiter can be settled. (S,M,J)

6. If the acid crystallizes, then either the solution was too weak or we made a mistake. We did not make a mistake; therefore, if the acid crystallizes, the solution was too weak. (A,W,M)

7. If a man has a talent and cannot use it, he has failed. If he has a talent and learns somehow to use the whole of it, he has gloriously succeeded and won a satisfaction and a triumph few men ever know. (Thomas Wolfe) He has not won a triumph few men ever know; therefore, either he does not have a talent or he has not learned to use the whole of it. (T,U,F,L,G,W,K)

8. The fact that animals are less intelligent than we does not imply that we may disregard their welfare. If we disregard their welfare, then we are inhumane and no better than animals ourselves. Therefore, if we disregard their welfare, then it is not the case that animals are less intelligent than we. (A,D,I,B)

9. This argument is invalid if and only if it can have true premises and a false conclusion. This argument has a false conclusion; therefore, it is invalid. (I,T,F)

10. If people earn different amounts and everyone pays the same amount in taxes, then those who earn more keep more and those who earn less keep less. If those who earn more keep more and those who earn less keep less, then the tax laws are unfair. Therefore, either people do not earn different amounts or if everyone pays the same amount in taxes, then the tax laws are unfair. (P,E,M,L,T)

11. T v O   T ⊃ O   ∴ O ⊃ −T

12. A v B   B ⊃ C   ∴ −(A + C)

13. M + N   −M v L   −P ⊃ −L   ∴ P + N

14. −(K + L)   R ⊃ (S + L)   R   ∴ −K

15. P ⊃ Q   Q ⊃ (S v F)   −S + −F   ∴ −P

16. A ≡ T   −A v −M   M   ∴ T

17. (E + F) + L   (F v G) + −(F + G)   ∴ −G

18. J ⊃ V   H ⊃ J   M ⊃ H   ∴ M ⊃ V

19. −(I + O) v T   ∴ I ⊃ T

20. D + [T ≡ (M v R)]   −T   ∴ −M + −R

6.3 Tautologies, Contradictions, Equivalences

In addition to evaluating arguments, truth tables can be used to identify types of statements and types of relations between statements. The types of statements are tautologies, self-contradictions, and contingent statements, and the types of relations are equivalences and contradictions.

Types of Statements

A tautology is a statement whose truth-value must be true, a self-contradiction is a statement whose truth-value must be false, and a contingent statement is one whose truth-value may be either true or false. In truth-functional logic these concepts of logical types of statements are given truth-functional definitions as follows:

Tautology: *A compound statement whose truth-values all are T's.*

Self-contradiction: *A compound statement whose truth-values all are F's.*

Contingent statement: *A statement whose truth-values include at least one T and at least one F.*

A tautology is a statement whose truth-values are always T and cannot be F; it is a *necessary truth*. By using a truth table we can easily demonstrate that a statement is a tautology, for the table will show that its truth-values are T's only. Consider this example:

Example 7

The snake is cold-blooded, or the snake is not cold-blooded.

	S	v	−S
	T	**T**	F
	F	**T**	T

Here is another example:

Example 8

It is not the case that something is solid and not solid.

−	(S	+	−S)
T	T	F	F
T	F	F	T

You may recognize these types of statements as examples of the laws of excluded middle and contradiction, respectively. Any statement of either of those forms is a tautology.

A self-contradiction is a statement whose truth-values are always F and cannot be T; it is a *necessary falsehood*. The truth table shows that these statements have only F for their values:

Example 9

It is not the case that everything is heavy or not heavy.

−	(H	v	−H)
F	T	T	F
F	F	T	T

Here is another example:

Example 10

```
P   +   -   (Q  ⊃  P)
```

P	+	-	Q	⊃	P
T	F	F	T	T	T
F	F	T	T	F	F
T	F	F	F	T	T
F	F	F	F	T	F

Contingent statements are those whose truth-values may be T or F; a truth table shows whether a statement is contingent, as in this example:

Example 11

If the paintings arrive, then we will not leave.

```
P   ⊃   -   W
```

P	⊃	-	W
T	F	F	T
F	T	F	T
T	T	T	F
F	T	F	F

Since there is at least one T and at least one F in the column for this statement, it is shown to be contingent.

Types of Relations: Equivalences, Contradictories

There are two important relationships among statements: statements may be equivalent or contradictory.

> Equivalences: *Two or more statements are logically equivalent if and only if for every assignment of truth-values to their components their truth-values are exactly the same.*

> Contradictories: *Two statements are contradictories if and only if for every assignment of truth-values to their components their truth-values are exactly the opposite.*

Equivalence occurs when two or more statements have exactly the same truth-values for every assignment of truth-values to their components. Their values may be true or false, but they are true or false under exactly the same conditions. The truth table shows this clearly:

Example 12

	P	⊃	Q			–	P	v	Q	

Truth table (P ⊃ Q):

P	⊃	Q
T	**T**	T
F	**T**	T
T	**F**	F
F	**T**	F

Truth table (– P v Q):

–	P	v	Q
F	T	**T**	T
T	F	**T**	T
F	T	**F**	F
T	F	**T**	F

Notice that each occurrence of the same simple statement is given the same initial assignment of values, just as was done earlier when we displayed the truth-values of compounds. The table reveals that the two statements above are logically equivalent and are therefore interchangeable. As we see in the next chapter, the particular example above is a very useful equivalence. It is called *material implication,* and it allows us to change a conditional statement into a disjunction, and vice versa. To do so, we simply follow the pattern exhibited in the equivalence above: the antecedent is negated, the '⊃' changes to the 'v', and the consequent stays the same. Below are examples of this equivalence:

$$(P \supset Q) \lor S \;\equiv\; (-P \lor Q) \lor S$$
$$-P \supset Q \;\equiv\; --P \lor Q$$
$$(P + Q) \supset R \;\equiv\; -(P + Q) \lor R$$

The following two equivalences are also very useful. They are called *DeMorgan's rule:*

$$-(P + Q) \;\equiv\; -P \lor -Q$$
$$-(P \lor Q) \;\equiv\; -P + -Q$$

Among other things, these two equivalences allow us to eliminate parentheses and change disjunctions to conjunctions, and vice versa. Another important equivalence that we have already used is the *rule of double negation:*

$$--P \;\equiv\; P$$

This rule tells us that any statement is logically equivalent to the negation of its negation.

Contradictories are statements whose truth-values are exactly opposite for every assignment of truth-values. When one is true the other is false. Here are some examples:

Example 13

Truth table (P ⊃ Q):

P	⊃	Q
T	**T**	T
F	**T**	T
T	**F**	F
F	**T**	F

Truth table (P + –Q):

P	+	–	Q
T	**F**	F	
F	**F**	F	
T	**T**	T	
F	**F**	T	

Example 14

```
P + Q    – P . v –Q

T  T  T     F      F  F
F  F  T     T      T  F
T  F  F     F      T  T
F  F  F     T      T  T
```

Exercise 6.3A   Tautologies, Self-contradictions, Contingencies.   Use truth tables to determine what type of statement each compound listed below is.

1. P ⊃ (P v Q)   2. (P ⊃ Q) + (−P v Q)
3. −P + (P + Q)   4. P ⊃ (P v −P)
5. (P ⊃ −Q) ≡ (P + Q)   6. P + −(−Q v P)
7. (P v Q) v −Q   8. −(Q + −P) ≡ (Q ⊃ P)

Exercise 6.3B   Equivalences and Contradictories.   Use truth tables to determine whether the following pairs of statements are equivalences, contradictories, or neither.

1. P ⊃ Q   −(P + −Q)
2. −P v −Q   P ⊃ −Q
3. −(P + −Q) v S   (−P v Q) v S
4. P + Q   Q + P
5. P ≡ Q   (P ⊃ Q) + (Q ⊃ P)
6. P + −Q   −Q ⊃ −P
7. −(P + Q)   −P v −Q
8. −(P v Q)   −P + −Q
9. −P ⊃ Q   P v Q
10. (P ⊃ Q) v −(−R ⊃ S)   (−P v Q) v (R v S)
11. P ⊃ Q   Q ⊃ P
12. P ⊃ Q   −Q ⊃ −P

Summary

In this and the previous chapter we have studied the fundamentals of truth-functional logic. First, we distinguished between simple and compound statements, and then we examined five common logical operators by which compound statements are formed from simple statements. We learned how sentences from ordinary language may be translated or symbolized using the standard truth-functional symbols. We used the truth table method for displaying the truth-values of compound statements and, by extension, for determining the validity of arguments. We also learned how to use the shortcut version of the truth table called the indirect truth table method. Finally, the logical types of statements and the logical relations between statements were demonstrated using the truth table method.

You now have a basic understanding of another important logical system besides categorical logic. It would be valuable at this point if you chose some arguments from previous chapters and evaluated them using the techniques of both categorical and truth-functional logic.

Review Questions Chapter 6

1. When you use the truth table method to determine validity, what exactly do you look for?

2. Describe the theory behind the indirect truth table method for evaluating arguments.

3. If you are using the indirect truth table method and you have an argument that, according to a trial assignment, cannot be given a consistent set of truth-values, is that argument shown valid or invalid?

4. Suppose you are using the truth table method and in one row there are all T's. Is that argument valid or invalid?

5. Define the following terms:

    (a) tautology   (b) contradictory

    (c) contingent statement   (d) self-contradiction

    (e) equivalence

6. How do you identify the concepts in question 5 with the aid of truth tables? What do you look for in the table?

7. Do all tautologies have the same truth-value?

8. Describe what the following equivalences enable you to do:

    (a) material implication   (b) DeMorgan's rule

    (c) the rule of double negation

9. Do you believe a computer could be programmed to evaluate arguments using the truth table method? Explain your answer.

10. The indirect truth table method is less mechanical than the full-blown truth table method and seems to require more thinking. Do you believe that a computer could be programmed to use the indirect truth table method just as well as the truth table method? Explain your answers.

True or False?

1. An argument is shown to be invalid if there is a row in its truth table in which the values for the premises are F.

2. A statement and the negation of its contradictory are logically equivalent.

3. If two statements are logically equivalent, then either may be used in the place of the other.

4. One must choose carefully whether to use the truth table method or the indirect truth table because they do not give the same results.

5. If a statement is not a tautology, then it is a self-contradiction.

CHAPTER SEVEN
Formal Deduction

This chapter introduces the principles of formal deduction and explains how validly to deduce the conclusion of an argument from its premises. Several valid argument forms, the *rules of inference* and the *equivalences,* are also presented.

7.1 Introduction

The advantage of truth tables is that they are almost completely mechanical and require very little creative thinking. The disadvantage of truth tables is that they are impractical and cumbersome for arguments involving several simple statements. The indirect truth table is more efficient for longer arguments, but several trials may be required before an argument can be shown to be valid. Furthermore, neither method explicitly shows the steps in reasoning. The method of formal deduction has distinct advantages over the truth table methods, particularly for longer arguments or those involving several premises. Furthermore, each step of reasoning leading from premises to conclusion is explicitly written out in deduction and can be examined.

Formal deduction is a procedure for validly deriving a conclusion from given premises according to certain valid argument forms called the *rules of inference* and the *equivalences*. A deduction consists of a sequence of statements each written on a separate line. Each line contains a statement that is either a premise of the argument or a valid deduction from the lines above it, deduced by the rules of inference and the equivalences. The deduction of the argument is complete when its conclusion is shown to be validly deducible from the premises by a sequence of steps, each one of which is an intermediate, validly deducible conclusion.

The key to constructing formal deductions lies in learning how to use the rules by which deductions are made. In this account of formal deduction we learn eighteen rules of deduction: eight rules of inference and ten equivalences (sometimes called *rules of replacement*). These represent two families of rules whose differences will become clear later. Each rule represents a valid argument form whose validity can be demonstrated by the truth table method. In our discussion the symbols p, q, r, and s are used to stand for *any* statement, either simple or compound. Thus, in studying the formulas for each rule, keep in mind that *the symbols p, q, and so on, may be instantiated by simple or compound statements*. The abbreviation for each rule is shown in parentheses.

7.2 The Rules of Inference: Group I

Let us begin by examining a group of some of the simpler rules of inference, namely, simplification (Simp), *modus ponens* (MP), *modus tollens* (MT), and disjunctive syllogism (DS).

1. Simplification (Simp)

$$p + q$$
$$\overline{\qquad\qquad} \quad or \quad \frac{p + q}{}$$
$$\therefore p \qquad\qquad\qquad \therefore q$$

According to simplification, if you are given a conjunction as a premise, then either one of the conjuncts is validly deducible. That is, if you have $p + q$ as a premise, then p follows as a valid deduction. Similarly, from $p + q$ you can deduce q. Consider how this rule of inference is used to deduce the conclusion of the following simple argument:

Example 1

Hydrogen is a gas, and ammonia is a liquid.
Therefore, hydrogen is a gas.

First, the argument is represented in truth-functional symbols as follows:

$$H + A$$
$$\therefore H$$

Next, the argument is written out with each premise on its own numbered line. Each premise is identified as such by the word 'premise' at the end of the line. The conclusion to be deduced is written on the same line as the last premise and is identified as the conclusion by a slash '/' separating it from the last premise and the three-dot symbol '∴' for 'therefore'. Thus, the argument as first written out shows each premise and the conclusion that is to be deduced.

1. $H + A$ premise   / $\therefore H$

This format shows that we want to deduce H from the premise H + A. In this example the conclusion is deducible from the premise by the use of one rule, simplification. Since we have H + A as a premise and simplification provides that either conjunct follows, we can deduce H. The deduction is written as follows listing the rule of inference and the number of the line used from above.

1. $H + A$ premise   / $\therefore H$
2. H 1, Simp

Each line must include a justification: either that it is given as a premise or that it is derivable from lines above according to a specified rule of inference or an equivalence.

The formulas for the rule of simplification state that any compound statement that is a conjunction may be simplified. Thus, the examples below are legitimate uses of simplification:

Example 2

1. $(T \lor B) + -S$ premise
2. $T \lor B$ 1, Simp

Example 3

1. $(M + Y) + H$ premise
2. $M + Y$ 1, Simp
3. M 2, Simp

The example below is not a legitimate use of simplification, because the statement deduced, T, is not a conjunct:

Example 4

1. $(T \lor B) + -S$ premise
2. T

2. *Modus Ponens* (MP)

$p \supset q$

p

_____

$\therefore q$

Modus ponens is a rule of inference that operates with a conditional as one of the premises: $p \supset q$ states that if you have p then you may conclude q. The second premise states that you do have p; therefore, q follows. Any argument with a conditional as one premise and the antecedent of the conditional as another premise is a candidate for the rule of *modus ponens*. All the arguments below conform to this valid argument form:

Example 5	*Example 6*	*Example 7*
$A \supset B$	$-S \supset R$	$-T \supset -V$
A	$-S$	$-T$
_____	_____	_____
$\therefore B$	$\therefore R$	$\therefore -V$

Example 8	*Example 9*
$-(P + Q) \supset R$	$(P + Q) \supset (S + T)$
$-(P + Q)$	$(P + Q)$
_____	_____
$\therefore R$	$\therefore S + T$

In each argument above you are given the antecedent of the conditional; therefore, the consequent follows. Consider the following example:

Example 10

If it rains, then my car is wet.	$R \supset W$
It rains.	R
_____	_____
Therefore, my car is wet.	$\therefore W$

From the conditional $R \supset W$ and the antecedent R as premises, according to *modus ponens*, W must follow. Consider the truth-functional meaning of the '$\supset$'. If, for example, $R \supset W$ has the truth-value T and R has the truth-value T, then W must also have the truth-value T. Thus, the conclusion W is deducible from the premises by *modus ponens*, written as follows:

1. $R \supset W$ *premise*
2. R *premise*   / $\therefore W$
3. W 1,2, MP

Notice that the last line of the deduction indicates the rule employed and the line numbers of the statements used in that step of the deduction.

3. *Modus Tollens* (MT)

$p \supset q$

$\underline{-q \qquad\qquad\qquad}$

$\therefore -p$

Like *modus ponens, modus tollens* is a rule of inference that operates with a conditional as a premise. In this case, however, the second premise is a negation of the consequent. Given a premise of the form $p \supset q$, if you have the negation of the consequent, then the negation of the antecedent must follow. Again, consider the truth-functional meaning of the '$\supset$'. If the '$\supset$' has the truth-value T and the consequent has the truth-value F, then the antecedent must have the truth-value F. Thus, the argument form *modus tollens* permits us to deduce the negation of the antecedent from a conditional and the negation of the consequent. Each of the following examples exhibits the *modus tollens* argument form:

Example 11	*Example 12*	*Example 13*
$-A \supset B$	$(P + Q) \supset S$	$-S \supset -R$
$-B$	$-S$	$--R$
$\therefore --A$	$\therefore -(P + Q)$	$\therefore --S$

In each example the premises are a conditional and the negation of the consequent, from which the negation of the antecedent can be validly deduced.

Consider this example:

Example 14

If it rains, then my car is wet.	$R \supset W$
My car is not wet.	$-W$
Therefore, it does not rain.	$\therefore -R$

Here is how the deduction is written:

1. $R \supset W$ *premise*
2. $-W$ *premise*   / $\therefore -R$
3. $-R$ *1,2, MT*

Line (3) shows that $-R$ is deducible from lines (1) and (2) by *modus tollens*.

4. Disjunctive Syllogism (DS)

$p \lor q$

$-p$

_____

$\therefore q$

or

$p \lor q$

$-q$

_____

$\therefore p$

The disjunctive syllogism is a valid argument form in which the premises are a disjunction and the negation of one of the disjuncts. Since a disjunction is true if and only if at least one of its disjuncts is true, if one part is false, then the other part must be true. The following are examples of this argument form:

Example 15

$-p \lor -q$

$--p$

_____

$\therefore -q$

Example 16

$(R + S) \lor T$

$-T$

_____

$\therefore R + S$

Example 17

$(-N \supset L) \lor (A + B)$

$-(-N \supset L)$

_____

$\therefore A + B$

Consider the following example:

Example 18

The Steelers win the championship, or the Cardinals go to the Super Bowl.	$S \lor C$
The Steelers do not win the championship.	$-S$
Therefore, the Cardinals go to the Super Bowl.	$\therefore C$

If you are given as premises $S \lor C$ and $-S$, it follows that C. Consider that the statement $S \lor C$ has the truth–value T and that the premise $-S$ also has the truth–value T. In order for a disjunction to have the truth–value T, at least one of its component parts must be T. Since we can deduce from the premise $-S$ that S has the truth–value F, then for $S \lor C$ to have the truth–value T, C must have the truth–value T. In short, C follows from the premises given.

Let us examine a deduction using more than one rule of inference. Here is a more complex argument:

Example 19

The Australians and the Belgians have made it to the finals of the World Soccer Cup. If the Australians have made it to the finals, then the Canadians did not win their game. Either the Canadians won their game or the Danes did not win theirs. Therefore, the Danes did not win their game.

First, we symbolize the argument by writing out each premise on a line with the conclusion indicated last.

1. $A + B$ *premise*
2. $A \supset -C$ *premise*
3. $C \lor -D$ *premise*   / $\therefore$ $-D$
4. ?

How can $-D$ be deduced from the premises? It helps to locate the symbol representing the conclusion (or the simple statements of the conclusion) in the lines given as premises. (The symbols for the conclusion do not all have to be located somewhere in the premises. As we will see, one rule of inference—the rule of addition—allows us to add a statement to a disjunction.) In the example we see that $-D$ occurs in premise (3). How can we separate $-D$ from that disjunction?

Notice that premise (3) gives us $C \lor -D$. If we could deduce $-C$, then we could deduce that $-D$ must be the true disjunct in premise (3). Notice that premise (2) tells us that if A is true then $-C$ is true. And we are given A in the conjunction of premise (1). Thus, it appears that we can deduce $-C$. Our first valid step is to deduce A from premise (1). Premise (1) gives us $A + B$. Since a conjunction is true if and only if both its parts are true, by the rule of simplification, A must be true.

4. A *1, Simp*

Now, from A in line (4) and premise (2) $A \supset -C$, we can deduce $-C$. The conditional $A \supset -C$ means that if we have A then we have $-C$; and we do have A from line (4). Therefore, we can write line (5) using the rule *modus ponens:*

5. $-C$ *4,2,MP*

Thus far, we have deduced $-C$. Now we can deduce that C is false because we have deduced $-C$. Thus, given that C is false and that $C \lor -D$ is a premise, it follows that $-D$ must be true. Thus, the conclusion $-D$ can be deduced. The rule for the final step is disjunctive syllogism. The whole formal deduction can be written as follows:

1. $A + B$ *premise*
2. $A \supset -C$ *premise*
3. $C \lor -D$ *premise*   / $\therefore$ $-D$
4. A *1, Simp*
5. $-C$ *4,2, MP*
6. $-D$ *5,3, DS*

Each line of the deduction is either a premise or a valid deduction from the lines above it. On the right of each line is the justification for that line. The justification either indicates that the line is a premise or shows the numbers of the previous lines appealed to and the rule used to deduce the line. Since each intermediate step validly follows from the steps before it, the conclusion is validly deduced from the premises of the argument.

For practice using the rules of inference in group I try working through the following examples. See if you can identify the rules used in the deductions by examining the lines listed before the blanks.

Example 20

1. M v P   *premise*
2. −M   *premise*   / ∴ P
3. P   1,2, _____

Example 21

1. H + −T   *premise*
2. T v (A + J) *premise*   / ∴ J
3. −T   1, _____
4. A + J   2,3, _____
5. J   4, _____

In example 20, line (3) is deduced from (1) and (2) by *disjunctive syllogism*. The premise M v P is true if at least one disjunct is true. From premise (2) −M we can deduce that M is false. Since M is false and M v P is true, then P must be the true disjunct. Thus, P.

In example 21, since H + −T is given as a premise, it follows that −T is deducible. Thus, line (3) is deduced from (1) by *simplification*. The premises T v (A + J) and −T allow us to infer A + J by *disjunctive syllogism*. Finally, the conclusion J is deducible from A + J, again by the rule of *simplification*.

Now try the exercises.

Exercise 7.2A   The Validity of Rules of Inference, Group I.   Use truth tables to demonstrate the validity of the following rules of inference.

1. Simplification: $p + q$ $p + q$
                                _____   _____

                                ∴ p ∴ q

2. *Modus ponens:* $p ⊃ q$
                                p
                                _____

                                ∴ q

3. *Modus tollens:*

$$p \supset q$$
$$\frac{-q}{}$$
$$\therefore\ -p$$

4. Disjunctive syllogism:

$$p \lor q$$
$$\frac{-p}{}$$
$$\therefore\ q$$

$$p \lor q$$
$$\frac{-q}{}$$
$$\therefore\ p$$

Exercise 7.2B   Deductions with the Rules of Inference, Group I.   Use the rules of inference from group I to deduce the conclusions of the following arguments. Use the translation cues provided.

1. France is a member of NATO, and Great Britain is a member of NATO. Therefore, Great Britain is a member of NATO. (F,G)

2. If France is a member of NATO, then Great Britain is a member of NATO. France is a member of NATO. Therefore, Great Britain is a member of NATO. (F,G)

3. Zaire is in central Africa, or Tanzania is in central Africa. Tanzania is not in central Africa. Therefore, Zaire is in central Africa. (Z,T)

4. Minnesota is north of Arkansas. If Minnesota is north of Arkansas, then Iowa is north of Arkansas. Therefore, Iowa is north of Arkansas. (M,I)

5. If the major industry of Alaska is salmon fishing, then most of the salmon sold in U.S. markets is from Alaska. But it is not true that most of the salmon sold in U.S. markets is from Alaska. Therefore, the major industry of Alaska is not salmon fishing. (A,S)

6. 1. A + T   premise
    2. T ⊃ P   premise   / ∴ P

7. 1. G ⊃ P   premise
    2. S + −P   premise   / ∴ −G

8. 1. T ∨ E   premise
    2. −T   premise   / ∴ E

9. 1. K ∨ N   premise
    2. −K + O   premise   / ∴ N

10. 1. D ⊃ I   premise
     2. D   premise   / ∴ I

7.3 The Rules of Inference: Group II

The remaining four rules of inference we will study are hypothetical syllogism (HS), addition (Add), conjunction (Con), and constructive dilemma (CD).

5. Hypothetical Syllogism (HS)   The hypothetical syllogism is an argument consisting of two conditionals. The statement that is the consequent of one conditional occurs as the antecedent of the other conditional.

$p \supset q$

$q \supset r$

_____

$\therefore p \supset r$

Thus, if p implies q and q implies r, then p implies r. Any argument with that form is a valid argument. Consider the following example:

Example 22

If Max passes physics, then Max majors in science.	$P \supset S$
If Max majors in science, then Max gives up French.	$S \supset F$
Therefore, if Max passes physics, then Max gives up French.	$\therefore P \supset F$

1. $P \supset S$ premise
2. $S \supset F$ premise   / $\therefore P \supset F$
3. $P \supset F$ 1,2, HS

Given $P \supset S$ and $S \supset F$, it follows that $P \supset F$ by the rule of hypothetical syllogism. A truth table shows that whenever the premises $P \supset S$ and $S \supset F$ have the truth-values T, the conclusion $P \supset F$ also has the truth-value T. Thus, the argument is a valid one.

6. Addition (Add)

p

_____

$\therefore p \vee r$

Given any statement (simple or compound), a disjunction can be validly deduced with that statement as one of the disjuncts. Thus, if p is assumed true, then $p \vee r$ is deducible, because a disjunction is true if and only if at least one of its parts is true. The following arguments are valid according to the rule of disjunctive syllogism:

Example 23

$-S + T$
_____
$\therefore (-S + T) \vee Q$

Example 24

$A \supset B$
_____
$\therefore (A \supset B) \vee (X \supset Y)$

In these examples the initial disjuncts are compounds, $-S + T$ and $A \supset B$, respectively, the rule of disjunctive syllogism permits forming disjunctions from simple or compound statements. However, a compound statement may not be broken apart in order to form a disjunction. Thus, it is not valid by the rule of addition to deduce a disjunction of this form:

Example 25

$-S + T$
_____
$\therefore -S \vee Q$

Example 26

$A \supset B$
_____
$\therefore B \vee (X \supset Y)$

The rule requires that the entire statement be used as the initial disjunct.

7. Conjunction (Con)

p

q
_____
$\therefore p + q$

A conjunction, you recall, is true if and only if all its conjuncts are true. Thus, a conjunction may be validly formed from two or more true statements. According to the rule of inference called conjunction, if a statement p occurs by itself on a line (as a premise or as a deduction from lines above it) and a statement q occurs by itself on a line (as a premise or as a deduction from lines above it), then a conjunction may be deduced consisting of p and q. For example, consider how conjunction is employed in this deduction:

Example 27

1. $H \supset P$ premise
2. H premise   / $\therefore H + P$
3. P 1,2, MP
4. $H + P$ 2,3, Con

Notice that line (3) P is derived from lines (1) and (2) by *modus ponens*. Thus, statements H and P both occur alone either as premises or as deductions from lines above, so the conjunction of H + P can be obtained following the rule of conjunction.

8. Constructive Dilemma (CD)

$(p \supset q) + (r \supset s)$

$p \lor r$

_____

$\therefore q \lor s$

Constructive dilemma is, in effect, a variation on the *modus ponens* argument. Notice that it involves a conjunction of two conditionals as one premise and a disjunction of the antecedents of each conditional as the other premise. From two such premises it is valid to infer the disjunction of the consequents of each conditional. Consider the following deduction:

Example 28

1. $(S \supset G) + (C \supset D)$	*premise*	
2. $S \lor C$	*premise*	
3. $-D$	*premise*	/ $\therefore$ G
4. $G \lor D$	*1,2, CD*	
5. G	*3,4, DS*	

Line (4) G v D is derived from (1) and (2) by *constructive dilemma*. Notice the characteristic pattern: (1) is a conjunction of two conditionals, and (2) is a disjunction consisting of the antecedents of the conditionals. Thus, the disjunction of the consequents is deducible. G is deduced from (3) and (4) by *disjunctive syllogism*.

In this section we have examined eight rules of inference: simplification (Simp), *modus ponens* (MP), *modus tollens* (MT), disjunctive syllogism (DS), hypothetical syllogism (HS), addition (Add), conjunction (Con), and constructive dilemma (CD).

_____

Exercise 7.3A   The Validity of Rules of Inference, Group II.   Construct truth tables to demonstrate that the following rules are valid argument forms.

1. Hypothetical syllogism: $p \supset q$

$q \supset r$

_____

$\therefore p \supset r$

2. Addition: p

_____

$\therefore p \lor q$

3. Conjunction: p

q

_____

$\therefore p + q$

4. Constructive dilemma: $(p \supset q) + (r \supset s)$
                              $p \lor r$
                              _____

                              $\therefore q \lor s$

Exercise 7.3B   Complete the Deductions.   In the blank space write the rule of inference from either group I or group II by which the line has been deduced. The line numbers are provided as hints.

1.   1. A ∨ B   premise
      2. −B   premise   / ∴ A
      3. A   1,2, _____
2.   1. B ⊃ (C + P)   premise
      2. B   premise   / ∴ C + P
      3. C + P   1,2 _____
3.   1. − −S   premise
      2. R ⊃ −S   premise   / ∴ −R
      3. −R   1,2, _____
4.   1. (X + Y) ∨ (Z + X)   premise
      2. −(Z + X)   premise   / ∴ X + Y
      3. X + Y   1,2, _____
5.   1. A ⊃ S   premise
      2. A   premise   / ∴ S
      3. S   1,2, _____
6.   1. R + T   premise   / ∴ R
      2. R   1, _____
7.   1. R + T   premise
      2. R ⊃ S   premise   / ∴ S
      3. R   1, Simp
      4. S   2,3, _____
8.   1. B ⊃ P   premise
      2. P ⊃ X   premise   / ∴ B ⊃ X
      3. B ⊃ X   1,2, _____
9.   1. −(A ⊃ P) ⊃ S   premise
      2. −S   premise   / ∴ − −(A ⊃ P)
      3. − −(A ⊃ P)   1,2, _____

10.　1. (D v S) ⊃ (P + Q)　　premise
　　 2. D v S　　　　　　　premise　　 / ∴ P + Q
　　 3. P + Q　　　　　　　1,2, _____
11.　1. (P + Q) + R　　　　premise　　 / ∴ P
　　 2. P + Q　　　　　　　1, _____
　　 3. P　　　　　　　　　2, _____
12.　1. S　　　　　　　　　premise
　　 2. S ⊃ (R + P)　　　　premise　　 / ∴ R
　　 3. R + P　　　　　　　1,2, _____
　　 4. R　　　　　　　　　3, _____
13.　1. C v −D　　　　　　premise
　　 2. −C　　　　　　　　premise
　　 3. E ⊃ D　　　　　　premise　　 / ∴ −E
　　 4. −D　　　　　　　　1,2, _____
　　 5. −E　　　　　　　　3,4, _____
14.　1. S v (P ⊃ T)　　　　premise
　　 2. P　　　　　　　　　premise
　　 3. −S　　　　　　　　premise　　 / ∴ T
　　 4. P ⊃ T　　　　　　1,3, _____
　　 5. T　　　　　　　　　2,4, _____
15.　1. L + (M v A)　　　　premise
　　 2. −A　　　　　　　　premise　　 / ∴ M
　　 3. M v A　　　　　　1, _____
　　 4. M　　　　　　　　2,3, _____
16.　1. T ⊃ Q　　　　　　premise
　　 2. S ⊃ Y　　　　　　premise
　　 3. T v S　　　　　　　premise　　 / ∴ Q v Y
　　 4. (T ⊃ Q) + (S ⊃ Y)　1,2, _____
　　 5. Q v Y　　　　　　　4,3, _____
17.　1. (N + A) ⊃ D　　　premise
　　 2. N　　　　　　　　premise
　　 3. A　　　　　　　　premise　　 / ∴ D
　　 4. N + A　　　　　　2,3, _____
　　 5. D　　　　　　　　4,1, _____

18. 1. (H ⊃ S) + (F ⊃ W)   premise
     2. H   premise   / ∴ S v W
     3. H v F   2, _____
     4. S v W   3,1, _____
19. 1. R v D   premise
     2. R ⊃ S   premise
     3. −D   premise   / ∴ S
     4. R   1,3, _____
     5. S   2,4, _____
20. 1. H + (G ⊃ T)   premise
     2. G   premise   / ∴ T
     3. G ⊃ T   1, _____
     4. T   2,3, _____

Exercise 7.3C Rules of Inference. Use the rules of inference from groups I and II to deduce the conclusions of the following arguments. Write the line numbers and the rules used.

1.   1. K ⊃ P   premise
     2. −P v D   premise
     3. −D   premise   / ∴ −K
2.   1. S + (R ⊃ J)   premise
     2. J ⊃ T   premise   / ∴ R ⊃ T
3.   1. S ⊃ P   premise
     2. −P + −A   premise   / ∴ −S
4.   1. A ⊃ B   premise
     2. A + (T v J)   premise   / ∴ B
5.   1. H + −T   premise
     2. T v (A + J)   premise   / ∴ J
6.   1. −L ⊃ B   premise
     2. L ⊃ S   premise
     3. −S   premise   / ∴ B
7.   1. [(A v B) + C] ⊃ (T v A)   premise
     2. −(T v A)   premise   / ∴ −[(A v B) + C]
8.   1. − −R ⊃ (R + S)   premise
     2. S ⊃ (−R v J)   premise
     3. − −R   premise   / ∴ J

9.　　1. −L　　　　　　　　　premise
　　　2. −L ⊃ (T + A)　　　　premise　　/　∴ T
10.　　1. C ⊃ [(P + J) v R]　　premise
　　　2. C + −R　　　　　　　premise　　/　∴ J
11.　　1. (R v T) ⊃ (T ⊃ L)　　premise
　　　2. (T ⊃ L) ⊃ S　　　　　premise　　/　∴ (R v T) ⊃ S
12.　　1. P + −−Q　　　　　　premise
　　　2. −Q v (P ⊃ J)　　　　premise　　/　∴ J
13.　　1. (S + A) v (P + M)　　premise
　　　2. (S + A) ⊃ R　　　　　premise
　　　3. −R　　　　　　　　　premise　　/　∴ P + M
14.　　1. Q ⊃ −R　　　　　　premise
　　　2. T ⊃ Q　　　　　　　premise
　　　3. T　　　　　　　　　premise　　/　∴ −R
15.　　1. (T ⊃ Q) + (S ⊃ P)　　premise
　　　2. T　　　　　　　　　premise　　/　∴ Q v P
16.　　1. L + (M ⊃ N)　　　　premise　　/　∴ L v R
17.　　1. T　　　　　　　　　premise
　　　2. (T + R) ⊃ S　　　　premise
　　　3. R　　　　　　　　　premise　　/　∴ S
18.　　1. A v −−B　　　　　　premise
　　　2. −A　　　　　　　　　premise
　　　3. S ⊃ −B　　　　　　premise　　/　∴ −S

7.4 Equivalences

In addition to the rules of inference, we also use ten equivalences in formal deductions. We know that if two statements are logically equivalent, we may validly infer one from the other. In effect, these equivalences allow us to replace a statement with its logical equivalent. They differ from the rules of inference in that, given any two equivalent statements, either one may be substituted for the other, and vice versa. They are "two-way" rules, whereas the rules of inference are "one-way" rules.

So, for example, it is not legitimate to employ the rule of addition in "reverse" as follows:

$$A \vee B$$
_____
$$\therefore B$$

Some of the ten equivalences are used frequently, others less so. We will examine the most commonly used equivalences and describe how they are employed in deductions. If you are ever in doubt about the correct use of an equivalence, simply construct a truth table to determine if the statements are indeed logically equivalent. Remember that two statements are equivalent if their truth-values are identical for every assignment of values. Abbreviations for the rules of equivalence are shown in parentheses.

9. Double Negation (DN) We have encountered this rule before. According to double negation a statement $--p$ is logically equivalent to p, and vice versa. Thus, whenever double negatives occur we may cancel them out or form a double negative from a statement. However, we must be careful to use this rule only in cases in which the double negatives apply to one and the same statement. The following statements, for example, are not candidates for the rule of double negation precisely because they do not exemplify the negation of a negation:

$$-(-A + B) \qquad -(P \supset -Q) \qquad -X + -Y \qquad -A \vee -(C + -D)$$

The following statements *are* candidates for double negation:

$$--A + B \qquad -(P \supset --Q) \qquad --X + --Y \qquad --A \vee --(C + -D)$$

Applying the rule of double negation, the statements above are logically equivalent to these:

$$A + B \qquad -(P \supset Q) \qquad X + Y \qquad A \vee (C + D)$$

Here are two examples showing how double negation may be used in deductions. The first example illustrates the use of double negation together with the valid argument form *modus tollens:*

Example 29   **Double negation with modus tollens**

1. $P \supset -Q$ *premise*
2. Q *premise*   / $\therefore -P$
3. $--Q$ 2, DN
4. $-P$ 1,3, MT

The second example uses double negation together with disjunctive syllogism:

Example 30 **Double negation with disjunctive syllogism**

1. $-P \vee R$ *premise*
2. P *premise*   / ∴ R
3. $--P$ 2, DN
4. R 1,3, DS

10. DeMorgan's Rule (DeM)   DeMorgan's rule allows us to switch a conjunction to a disjunction, or vice versa. The rule follows these forms:

First form: $-(p + q) \equiv (-p \vee -q)$
Second form: $-(p \vee q) \equiv (-p + -q)$

The first form captures our intuition that the construction 'not both p and q' is equivalent to 'not p or not q'. The second form captures the notion that 'neither p nor q' is equivalent to 'not p and not q'.

To understand the use of DeMorgan's rule, notice the changes that are made in the first form:

$$-(p + q) \equiv (-p \vee -q)$$

First p is negated; then q is negated; then the '+' is changed to 'v'. The original negation in $-(p + q)$ is "driven inside" the compound and distributed among the disjuncts. Thus, a negation of a conjunction is changed to a disjunction.

DeMorgan's rule (DeM):   p *is negated;* q *is negated;* + *changes to* v; *or* v *changes to* +.

By using DeMorgan's rule together with double negation we can formulate other useful equivalences, such as these:

STATEMENT   DeMorgan's   DOUBLE NEGATION

$-(-p + -q) \equiv (--p \vee --q) \equiv (p \vee q)$
$-(-p + q) \equiv (--p \vee -q) \equiv (p \vee -q)$

Finally, notice in the example below how DeMorgan's rule may be used by first applying double negation.

                   DOUBLE
STATEMENT   NEGATION   DeMorgan's

$(p + q) \equiv --(p + q) \equiv -(-p \vee -q)$

Now let's see how DeMorgan's rule can be used in deductions. First, consider an example using DeMorgan's together with double negation and disjunctive syllogism:

Example 31   *DeMorgan's with double negation and disjunctive syllogism*

1. $-(P + Q)$ *premise*
2. Q *premise*   / $\therefore -P$
3. $-P \vee -Q$ *1, DeM*
4. $--Q$ *2, DN*
5. $-P$ *4, DS*

Now consider DeMorgan's used together with addition:

Example 32   *DeMorgan's with addition*

1. $-P$ *premise*   / $\therefore -(P + Q)$
2. $-P \vee -Q$ *1, Add*
3. $-(P + Q)$ *2, DeM*

11. Material Implication (Impl)   The rule of equivalence called material implication allows us to replace a conditional with a logically equivalent disjunction, and vice versa.

$$(p \supset q) \equiv (-p \vee q)$$

Notice the changes: the antecedent is negated, the horseshoe '$\supset$' is changed to the '$\vee$', and the consequent remains the same.

> Material Implication (Impl):   *Antecedent is negated; $\supset$ changes to $\vee$; consequent stays the same.*

This example illustrates the use of material implication with addition:

Example 33   *Material implication with addition*

1. P *premise*   / $\therefore -P \supset Q$
2. $--P$ *1, DN*
3. $--P \vee Q$ *2, Add*
4. $-P \supset Q$ *3, Impl*

12. Material Equivalence (Equiv)   This equivalence changes the biconditional to a conjunction of two conditionals, or, used in reverse, it changes a conjunction of two conditionals to a biconditional.

$$(p \equiv q) \equiv [(p \supset q) + (q \supset p)]$$

Recall that the biconditional is an 'if . . . then' statement going in "both directions." Thus, changing a biconditional to a conjunction of two conditionals is simply forming an equivalent statement. Doing so allows us to simplify to that part of the biconditional that may be of some use to us in a deduction. Notice the use of material equivalence together with simplification in this example:

Example 34   Material equivalence with simplification

1. $P \equiv Q$	premise	/	$\therefore Q \supset P$
2. $(P \supset Q) + (Q \supset P)$	1, Equiv		
3. $Q \supset P$	2, Simp		

Consider now the use of material equivalence with implication and conjunction to form a biconditional:

Example 35   Material equivalence with implication and conjunction

1. $P \supset Q$	premise		
2. $-Q \vee P$	premise	/	$\therefore P \equiv Q$
3. $Q \supset P$	2, Impl		
4. $(P \supset Q) + (Q \supset P)$	1,3, Con		
5. $P \equiv Q$	4, Equiv		

13. Distribution (Dist)   One final equivalence worth close examination is distribution. In its first form distribution allows us to "distribute" a conjunct between two disjuncts. In its second form it allows us to distribute a disjunct between two conjuncts.

> First form: $[p + (q \vee r)] \equiv [(p + q) \vee (p + r)]$
> Second form: $[p \vee (q + r)] \equiv [(p \vee q) + (p \vee r)]$

Notice in the following example how distribution can be used with the disjunctive syllogism:

Example 36   Distribution with disjunctive syllogism

1. $P + (Q \vee R)$	premise		
2. $-(P + R)$	premise	/	$\therefore P + Q$
3. $(P + Q) \vee (P + R)$	1, Dist		
4. $P + Q$	2,3, DS		

The remaining equivalences are listed below, and all the rules of inferences and equivalences are shown in Tables 7.1 and 7.2.

Table 7.1   Rules of Inference

1. Simplification (Simp)	$p + q$ ———— $\therefore p$ or	$p + q$ ———— $\therefore q$

1. Simplification (Simp)

$$\frac{p + q}{\therefore p} \qquad \text{or} \qquad \frac{p + q}{\therefore q}$$

2. *Modus ponens* (MP)

$$\frac{\begin{array}{l} p \supset q \\ p \end{array}}{\therefore q}$$

3. *Modus tollens* (MT)

$$\frac{\begin{array}{l} p \supset q \\ -q \end{array}}{\therefore -p}$$

4. Disjunctive syllogism (DS)

$$\frac{\begin{array}{l} p \vee q \\ -p \end{array}}{\therefore q} \qquad \text{or} \qquad \frac{\begin{array}{l} p \vee q \\ -q \end{array}}{\therefore p}$$

5. Hypothetical syllogism (HS)

$$\frac{\begin{array}{l} p \supset q \\ q \supset r \end{array}}{\therefore p \supset r}$$

6. Addition (Add)

$$\frac{p}{\therefore p \vee q}$$

7. Conjunction (Con)

$$\frac{\begin{array}{l} p \\ q \end{array}}{\therefore p + q}$$

8. Constructive dilemma (CD)

$$\frac{\begin{array}{l} (p \supset q) + (r \supset s) \\ p \vee r \end{array}}{\therefore q \vee s}$$

14. Commutation (Com) $(p \vee q) \equiv (q \vee p)$
$(p + q) \equiv (q + p)$

15. Association (Assoc) $[p \vee (q \vee r)] \equiv [(p \vee q) \vee r]$
$[p + (q + r)] \equiv [(p + q) + r]$

16. Transposition (Trans) $(p \supset q) \equiv (-q \supset -p)$

17. Exportation (Exp) $[(p + q) \supset r] \equiv [p \supset (q \supset r)]$

Table 7.2 Equivalences

9. Double negation (DN)	$--p \equiv p$
10. DeMorgan's rule (DeM)	$-(p + q) \equiv (-p \lor -q)$ $-(p \lor q) \equiv (-p + -q)$
11. Material implication (Impl)	$(p \supset q) \equiv (-p \lor q)$
12. Material equivalence (Equiv)	$(p \equiv q) \equiv [(p \supset q) + (q \supset p)]$
13. Distribution (Dist)	$[p + (q \lor r)] \equiv [(p + q) \lor (p + r)]$ $[p \lor (q + r)] \equiv [(p \lor q) + (p \lor r)]$
14. Commutation (Com)	$(p \lor q) \equiv (q \lor p)$ $(p + q) \equiv (q + p)$
15. Association (Assoc)	$[p \lor (q \lor r)] \equiv [(p \lor q) \lor r]$ $[p + (q + r)] \equiv [(p + q) + r]$
16. Transposition (Trans)	$(p \supset q) \equiv (-q \supset -p)$
17. Exportation (Exp)	$[(p + q) \supset r] \equiv [p \supset (q \supset r)]$
18. Tautology (Taut)	$p \equiv (p \lor p)$ $p \equiv (p + p)$

Exercise 7.4A Equivalences and Rules of Inference. Use the equivalences and the rules of inference to make the following deductions. Write the line numbers and the equivalence or rule used for each step.

1.	1. A ⊃ B	premise	/ ∴ −A ∨ B
2.	1. −C + −D	premise	/ ∴ −(C ∨ D)
3.	1. −E	premise	/ ∴ −(E + D)
4.	1. Q	premise	
	2. −S	premise	/ ∴ −(−Q ∨ S)
5.	1. −A	premise	/ ∴ A ⊃ B
6.	1. −A	premise	
	2. C ⊃ S	premise	/ ∴ A ⊃ S
7.	1. −(A ∨ B)	premise	/ ∴ −B
8.	1. −(−S ∨ −R)	premise	/ ∴ S
9.	1. P ∨ −Q	premise	/ ∴ −P ⊃ −Q
10.	1. −F ⊃ −G	premise	/ ∴ F ∨ −G
11.	1. −P ∨ (−R ∨ S)	premise	/ ∴ P ⊃ (R ⊃ S)
12.	1. −P ∨ (R + S)	premise	/ ∴ P ⊃ (R + S)
13.	1. A ∨ C	premise	/ ∴ −A ⊃ C
14.	1. −S ∨ −(R + P)	premise	/ ∴ −S ∨ (−R ∨ −P)

15.	1. −S v −(R + P)	premise	/ ∴ S ⊃ −(R + P)
16.	1. −(R + S)	premise	/ ∴ R ⊃ −S
17.	1. −(R + S) v T	premise	/ ∴ (R ⊃ −S) v T
18.	1. A ⊃ (−B + −C)	premise	/ ∴ −A v −(B v C)
19.	1. −(S + R)	premise	/ ∴ S ⊃ −R
20.	1. D	premise	/ ∴ A ⊃ D
21.	1. A	premise	
	2. B	premise	/ ∴ A + (B v C)
22.	1. L + M	premise	
	2. S + A	premise	/ ∴ L + S
23.	1. A ⊃ B	premise	
	2. S + A	premise	/ ∴ B + S
24.	1. S	premise	
	2. R	premise	/ ∴ (S v T) + R

Exercise 7.4B   More Deductions.   The following deductions are more difficult. Use both equivalences and rules of inference to complete the deductions.

1.	1. −P v Q	premise	
	2. (P ⊃ Q) ⊃ R	premise	/ ∴ R
2.	1. A ⊃ C	premise	
	2. T v −(−A v C)	premise	/ ∴ T
3.	1. −P	premise	
	2. (P + R) v S	premise	/ ∴ S
4.	1. D + −A	premise	/ ∴ A ⊃ C
5.	1. (L + P) ⊃ Q	premise	
	2. −Q	premise	/ ∴ −L v −P
6.	1. (S + L) v −A	premise	/ ∴ A ⊃ L
7.	1. −(P + Q)	premise	
	2. Q	premise	/ ∴ −P
8.	1. T ≡ Q	premise	
	2. −Q	premise	/ ∴ −T
9.	1. R v (P + S)	premise	/ ∴ R v S
10.	1. −Q ⊃ −P	premise	
	2. −(R v −T)	premise	/ ∴ T + (P ⊃ Q)
11.	1. −(P v T)	premise	/ ∴ −T

12.   1. −S + −R   premise
       2. −(S ∨ R) ⊃ L   premise   / ∴ L
13.   1. A ≡ −C   premise
       2. −A   premise   / ∴ C
14.   1. K ≡ N   premise
       2. N ⊃ L   premise   / ∴ K ⊃ L
15.   1. −(A + B)   premise
       2. B   premise
       3. D ⊃ A   premise   / ∴ −D
16.   1. L + N   premise
       2. (L ∨ E) ⊃ F   premise   / ∴ L + F
17.   1. C ⊃ D   premise
       2. D ⊃ G   premise
       3. F ⊃ N   premise
       4. C ∨ F   premise   / ∴ G ∨ N
18.   1. −A ⊃ (B ⊃ C)   premise
       2. F ⊃ T   premise
       3. A ∨ (F ∨ B)   premise
       4. −A   premise   / ∴ T ∨ C
19.   1. (A ⊃ B) + (C ⊃ D)   premise
       2. A ∨ C   premise
       3. D ⊃ −S   premise
       4. A + S   premise   / ∴ F ⊃ B
20.   1. −H   premise
       2. −G ∨ H   premise
       3. (R + G) ∨ (S + A)   premise   / ∴ S
21.   1. P ⊃ (A ⊃ B)   premise
       2. D ∨ −B   premise
       3. −D + A   premise   / ∴ −P
22.   1. A ∨ B   premise
       2. −P ⊃ −A   premise
       3. −P   premise   / ∴ B

Exercise 7.4C   Symbolize and Deduce.   Translate the following arguments into symbolic form and then deduce the conclusion using the rules of inference and the equivalences. Use the translation cues provided.

1. If John keeps the house, then either Carol leaves or Mrs. Nussbaum will rent the room. If John is promoted, he will keep the house. John is promoted and Carol does not leave. Therefore, Mrs. Nussbaum rents her room. (J,C,N,P)

2. Either oxidation or reduction is the cause of the explosion. If the substance contains no potassium, then oxidation is not the cause of the explosion. The substance contains no potassium. Therefore, reduction is the cause. (O,R,S)

3. If the coalition collapses, then the Labor party will assume the leadership in the cabinet. If the Labor party assumes leadership, then the senate will not reorganize and no coalition members will be seated. If no coalition members are seated, then there will have to be an election of a new prime minister. There will be no election of a new prime minister; therefore, the coalition does not collapse. (C,L,S,M,E)

4. Eating meat is essential neither for survival nor for good health, nor is it a cost-efficient way of producing nutritious food. All of that implies that eating meat is not a necessity. Eating meat requires raising animals for slaughter. If this is so, and eating meat is not a necessity, then it is morally wrong to kill animals for food in these circumstances. Therefore, it is morally wrong to kill animals for food in these circumstances. (E,G,C,N,R,M)

5. If Fischer does not win the tournament, then Spassky wins. Spassky does not win. If Fischer wins, then neither Geller nor Krogius will play. Therefore, Geller will not play. (F,S,G,K)

6. Hydrogen and oxygen are gases. Silicon is not a gas. If hydrogen is a gas and silicon is not a gas, then either potassium is a liquid or it is a solid. If potassium is unlike silicon, then it is not a liquid. It is unlike silicon; thus, potassium is a solid. (H,O,S,P,I,U)

7. If people earn different amounts and everyone pays the same amount in taxes, then those who earn more keep more and those who earn less keep less. If those who earn more keep more and those who earn less keep less, then the tax laws are unjust. Therefore, either people do not earn different amounts, or if everyone pays the same amount in taxes, then the tax laws are unjust. (P,E,M,L,T)

8. If a man has a talent and cannot use it, he has failed. If he has a talent and learns somehow to use the whole of it, he has gloriously succeeded and won a triumph few men ever know. (Thomas Wolfe) He has not won a triumph few men ever know. So it follows that he has no talent or he's not learned to use the whole of it. (T,U,F,L,G,W)

9. It is false that film making is not an art form, because if film making involves the possibility for creativity, then it is an art form, and it does involve that possibility. (F,P)

10. Deregulation of the energy industry is now a fact. Neither the airlines nor the Bell System have benefited from deregulation. That may be concluded from the facts that deregulation of the energy industry implies higher expenses for the airlines and increased costs for the Bell System. In turn if there are higher expenses for the airlines and increased costs for the Bell System, then it's not true that either the airlines or the Bell System benefit from deregulation. (A,B,D,H,I)

11. Argument 10 above is either deductive or inductive and not both. Argument 10 above is deductive. Therefore, it is not inductive. (D,I)

12. If the Steelers win, then the Oilers lose, and if the Cowboys win, then the Broncos lose. Either the Steelers or the Cowboys win. The Broncos do not lose. Therefore, the Oilers lose. (S,O,C,B)

13. That peace is achieved in the Mideast is a necessary condition of the Mideast nations' engaging in successful negotiations. But neither is peace achieved nor are alliances formed. Therefore, the Mideast nations do not have successful negotiations. (P,M,A)

14. The choir will tour if and only if the administration funds the trip. If the administration funds the trip, then the expenses incurred by the new construction are not excessive. Those expenses are excessive if and only if the board decreases the year's budget. The board does decrease the year's budget, and so the choir will not tour. (C,A,E,B)

15. Most Indians are Hindus. Most North Africans are Moslems. Therefore, most Indians are Hindus and either most North Africans are Moslems or most Chinese are Buddhists. (I,N,C)

Review Questions Chapter 7

1. What are the advantages and disadvantages of the truth table method and the indirect truth table method?

2. What is a formal deduction?

3. What are the advantages of the method of formal deduction? Can you see any disadvantages to this method?

4. Which rules of inference involve the conditional? Which equivalences?

5. Which rules of inference involve the disjunction? Which equivalences?

6. Why is it valid to form a disjunction from a statement known to be true? That is, why is addition a valid argument form?

7. What rule would you use to change a disjunction to a conjunction?

8. What rule would you use to change a disjunction to a conditional?

9. According to material implication, $p \supset q$ is equivalent to $-p \lor q$. Explain how a conditional can be equivalently expressed as a disjunction.

10. According to DeMorgan's rule, we can change a disjunction to a conjunction. Thus, we should be able to change a conditional to a conjunction. Demonstrate how this can be done and check your answer with a truth table.

True or False?

1. If a conjunction is a premise or deducible from the premises, you may validly deduce either conjunct.

2. If a disjunction is a premise or deducible from the premises, you may validly deduce either disjunct.

3. DeMorgan's rule tells us, in effect, that 'neither p nor q' is equivalent to 'not both p and q'.

4. Whenever there are two "not" signs within a compound, you may eliminate them according to the rule of double negation.

5. Given the statement p you may deduce $q \supset p$ by addition, commutation, and material implication.

6. Every step in a deduction represents a conclusion drawn validly from premises.

CHAPTER EIGHT
Inductive Logic

This chapter examines *inductive strength,* the kind of inferential support possible in those arguments that are not deductively valid. We examine three types of inductively strong arguments: the *inductive generalization, the causal argument,* and the *argument from analogy.*

The title "Inductive Logic" implies that there is a logic of inductive reasoning that is distinguishable from the logic of deductive reasoning. That needs some explanation.

First, it is safe to say that all logicians agree that deductive reasoning is not the whole of logic. But if deductive reasoning is not the whole, what is the rest? Here logicians do not all agree. Some call the rest "nondeductive reasoning." Some may have other distinctions to make. We will call all reasoning that fails to be deductively valid "inductive." Therefore, according to some logicians, we use the term 'inductive' broadly, perhaps too broadly for them. What matters, however, is that we recognize and appreciate central forms of reasoning that are good yet not deductively valid.

Second, that logicians do not agree on what to call reasoning that is not deductive is not a mere disagreement over words. There is good reason why nondeductive—what we will call inductive—reasoning is a subject of controversy. The field of inductive reasoning is not homogeneous. Unlike deductive reasoning, much of which is fairly uniform and can be formalized symbolically, inductive reasoning consists of importantly different types of arguments. Facing inductive reasoning, one is like an early ornithologist (scientist who studies birds) wanting to develop a science of birds but overwhelmed by the variations in species. All have wings and lay eggs but beyond that the differences resist any easy generalizations.

Why is inductive logic so complex? There are several reasons. First, as we have defined it, it includes all reasoning that is not deductively valid reasoning. Thus, whenever we provide evidence or reasons from which the conclusion does not follow necessarily, we are reasoning inductively. For example, to consult a different physician for a second opinion is to obtain evidence that favors or disfavors the first physician's opinion. How is that new evidence to be weighed? To cancel a trip because of the weather is to make an inductive inference. To move one's bank account hoping to get higher interest rates and better service is to make an inductive inference. To vote for a Republican this time rather than a Democrat, to switch from butter to margarine, to change academic majors, to bet on the 49'ers, to research the causes of disease—all these are usually examples of nondeductive reasoning.

Second, inductive reasoning is usually about things that are not now observable, things we believe are or are not the case but which we cannot now check. Consider the examples above.

Third, inductive reasoning is always *a matter of degree*. Whereas an argument either is or is not deductively valid, an argument is *more or less* inductively strong. Whereas no new evidence, no new experiences, further strengthens deductive validity, new evidence or experience does strengthen or weaken an inductive argument. Since inductive reasoning is a matter of degree, it is more complex.

As a final note, if it is not already apparent, most everyday reasoning is inductive reasoning. Some of the most important areas of our lives and the beliefs and decisions we make about them involve inductive reasoning: our beliefs about how the world works, about human behavior, about the social policies we should adopt, and about the ways we should spend our time, to mention just a few. Thus, we are studying an area of immense importance when we study inductive reasoning.

8.1 Inductive Strength

In Chapter 1 we defined a good argument as one in which the premises are true and the conclusion follows from them. We also defined two senses in which a conclusion may be said to follow from the premises, deductive validity and inductive strength. In Chapters 2 through 7 we studied various techniques for determining deductive validity. In this chapter we will concentrate on those arguments that are not deductively valid yet may be inductively strong.

Recall from Chapter 1 that inferential support—the support premises pass to a conclusion—may range in strength from the strongest to the weakest. Deductive validity exemplifies the strongest support possible. Short of that, arguments descend in degrees of strength. Think of the analogy of boiling water and degrees of heat. The water either boils or it doesn't. Analogously an argument is either deductively valid or not. If the water isn't boiling, it still has some temperature ranging from very hot to cold. We have studied how to identify "boiling water." Now we will study how to identify "degrees of heat."

Let us define inductive strength as follows:

> Inductive strength: *An argument is* inductively strong *just in case, given its premises, (1) it is deductively invalid and (2) it is* more probable than not *that the conclusion follows.*

Let us say further that an argument lacks inductive strength, that is, it is *inductively weak*, given (1) above and failure to meet condition (2).

An argument is inductively weak *just in case, given its premises, (1) it is deductively invalid and (2) it is* more probable than not *that the conclusion* does not *follow.*

In contrast to the concept of deductive validity, inductive strength cannot help but appear vague. An inductively strong argument is one in which the conclusion is "more probable than not." In further describing inductive arguments we say such things as "it is very probable that," "it is highly unlikely that," "there is slight probability that," and so on. Compare the following examples of deductively invalid arguments.

Example 1	*Example 2*
Most MDs are conservatives.	*Few MDs are conservatives.*
Max is an MD.	*Max is an MD.*
Max is a conservative.	*Max is a conservative.*

It is clear that the conclusion is more strongly supported in example 1 than in 2. But it is not clear why that is so; neither is it clear just how much more probable the conclusion of 1 is in comparison with 2. How do we assess inductive strength? Is it possible to be more precise in the assessment of inductive strength? Let us consider the second question first.

One way to think about the probability of an inductive conclusion's following from its premises is to think about the way probability is described mathematically. The mathematical theory of probability assigns values ranging from 0 to 1 to statements and events. For example, statements that are always true and cannot be false are assigned a probability value of 1. On the other hand, statements that are always false and cannot be true have a probability of 0. Most statements fall somewhere between 0 and 1. A statement that is just as likely to be true as false is given a value of .5.

We can apply the mathematical description of probability to talk about arguments. An argument is a claim that, given the premises, the conclusion follows.

Thus, an argument can be viewed as a claim about the likelihood of the conclusion given the premises. A deductively valid argument is one in which, given the premises, the conclusion has to be true and cannot be false. Thus, the highest probability value, 1, is assigned to the conclusions of deductively valid arguments. An inductively strong argument, then, is one in which, given the premises, the conclusion has a probability value greater than .5 and less than 1. A weak argument has a probability value of less than .5. This helps us see that we are interested in identifying those arguments that have a degree of inductive support falling within the range less than 1 and greater than .5.

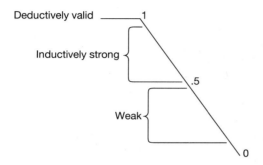

It is possible, then, to be more precise in describing the degree of probability of a conclusion, given its premises. However, applying the mathematical theory of probability to inductive arguments requires two things: (1) that we are able to assign numerical values to a premise or premises and (2) that we have a theory about how to assess the strength of different types of inductive arguments.

For example, we could assign a precise probability value to the argument in example 1 if we had statistical data describing the percentage of MDs who are conservative.

Example 3

Seventy-five percent of all MDs are conservatives.
Max is an MD.

_____

Max is a conservative.

In this example the conclusion has a probability of .75, so we ought to regard it as inductively well supported.

The calculation of mathematical probability goes beyond the scope of our study. For our purposes, we need to understand that it is possible to provide precision in the assessment of inductive probability and that doing so requires attention to the differences in kinds of inductive arguments. Consider the following examples.

Example 4

Seventy-five percent of 500 MDs interviewed are
conservatives.

Therefore, probably 75 percent of all MDs are
conservatives.

Example 5

When a mild electrical current is applied to a muscle,
the muscle contracts.

When the current stops, the muscle relaxes.

Therefore, the application of a mild electrical current to
a muscle is the cause of contraction.

Example 6

This mushroom looks and smells like a morel.

Morels are edible.

Probably, this mushroom is edible.

Each example above represents a distinctly different way in which premises bear on a conclusion. In example 4 a generalization is formed from premises describing some of the group. What determines whether it is a strong or weak generalization? In example 5 a cause and effect relationship is concluded from premises describing a correlation of events. In example 6 a property is attributed to something because it is similar to something else. These kinds of arguments are called *inductive generalization, causal argument,* and *argument from analogy,* respectively. Our purpose is to examine these three types and provide criteria for recognizing and assessing their inductive strength.

8.2 Inductive Generalization

Inductive generalizations are arguments with the conclusion that something is the case about all or many things on the basis of what is observed about some of them. They may be as commonplace as a neighbor's complaint that a recent scandal shows that all politicians are corrupt to elaborately designed statistical studies of public opinion. And they may vary in reliability from the irresponsible generalizations of prejudice to statistical calculations of probabilities and margins of error. Our concern is with what can be said in general about inductive generalizations: their typical forms, how they can be recognized, and how they can be assessed for inductive strength.

Let's focus on common features of inductive generalizations and develop a vocabulary for talking about them. Suppose we reason that all teachers in Boston are underpaid because all *those we have interviewed* are underpaid.

Example 7

All the teachers in Boston we interviewed are underpaid. Thus, all teachers in Boston are underpaid.

This example illustrates the basic features of an inductive generalization: (1) a conclusion describing what is inferred about all or many members of a larger group, called the *population,* based on (2) a premise or premises describing a subset, called a *sample,* of that population. A third element in an inductive generalization is (3) that characteristic observed in the sample and concluded to be true of the population. We will call this the *target characteristic.* It is that characteristic which, if this is a research project, we are seeking in our sample. In example 7 the target characteristic is "being underpaid."

The reasoning in an inductive generalization is that, although we have not observed all members of the population, we can *infer* their characteristics from information we have gathered from the sample. We reason *from what we have observed to a generalization about what we have not observed.* We can represent the form of an inductive generalization as follows:

FORM

All observed *A's are f. Thus, probably all A's are f.*

If we have more complex information about the sample, we may be able to make what is called a *statistical generalization.* For example, if our sampling showed that 40 percent of all those interviewed were underpaid, then we can argue statistically that:

Example 8

Forty percent of all Boston teachers interviewed are underpaid. Thus, it is likely that 40 percent of all Boston teachers are underpaid.

A statistical generalization has the form:

STATISTICAL GENERALIZATION

X percent of observed A's are f. Therefore, probably X percent of all A's are f.

In such an argument the premise or premises contain numerical data that characterize an observed sample of the population. The conclusion is an assertion of the probability that the same characterization will be true of the population.

How do we assess the reliability of an inductive generalization? How do we tell whether it is strong? Considering that an inductive generalization is an inference from some to all, common sense would suggest that the larger the sample, the stronger the generalization. After all, the more A's found to be *f*, the more likely all A's are *f*. There is truth to common sense here but the truth is below the surface. Consider this example:

Example 9

Of a sample of 60 percent of all Boston teachers, all of whom are primary grade teachers, all are underpaid. Therefore, it is likely that all Boston teachers are underpaid.

The sample, 60 percent of all Boston teachers, is remarkably large for a survey. If size were the definitive factor, then we should consider this a strong inductive generalization. But notice that the sample consists of primary grade teachers only. In spite of the fact that the sample is well over half of all teachers, can we be confident that what we learned about the salaries of primary grade teachers will be reflected in the salaries of all teachers? Our suspicion is that the salaries of primary grade teachers may not be representative of all teachers' salaries. This suggests that the size of the sample is less important than how representative it is. As a matter of fact, public opinion polls, such as Gallup polls and Nielsen TV ratings, are typically based on surveys of a very small number of people carefully selected to accurately represent the larger group. So the truth behind the commonsense idea that size determines reliability is really a function of the fact that size *may* increase representativeness. In the assessment of an inductive generalization it is the degree to which a sample is representative that matters most.

The more representative the sample, the stronger the inductive generalization. We have seen that it is much more important that a sample be representative than that it be large relative to the population. But what makes a sample *representative?*

A sample is representative *of a population to the degree that the target characteristics found in the sample occur with the same frequency or in the same proportion as they occur in the population.*

That defines representativeness, but how do we know when we have it? As you can see from the definition, one way to tell that a sample is representative is to examine the entire population! But if we could do that, we wouldn't bother with inductive generalization. So, in light of the fact that we want to infer rather than examine what may be the case about all members, how can we tell whether we have a sample whose characteristics are typical?

To tell whether a sample is representative we must already know something about the population and about how the target characteristic is related to other characteristics of members. In example 9, for instance, we assess the representativeness of that sample by using certain background information we already have. For example, we know that there are different levels of teaching and that salaries vary accordingly. We also know that salaries are influenced by such factors as seniority and school district. Thus, to be representative in this case, a sample should be composed with those differences taken into account. The fault with example 9 is that the sample lacks the variety that we know to be present in the larger population.

To consider how a representative sample is selected, let's design our own study. Suppose we want to determine what percentage of students at the university own automobiles. Suppose further that we believe that a sample consisting of 100 members will be sufficient. The method by which we compose that sample will bear on the reliability of our generalization. For instance, if we interview 100 students at the entrance to the parking lot, we are almost certain to have skewed results. On the other hand, if we interview 100 students near the campus bus stop, again our sample is not likely to be representative. What we need to consider is whether other characteristics of the members might bear on the occurrence of the target characteristic. In those two instances they do. Clearly, students found near a parking lot are more likely to be car owners. Students near a bus stop are not. Neither group gives us a representative sample. Thus, since where we select members bears on the results, it is best to avoid selecting members who have the characteristic of location in common. Our interviewers should take their data from various locations.

Simple random sampling   The science of statistics provides carefully devised procedures for designing samples. One of these, simple random sampling, is a commonly used way to achieve variety in our sample. If we can reasonably assume that car ownership is randomly distributed throughout the student population, then we may use a simple random sample. One way to do this would be to assign a number to each university student—something the registrar's office is likely to have done already—and to randomly select students with the use of a random number generator. Even simpler, we could pick 100 names out of a hat.

What makes either of these methods a *random* sample? The selection is random in the mathematical sense that each name has an even chance of being selected. The theory of a simple random sampling as a method for designing a representative sample assumes that (1) each possible member has an equal chance of appearing in the sample and (2) the characteristic sought is evenly distributed throughout the population. In our example we are able to use simple random sampling because we have assumed that the characteristic in question, car ownership, is likely to be distributed evenly throughout the population. If that is an acceptable assumption, then the generalization we infer about all the students has a high likelihood of being accurate.

Stratified random sampling   A more sophisticated method of sampling is appropriate when we know that the population consists of different groups and the groupings bear differently on the presence of the characteristic we are interested in. The generalization in example 7 above is more appropriately handled using this method, *stratified random sampling*. We know that teachers in Boston are not a homogeneous group but comprise instead several overlapping subgroups or *strata*. Therefore, a more representative sample will draw from those groups in proportion as they occur in the population. Suppose that 38 percent are primary grade teachers, 27 percent are secondary grade teachers, 19 percent are two-year college teachers, and so on. Suppose further that we factored in representative proportions of teachers at different levels of seniority for each strata. The final sample will consist of randomly selected members from each substrata and, thus, each strata. This sample, now quite complex, is more likely to reflect the characteristics we can expect to find throughout the population.

> Random Sample: *The random sample is a sample selected by a method that gives each element in the population an equal chance of being selected. The idea is that if each element has an equal chance to appear in the sample, then whatever characteristics are typically distributed throughout the group have the same probability of occurring in the sample.*

As the two sampling methods above show, assessing representativeness involves bringing background information to the argument. The more we already know about the population, the better we can assess the sample. If we know the population is diverse and we know that those differences bear on the presence of the target characteristic, then we know the sample must reflect that relevant diversity to be representative. Suppose, for example, we are interested in estimating the percentage of good eggs produced at an egg ranch. Suppose also that egg size is related to quality. Then the sample should contain a variety of sizes. On the other hand, those differences that make no difference can be ignored. For example, if the size of a marble makes no difference in its color and we are estimating the percentage of red marbles, a representative sample need not include variety of sizes.

To summarize: In order to assess the representativeness of a sample, we need to know (1) what different characteristics occur in the population and (2) whether those characteristics are relevant to the occurrence of the target characteristic. In general we can say that the more relevant diversity in the sample, the more representative it is. Interestingly enough, it also follows that the more relevant diversity in the population, the larger the sample will need to be to reflect that diversity. Thus, size is a function of the requirement for representativeness.

If strong inductive generalizations are ones that are based on representative samples, then weak ones are those that are not. A sample that is unrepresentative is called a *biased sample*. In statistics the concept of sample bias is mathematically defined. For our purposes a biased sample occurs when the sample fails to reflect relevant differences in the population either because it is too small or because it is not proportionately composed. One of the virtues of random sampling is that it avoids the likelihood of a biased sample. Nevertheless, sometimes an argument purportedly based on a random sample has members too much alike to be randomly selected. When a sample is biased the resulting generalization is unreliable and the argument is said to commit the *fallacy of hasty generalization* (see Chapter 9, section 9.11).

Other telling flaws in an inductive generalization have to do with the reliability of the premises themselves. Consider asking of the premises: How is the target characteristic defined? How is the information obtained? In example 7 the premise reports that so many teachers are underpaid. What does "being underpaid" mean in this example? Is it the subject's perception of his or her salary? Is it a measurement of subjects' salaries relative to the cost of living, to other comparable jobs, or to teachers elsewhere? If teachers are interviewed, as the example suggests, what questions are they asked? Consider the difference between being asked "How does your salary compare with that of other comparable jobs?" and "Are you underpaid?" The way in which a question is framed can affect the responses; thus, the way the information is obtained can introduce what is called *interviewer bias* into the results.

Summary: Inductive Generalization

1. *Inductive generalizations* are arguments concluding that something is the case about all or many things on the basis of what is observed about some of them. Presupposed in every inductive generalization is the idea that what we observe in the sample is likely to be true of all members of the group.

2. An inductive generalization consists of: (1) premises describing a *sample* (2) as having a *target characteristic* as reason for (3) a conclusion that all or some percentage of the *population* has that target characteristic.

3. The strength of an inductive generalization is a function of the representativeness of the sample. The more representative the sample, the stronger the argument.

4. A sample is *representative* of a population to the degree that the target characteristics found in the sample occur with the same frequency or in the same proportion as they occur in the population.

5. To assess the representativeness of a sample, we need to know (1) what different characteristics occur in the population and (2) whether those characteristics are relevant to the occurrence of the target characteristic. In general we can say that the more relevant diversity in the sample the more representative it is.

6. In general, a random sample is a sample selected by a method that gives each member in the population an equal chance of being selected.

    A *simple random sample* is a sample selected by a method that gives each member in the population an equal chance of being selected without regard to differences. The assumption is that if each member has an equal chance to appear in the sample, then whatever characteristics are typically distributed throughout the population have the same probability of occurring in the sample.

    A *stratified random sample* is a sample consisting of subgroups or strata in proportion as they occur in the population, with each member randomly selected. The assumption is that the occurrence of the target characteristic in the population is related to the occurrence of other characteristics. Strata are differentiated by relevant differences within the population.

7. A sample that is unrepresentative is called a *biased sample*. An inductive generalization based on a biased sample commits the *fallacy of hasty generalization*.

8. The premises describing what is learned about a sample may be unreliable if the target characteristic is not clearly defined or if the method of obtaining information adversely influences the results. Either is a case of *interviewer bias*.

Exercise 8.2   Inductive Generalization.   In the arguments below identify (a) the sample, (b) the population, and (c) the target characteristic. State whether (d) the sample is representative. If no judgment can be made, describe what information you need. Last, (e) given the premises discuss whether the argument is inductively strong.

Sample Exercise   According to a *New York Times* article on pelvic inflammatory disease (P.I.D.), a sexually transmitted disease affecting about one in seven women of reproductive age, Dr. Harold Kaminsky of the American College of Obstetrics and Gynecology reports that:

The men who passed the disease to the women often do not get treated. One study that looked at 60,000 cases of P.I.D. found that relatively few of the women's partners were treated. Because some of the women had more than one sexual partner at risk, the number of men treated should have been more than 60,000. In fact, only 29,000 were treated.

The argument is:

1. *A study of 60,000 cases of P.I.D. in women showed that only 29,000 men were treated.*
2. *P.I.D. is a sexually transmitted disease.*

---

3. *Therefore, men who pass the disease to women often do not get treatment.*

(a) The sample is the study of 60,000 cases of P.I.D. in which only 29,000 men were treated. (b) The population is the group of all cases of men and women with P.I.D. The report does not give us that number; it does tell us that about one in seven women have had the disease. (c) The target characteristic is men who have received treatment. (d) It is not clear whether the sample is representative. Although the sample is large, the report does not tell us how the sample was constructed. Presumably the data reflects reports of the disease made to the ACOG. (e) If we assume that most reports of the disease are reported to the ACOG, then we may conclude that the sample is representative. Therefore, the argument is a strong inductive generalization.

1. Pat has been counseling families for ten years and has never yet seen a family that does not exhibit some form of dysfunction. "There are no functional families," she says.

2. Debbie concluded that the nursing department can expect an attrition rate of about one-third of all freshmen nursing students each year, since about that many have failed or dropped out for the past three years.

3. Lauren says that she gets at least thirty minutes of happiness a day from her Barbie doll. When asked what she wanted for Christmas, she said she wants every six-year-old to have a Barbie doll so that each would have at least thirty minutes of happiness every day!

4. Having done a nonscientific survey of a two-square-mile tract of woodlands near his home, Tim concluded that there will be 40 percent fewer gypsy moth caterpillars feeding on the trees this coming spring. Following the same path through the woods at approximately the same time of year, Tim counted the number of egg cases on tree trunks visible from the path. The first count totaled 1,090 egg cases; the second count totaled 650.

5. Don has skied the same terrain every season for the past five years. He always sees at least one person skiing with reckless abandon. "These slopes are crawling with people who have no regard for safety. You take risks when you ski up here," he says.

6. After watching her real estate business slow to a standstill in winter and pick up in spring for the past six years, Mary Jane has concluded that from now on she'll close shop and spend winters in the Bahamas.

7. A survey by the American Academy of Actuaries reports that 72 percent of pension fund actuaries polled predict that half the baby boomers won't have the wherewithal to retire at age 65. The number of actuaries polled was 326; the number of registered actuaries in the nation is 7,854. The reasonable conclusion to draw is that well over half of all actuaries would agree that half of the nation's baby boomers will not be able to retire at age 65.

8. A recent study at a large teaching hospital involving 82 physicians and 75 patients found that there were 154 cases of resuscitation. Although 86 percent of the patients who received resuscitation were considered competent to make medical decisions, only 19 percent were asked for their consent prior to resuscitation being administered. From this study it is reasonable to conclude that the practice at most hospitals is to administer resuscitation without first discussing it with patients.

9. According to an essay by Mary McGrory, the American Bar Association aims to have its 129,000 law students throughout the country contribute 50 hours of public service before graduation. The ABA bases this recommendation on a report that 54 percent of law students at 100 out of 175 law schools voted in favor of mandatory public service.

10. From a one gallon jar filled with 1,000 variously colored gumballs, Teddy grabbed five handfuls for a total of 157. Sixty-three out of the 157 gumballs were red. Therefore, she concluded, almost fifty percent of all the gumballs in the jar are red.

11. The National Medical Care Expenditure Survey of 1977 conducted a survey, consisting of six household interviews, of over 40,000 individuals over an eighteen-month period during 1977 and 1978. Among their findings were that approximately 18 million Americans are without health insurance the

entire year, and as many as 34 million may be uninsured for some period of time during the year.

12. Macro Market Research of Burlington, Vermont conducted a phone survey of 508 Vermonters representing .1 percent of the total state population of approximately 500,000 people. Callers were selected through random digit dialing. The number of calls within each of the state's fourteen counties was proportional to the counties' population and distributed geographically according to population. Callers were given the names of candidates for election and asked which they would be inclined to vote for if the election were held today.

   For governor the survey showed that 49 percent were likely to vote for Richard Snelling, 29 percent for Peter Welch, and 21 percent were undecided. The margin of error is plus or minus 4.5 percent with a confidence level of 95 percent. That means that 95 times out of 100 this survey would produce results within 4.5 percent of these findings. Based on these statistics it is nearly certain that Snelling will be the state's next governor. (*Rutland Herald* news item)

13. To determine the percentage of Alameda County drivers wearing seat belts, toll booth operators were instructed to make observations of all drivers going through the toll at the Hill bridge. A survey of approximately 8,000 drivers over a twenty-four-hour period showed that 37 percent were wearing seat belts. County officials concluded that approximately 37 percent of all local drivers wear seat belts.

14. By randomly selecting names from the phone book, surveyors for Ace Phone Company asked people whether they owned an Ace phone. Out of 450 calls, 14 percent owned an Ace phone, 36 percent did not know, 2 percent hung up, and 48 percent owned another brand. Marketing researcher Victor Kay concluded that 14 percent of all area phone owners have an Ace and that Ace should print its name boldly across the front of each phone it produces. He is convinced, he argued, that a large percentage of those who "did not know" were Ace owners who couldn't find the label.

15. A survey of the buying habits of residents in Franklin County showed that the most commonly purchased commodities were coffee, long underwear, and ammunition. Researchers interviewed 500 rural residents during the month of January. Franklin County consists of approximately three thousand rural residents and 67,000 urban dwellers. On the basis of the survey, researchers recommended that area retailers are looking at an exciting untapped market, particularly in long underwear and ammunition.

8.3 Causal Arguments

Probably few interests in life occupy us as much as wanting to know how things work. We want to know why things happen, how to make things happen, how to avoid things from happening, and how to predict what will happen. Our lives consist of events and our success in life consists in part in our ability to explain, predict, and alter events. This is surely why newspapers, magazines, books, and everyday conversations are filled with discussions about what causes what. However, an interest in causes and effects is not the same as an interest in good reasoning about causes and effects. The latter is the subject of this section.

How do we identify strong causal arguments? In this section we will first clarify what a causal argument is. Then we will look at the kinds of arguments in which causal statements occur. From there we will see that our main concern is with causal statements as conclusions of arguments. Thus, we will focus on the strength or reliability of reasons supporting a causal conclusion and we will study John Stuart Mill's methods for identifying causal relations.

8.3A Causal Statements

Causal arguments, as we will illustrate shortly, consist of at least one causal statement as either a premise or the conclusion. Let's begin with an account of causal statements. A causal statement is a statement that asserts or denies that one thing or type of thing causes another or that one thing or type of thing is caused by another.

> A causal statement *is any statement that asserts or denies that "A causes B" in which A and B refer to things, people, events, states of affairs, or their types.*

Whatever is an instance of A in the schema "A causes B" is said to be the cause; whatever is an instance of B is said to be the effect. For example:

Example 10

Increased stress causes increased risk of heart attack.

Example 11

Increased stress does not cause increased risk of premature delivery in pregnant women.

Example 10 asserts a causal relationship. Example 11 denies one. Besides being assertions or denials, there is a distinction to be made between specific causal statements and causal generalizations. A *specific causal statement* asserts, for example, that some specific thing caused or is caused by some other specific thing.

> *Specific causal statement: A causes B*

where 'A' and 'B' refer to particular things or events. For example:

The power failure caused the loss of my document in the computer's memory.

The paint is drying slowly because of the high humidity.

The pesticide I used killed my neighbor's roses.

On the other hand, a *causal generalization* asserts or denies a causal relationship between *types* of things or events.

Causal generalization: A's cause B's

where A and B refer to types of things or events. For example:

Power failures are common causes of loss of data in a computer's memory.

Paints dry more slowly if the humidity is high.

Some kinds of pesticides harm flowering roses.

8.3B The Senses of the Word 'Cause'

In the most general terms, to assert that A causes B is to assert that A brings about, produces, or makes B happen. But if we look at various examples, we see that there are different senses of the word 'cause' in different causal statements.

Example 12

Power failures cause loss of data in a computer's memory.

Example 13

The presence of oxygen caused the combustion.

Example 14

Smoking causes cancer.

When we say that one thing causes another, sometimes we mean that one brings about the other, sometimes that one is required for the other to occur, and sometimes that one contributes to the occurrence of the other. A precise way to characterize these different senses is to use the concepts of necessary and sufficient conditions encountered in Chapter 5 (section 5.6). Recall that, given a statement of the form "If p, then q," p is a sufficient condition for q and q is a necessary condition for p.

Consider first the causal relationship asserted in example 12. How is the event of a power failure related to the effect, loss of data in a computer's memory? We know that if a power failure occurs during the operation of a computer, loss of data in memory will occur. We can say that a power failure is a *sufficient condition* for loss of data. However, if there is loss of data in a computer's memory, it does not follow that a power failure occurred. (Other causes are possible: you accidentally pressed "delete," for example.) Thus, power failure is not a *necessary condition* for loss of data. Example 12 illustrates a causal relationship in which the cause is a sufficient but not a necessary condition for the effect.

In example 13 the presence of oxygen is not sufficient for combustion; fuel is also required. But the presence of oxygen is a necessary condition, for without it there would be no combustion. The statement asserts a cause in the sense of a causally necessary condition for the effect.

Considering example 14, from what we know about the relationship between smoking and lung cancer, we know that the statement does not assert that smoking is a sufficient condition for lung cancer, since some people smoke but never get cancer. Neither does it assert that smoking is a necessary condition since not all causes of lung cancer are cases in which the person smoked. Rather, the causal relationship observed between smoking and lung cancer is that the incidence of lung cancer is higher in those cases in which a person smokes. Thus, smoking is a *contributing factor* or *partial cause* of lung cancer.

These examples illustrate three basic senses in which one thing may be said to cause another. They are summarized below.

In the case that A causes B, then:

(i) A is a *sufficient condition* for B if and only if given that A occurs, B occurs. If B does not occur, then A has not occurred.

   For example, a dead battery causes failure of the engine to start. That is, if the battery is dead, the car won't start.

(ii) A is a *necessary condition* for B if and only if given that B occurs, A occurs. If A does not occur, then B does not occur.

   For example, cessation of functioning in the human cerebellum causes the death of the person. That is, if a person is dead, then the cerebellum has ceased functioning.

(iii) A is a *partial cause* of B if and only if given factors f, g, h, the occurrence of A increases the likelihood of B, and A is neither sufficient nor necessary for B.

   For example, rapidly falling atmospheric pressure indicates the likelihood of precipitation. That is, if rapidly falling atmospheric pressure occurs along with other factors, then precipitation occurs.

As an example, consider how the concepts defined above are used in describing fog. Fog, the phenomenon in which visibility is reduced below 1 km by water droplets in the air, is the product of a number of factors occurring simultaneously. As the evening progresses, the earth radiates its heat into the atmosphere. If atmospheric pressure is high, permitting the warm air to ascend, the temperature to fall, and cooler air to be trapped near the earth, and if relative humidity increases in the absence of wind, fog is formed. No single factor is sufficient to produce fog. Rather the factors listed are *jointly sufficient* and some but not all are *individually necessary*. The occurrence of evening and the absence of wind, to be specific, are not necessary, since fog may occur as long as the surface temperature is cooler and the wind is bringing in moist air. Evening and the absence of wind, in our example, may be called *partial causes*.

Fog is a complex phenomenon because it occurs only if a number of factors are present. Some of the phenomena we would most like to understand—for example, disease, crime, educational success, economic shifts, environmental pollution, and so on—are significantly more complex. Crime, for example, is not a single phenomenon but a family of more or less closely related phenomena. Each kind of crime, furthermore, involves a network of factors. Even if we were to focus exclusively on a specific type of crime, arson, for example, we would find a number of contributing factors and few necessary conditions for cases of arson.

8.3C The Structure of Causal Relationships

Events take place against a background of circumstances. A woman falls in a store and breaks her hip because the floor is wet. But also at play are any number of other circumstances: the texture of the flooring; the high-heeled shoes she happened to be wearing, but might not have, had her others been repaired on time; the fact that she lingered at the meat counter; the custodian's being distracted by a spill in the next aisle and, thus, forgetting to get the caution sign; her age and increased vulnerability to fractures; the physical laws of falling bodies; the law of gravity, and so on. How do we begin to ferret out relevant causes?

In looking at the complexity of events, it is useful to apply some distinctions. First, we can distinguish between events that occur in sequence and events or circumstances that converge. In our example there are *causal chains* or sequences of events: something caused the woman to be at the store at that time, something caused her to linger at the meat counter, bringing her to the place where she stepped, slipped, fell, and was injured. But other factors converging at different places in that sequence also have bearing on the complex event: her other shoes being unavailable, the wet floor, the spill in the next aisle, and the absence of a caution sign. Independently occurring events converge to form a network of circumstances that make the accident possible. A diagram of the accident shows both causal chains and the convergence of circumstances.

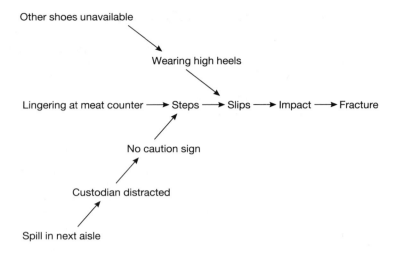

Second, we can distinguish causal factors in terms of their proximity or nearness to the effect in question. A *proximate cause* is a causal factor that occurs immediately prior to or simultaneous with the effect. In our example it seems that the proximate cause of the fractured hip is the impact of the woman's body on the hard floor which, in turn, was caused by slipping on water. Elaborating on the explanation we may specify other events as *intermediate causes,* say, the absence of a caution sign, or *remote causes* even further removed from the accident, say, the spill in the next aisle. Usually in explaining an event we single out an event or events immediately prior as bearing the weight of *the* cause. Although it may be true that the accident would not have occurred had some other events not taken place, we would probably not say that she fell and broke her hip because she lingered at the meat counter or because her other shoes were not repaired on time. And we would not say that the fall was due to the law of gravity.

> Proximate cause: *A causal factor that occurs immediately prior to or simultaneous with the effect.*
>
> Intermediate cause: *A causal factor whose occurrence links a more distant or remote cause to a proximate cause.*
>
> Remote cause: *A factor causally relevant to an effect but not immediately responsible for the effect. Typically, a remote cause is a cause occurring at some distance temporally or spatially from the effect.*

Adapting an illustration from Robert H. Blank's *Rationing Medicine,* we can see how the structure of very complex causal relationships might be displayed. Blank is illustrating the factors causally responsible for the crisis in health care.

A Model of Heath Care Policy in the United States

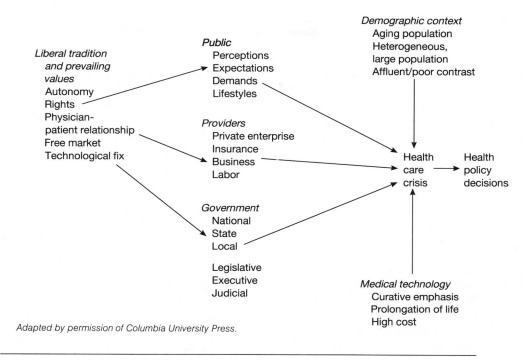

Adapted by permission of Columbia University Press.

Exercise 8.3A   Causal Structure   Using the concepts of causal chain, convergent events, proximate cause, intermediate cause, and remote cause, draw diagrams representing the following descriptions of events or circumstances.

Sample Exercise   Freezing followed by thawing followed by freezing causes the water to get under your shingles, freeze again, and then melt between the roofing boards. Pretty soon you have a leak in the roof.

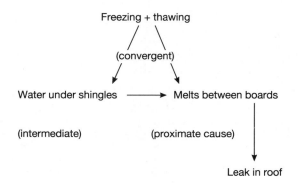

1. Max hit the baseball so hard it flew over the fence and broke Mr. Porter's picture window.

2. Maxine passed the history final because she stayed up all night studying.

3. The brilliant reds, yellows, and oranges of the leaves in fall result from the shortening of daylight hours which decrease the production of chlorophyll in the leaves.

4. The conflict over slavery caused the Civil War.

5. Sitting at a computer keyboard for prolonged periods can produce inflammation of the tendons in the wrist, arm, and elbow, a syndrome known as repetitive strain injury (RSI).

6. The car backfired, startling Mr. Potts, who dropped the can of paint on Fido, causing him to leap at Mrs. Potts, who was carrying the turkey dinner, which hit the floor with a splat.

7. The increase in consumer spending is directly affected by the availability of low interest rate borrowing. The interest rates local banks charge are in turn determined by their access to secondary mortgage holders. Secondary holders will buy groups of mortgages from local banks depending, ultimately, on the interest rates set by the Federal Reserve Board for loans to preferred customers.

8. The passenger in Ted's car was wearing a seat belt and, therefore, received only slight injury when Ted lost control of the car, due to poor visibility and icy roads, and hit a retaining fence that spun the car around and into a telephone pole.

9. Evelyn ran eight miles, causing repeated strain of her Achilles tendon. She packed her ankle in ice and prevented swelling, thus reducing the pain she otherwise would have experienced.

10. A recent study shows that, on the whole, working women tend to have fewer chronic ailments than housewives. Specifically, the incidence of chronic ailment is lower for women employed in nonindustrial jobs with a high degree of social interaction. Those in industrial occupations have a higher incidence of chronic ailment due to physical exertion and occupational hazards. The study suggests that the absence of daily social interaction is a significant factor in producing chronic ailments in women who are housewives.

Exercise 8.3B   Describing Causes   Using the concepts of necessary condition, sufficient condition, jointly sufficient condition, individually necessary condition, and partial cause, discuss the examples listed in Exercise 8.3A.

Sample Exercises

1. Max's hitting the baseball as he did is a sufficient condition for the breaking of the window but it is not a necessary condition, since the window's breaking can occur without Max's hitting the baseball.

3. If decreased production of chlorophyll occurs, the leaves change color. Thus, decreased production of chlorophyll is a sufficient condition for color change. Conversely, if there is color change, it must be that the leaves are producing less chlorophyll. Thus, decreased production is a necessary condition as well. Decreasing daylight seems to figure the following way: decreased daylight is a sufficient condition for decreased chlorophyll but not a necessary condition. Other factors might cause a tree to produce less chlorophyll. Thus, daylight is sufficient but not necessary for color change in leaves.

8.3D Types of Causal Arguments

A causal argument, we will say, is any argument in which a causal statement occurs either as a premise or a conclusion. Consider first causal statements as premises.

Example 15	FORM
Reduction in swelling causes relief of pain	*C's cause E's*
The swelling in my arm is diminishing.	*a C occurs*
Therefore, relief of pain will occur.	*an E will occur*

Example 16	
Reduction in swelling causes relief of pain.	*C's cause E's*
There is relief of pain.	*E occurs*
Therefore, the swelling in my arm is diminishing.	*C occurs*

Example 17	
Reduction in swelling causes relief of pain.	*C's cause E's*
Therefore, if relief of pain is desired, reduce the swelling.	*If E is desired, do C*

Each example employs a causal generalization as a premise, yet each illustrates a different kind of causal inference. In example 15 an inference is made to the occurrence of the effect, here symbolized by E. It is a *causal prediction*. In example 16 an inference is made to the occurrence of a cause. It is a *causal explanation*. Thus, given a causal generalization and a specific instance of a circumstance we can make an inference as to what will happen or what has happened. Example 17 illustrates a *causal prescription*. Given a causal generalization, we can conclude that if an effect is desired (or not desired), we should (should not) produce the cause. These three types are summarized below.

Causal predictions: given C, E will occur
(What will happen if C occurs?)

C's cause E's

a C occurs

E will probably occur

Causal explanations: E occurred because C occurred
(Why did E occur?)

C's cause E's

E occurs

C probably occurred

Causal prescriptions: If E is (is not) desired, do (not do) C
(How do we make E occur or prevent E from occurring?)

C's cause E's

If E is desired, do C
(Or: if E is not desired, do not do C)

Each type of causal argument above employs a causal generalization but none establishes, or concludes with, a causal generalization. Rather the strength of the argument forms above depends upon the reliability of the causal premise C's cause E's. In our examples, the prediction, explanation, and prescription all presuppose that reduction in swelling causes relief of pain. Such arguments are only as good as the evidence in support of the causal premise. This means that in assessing causal arguments of the kind illustrated above we are ultimately drawn back to those arguments that attempt to establish the relevant causal statement. Consider, as an example, how the causal generalization in the above arguments might be supported.

Example 18

Whenever swelling is reduced, pain is relieved.

Therefore, reduction in swelling causes relief of pain.

The example has the form:

Whenever event C occurs, event E occurs.

Therefore, events of type C cause events of type E
(that is, C's cause E's)

Example 18 illustrates a type of causal argument we will call a *causal conclusion*. We will say that a causal conclusion is an argument that employs premises to establish a causal statement. Since the arguments we have called predictions, explanations, and prescriptions employ causal statements as premises, we will focus on the assessment of those arguments in support of a causal statement. In the following section we will examine what have been called Mill's Methods for making and assessing causal conclusions.

Below is a summary of this section.

Causal statement: *A statement asserting or denying that one thing (or event) or type of thing (or event) causes or is caused by another thing (or event) or type of thing (or event).*

Causal argument: *An argument in which at least one causal statement occurs either as a premise or as a conclusion.*

Causal prediction: *An argument consisting of a causal generalization, an instance of a causal circumstance, and concluding that a specific effect occurs.*

Causal explanation: *An argument consisting of a causal generalization, an instance of an effect, and concluding that an instance of a specific cause explains the occurrence of the effect.*

Causal conclusion: *An argument consisting of premises in support of a causal statement.*

Exercise 8.3C   Types of Causal Arguments   In the following exercises (1) write the argument in *argument form,* (2) identify the causal statement, and (3) state whether the argument is a causal prediction, causal explanation, causal prescription, or causal conclusion. You may need to supply missing premises or conclusions. If so, mark them with an asterisk (*).

Sample Exercises

A. Some insects have the ability to survive freezing in winter by producing nucleating proteins in their body fluids. These proteins prevent ice crystals from spreading and causing cell destruction. Since mature green beetles reappear immediately with the first thaw, they have survived the winter by producing proteins that protect their body cells from freezing.

Answer
1. Some insects have the ability to survive freezing by producing nucleating proteins in their body fluids.

2. These nucleating proteins prevent ice crystals from spreading and causing cell destruction. *(Causal statement)*

3. Mature green beetles reappear immediately with the first thaw.

---

4. Therefore, they produce nucleating proteins that protect their body cells from freezing.

Statement 2 is a causal statement. The argument offers a *causal explanation* for the effect that mature green beetles reappear when temperatures thaw them out.

B. Since underwater weevils have been consistently found in those ponds that have an unusually diminished amount of milfoil weed present, it seems reasonable to conclude that the weevils are causing the disappearance of the milfoil weed.

Answer
1. Underwater weevils have been consistently found in ponds that have an unusually diminished amount of milfoil weed present.

---

2. Probably, weevils are causing the disappearance of the milfoil weed. *(Causal statement)*

Statement 2 is a causal statement. The argument is a *causal conclusion* providing evidence—the occurrence of weevils and diminishing weeds—in support of the causal statement.

1. Improper cabin pressure in an airplane causes earache. Several passengers have complained of earache; there is probably a problem with the cabin pressure.

2. Passing an electrical current through wire wrapped around a piece of metal produces an electromagnet. Thus, if you want to make an electromagnet, attach a battery to wire wrapped tightly around a piece of iron, for example.

3. Whenever an orange female cat is mated with a black male, the resulting male kittens will be orange and the resulting female kittens will be tortoiseshell. Thus, your black male and my orange female will probably produce no black kittens.

4. Fumbles in football cause more losses of games than any other player error. Since Mudd dropped the football, he will probably do it again, and the Tigers will lose this one.

5. According to Robert J. Samuelson in "Diapers: The Sequel," studies comparing cloth and disposable diapers show that the absorbent in disposable diapers draws moisture from the skin and reduces diaper rash. If you are interested in protecting your infant from diaper rash, you'd be wise to use disposable diapers.

6. Children who are born unable to hear often are also mute and require special attention to learn speech. This is because there seems to be corrective feedback between the part of the brain that hears sound and the part that controls speech. With the absence of sound, the child does not learn speech, at least not easily.

7. The mammalian eye may exhibit two types of nerve receptors, cone-shaped receptors for color vision and rod-shaped receptors for low-intensity light. Owls can hardly see in daylight because they have only rods; hens can hardly see at night because they have only cones.

8. High tide consistently occurs with the rising of the moon and subsides with its setting. Therefore, the tides are caused by the position of the moon.

9. Shaking a bottle filled with carbonated liquid releases the gas and increases the pressure inside the bottle. That is why the soda bubbled out and all over when you opened it.

10. If at night you see something out of the corner of your eye and then turn to look directly at it, it will seem to disappear. This is because the nerve receptors that are most sensitive to low light are displayed on the perimeter of the retina, not in the center.

11. It has recently been concluded that measurable levels of stress do not increase the likelihood of complications in pregnancy, based on a study correlating stress levels and the incidence of complications.

12. Fred's car went out of control and off the road because the roads were icy and, as we all know, ice on the road significantly reduces traction.

13. The fate that befell the Amerinds when they first came into contact with the European invaders is among the best-documented illustrations of the effects that epidemics in general and smallpox in particular have exerted on the course of wars. Shortly after the arrival of Cortez and his Conquistadores, smallpox spread like wildfire through the Indian population. As smallpox was then prevalent in Europe, the Spaniards had probably developed immunity to it through early exposure, whereas the Indians, who had no racial experience with it, proved very susceptible. By killing at least half the Indians and demoralizing them at a critical time, the epidemic certainly played a part as important as Spanish arms and valor in bringing about the conquest of the South American continent. (Rene Dubos, *The Mirage of Health*)

14. In light of the fact that Congress included significant increases in income tax in the new budget and that higher income tax results in decreased consumer spending and deepening recession, the likely result of the new budget will be to deepen the current recession.

15. According to *Newsweek,* "a new study headed by doctors from the University of Minnesota provided the strongest evidence yet that cholesterol does

indeed contribute to heart disease. The 838 subjects of the study had survived a previous heart attack and had cholesterol levels above 220. Half were told to modify their diets; some of them were given drugs. The other half underwent a surgical procedure to reduce absorption of cholesterol into the bloodstream. In the surgery group, cholesterol levels dropped to an average of 196, compared with 241 in the control group. Over a 10-year period the combined rate of second heart attacks or death from heart disease was 35 percent lower in the treated patients—and they required less than half as many cardiac operations as the controls. The study also showed convincingly, for the first time, that the progression of heart disease could be accurately forecast by X-rays taken to monitor plaque buildup inside the arteries." (*Newsweek,* 10/15/90)

Mill's Methods

John Stuart Mill (1806–1873), in his *System of Logic,* describes five methods for identifying causes and effects. They are the methods of agreement, difference, concomitant variation, residue, and the joint method of agreement and difference. We will examine the first four and comment on the last. Philosophers do not agree about the adequacy of Mill's methods. Some think Mill claims too much for them. But our purpose is not to enter the debate; it is to adapt the methods as seems reasonable to the assessment of arguments that conclude with a causal statement.

1. The Method of Agreement   According to the method of agreement, the cause of an event E is that circumstance which is common to all cases in which E occurs. Thus, to paraphrase Mill:

> Method of agreement: *If two or more instances of a phenomenon E have only one antecedent circumstance in common, then probably that antecedent circumstance is the cause or a partial cause of E.*

Reasoning that whenever a phenomenon occurs, the cause will be present, Mill's first method for identifying a cause tells us to look for an antecedent circumstance present in all those cases in which the phenomenon occurs.

Suppose, for example, that five friends have lunch at a restaurant and an hour later three get sick from food poisoning. The method of agreement suggests that we can identify the spoiled food causing the sickness by looking for the antecedent circumstance common to the three cases of illness.

Example 19

	Ate	Got sick
Denise	salad, roast beef, apple pie, tea	No
Amy	clam chowder, salad, apple pie, coffee	Yes
Beth	clam chowder, apple pie, Coke	Yes
Ellen	hamburger, fries, Coke	No
Clara	clam chowder, chicken, coffee	Yes

Following the method of agreement, we focus on those cases in which the illness occurred and look for a common element.

Case A: Amy's illness has antecedents: *clam chowder,* salad, apple pie, coffee

Case B: Beth's illness has antecedents: *clam chowder,* apple pie, Coke

Case C: Clara's illness has antecedents: *clam chowder,* chicken, coffee

The three cases of illness have only one circumstance in common: clam chowder. On the principle that the cause is probably that circumstance common to otherwise different instances of a phenomenon, it is reasonable to conclude that the clam chowder is, at least, a causal factor in producing the illness.

The form of an argument using the method of agreement is:

1. *Case A of phenomenon E has antecedent circumstances f, g, h, i.*

2. *Case B of phenomenon E has antecedent circumstances f, h, j.*

3. *Case C of phenomenon E has antecedent circumstances f, k, i.*

4. *Therefore, circumstance f is probably the cause or a partial cause of E.*

Although the case of the food poisoning illustrates Mill's first method, it seems contrived. Isn't it fortunate that *only one* dish was common to the cases of illness? What if there had been two or three common items eaten by those who got sick? Furthermore, isn't it possible that there are other circumstances common to the three? In fact, looking at our example, there are others: all three are women and, let us suppose, all three are wearing red. On what grounds, then, do we single out food items as antecedent circumstances and not, say, color of clothing? These questions require some discussion of the adequacy of Mill's first method. (Indeed, Mill's other three methods raise similar problems which, however, we will not stop to address. Let the present discussion suffice.)

Let's take the second problem above first. On what grounds do we single out food items as antecedent circumstances and not such things as wearing red? What is to count as an antecedent circumstance? In practice we distinguish between circumstances thought to be relevant to a phenomenon and those that are not. Wearing red, we say, is not relevant to getting sick after lunch. In other words, we form an *hypothesis*, a reasonable guess based on past experience, as to what circumstances are relevant candidates for the cause of a phenomenon. Using an hypothesis, we significantly narrow the field of antecedent circumstances and thus may apply a method like Mill's first method to isolate the cause. This qualification is required for the application of Mill's first method (and, with the appropriate changes, the others as well):

Given the hypothesis that antecedent circumstances f, g, h, i, etc., are causally relevant to E, then, according to the method of agreement, if two or more instances of a phenomenon E have only one antecedent circumstance in common, probably that antecedent circumstance is the cause or a partial cause of E.

Second, given two or more occurrences of a phenomenon E, how likely are they to have *only one relevant* antecedent circumstance in common? What do we do when two or more *relevant* antecedent circumstances are common to the otherwise different cases of E? In our example we may imagine that, besides each woman having clam chowder, each also ate apple pie. The first thing to notice is that the antecedent of Mill's method of agreement does not obtain: We do not have two or more instances of E with only one circumstance in common. Thus, in such a case Mill's first method does not identify the cause of E. We must turn to Mill's second method. Nevertheless, the first method does allow us to eliminate from further consideration all those circumstances not present in instances of E. It provides, in other words, positive evidence that the cause of E is, at least, among those antecedent circumstances common to E. We may state this as a modified version of Mill's first method:

> Modified method of agreement: *If two or more instances of a phenomenon E have antecedent circumstances f and g in common, then probably (f causes E) or (g causes E) or (f and g cause E).*

Naturally, this modified version can be rewritten to apply to cases in which there are more than two common antecedent circumstances. The essential point is that, while Mill's method of agreement may not be sufficient to identify *the* cause of a phenomenon, it does allow us to identify potential causes.

2. The Method of Difference   Using Mill's second method, the method of difference, we can continue the investigation. According to this method, we compare cases in which the phenomenon occurs with those cases in which it does not occur to discover in what way they differ. If there is a single antecedent circumstance present when the phenomenon occurs but absent when it does not occur, that circumstance is causally involved in the phenomenon. For example, you may conclude that touching the TV antenna is the cause of the clear picture on your TV screen when you observe that it is clear when you touch it but not clear when you take your hand away. Or, to take another example, you may conclude that it is the ham that causes the salty taste in your stew when you notice that the salty-tasting batch has ham in it while the other batch does not.

> Method of difference: *If an instance of phenomenon E and an instance in which E does not occur differ only in the presence of one antecedent circumstance with the instance of E, then that antecedent circumstance is probably the cause or a partial cause of E.*

The form of an argument employing the method of difference is:

> 1. *Case A of phenomenon E has antecedent circumstances f, g, h, i.*
> 2. *Case B without phenomenon E has antecedent circumstances g, h, i.*
> _____
> 3. *Therefore, circumstance f is probably the cause or a partial cause of E.*

By using the method of difference in conjunction with the method of agreement—actually what Mill calls the joint method of agreement and difference—we can handle the problem raised above: those cases in which two or more instances have *more than one* antecedent circumstance in common. Let's suppose that Amy, Beth, and Clara also have apple pie in common. By the method of agreement, we can say that the three cases of illness are caused by apple pie, clam chowder, or the combination of apple pie and clam chowder. Now we compare their cases with those in which one of the two antecedents is present yet the illness is not.

Example 20

Case A: Amy's illness has antecedents: *clam chowder,* salad, *apple pie,* coffee

Case B: Beth's illness has antecedents: *clam chowder, apple pie,* Coke

Case C: Clara's illness has antecedents: *clam chowder,* chicken, *apple pie,* coffee

Case D: Denise, no illness, has antecedents: salad, roast beef, *apple pie,* tea

By using the method of difference we see that the apple pie cannot be the cause of the illness because Denise had apple pie but did not get sick. Thus, of the two common antecedents, the apple pie may be eliminated as a cause.

When we use the method of agreement, we look for what is common to instances of a phenomenon we are investigating. Thus, we eliminate those antecedent factors not present in all cases in which the phenomenon occurs. When we use the method of difference, we look for some difference between instances of a phenomenon and instances without the phenomenon. Thus, we eliminate those antecedent factors present whenever the phenomenon fails to occur.

Below is the form of an argument employing both the method of agreement and the method of difference.

METHOD OF AGREEMENT AND METHOD OF DIFFERENCE

1. If f and g are common to E, then   (modified method of agreement)
   probably (f causes E) or (g causes E).

2. f and g are common to E.   (by observation)
_____

3. Therefore, probably (f causes E) or   (by 1 and 2, MP)
   (g causes E).

4. If circumstance g but not E, then   (method of difference)
   probably not (g causes E).

5. g and not E.   (by observation)
_____

6. Therefore, probably not (g causes E).   (by 4 and 5, MP)
_____

7. Therefore, probably f causes E.   (by 3 and 6, DS)

3. The Method of Concomitant Variation   Any number of things in our experience exhibit variations. Hot plates get hotter; people get physically stronger or weaker. Frequently we observe that such variations coincide with (are concomitant with) variations in other circumstances.

Example 21

The more Smith exercises, the stronger he seems to get.

Example 22

The higher the humidity, the longer it takes the paint to dry.

The fact that instances of two different kinds of phenomena consistently vary together provides some evidence that they are causally related. To paraphrase Mill:

Method of concomitant variation: If variations in phenomenon E coincide with variations in phenomenon P, then it is probable that E and P are causally related.

A virtue of the method of concomitant variation, Mill claims, is that it is particularly useful for those cases in which the method of difference cannot be applied. Mill's example is the phenomenon of the tides. Suppose we suspect that the moon's gravitational pull on the earth is the cause of the tides. In this case there is no possibility of applying the method of difference because we cannot get rid of the moon (which is what we'd have to do to see what effect, if any, that had on the tides). But what is possible, Mill says, is to observe the variations in the position of the moon and look for concomitant variations in the tides. Hence, we see that the tide rises with the rising moon and ebbs with the latter's setting.

Now the fact that two phenomena vary consistently is evidence that they are causally related but not evidence as to which is the cause and which the effect. Thus, for example, we should not conclude that the moon is causing the tides just because we observe a concomitant variation between the two. Odd as it may sound, perhaps the tides cause the moon to rotate! By itself the method of concomitant variation gives us only correlations of phenomena and, hence, evidence of a causal connection. In order to conclude which phenomenon is causing which, we need evidence beyond what the method of concomitant variation provides, evidence that is perhaps provided by the other methods.

In thinking about two phenomena that vary in relation to each other it will be useful to make a distinction. In some cases a phenomenon varies *simultaneously* with some other circumstance. For example, variations in humidity and paint drying time occur simultaneously. The moon's rotation occurs simultaneously with the changing of the tides. On the other hand, there are those phenomena that vary *subsequent to* variations in some other circumstance. For example, one's muscles get bigger subsequent to increased exercise. Next year's crop of insects varies with the severity of this year's winter.

About the second kind of case above, we can conclude that the antecedent phenomenon is the cause of the subsequent because we know that what comes after cannot be the cause of what comes before. If we know, in other words, that some phenomenon E has circumstance f *as an antecedent,* then we could reason that variations in E are caused by variations in f. Letting the symbols + and − represent increases or decreases, we can express the form of the argument by the method of concomitant variation as follows:

> *Case A: phenomenon E has antecedent f*
>
> *Case B: phenomenon E+ has antecedent f+*
>
> *Case C: phenomenon E− has antecedent f−*
>
> ———————————————————————
>
> *Therefore, probably variations in antecedent f cause variations in E.*

Of course, for those cases in which phenomena vary inversely, the form of argument would differ accordingly. For example, "phenomenon E+ has antecedent f−."

About those kinds of cases in which phenomena vary simultaneously, Mill suggests that, if possible, we try to produce variations in one phenomenon by controlling variations in the other. For example, in a tightly sealed room we vary the humidity and see whether that produces variations in drying time. Then we try the reverse. We speed up drying time by thinning the paint, say, to see if that alters the room's humidity. Or, as another example, we observe that increasing the temperature of a gas increases its volume but increasing volume does not increase temperature. Such experiments enable us to say which of two simultaneously occurring events is varying because of which.

Example 23

Given a balloon filled with air to a volume of 15 cubic inches at room temperature, say, 70 degrees, I then step outside into the cold, 20 degrees, and observe that the balloon nearly collapses. When I return to the warm house, the balloon resumes its previous volume.

Experiments in which we produce variations in some phenomenon by controlling others borrow from what we have learned with the method of difference. In effect, we try to produce a difference in one by making a difference in the other. In short:

Case A: phenomenon P increases (or decreases), E increases (or decreases)

Case B: phenomenon E increases (or decreases), P neither increases nor decreases.

Therefore, variations in P probably cause variations in E.

What finally entitles us to say that the moon causes the tides and not the reverse? We cannot experiment on the moon and the tides. However, in this kind of case the method of difference provides a way of testing the hypothesis that the tides cause the moon's variations. Comparing our moon with planets having a moon but no oceans, we conclude that the tides cannot be the phenomenon causing variations in the moon; it must be the reverse.

4. The Method of Residue Suppose we are investigating some complex phenomenon such as the increased incidence of AIDS in our community. Let us say that we already know certain facts: (1) that the AIDS virus is transmitted through exchange of body fluids, typically blood or semen; (2) that in all the cases of AIDS we have observed the antecedent circumstances have been either contaminated needles in IV drug use, unsafe sex, or blood transfusions; (3) we have established that IV drug use is a causal factor in 65 percent of the cases and unsafe sex is a causal factor in 25 percent of the cases. Thus, we can conclude that the remaining cases are caused by blood transfusion. Our argument is:

Example 24

1. All observed instances of AIDS have as their antecedent circumstances IV drug use, unsafe sex, or blood transfusion.

2. *IV drug use is a causal factor in 65 percent of cases of AIDS.*

3. *Unsafe sex is a causal factor in 25 percent of cases of AIDS.*

_____

4. *Therefore, blood transfusion is a causal factor in the remaining cases of AIDS.*

That argument illustrates Mill's method of residue, which he describes as follows:

> Method of residue: *Subtract from any phenomenon such part as is known by previous inductions to be the effect of certain antecedents, and the residue of the phenomenon is the effect of the remaining antecedents.*

An example of the form of an argument using the method of residue is this:

1. *Phenomenon E consists of parts e1, e2, and e3*

2. *E has antecedent circumstances f, g, and h*

3. *f causes e1*

4. *g causes e2*

_____

5. *Therefore, h causes (the residue) e3*

In short, if we know what part one antecedent plays in a complex phenomenon, we can infer the part played by the other. Suppose we want to clarify for ourselves what effect the strings are having in an orchestra, given that we can hear the horns well. Following the method of residue, we ask the horn section to sit out while the strings play.

The method of residue may be used to identify interfering causal factors as well. Suppose a patient is being given an antihypertensive drug that we know should have the effect of a reduction in blood pressure. Yet we observe that the patient is not responding as predicted. In searching for other antecedent circumstances we discover that the patient has been taking epinephrine to control a cold. Assuming that we can rule out other factors and given that the antihypertensive normally dilates blood vessels, we can reasonably conclude that the epinephrine is interfering. Letting f refer to the antihypertensive drug, g the epinephrine drug, and E reduced blood pressure, we are reasoning as follows:

1. *Antecedent circumstance f is known to cause E, i.e., all things being equal, in cases where f is present, E occurs*

2. *Case A: antecedent circumstances f and g, E does not occur*

_____

3. *Therefore, in case A, probably g causally interferes with f*

As the examples illustrate, the method of residue presupposes some causal knowledge of a phenomenon. Perhaps by means of the other methods, we have a partial understanding of the phenomenon. This method allows us to identify at least one, perhaps other causal factors contributing to the phenomenon.

Summary: Mill's Methods

Mill's methods provide four criteria for assessing the strength of arguments having a causal conclusion. In applying Mill's methods the following points should be observed.

First, Mill's methods assume that relevant circumstances or factors have been identified. That is, the use of Mill's methods requires a hypothesis about which kinds of circumstances are to be considered. Thus, in assessing an argument in support of a causal statement, we should consider whether a premise asserting that, for example, "in all instances of E, only antecedent circumstance f is present" is true. Are there relevant circumstances that have not been considered?

Second, consider the methods as *providing evidence* in support of or contrary to a causal claim. That is, if a causal claim—X causes Y—is supported by premises based on one of the methods, we will say that that causal claim is strengthened. Let us say, further, that a causal claim is given additional strength by premises based on more than one method.

Below is a shorthand summary with simple explanations, not rigorously expressed, of the four methods we have studied. In examining a particular argument use this general summary to direct you to the more detailed discussions above.

AGREEMENT

If a circumstance f is the only circumstance always present whenever E occurs, then we have supporting evidence for the conclusion that f is the cause of E.

Why? Because whatever is the cause of E will be present whenever E is present.

DIFFERENCE

If E occurs when f is present but not when f is absent, then we have supporting evidence for the conclusion that f causes E.

Why? Because the nonoccurrence of E is attributable to some difference in antecedent circumstances.

CONCOMITANT VARIATION

If one phenomenon varies consistently with another phenomenon, then we have supporting evidence that the two are causally related.

Why? Because if two variable phenomena are causally related, then they will exhibit concomitant variation.

(1) Given two phenomena that vary consistently, if one precedes the other, then we have supporting evidence that the former causes the latter.

(2) Given two phenomena that vary consistently, if by altering one we can produce concomitant variations in the other, then we have supporting evidence that the former causes the latter.

RESIDUE

If one or more parts of a phenomenon can be causally explained by one or more parts of the antecedent circumstances, then we have supporting evidence that the remaining part of the phenomenon can be causally explained by the remaining antecedent circumstance.

Why? Given a complex phenomenon represented as E1, E2, and E3 and antecedents f, g, and h; and given that E1 is causally explained by f, E2 is causally explained by g, then the only remaining factor to explain E3 is h.

Since these four methods provide evidence in support of a causal statement, we can say in summary that:

A causal conclusion is strong to the degree that it is supported by premises with evidence of one or more of Mill's methods.

Exercise 8.3D   Mill's Methods.   In the exercise below (1) identify the causal statement that is asserted; then (2) explain which method or methods are employed or should be employed to support the causal statement.

Sample Exercise   Researchers reported in *Scientific American* recently that some species of frogs are able to survive the winter by existing in a frozen state. Ice on the skin of the frog causes the liver to excrete large amounts of glucose into the blood system. The glucose in the blood acts to control the formation of ice crystals in the body and to prevent cellular collapse.
(1) The causal connection asserted in the passage is that between the presence of glucose in the frog's blood system and effects of freezing. (2) Mill's methods of agreement and difference are appropriate in this example. First, researchers have identified the glucose in the blood as the causal factor inhibiting the effects of freezing. Second, it would strengthen the causal claim to observe those cases in which the frog is frozen but the liver is prevented from excreting glucose into the blood.

1. Smith needs some more lavender paint. Previously he mixed red, blue, and white to make the shade he wanted. He knows that red and blue make purple, so he reasons that adding white must produce lavender.

2. Ralph reasons that his grades are improving over last semester's because this semester he is sleeping an extra hour each night.

3. Alice suspects that she is allergic to Bud's cat because every time she visits his house the cat is there and she starts sneezing. But when he visits her house, the cat isn't and she doesn't. Does she have good evidence for her suspicion? If so, by what method? If not, by what method can she confirm or disconfirm her suspicion?

4. Max plugged in the vacuum cleaner and flipped the on switch but nothing happened. Then he plugged in a lamp; it worked. Max concluded that the cause of the problem lies in the vacuum cleaner, not the electric outlet.

5. Kay-kay, a precocious three-year-old, reasoned that turning the knob on the stereo caused the music to get louder or softer because no matter how far or how fast she turned the knob, the sound changed along with it.

6. At the first weighing, the mother stepped onto the scale alone. Her weight caused the scale to show 150 lbs. At the second weighing, the mother stepped onto the scale holding her baby. Their combined weight registered 165 lbs. Thus, the weight of the baby, being the cause of the difference, is 15 lbs.

7. Comparing the cases in which women are employed in jobs involving a high degree of social interaction with cases in which women are not, we can conclude that, all things being equal, social interaction reduces the incidence of chronic ailment.

8. Seventeen customers reported being shortchanged during one week. All seventeen had receipts showing that Max was their cashier. It appears that Max is responsible.

9. Caffeine does not increase the risk of heart disease, for as a recent study shows, comparing caffeine users, users of decaffeinated products, and those who use neither, heart disease is as low for caffeine users as it is for those who use neither. The incidence of heart disease is slightly higher for those who use decaffeinated products.

10. Airplane crashes have a number of causes: equipment malfunction, weather conditions, pilot error, ground control error. Studies show that equipment malfunction, weather conditions, and pilot error account for 87 percent of airplane accidents examined in the past nineteen years. We conclude that 13 percent are due to ground control error.

11. If the cycle goes over a bump and the engine misfires, and then goes over another bump and the engine misfires, and then goes over another bump and the engine misfires, and then goes over a long smooth stretch of road and there is no misfiring, and then goes over a fourth bump and the engine misfires again, one can logically conclude that the misfiring is caused by the bumps. (Robert M. Pirsig, *Zen and the Art of Motorcycle Maintenance*)

12. The following letter to the editor appeared in the *New York Times*:
    "Studying Art with the Eye of a Physician" discusses the debunking of the theory that El Greco painted elongated figures because of astigmatism, a disorder in which the eyeball is more elongated than round. The proof that astigmatism did not cause El Greco to draw elongated figures is relatively simple:
    If he chose to draw a life-size man six feet tall, the man and his drawn image side by side would be the same length with or without astigmatism. An astigmatic person would perceive the length of the man and his life-size

image as equivalent. Any perceived distortion in length would apply to both the object and the drawn image.

I have noticed also that El Greco's elongation applied to vertical torsos, not to horizontal ones. If he were consistent, the hips of the reclining, horizontal figure would be 15 percent to 25 percent wider in the vertical direction. But I have not seen this in his paintings.

13. The following is an excerpt from a *New York Times* report on studies showing that "birds can calibrate their innate sense of magnetic north with the movement of celestial objects across the sky."

In a study performed by Kenneth P. and Mary A. Able of the State University of New York at Albany, 20 Savannah sparrows were divided into four groups and exposed to a rotating disk with dim lights resembling stars.

In the wild, young birds learn the location of true north by noting the axis of the rotation of the night sky.

But in the Ables' test, only one group of birds observed the rotation of the artificial stars at true north. For the other three groups, that point was located to the magnetic east, south or west.

When the birds were ready to migrate, they were placed in darkened boxes without the star patterns. Only the birds exposed to the "normal" pattern migrated south.

The others calibrated their compass to a point they believed to be north and veered off in the wrong direction.

In comparison, another group of sparrows raised seeing neither the actual sky nor the artificial patterns migrated according to magnetic north only.

14. According to a report in *Newsweek*:

People with two X chromosomes are usually female; an X and a Y make a male. But sometimes an XX is male and an XY is female. By studying these exceptions, researchers narrowed the search for the maleness gene to a smidgen of the Y—a piece that was absent from an XY female's Y, but present on an XX male's X. Researchers at the Imperial Cancer Research Fund in London used biochemical scissors to chop this smidgen of human DNA into 50 bits; they then mixed those bits with DNA segments from other mammals, male and female. Because a trait as basic as maleness is expected to have deep evolutionary roots and thus can be shared across species, the bit that found a match in every male was the best candidate for the masculinity gene.

15. A *New York Times* essay by William K. Stevens reports on a study showing that:

If a new analysis of the link between weather patterns in West Africa and the tropical Atlantic is correct, communities along the United States East Coast that experienced relatively few dangerous hurricanes in the 1970's and 1980's may face more frequent killer storms in the next two decades or so.

The analysis by William M. Gray of Colorado State University, an expert on tropical cyclones, found that when rain in the Western Sahel region of Africa is plentiful, more strong hurricanes develop in the Atlantic and strike the United States. The years from 1947 through 1969 were just such a time. In that period, the study found, 13 hurricanes with winds of more than 110 miles an hour slammed into the East Coast and Florida.

But when there is drought in the Western Sahel, fewer strong Atlantic hurricanes develop. According to this study, that was the case in the Sahel from 1970 through 1987, when only one storm with peak winds of more than 110 miles an hour struck the East Coast and Florida.

The study suggests that this relatively calm period is ending and that a more violent period is about to begin or may already have begun. And the potential for damage is greater now, Dr. Gray said. "There are more people and more development along the Atlantic Coast. . . . There is more property to damage."

8.4 Argument from Analogy

An argument from analogy draws a conclusion about something on the basis of an analogy to some other thing. For example, you may reason that since your last car was a Ford and it held up well, then your present car, also a Ford, will hold up well too. What is true of your previous car is likely to be true of your present car because they are both Fords. The reasoning is that if two or more things are alike in some respects, they are alike in some other respect. Letting A and B represent two different things, events, or practices and letting f, g, h, and j represent features or properties, we can represent the form of analogical reasoning as follows:

FORM OF ARGUMENT FROM ANALOGY

(A and B are analogous in that . . .)

A and B are both f, g, and h

A is also j

Therefore, probably B is j

Let us call the thing, event, or practice at issue in the argument the *subject*. In the formal expression above B is the subject. Let us call that to which the analogy is drawn the *analogue*. Further, let us call the feature j possessed by A and concluded to be possessed by B the *inferred feature*. Last, we will call the similarities that form the basis of the analogy the *common features*. Thus, the reasoning is that subject B has inferred feature j because B has common features f, g, h with A, the analogue. Although this is cumbersome, it will help in talking about this type of argument.

Consider now some examples of arguments from analogy and notice the assertion of an analogy between the subject of the argument and the analogue.

Example 25

The economic depression of the thirties was turned around by extensive federal jobs programs. We are cur-

rently in a similar economic situation, so it is probable that federal jobs programs are needed to solve the current economic problem.

Example 26

Machines are the products of intelligence. They are ordered systems consisting of parts deliberately designed to perform certain functions. The universe, too, is an ordered system, albeit on a much greater magnitude, consisting of parts perfectly adapted to certain ends. Thus, it is reasonable to conclude that the universe is also a product of intelligence.

Example 27

Just as no one is under an obligation to donate his or her kidney to a person who needs one to live, so no pregnant woman is under an obligation to donate the use of her womb to the person, the fetus, who requires it to live.

In each of the examples above a conclusion is drawn about the subject under discussion—the current economic situation, the universe, and the obligation of a pregnant woman to the fetus, respectively—on the basis of what is asserted to be true of an analogue, the previous economic depression, machines, and the obligation of persons with healthy kidneys to persons in need of a kidney. How do we assess such arguments? What do we look for in evaluating the strength of analogical reasoning?

The inductive strength of an analogical argument essentially depends on two considerations: (1) How does the possession of the common features bear on the possession of the inferred feature? Is being like A in virtue of features f, g, and h good reason for concluding that B also possesses j? (2) Is there any relevant dissimilarity between A and B? Is there a difference between the two that might bear negatively on B's possessing the inferred feature? A summary description of the inductive strength of the argument from analogy can be put as follows:

> *An argument from analogy is inductively strong to the degree that:*
> *(1) the common features are relevant to the inferred feature; and*
> *(2) there are no relevant dissimilarities.*

We will call these two considerations the criteria of inductive strength in arguments from analogy. There is a third consideration we must look at, the *extent of the similarity* between the subject and the analogue. However, we will see that the extent of similarity between subject and analogue is less important than whether the similarities are relevant and there are no relevant dissimilarities, that is, criteria (1) and (2) above.

Assessing an argument from analogy frequently requires that we attempt to make explicit information that is not provided in the premises. What are we told in the argument and, more importantly, what do we already know about the subject, the analogue, or the relevance of the purported analogy? Both examples 25 and 27 above are typical arguments; they leave much unstated. In assessing Example 25, for instance, we need to ask, what are the features common to the depression of the thirties and today's economic situation? Is it because of those features that federal jobs programs succeeded in changing the economy? Or are there relevant differences today that would make federal jobs programs ineffective? Given that background information is presupposed in the typical argument from analogy, if we were to make explicit and express formally those claims, then the form of an inductively strong argument from analogy is this:

1. *A and B are f, g, h.*

2. *A is also j.*

3. *Features f, g, and h are relevant to the possession of feature j.*

4. *There is no feature k possessed by B but not A that bears negatively on the presence of j.*

---

5. *Therefore, B is probably j.*

Premises (3) and (4) above express what is presupposed in a strong analogical argument. Thus, to the extent that an argument meets the criteria of relevant features and no relevant dissimilarities, it is strong. In what follows we will examine and illustrate statements (3) and (4) to see how they bear on the strength of analogical arguments.

(1) The similarities are extensive   The first premise in our construction of the form of an inductively strong analogical argument asserts that the subject and the analogue have some number of features in common. (The form of the premise lists three common features. This is only for illustration, of course.)

Now it would seem that the greater the similarity between two things, the stronger the argument, but in fact this consideration turns out to be less reliable than the other two. The situation with the extent of similarity is reminiscent of what we saw about sample size in inductive generalizations. But let's see why sheer number of similarities is, generally, no real virtue in an analogical argument.

Consider an example in which two things are said to be alike in a number of ways:

Example 28

In respect of color, shape, and size, an orange is more like a peach than a pineapple. Furthermore, oranges and peaches come from trees that are very similar in appearance, while the pineapple comes from a short, tough, lance-leaved shrub. The orange contains citric acid. Probably, a peach contains citric acid, whereas a pineapple does not.

In this example the extensive similarities mislead us; just the opposite is true of peaches and pineapples. Why does that argument fail in spite of the numerous similarities? It is because the stated similarities do not bear on whether a fruit has citric acid. The example suggests two points: (1) if the features two things have in common are *not* relevant to the inferred feature, then the number of common features does not matter; and (2) two things, like the orange and pineapple, may have few, if any, observable similarities, yet still be alike in possessing the inferred feature.

How, then, does extent of similarity bear on the strength of an analogical argument? It is important in three ways. First, just as a matter of probability, the greater the points of similarity between two things, the more likely a relevant similarity, if present, will appear in the set of common features. Thus, *extent of similarities* may be indirectly related to the criteria of (1) relevance and (2) no relevant dissimilarity.

Second, if we have no grounds for judging the relevance of common features to the inferred feature, then knowing only that two or more things are similar in a number of ways is positive evidence of further similarities.

Example 29

A and B are spherical, yellow, waxy, small, and light.
A is sweet-tasting. Probably B is sweet-tasting.

If all we know is that A and B are alike as described, then the conclusion drawn seems reasonable. Indeed, given the premises in example 29 it is reasonable to expect that A and B are of the same kind.

Third, having a number of similarities in common is usually what we expect of things that are members of the same kind. (Think of two or more Fords, gumballs, no. 2 pencils, Shetland ponies, etc.) Some arguments from analogy are based on a premise stating that the subject is a member of a kind. For example, the following argument illustrates this type of reasoning by analogy:

Example 30	FORM
Most sociologists are liberals.	*Most X's are j*
Max is a sociologist.	*B is an X*
Therefore, Max is probably a liberal.	*B is j*

Implicit in the argument is that Max shares common features with sociologists in virtue of being a sociologist. (If it sounds odd to you to say that Max is analogous to or similar to sociologists when, after all, he *is* one, consider that Max could only be a sociologist if he did in fact share some common features with them, such as, for example, the same kind of training.)

Although B's being a member of kind X provides some reason for thinking that B has some feature common to X's, nevertheless the argument assumes that B is typical of X's. The strength of an argument like example 30 depends on whether Max is a *typical* sociologist. Max might have those features that make him a sociologist, yet be a rather atypical one. Thus, while being a member of a kind is some positive evidence for an inference, again we see that the number of similarities between two things or types of things is less important than the kinds of similarities, the criterion expressed in (2) above. We need to consider that criterion next.

(2) The similarities are relevant to the inferred feature   If the conclusion of an analogical argument is strongly supported by its premises, then implicit, at least, in the premises is that the common features are relevant to the inferred feature. Let's focus on statement (3) in the formal expression of a strong argument.

1. *A and B are f, g, h*

2. *A is also j*

3. **Features f, g, and h are relevant to the possession of feature j**

4. *There is no feature k possessed by B but not A that bears negatively on the presence of j.*

Therefore, probably B is j

What makes common features relevant to the possession of the inferred feature? Features the subject and analogue have in common may be relevant to the inference in different ways. Let's consider four kinds of relevance, giving us four different kinds of analogical arguments. This classification is not exhaustive but it does illustrate some of the variations found in analogical reasoning. The four we consider are causal, statistical, moral and aesthetic analogies.

(2a) Causal Analogies   One way in which common features may be relevant is that they are *causally connected* to the inferred feature. Perhaps it is the case that features f, g, and h are causally sufficient or necessary for j. Consider this example.

Example 31

Although both Jalapeño and Serrano chiles are different in size and color, both contain the acid capsaicin. Jalapeños leave a strong burning sensation in the mouth. Probably Serranos do as well.

The acid capsaicin causes the burning sensation; thus, having that acid in common with Jalapeños provides good evidence that Serranos are hot too.

A common method of reasoning in science is to explore one phenomenon by means of what is purported to be an analogue called a model. For example, one very important and deservedly controversial area in which analogical reasoning is assumed to be valuable is in scientific research using animals to gain information about humans. Regarding the animal as a model of human physiology, researchers draw conclusions about, for example, human susceptibility to disease on the basis of the animal's susceptibility to disease. The inferences made are causal analogies.

In the following example a physical model is used as evidence of the activity of atoms.

Example 32

In support of the theory of molecular motion, Einstein attempted to produce an observable mechanical consequence of the action of atoms. Searching for phenomena large enough to be viewed through a microscope yet small enough to respond to the mechanical actions of atoms, he found it in the phenomenon known to biologists as Brownian motion. If one suspends a fine powder . . . in a liquid and studies the grains through a microscope, he notes that they are in continual trembling, random motion. (Adapted from Contemporary Physics *by David Park)*

(2b) Statistical Analogies   Another way in which common features may be relevant to the inferred feature is that they are frequently found together. A frequently occurring correlation of features gives some evidence for inferring the one whenever the other or others are present. Since such correlations can be studied and described statistically, we can call analogical arguments based on correlations statistical analogies. Our observations suggest that the probability is high that whenever features f, g, and h are present, the inferred feature j is also present.

Example 33

In district 4 the majority of residents have incomes above $80,000. They almost always elect the Republican candidate in their district elections. District 6 is also populated with high-income residents; therefore, they will probably vote Republican.

Example 34

A study of physicians' attitudes toward patient autonomy showed that physicians at Boston University Medical Center, a teaching hospital, rated patient autonomy an important value. Physicians at an equally large but nonteaching metropolitan hospital rated patient autonomy as having less value in their practice. Since the Dartmouth hospital is a large teaching hospital, we should expect physicians' attitudes like those of the BU hospital.

(2c) Moral Analogies   To draw a moral conclusion on the basis of an analogy is to reason that what is morally true about one case is true about another because they are similar cases. It is presupposed that features f, g, and h support the same moral judgment about the subject as is made about the analogue. For example, since case A is a case of lying and therefore morally wrong, case B, also a case of lying, is also morally wrong. Consider these examples.

Example 35

A pet of any sort is certainly as dependent on its owner as a child is on its parents. Neither pet nor child can live and develop well without basic attention to its needs, consistency in treatment, and affection. Thus, since what's good for a child should always be considered, so also what's good for a pet should be considered.

Example 36

Since Smith was punished with a fine and two months in jail for driving while intoxicated, Jones, who committed the same offense, should receive the same punishment.

Example 37

Recently the parents of a child dying from kidney failure made their plea for a kidney donor on national television. Some weeks later the host of that show proudly announced that a donor had been located and the child was doing well after a successful transplantation of a new kidney. There is a serious injustice in a case like this, an injustice to those children and parents who happen not to have access to national television but who wait patiently and bravely, following the nationally agreed-upon rules for allocation of organs. There is a child just like the child of those TV parents, whose turn was taken by someone else.

In example 37 the argument is that an injustice is done when two similar cases are not given the same treatment.

(2d) Aesthetic Analogies To draw an aesthetic conclusion about something is to conclude that it has or lacks aesthetic merit or some particular aesthetic quality. You might support your conclusion on the basis of an analogy to a case you think is uncontroversial. For example, since performance A was dynamic, sensitive, and intelligently executed and you judged it aesthetically good, then performance B, also dynamic, sensitive, and intelligently executed, should also be judged aesthetically good. Consider these examples.

Example 38

The movie Lethal Weapon II *is worth seeing because it has the same actors as* Lethal Weapon, *and it maintains the same fast-paced excitement and comic irony that we saw in the first one. Much of the success of the first version is due to the improbable pairing of actors Mel Gibson and Danny Glover, playing two opposite personality types.*

Example 39

These two shades of turquoise and orange will really liven up your kitchen and make it cheerful and inviting. Just look at how exciting these colors look together when you hold up these samples in the light.

Example 40

On the current Metropolitan Museum exhibit "Mexico: Splendors of Thirty Centuries," a Newsweek *reporter writes: "The whole idea of . . . squeezing the art history of an entire nation of nearly 90,000,000 people and three distinct civilizations into part of a floor of the Met seems a little sad, if not absurd. Would the Italians have sat still for a few galleries each of imperial Rome, the Renaissance and the industrial age?"*

In this example it is argued that the exhibit is aesthetically flawed because the cultures it represents are as complex as the Italian cultures and a similar presentation of the Italians would be aesthetically flawed.

(3) There are no relevant dissimilarities Let us focus on the second criterion of a strong inductive analogy by considering statement (4) in the formal account:

*(4) There is no feature k possessed by B but not A
that bears negatively on the presence of j.*

If there is a dissimilarity between the subject and the analogue, then there is some feature possessed by one and not the other. Differences as such do not create a disanalogy; differences are to be expected. For instance, in example 28 it matters little that oranges and pineapples come from plants that are so different in appearance. However, when a difference bears negatively on the possession of the inferred feature, a disanalogy exists. For example, in thinking about example 27 above—where it is argued that mothers have no more obligation to bring a fetus to term than healthy people do to those who need a kidney transplant—it is arguably a relevant difference that a fetus may have a right to use the mother's womb, whereas a donor hardly ever has a right to another's kidney. If that difference can be supported, then criterion (2) has not been met and the argument is weakened. Consider this example.

Example 41

*Maxine has demonstrated that she knows how to apply
CPR (cardiopulmonary resuscitation) and how to remain calm and controlled in simulated cases of cardiac
arrest using a dummy. Therefore, she can be expected
to treat actual cardiac patients effectively and calmly.*

The argument concludes that Maxine can be expected to handle actual cardiac patients effectively because she has done so in demonstrations with dummies. Yet there
is certainly a significant psychological difference between treating a dummy and
treating a person who might die because of one's actions. An awareness of that risk is
liable to produce anxiety and affect Maxine's behavior; she may freeze or fail to remember the proper procedure. Suppose, however, the analogy had been constructed
on the basis of Maxine's performance in some previous case of actual cardiac arrest.
No disanalogy could be raised and the argument would be stronger. As it is, example 41 fails to meet criterion (2).

We show that an argument from analogy is weak or at least weakened by
showing that there is a relevant difference between the cases. Conversely, we add
strength to an argument by showing that no such relevant difference exists. For example, in defense of example 41 two kinds of replies are appropriate. One is to show
that the purported dissimilarity, the anxiety, is not adversely relevant to proper behavior in actual cases. Repeated practice does not reduce anxiety but it does ensure
proper behavior. She will be frightened but her actions will be almost automatic.
Another reply is to argue that the adversely relevant factor, anxiety, does not usually
occur in people who have been so thoroughly tested as has Maxine. She is unlikely
to be frightened. In short, the debate about the strength of an analogy is likely to
turn on whether the relevant negative feature is present or whether, being present, it
does indeed make the inferred feature less probable.

Summary: Argument from Analogy

1. An argument from analogy draws a conclusion about one thing on the basis
of an analogy to some other thing.

2. The form of an argument from analogy is:

A and B are both f, g, and h

A is also j

Therefore, probably B is j

3. The terms we employ to talk about the argument are the following.

Subject: That person, thing, or event, represented by B, about which a conclusion is drawn.

Analogue: That person, thing, or event, represented by A, to which B is claimed to be analogous.

Common features: Those features, here f, g, h, possessed by both A and B that are the basis for the analogy.

Inferred feature: That feature, j, present with A and concluded as belonging as well to B.

4. There are two criteria of the inductive strength of an argument from analogy. They are:

   (1) the common features are relevant to the inferred feature; and

   (2) there are no relevant dissimilarities.

5. A common feature is relevant to the presence of the inferred feature if it increases the likelihood of the presence of the inferred feature. Specifically, common features may be relevant to an inferred feature in ways such as the following.

   Causal analogy: Common features are causally connected to the presence of the inferred feature.

   Statistical analogy: Common features are statistically correlated with the presence of the inferred feature.

   Moral analogy: Common features justifying a moral judgment about the analogue justify the same moral judgment about the subject.

   Aesthetic analogy: Common features justifying an aesthetic judgment about the analogue justify the same aesthetic judgment about the subject.

Exercise 8.4   Arguments from Analogy.   Identify the subject and analogue. Discuss whether the analogy is relevant or irrelevant by supplying, where necessary, background information about common features. Given the information provided, would you judge it to be inductively strong? If not, why?

Sample Exercise   A *Newsweek* article reports concerns over the use of mercury in dental fillings. At a meeting of the American Physiological Society scientists presented evidence that mercury "seriously compromises" organ systems in test animals. Researchers at the University of Calgary placed twelve amalgam fillings in the mouths of six ewes. Within two months, the test animals experienced a loss of kidney function of between 16 percent and 80 percent; control animals suffered no loss. And in the first study in primates, the Calgary team reports that in monkeys the mercury winds up in the kidneys, intestinal tract, and jaws. Canadian and American researchers concluded that mercury in fillings should be banned immediately.

Subject: humans; *analogue:* ewes and primates. Argument: Mercury amalgam fillings cause organ problems in ewes and primates. Ewes and primates are like humans. Therefore, mercury amalgam fillings probably cause organ problems in humans. Therefore, they should be banned.

Relevant analogy? We might wonder how alike ewes and humans are but primates are the closest, physiologically, of all animal groups to humans. The study reports no relevant dissimilarities. It is reasonable to conclude that this is a strong analogical argument.

1. Police officers routinely practice the use of their service revolvers at a firing range. An officer who does well in target practice ought to do well in actual situations requiring the use of a revolver.

2. Like a religion, dianetics has a comprehensive body of beliefs about what we are, where we came from, our purpose, a diagnosis of our ills, and a prescription for how to live well. Furthermore, like a religion it postulates supernatural forces at work in human nature. The science of dianetics purports to be a science but it should be classified as a religion.

3. Organisms—plants and animals of all varieties—are highly organized systems composed of parts that cannot exist independently, that work together harmoniously, and whose activities are irreversible. Every organism we know of is the product of the natural processes of chemical interaction and biological reproduction. The universe is like an organism, for what we see in it is exactly what we see in them. Thus, it is probable that the universe is a product of natural processes.

4. I wouldn't buy a Zephyr. Marie bought a new one, and within a year she had to have the transmission completely replaced.

5. The other day Dad and I happened to see Madonna on TV and Dad said she was pretty. So when I saw this tie with a picture of Madonna on it, I knew it would be a perfect present for him to wear at Bab's wedding on Saturday!

6. The problem with Bart Simpson is that he looks like a pencil eraser with eyeballs. Anybody with those looks has got to be a lot of trouble.

7. When I observe myself, I see that if fire touches me I jump and feel pain. What I see in others is that when fire touches them, they also jump. Since they behave as I do, and since they are so much like me, I reason that they too feel pain.

8. Konrad Lorenz, a pioneer in the study of animal behavior, has observed that many species of animals are innately aggressive. Given that humans are animals too, the same conclusion about us seems to follow.

9. Cats lack the special nerve cell that in humans is believed to be responsible for color vision. Since they lack that nerve cell, and since they are like us in so many other ways, it is likely that on this score they differ. They don't see color as we do.

10. Consider a child who reacts to a first stimulus of thirst by drinking from his glass of milk. One day the glass is filled with buttermilk, and the child receives an unexpected second stimulus. The next time he is thirsty he may refuse his milk until convinced that it is not buttermilk.

When a household appliance is plugged in, the outlet provides the necessary electric current. This is normal behavior; it corresponds to the child habitually drinking his milk. Then one day a defective lamp is plugged in and the fuse burns out. The burnt fuse corresponds to the child's memory of the buttermilk. The outlet will no longer provide current to appliances until the memory has been removed by inserting a new fuse. Both the child and the electric circuit have "learned by experience." (Marshall Walker, *The Nature of Scientific Thought,* p. 14)

11. The tackling dummy constitutes a material model of a football player because its inertia corresponds to the inertia of the player. The coach can use it to make predictions. "If our 140-pound center tends to bounce off the tackling dummy, he will probably bounce off an opposing player also." The dummy may look somewhat like a football player, but such a resemblance is irrelevant. (Marshall Walker, *The Nature of Scientific Thought,* p. 3)

12. Just as we see that fallow land, if rich and fertile, teems with a hundred thousand kinds of wild and useless weeds, and that to see it work we must subject it and sow it with certain seeds for our service; and as we see that women, all alone, produce mere shapeless masses and lumps of flesh, but that to create a good and natural offspring they must be made fertile with a different kind of seed; so it is with minds. Unless you keep them busy with some definite subject that will bridle and control them, they throw themselves in disorder hither and yon in the vague field of imagination. (Montaigne, "Of Idleness")

13. We can point to the fact that the nervous systems of all vertebrates, and especially of birds and mammals, are fundamentally similar. Those parts of the human nervous system that are concerned with feeling pain are relatively old, in evolutionary terms. Unlike the cerebral cortex, which developed only after our ancestors diverged from other mammals, the basic nervous system evolved in more distant ancestors common to ourselves and the other "higher" animals. This anatomical parallel makes it likely that the capacity of animals to feel is similar to our own. (Peter Singer, *Practical Ethics*)

14. Regarding the use of scientific experimentation on animals, Peter Singer argues in *Animal Liberation:* If experimentation on retarded, orphaned humans would be wrong, why isn't experimenting on nonhuman animals wrong? What difference is there between the two, except for the mere fact that, biologically, one is a member of our species and the other is not? But *that,* surely, is not a morally relevant difference. . . .

15. Since the probability of winning 1 million dollars in the national clearinghouse sweepstakes is 1 in 70,000 and the MacDonald's sweepstakes is also a national lottery for a million dollars, it is likely that it, too, has a winning ratio of 1 in 70,000.

16. Suburban residents interviewed outside Albany said, eight times out of ten, that education should have priority in local funding. Troy is a suburb of Albany, so probably residents of Troy support giving priority to education.

Summary

1. An argument is *inductively strong* just in case, given its premises, (1) it is deductively invalid and (2) it is more probable than not that the conclusion follows. An *inductively weak* argument is one that is deductively invalid and it is more probable than not that the conclusion does *not* follow.

2. *Inductive generalization:* An argument with the conclusion that something is the case about all or many things on the basis of what is observed about some of them.

   An inductive generalization is inductively strong *to the degree that the sample on which the generalization is based is representative of the population. Otherwise it is inductively weak.*
   Criterion of inductive strength: representativeness of the sample.

3. *Causal arguments:* arguments in which at least one causal statement (a statement of the form "X causes Y") occurs as a premise or as the conclusion.

   Causal conclusion: *an argument consisting of premises in support of a causal statement.*
   A causal conclusion is inductively strong *to the degree that its premises describe evidence from one or more of Mill's methods. Otherwise it is inductively weak.*
   Agreement: If f is present whenever E occurs, then probably f causes E.
   Difference: If f is present whenever E occurs, but absent whenever E fails to occur, then probably f causes E.
   Concomitant variation: If f varies consistently with E, then f and E are probably causally related.
   Residue: If f causes E1, g causes E2, then the remaining factor h probably causes the remaining effect E3.
   Criterion of inductive strength: premises with evidence from one or more of Mill's methods.

4. *Arguments from analogy:* An argument in which a conclusion is drawn about one thing on the basis of an analogy to some other thing.
   An argument from analogy is inductively strong to the degree that the common features are relevant to the inferred feature and there are no relevant dissimilarities.

   Criteria of inductive strength:
   (1) common features are relevant to the inferred feature; and
   (2) there are no relevant dissimilarities.

Review Questions Chapter 8

1. According to your text, what are the features of an inductive generalization and the terms used to refer to them?

2. What is the difference between a simple random sample and a stratified random sample?

3. What is a random sample? Explain how random sampling improves the likelihood of obtaining a representative sample.

4. Briefly explain these terms as they are used in your text:
    a. causal statement
    b. causal prediction
    c. causal explanation
    d. causal argument
    e. proximate cause

5. In your own words, explain Mill's:
    a. method of agreement
    b. method of difference
    c. method of concomitant variation
    d. method of residue

6. What, according to your text, are the terms used to talk about the elements of an argument from analogy?

7. What are the criteria for inductive strength in arguments from analogy?

8. Given that we assign numerical values to arguments ranging from 0 to 1 (0 being the worst), explain in your own words how you would arrange deductively valid, deductively invalid, strong, and weak inductive arguments.

True or False?

1. Given that the car starts whenever the temperature, with wind chill, is above freezing, but fails to start when the temperature is below freezing, you could infer by the method of agreement that the freezing temperature is causing the car failure.

2. If a person reasoned that her chemistry class will be difficult because it is a lab class like biology and biology was difficult, then she would be making an inductive generalization.

3. Two criteria of a strong causal conclusion are that a phenomenon has been found present in all cases in which circumstance C is present and absent in all cases in which C is absent.

4. Causal arguments are arguments that include a causal statement as a premise or conclusion.

5. In the statement "Bovine growth hormone (BHG) causes increased milk production," a sufficient condition of increased production is the introduction of BHG.

6. Strong inductive generalizations require large samples.

7. A moral analogy is a kind of argument in which a moral conclusion is supported by some moral authority.

8. A sample is randomly constructed if every member of the sample is of the same generic type.

9. According to your text, every inductively strong argument is inductively invalid.

10. If an argument fails to be deductively valid, it fails to be a good argument.

CHAPTER NINE
Informal Fallacies

This chapter presents a survey of several common *informal fallacies*—errors in reasoning that we can detect only by examining the content or meanings of the words in the argument. The study of informal fallacies is one of the major enterprises of *informal logic*.

A *fallacy* is an error in reasoning. Both deductive and inductive arguments may be fallacious. Some fallacies are detectable by an examination of the *form* of the argument; they are called *formal fallacies*. (The techniques for evaluating deductive validity that we learn in categorical and truth-functional logic enable us to recognize many sorts of formal fallacies.) All other fallacies are called *informal fallacies,* and they must be detected by an examination of the *content* of the argument.

Logicians have distinguished many types of informal fallacies, although they have by no means agreed on uniform classifications. Nevertheless, certain common types are recognized fairly universally, and these are the ones surveyed in this chapter. Many informal fallacies are traditionally referred to by their Latin names, so those Latin names appear in parentheses in the headings.

9.1 Appeal to Authority
(*Argumentum ad Verecundiam*)

An *appeal to authority* is an argument in which the testimony of someone believed to be an authority is cited in support of a conclusion. The fallacy occurs when the person cited is not in fact an authority on the matter or for some reason should not be relied upon. Here are three examples:

Example 1

Well, I wouldn't listen to Bishop Desmond Tutu's version of the situation in South Africa, because Jerry Falwell says that Tutu is a phony.

Example 2

According to my physics professor, Emily Dickinson's poetry is for the birds. That's good enough for me.

Example 3

Marvis Frazier is America's greatest boxer. I have that on the authority of Marvis's father, Joe Frazier.

The underlying idea of such arguments is that some statement S is true because some authority A has said it is true. The argument's basic structure is this:

Authority A asserts that S.

Therefore, S.

You see immediately that such an argument is neither valid nor inductively strong, since the mere fact that someone asserts S neither makes it so nor makes it probable. Typically, however, the arguer believes more than the mere fact that A asserts that S. The arguer very likely is assuming such things as that A is someone who knows what he or she is talking about regarding S, or that A is speaking without bias, or that A is telling the truth. If those or similar assumptions are well founded, then the appeal to authority A *may* constitute good—that is, nonfallacious—reasoning. Not all appeals to authority are fallacious; some may be inductively strong. After all, we should accept the testimony of qualified and unbiased experts, for we cannot be experts in every field ourselves.

The fallacy of appeal to authority occurs when the authority cited is not qualified in the relevant matters or, less typically, is not free from adverse influences. Thus, the arguer is relying upon the assertions of someone who is not truly in a position to know.

To identify the fallacy of appeal to authority, we ask two questions: (1) Is the authority in fact a *qualified* authority about matters related to S? (2) Is there any good reason to believe that the authority may be biased in matters related to S? Regarding example 1 given above, we should ask, Is Jerry Falwell qualified to claim that Bishop Tutu is a phony? Is Falwell an expert on South Africa and the political representation of the protesters? Regarding example 2, we should ask, Is a physics professor likely to be an authority on American poets? And regarding example 3, although we know that Joe Frazier *is* a boxing expert, we may ask if he is impartial when it comes to his own son.

A common variation on the appeal to authority is an appeal to a magazine or newspaper article or a radio or TV program. Consider this example: 'They've found a cure for cancer. I read about it in *Popular Mechanics*'. In such cases we ought to ask the same question: Is the source cited a reliable one in this matter? Ordinarily, we should be very suspicious of medical breakthroughs reported in *Popular Mechanics*, though not of such breakthroughs reported in, say, *The Journal of the American Medical Association*. On the other hand, we would not expect to get reliable advice on automobiles in a medical journal. The fallacy occurs when an argument is supported by reference to a publication or program not known for specialization on the subject.

In summary, not all appeals to authority are fallacious. The fallacy occurs when an arguer appeals to someone who is not an expert in the field for which he or she is cited as support or who is not unbiased.

To recognize the appeal to authority, look for an argument based primarily on the premise that some person (or some publication) reports that S is true. The fallacy occurs when the person (or publication) is not relevantly qualified or is not speaking without bias.

9.2 Appeal to the People (*Argumentum ad Populum*)

The *appeal to the people* fallacy is a variation on the appeal to authority. It consists in arguing that some statement S is true because most people believe S. It is, in effect, an appeal to commonly or traditionally held beliefs. Many advertisements recommend a product by asserting that "everyone uses it," as for example, in this ad for Ford trucks:

Example 4

America's best-selling pickups: Ford.

The unstated premise is that the best-selling pickup truck is the *best* pickup truck, and the conclusion is that since you ought to buy the best, you ought to buy a Ford. But of course the fact that Ford sells the most pickups entails neither that Fords are the best nor that you ought to buy one.

Here are some other examples of the appeal to the people:

Example 5

Well, for centuries people have believed in God, and I just don't see how so many people could be mistaken. So that's why I choose to believe.

Example 6

Working one's way through college is a cherished American concept. (Dr. Newman, former president of the University of Rhode Island)

In the first example the arguer bases a decision to believe in God on the fact that, as he or she claims, people throughout the centuries have so believed. The implicit inference of Dr. Newman's statement is that working one's way through college is good because it is "a cherished American concept." Both arguments commit the fallacy of appeal to the people.

To recognize the fallacy of appeal to the people, look for an argument in which the conclusion is based on assertions about commonly or traditionally held beliefs.

9.3 Appeal to Force (*Argumentum ad Baculum*)

An *appeal to force* is an argument based upon a threat. Arguers using this type of appeal try to persuade you by pointing out their power over you or by warning you of the bad consequences of refusing to accept their argument. Consider these examples:

Example 7

Ladies and gentlemen of the jury, if you do not bring in a verdict of guilty, you may be this killer's next victim!

Example 8

Look, I give out the grades in this course, so I guess I should know that your answer is wrong!

Example 9

Smith, we can't have this statement on expenditures coming to the attention of the president. You've been the

*accountant here for nearly twenty years. It would be a
shame to ruin all that now. I think it would be wise of
you to take another look at the books, don't you?*

Rather than offering a relevant reason for the conclusion, the arguer poses a threat to the listener, saying, in effect, "Accept my conclusion or you'll be sorry." Obviously, the fact that the arguer poses a threat does not make the arguer's conclusion true or even probably true.

*You may recognize the fallacy of appeal to force by the presence of a threat either ex-
plicit or, as in the third example above, subtly disguised.*

9.4 Appeal to Pity
(*Argumentum ad Misericordiam*)

Someone offering an *appeal to pity* is reasoning, in effect, "You should accept my conclusion out of pity." Such arguers urge you to believe something by arousing your sympathy for them or their cause. For example, imagine an attorney defending his client to the jury:

Example 10

*There is no question that what this young man did is
intolerable and repugnant. He admits it himself. But
you're not here to evaluate this man's conduct morally;
you're here to try him and determine his guilt or inno-
cence. And as you think this over, I want you to think
hard about this young man, his home life and his future, which you now hold in your hands. Think about
his broken home, never knowing his father, being left
by his mother. Think about the poverty he's known,
the foster homes, the birthdays going unnoticed, and
the Christmas he's never had. And think hard about
what life in prison will do to him. Think about these
things, and I know you will acquit him of this crime.*

This clever lawyer makes quite a case for his client's miserable and unfortunate life. Although all of it may be true, it would be fallacious to conclude that the defendant is *not* guilty because his life has been hard or because finding him guilty would add to his misery.

To recognize the fallacy of appeal to pity, look for premises that appeal to your sympathy.

9.5 Appeal to Ignorance
(*Argumentum ad Ignorantiam*)

When arguers claim that some statement S is true because, they say, we have failed to show that S is false, they are guilty of the fallacy of *appeal to ignorance*. If they argue that S is false because we have failed to show that S is true, they are also guilty of this fallacy. In each case the lack of proof or good evidence for the truth (or falsity) of S is used as a reason for concluding that S is false (or true). The two forms of the appeal to ignorance look like this:

We do not know that S is false.

Therefore, S is true.

We do not know that S is true.

Therefore, S is false.

Consider this example:

Example 11

Well, I've examined all the arguments for the existence of God, and I've seen that none of them proves that God exists. That's reason enough for me: there is no God!

The speaker concludes that there is no God because there are no successful proofs of God's existence. But the absence of a successful proof of God's existence does not justify concluding that there is no God. What the speaker *is* justified in concluding is that we do not know.

Similarly, some people have been behaving irrationally about the disease AIDS. For example, several Hollywood actors have refused to play scenes opposite potential AIDS carriers. Scientists say that although their research has not proven that AIDS *cannot* be transmitted by casual contact, neither has it produced evidence that it *can* be transmitted by such contact. Yet some people interpret this as follows:

Example 12

Scientists have not proven that AIDS cannot be transmitted through casual contact. Therefore, we should avoid casual contact with suspected AIDS carriers.

Here the fact that the possibility of contracting the disease through casual contact has not been disproven is taken as a reason for acting on that possibility.

The lack of evidence that S is true (or not true) should not, in most cases, be taken as proof that S is not true (or true). However, there are at least two kinds of cases that resemble the appeal to ignorance in which a lack of evidence may justify the conclusion that S is true (or not true). In a court of law the failure to establish that a person has committed a crime is considered sufficient to allow us to conclude that the person is not guilty. Thus, lawyers may argue that their clients are innocent because there is no evidence of their guilt. Notice, however, that finding a person innocent or not guilty in a court of law is not a determination that the person did not commit the crime; it is a determination that the evidence does not justify a judgment of guilt. So if we concluded that a defendant did not commit the crime because he or she was found not guilty, we would be committing the fallacy of appeal to ignorance. Similarly, in scientific reasoning a failure to disconfirm or disprove a hypothesis lends support to the hypothesis, although it does not usually justify concluding that the hypothesis is true. Rather, each failure to disconfirm the hypothesis indicates that it is more probable.

The second kind of case in which a lack of evidence may justify a conclusion about a statement is one in which investigation can be expected to tell us what is or is not so. For example, the fact that X rays reveal no evidence of a fracture is a good reason for concluding that there is no fracture, since we can expect a fracture to show up on X rays. Or consider the case of the Loch Ness monster. The fact that repeated searches have produced no evidence of this monster makes it probable, though not certain, that it does not exist. If there were a Loch Ness monster, we would expect some indication of its presence. As you can see, these are cases in which the results of an investigation are relevant to the truth-value of a statement. The fallacy of appeal to ignorance occurs when the lack of evidence or proof is not relevant to the conclusion but the arguer believes that it is.

To recognize the fallacy of appeal to ignorance, look for a conclusion based upon an absence of proof or evidence. Be aware of the two types of cases in which lack of evidence for S is relevant to the truth or falsity of S.

9.6 *Ad Hominem*

An *ad hominem* argument is an attack upon the person rather than the person's ideas. The name of this fallacy comes from the Latin and means literally "against the person." There are three common types of *ad hominem* arguments: abusive, circumstantial, and *tu quoque* ("you, too!").

The *ad hominem* abusive argument is an attack on the opponent's character implying that what he or she says should not be believed because of this character flaw. Consider these examples:

Example 13

Well now, you've all heard Professor Clark tell us
about the theory of evolution. But I'm not surprised
that he neglected to tell you that he is a godless atheist!
How can this man speak the truth, I ask you?

Example 14

*Ted Kennedy says he'd make a good president. But he's
no man for the White House; not only has he been
divorced, but he's a Catholic and divorced!*

The abusive *ad hominem* argument, in effect, involves two claims: first, that the opponent possesses a certain undesirable or negative characteristic and, secondly, that
the opponent's words or abilities are not to be trusted because of that characteristic.
Thus, an abusive *ad hominem* argument may be fallacious either because the person
does not possess the characteristic ascribed to him or her or because possessing that
characteristic is not relevant to the truth of his or her statements. For example, the
fact—if it is one—that Professor Clark is an atheist does not make it even probable
that what he has said is false. Similarly, the fact that Ted Kennedy is a divorced
Catholic does not make it probable that his claim that he would be a good president
is false. The underlying idea of this type of argument can be exposed as follows:

> *Whatever anyone with undesirable characteristic X says
> is probably not true.*
>
> *Person A has undesirable characteristic X.*
> _____
>
> *Therefore, whatever A says is probably not true.*

To identify the ad hominem *abusive fallacy, look for an attack on the person's character
rather than the person's statements.*

The *ad hominem* circumstantial argument implies that the opponent has special,
usually self-interested, reasons for his or her claims. Thus, the argument attempts to
refute the person's statement not by offering reasons against it but by suggesting that
the person himself does not have good reasons or honest motives for the position.
Here are some examples:

Example 15

*The auto industry lobbyists have been arguing that tax
reform is unnecessary. But just remember this: it is the
auto industry that stands to benefit the most if there is
no change in the current tax laws.*

Example 16

*I'm not surprised that your mechanic recommends a
complete engine overhaul. Do you know how much
money he stands to make from that?*

Rather than offering reasons against the others' claims, these speakers suggest that
the persons are not to be believed because they have self-interested motives. In the

first example, for instance, the speaker implies that the auto industry lobbyists would not be arguing against tax reform if they did not stand to gain from it. Thus, the speaker argues that we should not accept the lobbyists' position because they do not have logically relevant reasons for it.

The structure of the *ad hominem* circumstantial argument may be represented as follows:

Person A has self-interested reasons for asserting S.

Therefore, S is probably not true.

The fallacy is apparent if you consider that even if the charge of self-interested motives is true, it still does not follow that what the person says is not true or even probably not true.

To identify the ad hominem *circumstantial fallacy, look for an argument that claims that the opponent advances his or her argument not because it is true but because the opponent has some other, usually ulterior, motive for wanting his or her argument accepted.*

The *ad hominem tu quoque,* or "you, too!", argument is an argument in which one defends oneself by accusing one's attacker, usually of a similar wrongdoing. For example, suppose you have been accused of cheating on a test. If you respond to your critic by saying, "Well, I saw you cheating, too!", you are committing an *ad hominem* fallacy. Your defense is, in effect, to accuse your attacker. But even if you are correct in your accusation, you have not defended yourself against the charge. The fact that someone else has done wrong does not excuse you from doing wrong. Appropriately, this fallacy is sometimes called the fallacy of "two wrongs make a right." Here are some other examples:

Example 17

Yes, I admit, I did lie to you about last night. But you've lied to me.

Example 18

Congressman Pyle accuses me of wasting taxpayers' money on political junkets. Well, you'll be interested to know that he has the track record in Congress for so-called working vacations. Working in the Bahamas! Come now, Mr. Pyle.

To identify the fallacy of ad hominem tu quoque, *look for an argument that attempts to offer a defense by accusing the accuser of a similar wrongdoing.*

To identify an ad hominem *fallacy in general, look for an argument that attempts to offer a defense or a response by attacking the opponent rather than the opponent's argument.*

9.7 False Cause

The fallacy of *false cause* is committed when an arguer concludes that one event or thing A causes another event or thing B when in fact there is no good evidence of a causal relation. In Chapter 8 (sec. 8.3) we saw that evidence supporting a causal statement is strong to the degree that it conforms to one or more of Mill's methods. Absent that the fallacy occurs. One common type of false cause, called *post hoc, ergo propter hoc* (Latin for "after this, therefore because of this"), consists of concluding that A causes B because A *preceded* B. The fallacious reasoning is obvious: Because one event A occurs before another event B, it does not follow that A causes B. Here is an example:

Example 19

Statistics show that nearly every heroin user started out by using marijuana. It's reasonable to conclude, then, that marijuana smoking naturally leads to the harder drug.

The arguer asserts that the majority of heroin users tried marijuana before using heroin, which may be true. However, the arguer concludes that smoking marijuana leads to using heroin, which has in fact been shown to be false. The arguer is mistaking the concurrence of two things for a causal connection.

Another example illustrates a common feeling of guilt and, hence, responsibility that people may have when they have wished misfortune on others:

Example 20

Last night I was so angry at my brother I wished he was dead. And now he's in the hospital. God, if only I hadn't thought that. It's all my fault. I'll never feel hatred again, not of anyone!

Although the speaker in the example may simply regret having had ill feelings toward his brother, if, on the other hand, he literally believes that his wishing misfortune on his brother contributed to the misfortune, then he is guilty of the fallacy of false cause. There is no good reason to believe in this case that wishing it so has caused it to be so.

Another type of fallacy of false cause may be called *oversimplification*. This fallacy occurs when an arguer explains the occurrence of some event or phenomenon in terms of one (or more) of its least important causes. Suppose, for example, that some event E is caused by a combination of several factors, A, B, C, and D. The arguer asserts that E is caused by A and then proceeds to show how A can be eliminated. The arguer appears to have a solution to the problem regarding E when, in fact, the other, more important causal factors are being neglected. Thus, the arguer oversimplifies what is really a complex matter. Consider this example:

Example 21

> *I blame the television media for the epidemic of hijack-*
> *ings, kidnappings, and other acts of terrorism. If we*
> *would stop televising terrorist acts, they'd stop.*

The arguer implies that televising terrorist acts causes more terrorist acts. It may be true that television coverage partially contributes to terrorism by giving the terrorists the attention they seek for their causes, but the speaker neglects other, more important causes. Is it really likely that terrorism would cease if the media refused to provide television coverage? Thus, although the element of truth in this argument may draw us in, the arguer's solution to the problem is on examination naive.

To identify the fallacy of false cause, look for the claim that one thing or event B is caused by or explained as the result of some other thing or event A. Then consider whether there is any good evidence that A causes B. The variation called oversimplification can usually be spotted when an arguer proposes a solution to a problem while at the same time overlooking other causal factors.

9.8 Slippery Slope

The fallacy of *slippery slope* is actually a variation of the fallacy of false cause; it involves a claim that a chain of causal events will occur. This fallacy is committed when a person argues that some event or practice he or she disapproves of will trigger a sequence of events ultimately leading to some undesirable consequence. The reasoning is that since we do not want the undesirable consequence, we ought therefore to oppose the initial event or practice. The fallacy in the reasoning consists in the false assumption that the chain of events will in fact occur.

One well-known example of the fallacy of slippery slope is the *domino theory,* the theory that the loss of one country to communism will lead, like the fall of a series of dominoes, to the communist takeover of others, with ultimately disastrous consequences for the United States. This theory was often heard in an attempt to justify the Vietnam War. The argument was that if we did not stop the communist takeover in Vietnam, communism would spread to the neighboring countries of Cambodia, Laos, and Thailand and we would eventually lose our political influence in Southeast Asia. Opponents of the war in Vietnam argued that such a series of events was not likely to occur. They argued, in effect, that the domino theory exemplified the fallacy of slippery slope.

Here is another example:

Example 22

*You've all heard of grade inflation. Well, I want to
speak to you about grade depression: the serious harm
we do to students by grading them too hard rather than
too easily. What does it do to students to measure them
by too strict a standard? It frustrates them. It conditions
them to expect failure. They recoil from responsibility,
always taking the easy route rather than learning to
challenge and hence improve themselves. They develop
habits of dependency, and many develop the symptoms
of neurosis and other psychological disorders. Can we
afford a generation of weak, dependent people unsuited
for the demands of contemporary society?*

In this example the arguer opposes a strict grading policy by claiming that it will
ultimately lead to "a generation of weak, dependent people." The first step in the
causal chain—that strict grading leads to frustration—is perhaps plausible. But from
that point on the series of occurrences is unlikely. There is no good reason to believe
that harsh grading will lead to expectations of failure, withdrawal from responsibility, and eventually dependency or neurosis. Thus, the arguer commits the fallacy of
slippery slope.

*To recognize the slippery slope fallacy, look for an argument claiming that a cer-
tain practice or event will initiate a series of events ultimately leading to some undesirable
consequence.*

9.9 Either/Or Fallacy

The *either/or* fallacy, sometimes called *false dichotomy*, consists of mistakenly
assuming that there are only two possible solutions to some problem or that solving
some problem consists of choosing between only two alternatives. The argument
moves by showing that one of the alternatives is false or unacceptable and concludes
that the other must be true. (We can imagine variations of the either/or fallacy in
which an argument rests on the mistaken assumption that only three alternatives or
four alternatives are available. The fallacy in each case consists in overlooking some
other, less extreme alternative.) Here is a typical example:

Example 23

*As I see it, either we enforce the death penalty or we
eventually find the convicted murderer out on parole.
We cannot have murderers going free, so we had better
start enforcing the death penalty.*

Let's expose that argument and examine its form.

> 1. *Either we enforce the death penalty or we eventually find the convicted murderer out on parole.*
>
> 2. *We cannot have murderers going free.*
> _____
> 3. *Therefore, we must enforce the death penalty.*

The form of the argument is:

> *Either X or Y.*
>
> *Not Y.*
> _____
> *Therefore, X.*

Notice that this is a valid argument form—assuming the premises are true, the conclusion must be true. Therefore, the fallacy does not consist in the use of an invalid argument form. It consists rather in a false premise—the premise stating that only two alternatives are available, the death penalty or parole for murderers. The either/or fallacy consists in assuming a false dichotomy; the arguer overlooks other possible alternatives. In the case of the example above, the arguer neglects the possibility of mandatory life imprisonment without the chance for parole.

Here are some other examples:

Example 24

I don't like Smith any more than you do, but voting for him is better than voting for Brown.

The speaker assumes one has only two choices, whereas, one could choose some other candidate, write in a name, or not vote at all.

Consider this attempt to justify the government's policy of refusing to negotiate with terrorists holding Americans hostage:

Example 25

Either we give in to these terrorists' demands and jeopardize the lives of thousands of Americans, or we refuse and risk the lives of the hostages. Well, I for one will not risk the lives of Americans all over the world. So we must not give in to these terrorists.

And consider this attempt to justify subjecting animals to head injuries for research purposes:

Example 26

*The idea of deliberately causing trauma, deliberately
injuring the head of a living baboon, is extremely distasteful. But if we are not allowed to continue this
research, then we will simply not learn how to treat
human beings with head injuries. It is unfortunate, but
it must be done.*

In studying the examples above, consider whether there may not be other alternatives the speaker is overlooking. If you can describe such alternatives, then you
have a way of showing the fallacious either/or reasoning of the argument.

To identify the either/or fallacy, look for an argument that makes the false assumption
that there are only two alternatives (or perhaps three or more) available and that one must be
taken because the other is unacceptable.

9.10 Equivocation

The fallacy of *equivocation* occurs when the conclusion of an argument rests
upon the equivocal use of a word or phrase, that is, its use in two different senses.
Consider this example:

Example 27

1. Philosophy is an art.

2. Art is studied by art historians.

---

3. Therefore, philosophy is studied by art historians.

The premises of the argument are plausible, and the argument appears to be valid.
However, the word 'art' is used in two different senses. In its first occurrence it refers
to a skill requiring creativity and imagination, whereas in its second occurrence it
refers to the fine arts or the cultural institution involving the fine arts. When we
rewrite the argument replacing 'art' with those different meanings, it becomes obvious that the argument is not valid:

1. Philosophy is a skill requiring creativity and
imagination.

2. The fine arts *are studied by art historians.*

---

3. Therefore, philosophy is studied by art historians.

Although it may be true that art historians study the fine arts, it is not true that art historians study all skills involving creativity and imagination; and so it is not true that philosophy is studied by art historians.

Consider this second example:

Example 28

Logic is the study of argument. Well, that's one course I could ace. I know all about arguments. I've learned from experts. You should hear the arguments my parents have.

The speaker concludes, in effect, "I would do well at the study of argument because I know all about arguments." The word 'argument' is being used here in two different senses. In the first occurrence it means 'reasoning', and in the second it means 'quarreling'. Substituting the two senses of the word clarifies what is in fact being said: I could do well at the study of *reasoning* because I know all about *quarreling*. That, of course, does not follow.

A rather farfetched but dramatic instance of the fallacy of equivocation occurs in Shakespeare's play *Macbeth*. Macbeth has been told by the three witches that "none of woman born / Shall harm Macbeth." Macbeth reasons as follows:

Example 29

*". . . for none of woman born shall harm Macbeth."
Since all persons are born of woman, it follows that I shall not be harmed by anyone.*

Believing that he cannot be harmed by anyone, Macbeth confidently confronts his rival Macduff in the following exchange:

Macbeth: *Let fall thy blade on vulnerable crests.
I bear a charmèd life, which must not yield
To one of woman born.*

Macduff: *Despair thy charm,
And let the angel whom thou still has served
Tell thee, Macduff was from his mother's womb
Untimely ripped.*
(Macbeth, Act 5, Sc. 8)

Macbeth is the victim of the fallacy of equivocation. In one sense of the phrase 'of woman born', what the witches said was true: Macbeth shall not be harmed by anyone *born naturally*. Unfortunately, and quite understandably, Macbeth took them to mean: Macbeth shall not be harmed by anyone *conceived and carried by a woman*.

To identify the fallacy of equivocation, look for reasoning that involves a shift between two or more senses of a key word or phrase in the argument.

9.11 Hasty Generalization

The fallacy of *hasty generalization* occurs when a generalization is formed on the basis of an unrepresentative sample. As we saw in Chapter 8 (sec. 8.2), to be accurate, a generalization about a group should be based upon a sample reflecting the diversity of that group. One way to ensure a representative sample, in some cases, is to select as large a sample as possible. The more people polled, for example, the more likely it is that the results truly represent the group. However, an accurate generalization does not necessarily require a large sample. In Gallup opinion polls, generalizations are typically based on surveys of a very small number of people. However, the pollsters are careful to select a typical or representative group of people for their sample. Consider these two examples:

Example 30

I've surveyed twenty-five students—each from a different campus organization—out of a student body of two thousand, and all of them prefer to use the activity fund for a film series. So probably the majority of all students would prefer a film series.

Example 31

I've spoken to the members of the campus Audubon Club, and they prefer to use the activity fund for a film series on birds. So probably a majority of the two thousand students would prefer a film series on birds.

The arguer in the first example forms a generalization about the preferences of two thousand students on the basis of a sample drawn from various campus groups. It is reasonable to assume that this sample accurately reflects the diversity of opinion among the students. Thus, this generalization does not commit the fallacy of hasty generalization. In the second example, however, the generalization is based solely upon a survey of one, rather select group, the members of the Audubon Club. Although their preferences should be considered, it is not likely that their group is representative of the student body as a whole; neither is it a random sample of opinions. Thus, the generalization rests on an unrepresentative sample.

Here is another example to consider. Columnist Ann Landers conducted an informal survey in which she asked her women readers to reply to this question: "Would you be content to be held close and treated tenderly and forget about 'the act'?" She reports that 100,000 women responded, with 72 percent answering yes. Among the conclusions she draws is the following:

Example 32

The most surprising aspect of this survey was that 40 percent of the yes votes were from women under forty years of age. What does this say about the sexual revolution? It says, in the boudoir at least, it has been an abysmal failure.

Landers reports that 72,000 women answered yes and that of that group, 42 percent, or 28,800, were under forty years of age. She concludes that the sexual revolution "has been an abysmal failure" on the basis of the 28,800 women under forty who answered yes. Setting aside problems with the survey question itself and, in particular, the meaning of a yes answer, can we say that her sample of 28,800 women is large enough to support a generalization about a majority of the nation's approximately 2 million women under forty years of age? Although it is a significant sample, we may wonder whether it is indeed representative of the nation's women under forty. Landers provides no further information about the makeup of the sample. We know only that it is composed of women forty years or under who read the survey and responded. Lacking such information we cannot conclude that it is an accurate generalization, and we may suspect the fallacy of hasty generalization.

To identify the fallacy of hasty generalization, look for a conclusion that generalizes over a group. Notice whether the basis for the generalization is both representative of the group and sufficiently large to justify the generalization.

9.12 Fallacy of Composition

The fallacy of composition and the fallacy of division consist of fallacious reasoning about the relationship between a whole and its parts or a group and its members. They are sometimes called the part/whole fallacies. The fallacy of *composition* occurs when an arguer *mistakenly* concludes that the whole must have some characteristic because each part or member has the characteristic. Letting W stand for the whole and f for some feature, we can represent the form of this type of reasoning as follows:

Each member of W is f.

Therefore, W is f.

Here is an example:

Example 33

Each member of the orchestra is excellent, so the orchestra is excellent.

The assumption of the argument is that what is true of the parts is true of the whole. However, that assumption is often false. It is false, for instance, in many of those cases in which "the whole is *more than* the sum of its parts." In the example above, an orchestra is not excellent simply because each musician is excellent. It is excellent because, in addition, the musicians work well together. Thus, the fact that the members are individually excellent does not itself justify inferring that the orchestra is excellent. More needs to be supplied to save the argument from the fallacy of composition.

Here are some other examples:

Example 34

The pink sweater is gorgeous. The purple skirt over there is smashing. I love those red shoes in the window, and how about that terrific yellow vest on the mannequin! Let's face it, it will make a great outfit for you!

Example 35

Smoking this cigarette surely can't harm me. So how can smoking cigarettes harm me?

Example 36

The movie Cleopatra *must be great. After all, it stars Elizabeth Taylor, Richard Burton, Rex Harrison, and Hume Cronyn—each a superb actor.*

To recognize the fallacy of composition, look for an argument that moves from a claim about the parts or members of a group to a conclusion about the whole. Consider then whether it is justifiable to attribute what is true of the parts to the whole.

9.13 Fallacy of Division

The fallacy of *division* is fallacious reasoning from the whole to the parts. It is, in effect, the reverse of the fallacy of composition. In this case the arguer mistakenly concludes that each part or member of the whole must have some characteristic because that characteristic is possessed by the whole. Letting W stand for the whole and f for some feature, we can represent the form of this argument as follows:

W is f.

Therefore, each member of W is f.

Here are some examples:

Example 37

The union voted to strike. Therefore, every member of the union voted to strike.

Example 38

Humans are the only animals capable of philosophical thinking. Thus, every person is capable of philosophical thinking.

Example 39

Tornadoes are common in the Midwest. Therefore, since Kansas City is in the Midwest, tornadoes are common in Kansas City.

Example 40

The team won a trophy. Therefore, every player won a trophy.

In the first two examples the characteristics of the group as a whole—having voted to strike and being capable of philosophical thinking, respectively—are erroneously attributed to the members composing the group. As the examples illustrate, a group may have characteristics *as a group* that are not possessed by all members taken individually. The last two examples illustrate how a characteristic possessed by the group is not necessarily possessed by *any* member. For example, although tornadoes may be common in the Midwest, it does not follow that tornadoes are common in Kansas City or in any particular city in the Midwest. Likewise, that the team won a trophy does not mean that every member or any member won a trophy. Thus, what is true of the whole is not necessarily true of the parts.

To recognize the fallacy of division, look for an argument that moves from a claim about a whole or a group to a conclusion about one or all of the members of the whole. Then consider whether it is justifiable to attribute what is true of the whole to its parts.

9.14 False Analogy

An argument from analogy draws a conclusion about something on the basis of an analogy with or resemblance to some other thing. The assumption is that if two or more things are alike in some respects, they are alike in some other respect. Letting A and B represent two different things, events, or practices and letting f, g, h, and j represent features or properties (any number of features is possible), we can represent the form of the argument from analogy as follows:

> *A and B are both f, g, and h.*
> *A is also j.*
> ———————————————————————————
> *Therefore, probably B is j.*

As we saw in the previous chapter (sec. 8.4), the strength of an argument from analogy depends on (1) the relevance of the possession of features f, g, and h to the possession of feature j and (2) there are no relevant dissimilarities. If either criterion is not satisfied, then the argument commits the fallacy of *false analogy*. For example, the following argument lacks a relevant resemblance:

Example 41

Professor Hart teaches philosophy, and he is no fun at parties. Professor Milton teaches philosophy too, so he is probably no fun at parties either.

Now consider a variation on this argument with the addition of further points of resemblance between the two professors:

Example 42

Professor Hart teaches philosophy, has a pet cat, reads German, drives a foreign car, likes to cook, and is no fun at parties. Professor Milton teaches philosophy, has a pet cat, reads German, drives a foreign car, and likes to cook. So he is probably no fun at parties either.

The resemblance is stronger, yet the features that the two professors have in common are not relevant to the further feature of being no fun at parties. A strong resemblance or analogy is not by itself sufficient to warrant the conclusion.

On the other hand, the same conclusion is more probable if it is based upon points of resemblance that *are* relevant to the feature in question, as in this example:

Example 43

*Professors Hart and Milton both teach philosophy.
Both are only happy when talking about philosophy.
Both frequently get into lengthy, abstract debates on
nearly any subject with anyone. Professor Hart is no
fun at parties. So Professor Milton is probably no fun
at parties either.*

Not only is the analogy between Hart and Milton more complete, but the characteristics they are said to have in common do provide a reasonable basis for the conclusion that Milton is no fun at parties.

The first two examples above illustrate simple cases of the fallacy of false analogy. Let's consider a more difficult and more typical example:

Example 44

Regarding Iowa House Minority Leader Delwyn
Stromer's proposal to get teenagers drunk in
order to teach them their drinking limitations, a
letter to the editor in the September 22, 1985, *Des
Moines Register* contained this statement:
     *Perhaps Stromer would also be an advocate of
Russian roulette to teach gun safety.*

The writer's argument can be exposed as follows:

1. *It is foolish to advocate Russian roulette to teach gun
   safety.*
2. *Getting teenagers drunk to teach them their drinking
   limitations is like using Russian roulette to teach
   gun safety.*

---

3. *Therefore, getting teenagers drunk to teach them
   their drinking limitations is foolish.*

The analogy between getting teenagers drunk and Russian roulette is faulty. Getting teenagers drunk in the proposed experimental setting is not potentially fatal and could be conducted without harm. Russian roulette *is* potentially fatal and could not be conducted in such a way as to ensure no harm. Thus, the argument does not succeed in raising a legitimate objection to Stromer's proposal.

Consider another example:

Example 45

*A study conducted in Argentina has shown that the
IQs of mentally defective children can be raised 12 to
25 points by administering large doses of vitamin E.
The implications of this study are astounding. If it*

*works for retarded children, just think what it would do
for normal children! We could greatly improve the IQs
of the next generation of young people and, perhaps,
raise the level of intelligence of our people for generations to come.*

The argument assumes that mentally defective children and normal children are enough alike that what will work for the former will work for the latter. The obvious neurological differences are discounted, as though they were no factor in the children's body chemistry. We ought to be suspicious of this. It is very likely that the neurological differences are such that large doses of vitamin E will not have the same effects on normal children. It is possible, that is, that the addition of vitamin E makes up for some chemical deficiency in abnormal children or, perhaps, inhibits some of the symptoms of their mental condition; whereas normal children have no such deficiency or no mental condition that is inhibited by the vitamin. Whatever the case, the neurological differences between the mentally defective and the normal child are important enough to make us suspect the fallacy of false analogy.

To recognize the fallacy of false analogy, look for an argument that draws a conclusion about one thing, event, or practice on the basis of its analogy or resemblance to others. The fallacy occurs when the analogy or resemblance is not sufficient to warrant the conclusion, as when, for example, the resemblance is not relevant to the possession of the inferred feature or there are relevant dissimilarities.

9.15 Begging the Question

Begging the question is the fallacy of assuming as true the very point under question. Suppose the question is whether God exists, and a person argues for the affirmative on the grounds that 'God's existence is clearly stated in the Bible, and the Bible is the divine word of God'. The arguer is not providing an independent reason for God's existence; rather the arguer is assuming the existence of God already in the reasons he or she gives. This is made clear by exposing the argument:

Example 46

1. The Bible asserts that God exists.

2. The Bible is the divine word of God.

3. Therefore, God exists.

The argument is valid. Indeed, arguments that beg the question are usually valid. However, premise (2) is true only if the conclusion (3) is true. In other words, the premise does not offer independent support for the conclusion; it assumes the conclusion. Thus, the argument assumes the very thing that it purports to prove. A person using an argument of this form is often said to be guilty of "circular reasoning," for, as you can see, the support for the conclusion is itself supported *by* the conclusion.

There are various forms of question begging. The example above illustrates the type of question begging in which the premise itself rests upon or assumes the conclusion it is meant to support. Usually the fallacy is not as obvious as this. In other cases question begging occurs when the arguer uses a premise that is merely a restatement of the conclusion. The premise asserts the conclusion in different words, perhaps so subtly that the arguer may not notice. Consider this example:

Example 47

It is plain to see that suicide is morally wrong because, as any thinking person will admit, no one is ever justified in taking his or her own life.

The example claims that suicide is morally wrong because it is not justified. Saying that it is not justified is merely another way of saying that it is morally wrong. Thus, the arguer has not advanced the issue, for the issue is precisely whether suicide *is* morally justified.

Question begging also occurs when a question is expressed in such a way that a certain position or a certain answer is already assumed. Consider these two examples:

Example 48

I'm sorry I missed your class today, Professor Hart. Did I miss anything important?

Example 49

Mr. President, are you going to support further unnecessary military spending?

The first question carries the implication that nothing of importance takes place in the class and missing it is thus of little consequence. The second question assumes, before hearing the president's answer, that the military spending is unnecessary. A related form of question begging is called the *complex question,* so called because it typically hides more than one question and assumes an answer, usually incriminating, to one of them. The classic humorous question 'Are you still beating your wife?' is a complex question. It actually involves two questions:

1. *Do you beat your wife?*
2. *Given that you beat your wife, do you still do it?*

The original question leaves the respondent no simple yes or no reply, for it assumes already that the answer to (1) is yes. Notice that if the respondent says no, the implication is that he *did* beat his wife. If he answers yes, then again he implies that he beats his wife. Thus, either way he incriminates himself. The only response to such a question is to refuse to answer it as stated and to take it apart, as it were, so that it can be dealt with. Thus, one might say, 'You assume that I beat my wife; and I have never beaten her'.

To recognize the fallacy of begging the question, look for an argument, reply, or question that assumes already the very issue under debate. Be aware that a question-begging argument may appear to offer legitimate, independent support, but on closer examination a premise in fact either itself rests upon the conclusion or restates the conclusion in different words.

9.16 Straw Man

The *straw man* fallacy occurs when an arguer responds to an opponent's argument by misrepresenting it in a manner that makes it appear more vulnerable than it really is, proceeds to attack that argument, and implies that he or she has defeated the opponent. It is called the straw man fallacy because, rather than attacking the "real man," the opponent sets up and knocks over a "straw man."

One form of the straw man fallacy involves a misrepresentation of an opponent's position as much too strong and therefore unacceptable. For example, in the argument below the arguer interprets an inductive argument as a deductive argument and shows that it is invalid.

Example 50

Don't be fooled by statistics showing some sort of correlation between smoking and lung cancer. Any logic student can tell you that it does not necessarily follow that a person will get cancer from smoking cigarettes.

The arguer misrepresents a causal correlation between smoking and lung cancer as a necessary connection and then easily provides an argument against it. The arguer thus appears to have a relevant response to the opponent's position, when in fact no such necessary connection is intended by the opponent.

Another example of interpreting an opponent's position in an unacceptably strong way is this:

Example 51

Councilman Winters says that all homeowners should be required to put fences around their swimming pools in order to warn children. But we all know that any child who really wants to get to a neighbor's pool will find some way to get over any fence.

The arguer is probably right, but Councilman Winters does not claim that putting up fences makes it impossible for children to gain access to pools. The arguer is unfairly interpreting Councilman Winter's argument as involving an extremely strong and rather implausible claim.

Another form of the straw man fallacy occurs when an arguer represents an opponent's position as crucially depending upon some rather minor point which he or she then proceeds to attack. In this kind of case the arguer's response attributes too little to the opponent. Consider this example:

Example 52

Robert Ardrey and others have argued for the theory of evolution by adducing evidence that humans evolved from a rather smallish, apelike hominid, Australopithecus africanus, *who, they say, was an aggressive, territorial hunter and carnivore. In their zeal to establish this theory of theirs, they overlook one crucial fact: we are not all carnivores! How does their theory of descent from the apes account for the fact that many humans, indeed, most humans in the world, live on a diet of vegetables and grains, not meat?*

The arguer misconstrues the theory of evolution as dependent on a rather minor point—that the hominids from which we evolved were carnivores—which can then be refuted.

Consider one final example of the straw man fallacy:

Example 53

Mr. Hunter: *Among the reasons I have for supporting sport hunting is that it is in point of fact beneficial to the species. If we abolished sport hunting, then the deer populations in many parts of the country would multiply without check, leading to massive starvation as the deer placed impossible demands upon their habitat. There would simply be too many deer and not enough food for them all.*

Mr. Audubon: *Well, that's the most foolish and cruel argument I've ever heard. How can it be good for a deer to shoot him?*

Mr. Audubon distorts the argument by interpreting it to mean that it is beneficial to the particular deer, whereas the argument claims that it is good for the species as a whole.

To recognize the straw man fallacy, look for a response that misrepresents an opponent's argument in order to defeat it more easily. The arguer appears to be attacking the opponent's position, but in fact the arguer is attacking a misrepresentation of it.

9.17 Red Herring

The fallacy of *red herring* gets its name from the practice of using a herring, a particularly smelly fish when cooked, to divert hunting dogs from the scent of a fox. To commit the fallacy of red herring in an argument is to draw attention away from an issue by raising some other, seemingly related issue. In so doing, the arguer attempts to sidetrack the opponent's argument, as in this example:

Example 54

Friends and neighbors, I urge you to defeat the proposal to make jail sentences mandatory for drunk drivers. My opponent claims that it will reduce the number of accidents caused by drunk drivers. But if we really want to reduce traffic accidents, then we should stand behind those men and women whose chief responsibility is our safety. I am referring, of course, to our valiant police officers. What we need to do is increase their salaries, beef up the police force, and, most importantly, stop butting into their business with troublesome proposals!

The issue is whether mandatory jail sentences should be used to combat drunk driving. The arguer does not advance the issue but instead diverts attention to the issue of supporting the police force. The tactic is clever because it raises an issue of loyalty that is likely to capture a crowd's attention and sympathy.

Here is another example:

Example 55

I agree with my opponent that pornography is a national problem, and I am almost persuaded by his argument that women are being degraded and victimized by pornography. I say, almost persuaded . . . until I remember the facts that my opponent obviously overlooks: namely, that the people of South Africa are not merely degraded and victimized, they are deprived of every right due a human being. And what I don't understand is how we convince ourselves that our so-called national problem takes precedence over genuine oppression and suffering.

Although the speaker may well have a point about the relative unimportance of pornography in comparison with the situation in South Africa, and although it is interesting to ask how we determine our priorities, nevertheless, this response is not relevant to the issue at hand. The question is not, Should we devote our time and energy to the consideration of pornography? but, Does pornography pose a serious moral harm to society or segments of society? Thus, this response involves the fallacy of red herring.

To recognize the fallacy of red herring, look for an argument in which the speaker responds by directing attention away from the issue to other, seemingly related issues.

9.18 Inconsistency

The fallacy of *inconsistency* involves reasoning from inconsistent premises, that is, statements that cannot be simultaneously true. For example, the statements 'Love is the desire for what is good' and 'Love is not the desire for what is good' are clearly inconsistent. It is impossible for both to be true.

The above example illustrates what we may call *explicit* inconsistency, because the inconsistency is readily apparent: one statement is the denial of the other. Such cases of inconsistency are rare, since they are so easily recognized. More common is what can be called *implicit* inconsistency. Two statements are implicitly inconsistent if one or both imply statements, one of which is the denial of the other—that is, if what follows from one is explicitly inconsistent with the other. For example, in President Reagan's 1984 campaign for the presidency he promised, on the one hand, to achieve a balanced budget without diminishing funds to other government programs and, on the other hand, to increase the defense budget without raising taxes. Many critics charged Reagan with inconsistency on the grounds that increasing defense spending without cutting into other programs would require more federal money at the same time that attempting to balance the budget without raising taxes would decrease the amount of federal money. Thus, Reagan appeared to be endorsing (1) an increase in federal spending and (2) no increase in federal spending. Without explaining how both goals could be achieved, Reagan was guilty, critics claimed, of an inconsistency.

Consider another example of an implicit inconsistency:

Example 56

Senator: *Parents are the sole authority on the education of their children. Nothing we do should restrict the rights of parents to determine the kind of education they want for their children.*

Interviewer:	Senator, does the state, as a major contributor to the funding of education, have an interest in the content of education?
Senator:	Most certainly it does. One of the primary responsibilities of the state is to ensure a quality and equal education for all children. That is why we give the state the authority to license teachers, determine educational goals, and monitor the use of funds in education.

The senator is inconsistent. It cannot be the case that parents are the sole authorities on education and that the state has the authority to regulate education. Even if by a happy accident the wishes of parents and the decisions of the state coincide, the senator's position is inconsistent. He maintains that (1) the parents have the sole right to determine the quality of education and that (2) the state has the right to determine the quality of education. If (1) is true, then it follows that (3) the state does not have the right to determine the quality of education; and (3) is the denial of (2).

The fact that speakers assert one thing at one time and its denial on another is not in itself sufficient to charge them with inconsistency. Speakers may change their minds, in which case they do not assert both the statement and its denial. Rather, they conclude that one of the statements is false. For example, when it was learned that the hijackers of the ship Achille Lauro were likely to be turned over to the PLO, President Reagan was asked if he would accept the PLO's claim that it would bring the hijackers to justice. Reagan said that he would. Later in the day, however, he responded to the same question by saying that he would not. He explained to the reporters that he had considered the matter further and concluded that he spoke hastily the first time. At no time did he maintain that it both was and was not acceptable to him. Thus, Reagan cannot be charged with inconsistency in his remarks.

What is wrong with inconsistency? From the practical standpoint the most obvious answer is that we cannot rely on a person who argues inconsistently or maintains inconsistent positions. If a politician asserts S on one occasion and not-S on another, without explaining it as a change of mind, then we do not know what the politician thinks or will do. Such a person is unreliable, if only regarding that issue. But there are two other reasons why inconsistency is a serious error in reasoning.

First, arguments with inconsistent premises necessarily fail to be good arguments because it cannot be the case that all premises are simultaneously true. Secondly, an argument with inconsistent premises does not distinguish good reasoning from bad because *any* statement can be validly deduced from inconsistent premises. Suppose, for example, we have as premises the two statements 'It is raining' and 'It is not raining'. We can validly deduce any statement whatsoever. Consider the following nested argument:

Example 57

1. *It is raining.*

---

2. *Therefore, it is raining or Mexico is north of the United States.*
3. *It is not raining.*

---

4. *Therefore, Mexico is north of the United States.*

The inference from (1) to the conclusion (2) is a valid deduction. Given that it is raining, it necessarily follows that (2) 'It is raining *or* Mexico is north of the United States'. Notice that (2) does not assert that 'It is raining' is true *and* 'Mexico is north of the United States' is true. It asserts only that one *or* the other is true. Thus, from a statement S assumed to be true we may always combine it with any other statement P in a statement of the form 'S or P'. Now premise (3)—the denial of (1)—asserts that it is not the case that it is raining. Thus, since 'It is raining' is false and 'It is raining or Mexico is north of the United States' is true, 'Mexico is north of the United States' must follow as a valid inference. From inconsistent premises we have validly deduced (4). The significance of this is that inconsistent arguments are particularly pernicious. Any argument form from which *any* statement (including S and not-S) is deducible is one that necessarily fails to distinguish good reasoning from bad. It is understandable, then, that inconsistency is the logician's nightmare. Imagine working long and hard to establish some highly important thesis only to discover that one's premises are implicitly inconsistent.

In order to recognize the fallacy of inconsistency, look for an argument with premises that are either implicitly or explicitly inconsistent.

Summary

The following summary is no substitute for the detailed explanations given in this chapter. Use the summary as a quick reference when you are explaining the fallacious reasoning in the exercises.

1. *Appeal to authority:* an argument that relies upon the assertions of someone who is not relevantly qualified or is not speaking without bias.
2. *Appeal to the people:* an argument in which a conclusion is said to be true because it is commonly or traditionally believed.
3. *Appeal to force:* An argument in which a threat is used to win the listener's acceptance of the conclusion.
4. *Appeal to pity:* an argument in which an appeal to the listener's sympathy is used to win the listener's acceptance of the conclusion.
5. *Appeal to ignorance:* an argument in which it is concluded that some statement is true (or false) because there is no evidence that the statement is false (or true).

6. *Ad hominem:* an argument that attacks the person rather than the person's ideas.

   Abusive: reasoning that a person's arguments are not to be believed because the person is of poor character.

   Tu quoque: excusing or defending oneself by accusing one's critic of a similar wrongdoing.

   Circumstantial: reasoning that a person's arguments are not to be believed because the person has ulterior motives.

7. *False cause:* an argument that concludes without justification that one thing or event causes another.

   Post hoc, ergo propter hoc ("After this, therefore because of this"): concluding that one thing or event, A, causes another, B, because A preceded B; whereas, from the fact that A precedes B it does not follow that A causes B.

   Oversimplification: proposing a solution to a problem that oversimplifies the matter by overlooking other important causal factors.

8. *Slippery slope:* an argument that reasons without justification that some thing or event will cause a series of events ultimately leading to some undesirable consequence.

9. *Either/or:* an argument involving the mistaken assumption that there are only two alternatives available and that one must be taken because the other is unacceptable.

10. *Equivocation:* an argument in which the conclusion rests upon the use of a word or phrase in two different senses.

11. *Hasty generalization:* an argument in which a generalization is formed on the basis of an unrepresentative sample.

12. *Fallacy of composition:* an argument involving the mistaken assumption that what is true of the parts or members of a whole is true of the whole itself.

13. *Fallacy of division:* an argument involving the mistaken assumption that what is true of the whole is true of the parts or members of the whole.

14. *False analogy:* an argument that reasons that if two things are alike in certain respects, then they are alike in some other respect. The fallacy occurs when the analogy is not relevant to the possession of the inferred feature or there is a relevant disanalogy.

15. *Begging the question:* an argument that assumes as true the very point under question. Question begging occurs when a premise assumes the truth of the conclusion or the conclusion is a restatement of the premise.

    Complex question: a question framed in such a way that the answer is already assumed.

16. *Straw man:* a rebuttal to an argument in which the speaker misrepresents the opponent's argument as more vulnerable than it is and then proceeds to attack that misrepresentation.

17. *Red herring:* a rebuttal to an argument that diverts attention away from the main issue by raising other, seemingly related issues.

18. *Inconsistency:* an argument based on inconsistent premises, that is, premises that cannot be simultaneously true.

Exercise 9.1A   Identifying Fallacies.   In the arguments below identify the fallacy and give a short explanation for your judgment.

1. Those who keep quiet about this funding won't have to look for other jobs. Do you all understand?

2. I know your doctor says you need your appendix removed, but according to *Reader's Digest* people with your symptoms just need a change in their diet. So forget about having your appendix out.

3. Certainly Leo Tolstoy was a great novelist, and I admit his stories are excellent. But if we are supposed to take his sermonizing on the value of unselfishness and love for humanity as a prescription for the good life, then I strongly object. If the man has a philosophy, it is not worth the paper it's written on for the simple reason that he was himself a failure at living unselfishly and benevolently.

4. I don't have any mice in my house. I haven't seen a single one.

5. Aw, c'mon, go out with me. My ship's been out at sea for six months, and I haven't seen a girl in all that time.

6. Well, I don't like Hollings, but either I vote for him or I vote for Miller, and you know what I think about Miller.

7. People have no reason to be afraid of love, for love is just a four-letter word.

8. It's no wonder there's so much divorce, crime, and political corruption in our nation today. Have you seen what's on TV these days?

9. I can't understand why people talk about how beautiful California is. Last summer I spent three days at a convention in Los Angeles, and I can tell you, California is not beautiful. There are too many people, too many cars, too much concrete, not enough fresh air, and not enough peace and quiet.

10. I believe that God's word is our commandment, for he is all-good and he knows what is right and wrong. After all, he created us and gave us the freedom to act as we choose; so it is up to each individual to follow his or her idea of what is right.

11. Studying philosophy is a dangerous thing to do. It makes you critical, which in turn makes you skeptical of your religious beliefs. And once you've begun to lose faith in your religion, it's a small step to atheism and immorality, and a life of immorality is damned.

12. I find the proposal to permit students to take part in the development of the college curriculum utterly ridiculous. How can students be in a position to judge which courses are worthwhile and which are not before they have had those courses? It's preposterous!

13. Simpson, it has come to my attention that some of the employees want to form a union. Their representative tells me that they are not satisfied with

their working conditions. Well, some people are never satisfied and never think of anyone but themselves. You can tell them for me that it will be a cold Fourth of July before we cater to the whimperings of malcontents.

14. George: That must be a pretty heavy book you're carrying.
    Jeff: It ought to be; it's got the weight of authority in it.

15. I know my paper is late, Professor Hart, but my roommate was sick last night, and my folks'll kill me if I flunk this course.

16. Max: Maestro, tell me, what is the secret of composing a beautiful symphony?
    Maestro: Ah, that's easy. Just make sure that you select only beautiful notes.

17. Professor Scott, my American Literature professor, warned us about the dangers of nuclear power plants, so I'm voting against proposition N, the nuclear power plant initiative.

18. I don't see why you get down on me for smoking pot. You guys have a couple of martinis every night.

19. If you don't accept Christ in your heart this very night, you will lose your immortal soul.

20. Max: Are you going out with that cheerleader this weekend?
    Fred: Yep.
    Max: Wow! What did she say when you asked her out?
    Fred: She didn't say no.
    Max: Well, what *did* she say?
    Fred: She didn't say anything.

21. A: Do you see what I'm saying?
    B: No, how could I? We can only see what is visible.

22. Ginger: I believe in the theory of reincarnation.
    Diane: What is that?
    Ginger: Well, it is the idea that we never *really* die. What happens at death is that our soul leaves the body and is reborn into another human body to live another life. So we always come back and never really die.
    Diane: So you mean we're sort of recycled?
    Ginger: Yes, in a sense.
    Diane: Well, that's got to be false. If we all just keep coming back, then what are we having funerals for?

23. No one on the weight-lifting team can lift more than 250 pounds, so the team won't be able to push that 2,000-pound car.

24. The sign read, "All you can eat for a dollar," but when I went back for more the manager said, "No more! That's all you can eat for a dollar."

25. Sure I was speeding, officer, but so were you! How else would you ever have caught me?

26. My opponent argues that women do not have the right to choose abortion. That means he denies that women have the right to control their own bodies,

and he thus endorses a kind of sexual discrimination. Well, we've worked too long and too hard to ensure equality between the sexes to revert back to that kind of unjust treatment of women.

27. I recommend that we not rehire Professor Buzz. We simply can't have teachers who cannot keep discipline in the classroom. Professor Buzz is cross-eyed and, as everyone knows, a cross-eyed teacher cannot control his pupils.

28. We haven't heard any sounds from the rubble of that collapsed building, so we figure that no one remains alive inside.

29. My art professor, Mr. Crowley, recommends using marble slab for the lithos. So you should use it, too.

30. Art: Well, I've decided to take the course in philosophy of art because I already have a theory worked out. It's that all art is the communication of emotion.
    Phil: That's interesting. Does it matter what kinds of emotion art communicates?
    Art: Yes, it does. Good art communicates only noble and fine emotions.
    Phil: And bad art? What does it communicate?
    Art: Aha! That's just it! Bad art doesn't communicate at all.

31. Plato said that man is the rational animal. Aristotle said that man is the featherless biped. Both of them were wrong. After all, not everybody is rational and not everybody has two legs. Those Greeks!

32. Baba Jag Dish: Well, you see, it is terrible. The bhagwan should not be arrested and put in jail. He is a holy man.
    Phil: Oh, really? So holy men shouldn't be put in jail?
    Baba Jag Dish: Of course not, otherwise he would not be a holy man.
    Phil: Sure. And I wouldn't be a logic student if I accepted that!
    Baba Jag Dish: Goodness. What did I do?
    Phil: You just committed the fallacy of _____.

33. Well, I was shocked to learn from my daughter that racial discrimination is being *taught* at her college. In her last letter she said that her art teacher is teaching them to make discriminations on the basis of color.

34. When people have typhoid fever, we quarantine them so that others will not be infected. Malaria is certainly as serious a disease as typhoid, so we should quarantine malaria patients, too.

35. Of course there are extraterrestrials. Haven't you read that article in the *National Enquirer* about those UFOs spotted in Texas last month?

36. Every year a few Snowy Owls are spotted in Nebraska. So every year a few Snowy Owls are spotted in Omaha, because Omaha is in Nebraska.

37. Son, I have to tell you that I strongly disapprove of your living with your girlfriend. People just do not do that.

38. Special Investigator Griffin Bell's committee concluded that there was no evidence of wrongdoing on the part of top executives at E. F. Button, so we may all rest assured that Button's top executives had nothing to do with those illegal practices.

39. I read in the obituary column this morning that the multimillionaire J. P. Vanderbilt died, leaving his entire estate to his brothers. Well, since we are all brothers under the skin I expect I'm entitled to my share of his millions.

40. Phil: The philosopher Spinoza said that if we know God then we know all things, because God *is* all things.

   Max: That sounds very nice, Phil, but you're surely not going to believe a man who is an avowed pantheist.

Exercise 9.1B   More Informal Fallacies.   The following excerpts from letters to the editor and from newspaper and magazine articles contain fallacious reasoning. Some excerpts may contain more than one fallacy. State what fallacy or fallacies you find in the passages, and give an explanation for your judgment.

1. Gerald F. Uelmen describes an incident in which Justice Oliver Wendell Holmes, Jr., hearing a motion for a continuance of a murder trial by a lawyer named Swasey, appears to commit a fallacy. Justice Holmes speaks:
   "Mr. Swasey, the record shows that the trial of this case has at your request been continued once. Last summer, when I was in England visiting the law courts, Mr. Justice Stephen commented to me on the importance of speedy trials in the administration of justice, particularly in capital cases while witnesses were available, evidence fresh in the mind, and before suggestions could create false psychological memories."
   As Holmes paused before ruling, Swasey inquired, "Has Your Honor read the morning papers?" An annoyed Holmes inquired what bearing the morning papers could possibly have on the motion. "None," replied Swasey, "but they do report that yesterday Mr. Justice Stephen was judicially committed to an institution for the feeble-minded." Amidst harrumphs, Holmes granted the motion. (*New York Times*)

2. *A letter to the editor of the St. Joseph Gazette claiming that spanking children leads those same children to become child abusers when they grow up gives this argument:* To say it is proper to whip a child mildly, is like saying it is all right to steal a few things, just don't carry it too far.

3. Despite the fact that the case against cigarette smoking has by no means been proven, the tobacco industry has in recent years suffered a notable degree of harassment: It has stopped advertising cigarettes on television. It has had to print on its packs the flat assertion that smoking "is dangerous" to one's health. We have seen effective and often very creative anti-smoking ads. Some magazines won't accept cigarette advertising. Some periodicals won't publish articles which tend to exonerate tobacco. Aboard commercial airlines and on interstate trains and buses, it is not only permissible to segregate smokers; it is federally mandated. (Smokers usually have to sit in the back of the plane where there is more engine noise and more chance of being served a cold meal.) Recent lawsuits have sought to ban smoking in the New Orleans Superdome and to limit it in federal office buildings. And sales and excise taxes, particularly at state and local levels, have climbed to the sumptuary

point in many places. (James Council, "The Case for Tobacco," in *The Language of Argument,* by Daniel McDonald)

4. A few of us just get kind of sick and tired of the Catholic Church and our U.S. government always being fair game. Every Christian owes his Christianity, and a word of appreciation, to the treasury of faith, history and tradition due to the uninterrupted Catholic lineage leading back to Christ. And every American owes his freedom, and rights and thanks to the continuity of our government. It is the greatest success story in the history of the world, and the envy of those who cannot share it. (Letter to the editor, *Des Moines Register*)

5. *Phyllis Schlafly, spokesperson for the pro-life position on abortion, accused women working for abortion rights of wanting* to protect women's rights to kill their babies. That isn't what American women really want. (*U.S. News & World Report*)

6. Unless the homosexuals end their perverted way of life, which is unlikely, we can forget a nuclear holocaust and prepare for the AIDS holocaust. Something has to be done. Should the AIDS cases be allowed to roam freely like walking time bombs, or should they be isolated, as discussed on TV, in their own colony as was done in the past with leprosy cases? (Letter to the editor, *Riverside Press-Enterprise*)

7. Religion *is* being taught in our public schools today, and the government's own brand of "brainwashing" is going on. It is called secular humanism. (Letter to the editor, *Des Moines Register*)

8. One reads a lot about Social Security going broke, or being done away with. Young people complaining about their taxes being too high, and that they will never get anything out of the money they put into it. They could be wrong; most young people are getting more out of Social Security right now than they may think. If we didn't have Social Security the incomes of people who are receiving $20–30–40–50 thousand a year wouldn't be receiving that kind of pay, but more like 20–30–50 cents an hour. I know, because that is the wages the people were receiving in the day before Social Security came into being, if they had a job at all. (Letter to the editor, *Riverside Press-Enterprise*)

9. While I certainly don't feel the Japanese attack on Pearl Harbor was justified, I can't believe there is so little knowledge of what actually took place. Several books now out tell of how Roosevelt was simply a frontman for the industrialists who were hoping to reap fat profits from war. Roosevelt cut off trade with Japan, refused to negotiate with her, and when he got word she was going to attack Pearl Harbor, deliberately withheld the information. . . . Later, Truman deliberately ignored the overtures to surrender by Japan and dropped the A-bombs. All governments are usually run by those who put profits above freedoms and life, and an ill-informed, apathetic public allows it. (Letter to the editor, *Riverside Press-Enterprise*)

10. [Black Muslim leader Louis] Farrakhan calls Judaism a "dirty religion." Jewish teachers believe the Old Testament is the inspired word of God. Christian teachers believe both the Old and the New Testaments are the inspired word

of God. Therefore by implication Farrakhan really says that the Judeo-Christian religion is dirty.

Farrakhan is evil, Farrakhan is satanic. I am very distressed more Christian leaders did not make an outcry against this evil man and his sinful remarks. (Letter to the editor, *Riverside Press-Enterprise*)

11. *Regarding the "Farm Aid" benefit designed to help alleviate the U.S. farm crisis, one writer made the following comment in the letters to the editor column:* Only a man of Willie Nelson's caliber can understand who really feeds the world—the American farmer.

12. Until we as a nation, take a stand against any kind of corporal punishment of our children, we will continue to abuse them in the name of discipline. (Letter to the editor, *St. Joseph Gazette*)

13. *Ann Landers commented as follows on a survey in which she asked people to answer yes or no to the question, "Would you be content to be treated tenderly and forget about the 'act'?":* If my survey had any value, it was in the revelation that a great many women choose affection over sex. Those yes votes were saying, "I want to be valued. I want to feel cared about. Tender words and loving embraces are more rewarding than an orgasm produced by a silent, mechanical, self-involved male." (*Family Circle,* June 1985)

14. *The following letter was in response to an editorial by Mary McGrory in which she argued that AIDS is not God's punishment for homosexuality because it is also being contracted by those who are not homosexuals.* Never once as a Christian have I thought that AIDS was God's punishment of homosexuals. I always have thought of AIDS as being a good example of what happens when a person puts his own interests and pleasures ahead of what God's will is on the matter. God did not bring AIDS upon homosexuals and drug addicts; they brought it upon themselves by means of an unclean, unbiblical lifestyle. That mainstream people and even children are contacting AIDS only points out the fact that many people must pay the price for the reckless behavior of a few. (Letter to the editor, *Omaha World Herald*)

15. *On a television interview regarding his new book,* Macdougal's Medicine, *Dr. Macdougal answered questions from callers. Two separate callers asked about having surgery to remove a suspicious lump.*

To the first caller: Have the lump removed. If the tumor hasn't spread, then by all means remove it. If it has spread, then don't let yourself be disfigured by surgery which won't save you.

To the next caller: If there are no symptoms from this breast tumor, then follow the advice of the doctor who told you to wait. You can always have the surgery later. The one thing about surgery is that it's a last-ditch effort in most cases. You can always have it done later.

16. We dare to challenge the seat-belt law because it is an infringement on our personal freedom, and no excuse that it saves money in any way is going to change that fact. It's not what I fought for in World War II. We have a state government in Lincoln that is doing its best to create a police state. (Letter to the editor, *Omaha World Herald*)

17. In reference to the Farm Aid concert, I feel that the true impact of the farmers' plight on the world is being missed. Our country feeds the world, and as more and more individual farmers go under their land is being bought up by large conglomerates.

At the current rate of farm loss, soon our food will be controlled by a selected few just like the oil and other natural resources. This will create the interesting shortages we have seen, such as the gas shortage of the 70's. Isn't it interesting that at 50 cents a gallon there's no gas, but now at $1.50 you can have all you want?

Since most of the rest of the world spends over 50 percent of their gross income on food, and we in this country spend far less, we might be in store for some catastrophe that will send bread to $3 a loaf if you can get it. Remember if you feed people you own them and we have a country that is supposed to be run by the people and for the people, so for God's sake we must make sure that the production of our food stays in the hands of the people, not the conglomerates. (Letter to the editor, *Des Moines Register*)

18. If it were really demonstrated that cigarettes are *the* cause of cancerous growths, the tobacco industry would join the rest of the world in rejoicing that the cause of cancer had at last been identified. It would celebrate the medical breakthrough which would bring protection and new hope to everyone, including tobacco people. It would be most happy to stop cigarette production and diversify into new areas. (James Council, "The Case for Tobacco," in *The Language of Argument,* by Daniel McDonald)

19. Apartheid, when all is boiled down, is one group of people (in this case, the white minority) deciding that another group of people (the black majority) have no rights and are therefore somewhat less than fully human. It's an ugly story, but unfortunately, it's not unlike many in history. It seems to happen quite often. For one group of people to gain or keep their rights, another group must be put on a subhuman level.

On Jan. 23, 1973, our Supreme Court again classified a group of individuals as being nonpersons. This time the target was the unborn citizens of our nation. From that day on, for any reason deemed necessary by the mother, an unborn child could be eliminated. I find it more than ironic that mankind must always deny segments of society their personhood in order to either destroy or enslave them.

I will admit that many of us in this country are the victims of pro-abortion rhetoric. We've been pacified with the terms fetus and non-viable to describe the unborn child so that we don't conjure up mental pictures of a baby, fully formed, yet tiny and defenseless. We must make them less than human before we can destroy them.

Apartheid—an ugly, shameful issue.

Abortion—is there any difference?

(Barb Malek, "Apartheid's Link to Abortion," *Omaha World Herald*)

20. In scientific minds, vitamin E may be related to fertility and reproduction, said an article in *Medical World News* for April 18, 1969. But a famous ball player, Bobby Bolin of the San Francisco Giants, credits the vitamin with keeping his pitching arm in condition. He developed a sore shoulder in 1966,

resulting in a poor pitching season for two years. He began to take vitamin E. The article said that he expected to be a "regular starter" at the beginning of the 1969 season, and that vitamin E was responsible for the good news. (Ruth Adams and Frank Murray, "Vitamin E in the Hands of Creative Physicians," in *Vitamin E, Wonder Worker of the 70's*)

21. Liberal Democrats have convinced themselves that their recent debacle at the polls is no more than a choice of the wrong messenger [Mondale], that it can be cured with cosmetics and imagery.

    No, the Democratic Party is too emotionally committed to the liberal special interests to make a meaningful "move to the center," and, for that reason, look for Teddy, Gary or Mario at the helm of the *Titanic* in 1988. (Letter to the editor, *U.S. News & World Reports*)

22. We have an obligation to stop playing games, hiding behind euphemisms, arguing over shades of meaning of the word "viability" and face a very distasteful fact: when we perform an abortion, we are destroying a life. We may choose to do that—some of us do choose to do it—but abortion is murder and there is no way we can, if we are honest, deny that revolting fact. (William A. Nolen, M.D., *The Baby in the Bottle*)

23. Apparently Secretary of State George Schultz does not believe in God for he has said that we must ensure that there is "no escape from justice" for the terrorists responsible for the recent shipjacking of the Achille Lauro. If he believed in God, he'd know that God brings all men to justice no matter what *we* do. If he thinks they might escape justice, then he cannot be a believer in a God of justice; it's that simple.

24. In regard to a recent article . . . about the intolerable conditions in the county jails and the statistics on inmate population increases: One comment was that inmates were forced to eat near toilets and urinals in their cells. Oh, for shame! Who forced them into jail! It would be nice if they could be housed in Motel 6 and have catered meals plus a membership in Jack LaLanne's. But in my and other law-abiding citizens' books, they are getting their just desserts. The solution is simple: Stay out of jail. (Letter to the editor, *Riverside Press-Enterprise*)

25. There was Live Aid and there is Farm Aid and there is, apparently, going to be AIDS Aid, all which seems designed by the entertainment industry to try to disguise its squalid role as corrupter of the young.

    What's a nice little three-letter word like aid doing hustling funds in these electronic Woodstock-Altamonts? What it is doing is helping a cold-hearted, contemptibly exploitative, multi-billion-dollar international industry defend itself against plausible charges of child abuse. The true recipients of the aid are the performers and their entourages and the big corporations that peddle their stuff.

    The only way to counter this kind of mischief is resolutely to ignore in future any public spectacle, electronic or otherwise, that employs the word "aid," however worthy the cause. (David Wilson, article)

26. A Romanian farm journal reports that extremely large amounts of vitamin E, plus vitamin A, were given to 77 sterile cows. Within one to one and a half months, their sexual cycles were restored, and 70 percent of them conceived. (Ruth Adams and Frank Murray, "Vitamin E in the Hands of Creative Physicians," in *Vitamin E, Wonder Worker of the 70's*)

27. *Jerry Falwell of the Moral Majority sent out a poll soliciting viewers' opinions on the presence of violence and sex on television. Respondents were asked to answer the following questions and then send a donation to the Moral Majority to "help clean up television once and for all!"*

Please answer each of the questions below by checking the appropriate box:

1. Are you in favor of America's children being subjected to the presentation of homosexuality as an acceptable lifestyle in prime-time television?

2. Do you favor the showing of obnoxious and edited R-rated movies on network television?

3. Are you in favor of television programs which major in gratuitous violence such as murder, rape, beatings, etc.?

4. Are you in favor of cable television now bringing hard-core pornography into America's living room?

28. Seventy-five percent of the people in California believe the death penalty is a protection which they need and are entitled to. Now, this question is not subject to any scientific analysis; not something one person knows a great deal about and another person knows nothing about. You can't come up with a right answer by using a slide rule. Everyone in this room, and most of the citizens in this state are just as well qualified to arrive at a correct conclusion in this as I am, or as is Professor Amsterdam, or as is Governor Brown. This is not something that's subject to expert testimony. I think every citizen has a stake in this and the fact that 75 percent of our citizens support the reenactment of the death penalty is significant. (Evelle J. Younger, "Capital Punishment: The People's Mandate," Address of the California Attorney General to the Commonwealth Club of California, July 1977)

29. The extraordinary courageous action of the citizens who captured the "Night Stalker" and those providing vital information leading to the arrest, are really entitled to any reward previously offered; however I believe if I had been in the position of these noteworthy captors, I would have killed him myself. . . . Of course, I realize the decision to take the law into my own hands would be wrong, but equally wrong would it be to let this criminal be released after a prison term—to kill again and again. (Letter to the editor, *Riverside Press-Enterprise*)

30. Prior to World War II, we heard nil about Alzheimer's [disease] and we hardly heard of anyone who acquired it. At this point in time, post–WWII, we tossed out iron and enamel cookware for aluminum cookware and bakeware. Then the popular new TV dinners wrapped in aluminum foil, ice cream bars, not to forget soda pop and beer in aluminum cans. We also receive a lot of aluminum into our system through buffered aspirins, and stomach anti-acids and underarm deodorants. We are taking a lot of a toxic poisonous substance aluminum which affects the ions of the brain. Was the overuse of aluminum and the upsurge of so much Alzheimer's disease surfacing coincidental? (Letter to the editor, *Riverside Press-Enterprise*)

31. Another argument, a favorite of those who oppose the death penalty, is that we can accomplish the same thing by life imprisonment without possibility of parole. There are several things wrong with that. There is no such thing in our nation or in our state as true life imprisonment, nor should there be. The

governor has, and always should have, the power to commute. That's the safety valve that will work when everything else fails. So I wouldn't be in favor of, if we could, and it would be impossible, to try and take away the governor's power to commute. Given that power to commute, there's no such thing as life imprisonment. (Evelle J. Younger, "Capital Punishment: The People's Mandate," Address of the California Attorney General to the Commonwealth Club of California, July 1977)

32. The Bible is 100% error-free. Its interpreters do not, however, share in that accuracy rating. (Letter to the editor, *Time*)

33. Frederick J. Stare, a founder and chairman of the Department of Nutrition at Harvard University's School of Public Health, remains one of the country's leading defenders of sugar in our diet. He thinks the substance has been "unduly maligned." He applauds it as "the least expensive important source of calories" and "an important nutrient and food." General Foods Corporation, the second-largest user of sugar in the country, paid for the Nutrition Research labs at Harvard's School of Public Health. Other contributors to Harvard's Department of Nutrition—Amstar, Domino Sugar, Coca-Cola, Kellogg, the International Sugar Research Association, and the Sugar Association—are no more eager for the true sugar story to emerge. (Jeanne Shinto, "Is Our Diet Driving Us Crazy?" *The Progressive*)

34. *The following exchange took place on the Dick Cavett Show during an interview with G. Gordon Liddy who spent five years in prison in connection with the Watergate burglary:*

    Cavett: You spent several years in prison and we hear about the high incidence of homosexuality. Did you find it hard to adjust to the homosexuality there?
    Liddy: No.
    Cavett: You heard it, folks. He said he had no trouble adjusting to homosexuality in prison.

35. We can talk and plan and agonize about child abuse until the cows come home, but we shall never approach the cure until we stop planting the seeds. Every time we strike a child and tell him it is for his own good that we must whip him to make a good child of him, we have planted a seed of belief that violence to the body will control actions; will control others. That tiny seed becomes a monstrous tree that is resulting in a violent society. (Letter to the editor, *St. Joseph Gazette*)

36. *Political cartoonist Jules Feiffer attributes the following reasoning to Jerry Falwell:* South Africa is part of the free world. The free world is in a mortal struggle with the communist world . . . which enslaves its people. If South Africa frees its blacks, they will take over the government. They will join the communist world, which enslaves its people. So in order to remain part of the free world . . . South Africa must continue to enslave its blacks.

37. In fairness, any legal effort to curtail cigarette smoking on the ground that it may be a health hazard, should also work against other possible health hazards: There should be no television advertisements for wine or beer. Every bottle of whiskey and of cough syrup should bear a health warning. T-bone steaks should carry a printed brand warning of cholesterol. It should be illegal for a restaurant to serve pecan pie to anyone who is twenty pounds

overweight. To avoid danger to health, no one should be allowed to buy a gun—or a football—or a king-size bottle of aspirin. Clearly, very heavy regulations should govern the sale of something as deadly as an automobile. No one should be permitted to sunbathe on the beach or to shop in high-crime areas. (James Council, "The Case for Tobacco," in *The Language of Argument,* by Daniel McDonald)

38. *The New Republic* refers to fetuses as "not yet self-conscious." On what grounds does *The New Republic* say that fetuses are not "self-conscious"? A sixteen-week-old fetus will kick and squirm if prodded by a needle. That, it would seem to me, is very simple evidence that the fetus is self-conscious. Perhaps a sixteen-week-old fetus does not spend time, as it bobs around in the amniotic sac, thinking about the meaning of life or musing on the works of Plato, but neither does a two-year-old toddler. (William A. Nolen, M.D., *The Baby in the Bottle*)

39. I am a Christian woman, and I am also a feminist. I am writing to share with all your readers the fact that there *are* Christian sisters who, though they believe abortion is wrong, *uphold a woman's right to do with her body as she wishes.* This is a point I cannot get across to most fanatical Christians, especially men. I hope that non-Christians aren't lumping all Christians in with Jerry Falwell and Ronald Reagan, because that is not accurate. I am appalled by the Moral Majority, and it frightens me that they are trying to change the current abortion laws. Christians have a nasty habit of imposing their views and doctrine upon people, and this marriage of religion and state is not good. (Letter to the editor, *Ms.* magazine)

40. Frankly I don't think it matters whether porn is degrading to women. It's a society of many voices and I don't want any of them silenced. (Al Goldstein, publisher of *Screw* magazine)

41. Cartoonist Walt Handelsman charges MTV with what fallacy?

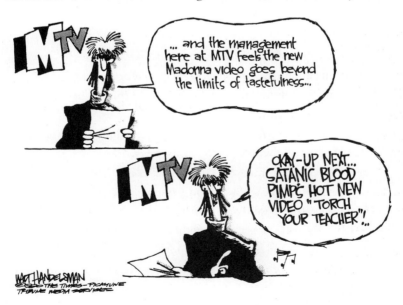

42. It [the pope's position against birth control] is insane, yet it reflects the ambition of the Catholic Church for power by sheer numbers. Each female member of every diocese becomes a baby factory, by papal decree—being urged to produce as many children as possible in her lifetime. This pressure makes the Catholic Church the greatest menace in the world today. . . .

    The Catholic churches . . . should be picketed until the pope and the church renounce their stand against birth control and do as other churches do: preach Christianity, love for their fellow man, and follow in the footsteps of Jesus Christ. (Letter to the editor, *Riverside Press-Enterprise*)

43. I was filled with awe and admiration when I read of the determination of the men searching for the killer bees. Why couldn't we conduct just such a thorough search for missing children? Why couldn't we search every single home in the United States for these children? I think very few people would object to a legal search. (Letter to the editor, *Riverside Press-Enterprise*)

44. What mergers are doing to America is a national disgrace. They are the real reason the U.S. can no longer produce goods of quality at a reasonable price. Why produce goods when mergers are the product? Keep on merging, America; the Orient loves it. (Letter to the editor, *U.S. News & World Report*)

45. Many people fear that Fundamentalists will influence the passage of laws that infringe on their personal choices. However, this claim can never be an argument against the movement since all laws quite properly limit the individual's freedom for the collective good. (Letter to the editor, *Time*)

Review Questions Chapter 9

1. What is a fallacy?
2. What is the difference between formal and informal fallacies?
3. What is fallacious about the *ad hominem, tu quoque* argument?
4. What is the difference between the straw man and the red herring fallacies?
5. What fallacies do the following phrases express?

    a. If we cannot show that S is true, we may conclude that S is not true.

    b. What is true of the whole is true of its parts.

    c. Accept my conclusion if you know what is good for you.

    d. Don't believe him; he's not a good person.

    e. This must be true because so many people believe it.

    f. A and B are always observed together, so A must cause B.

    g. Believe what I say, I need your support.

    h. If A and B are alike in those respects, they are probably alike in this respect.

i. This premise is true only if the conclusion is true.

j. Refuting a misrepresentation of an opponent's argument.

True or False?

1. An argument that cites an authority in support of its conclusion is always fallacious.

2. The fallacy of composition consists of reasoning that what is true of the whole is true of the parts.

3. The fallacy of hasty generalization consists of generalizing over a small sample.

4. If a person asserts S and then asserts not-S after changing his or her mind, the person is not guilty of inconsistency.

5. The domino theory is a good example of the fallacy of begging the question.

6. Arguments from analogy are always fallacious.

7. An arguer who uses a word in two different senses is not necessarily guilty of the fallacy of equivocation.

8. Any statement whatsoever is validly deducible from inconsistent premises.

9. The fallacy of slippery slope may be thought of as an assertion of a series of causal connections, at least one of which commits the fallacy of false cause.

10. At the heart of the either/or fallacy is the mistake of overlooking some other possible alternative.

CHAPTER TEN
Evaluating Extended Arguments

This chapter describes a procedure for evaluating
extended arguments. The treatment involves a
closer examination of exposing arguments by
using the skills of rewriting sentences, paraphrasing, and supplying missing parts. Then
we will consider how premises may be evaluated
for truth-value and illustrate the procedure in its
entirety.

10.1 A Procedure for Argument Evaluation

The purpose of argument evaluation is to decide by examination whether an
argument is good. But, as we have seen throughout the text, a number of steps are
involved in such a decision. First, we need to expose the argument by identifying
premises and conclusions and, in the process, the inferences. Second, we determine
the validity or strength of the inferential support that premises pass to conclusions.
And third, we assess the truth-values of the premises. If we think of evaluating an
argument as a procedure consisting of steps, we can see clearly what we have learned
thus far and what we have yet to learn (see Figure 10.1).

Figure 10.1   Evaluation Flowchart

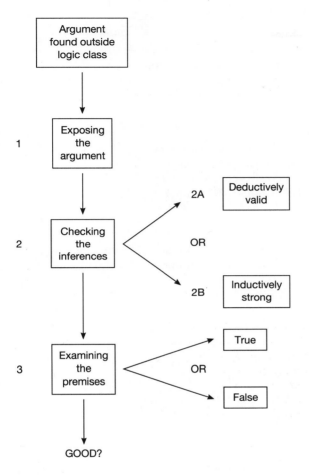

Throughout this text we have concentrated on Step 2, learning how to determine the degree of inferential strength that premises pass to a conclusion. Specifically, we have learned how to determine 2A, deductive validity or invalidity and 2B, criteria for assessing inductive strength. What we have to develop more fully are Step 1, how to expose the arguments in a lengthy passage and Step 3, how to examine premises for truth-value. This chapter addresses these two steps and then illustrates the procedure of argument evaluation from beginning to end. Let's begin by focusing on Step 1, exposing lengthy or extended arguments.

10.2 Introduction to Exposing Extended Arguments

Most arguments found in essays, newspapers, conversations, and so on are *extended arguments*. (See Chapter 1, p. 15 and also Chapter 4 on sorites, p. 100.) That is, the passage contains an overall argument supported by one or more subsidiary arguments. For instance, we encountered this example in Chapter 1:

Example 1

① *Cats make good pets and* ② *cats make good anatomical subjects. Therefore,* ③ *some good pets make good anatomical subjects. Since* ④ *good anatomical subjects are in high demand in medical schools, it follows that* ⑤ *some good pets are in high demand in medical schools.*

Recall that we have two different formats for showing the structure of an argument: argument form and diagraming. The argument in example 1 could be written in argument form as follows:

1. *Cats make good pets.*
2. *Cats make good anatomical subjects.*

---

3. *Some good pets make good anatomical subjects.*
4. *Good anatomical subjects are in high demand in medical schools.*

---

5. *Some good pets are in high demand in medical schools.*

The argument in example 1 also could be written in diagram form as follows:

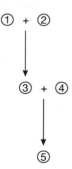

(Notice that it would be easy at this point to translate the statements into categorical forms and assess the argument for deductive validity as a sorites.) Either format above shows us that the argument supporting the conclusion ⑤ contains a subsidiary argument for statement ③. In other words, example 1 involves two inferences. The argument form format uses the line separating statements to show an inferential relationship. The diagram format uses the arrow to show an inferential relationship. Thus, we can define an extended argument technically as any argument that consists of two or more inferences as shown by either format.

Example 1 is easy to expose, but arguments found outside logic class are usually not that easy. They often consist of several paragraphs and several subsidiary arguments. The kinds of essays, speeches, and letters to the editor so often found in ordinary discourse are frequently difficult to expose because they present special problems.

Some of the special problems encountered with extended arguments are the following. A lengthy passage may include sentences that, on the surface, are not statements; we may need to rewrite them as statements. The passage may contain sentences that serve no purpose in the argument; we may disregard them. Or the passage may leave out statements that need to be supplied. Thus, since the purpose of exposing an argument is to make explicit what a person is arguing and how, we may have to edit an argument, that is, rewrite statements, paraphrase passages, omit some sentences, and supply missing parts.

But *how explicit should we be?* Given a lengthy speech or essay, how much detail do we need to include in our exposure of the argument? Every claim the arguer makes or something less than that? Here is a reasonable answer. In the first place, we know that we must provide at least as much detail as necessary for us to say what and how the argument is made, that is, enough detail so that we can pass to steps 2 and 3. In the second place, we need to be able to choose whether to give a detailed or a short account of an argument. Which we choose to do depends on how important the argument is. Those arguments that address vital concerns deserve close attention; others perhaps do not.

Proficiency in exposing extended arguments involves the important skills mentioned above: the skills of rewriting statements, paraphrasing, omitting sentences that serve no inferential purpose, and supplying missing parts. Not every extended argument requires these tasks but we do not have mastery of handling arguments without them. Therefore, in the following sections we will concentrate on those skills.

10.3 Omitting, Rewriting, and Paraphrasing

Omitting Sentences

Some sentences in an argument serve no inferential purpose. That is, they state neither premises nor conclusions. They may, on the other hand, serve to explain, illustrate, clarify, or provide some contextual information. Consider the following letter to the editor from *Scientific American:*

Example 2

> *I am a member of People for the Ethical Treat-ment of Animals as well as other groups dedicated to a more compassionate interpretation of our world.* I see an animal, or a plant for that matter, as a living organism that is unique by the fact of its life force. Creatures have only one life to live (Shirley MacLaine notwithstanding) and should be allowed to do so with dignity and in their natural environments.
>
> I am confused by the photograph of the researcher feeding the chimpanzee: he is spoon-feeding it as one might feed a baby, and he obviously cares about its health, yet the chimpanzee is peering through a small opening like one in a jail-cell door. Would that same researcher force his child to live under such conditions or subject himself to such deprivations?

The opening sentence (called out in underline) of this argument is neither a conclusion nor a premise. Rather it serves to identify the writer. In exposing the argument of the letter, we may omit the opening sentence.

In Brian Duffy's essay, "Mass Media: Marketing Marketing," he argues that during the eighties "the planet seemed finally to conclude that if it wasn't on TV, it wasn't real." The excerpt below states a premise of his argument followed by an illustration (underlined).

Example 3

> *Before the 80s, network news gave TV its excuse for existing. In the 80s, the point of TV news was simply to sell TV. And so we had Cable News Network—all the news, all the exhausting time. And what images! What theatrics! Grenada, Jessica McClure, Oliver North. We savored these TV moments. But we were numb from the hairline down.* (U.S. News & World Report)

The underlined sentences explain what he means by saying that the point of TV news in the eighties was to promote TV. We need not include these sentences in the exposition of the argument.

In the excerpt below, author Howard Morland in his *Newsweek* essay "Why War is Ignoble" opens with a claim that he proceeds to illustrate.

Example 4

Whenever young Americans depart for overseas battlefields, older men seem to envy them the adventure. On the eve of the Vietnam War, my college dean told me he was sorry he had not come under fire during his wartime service in the Pacific. He wanted to know how he might have responded to the test of combat. He assumed I would understand, and his regrets may have led me to later join the Air Force rather than seek a draft deferment.

The author's remarks are autobiographical and do not provide reason for accepting the opening statement. In exposing the paragraph, it is reasonable to omit the underlined portions.

It is not always easy to determine whether sentences or passages provide inferential support or not. The following example illustrates such a passage. In a letter written to the editor of *Rider*, a magazine for motorcyclists, on the practice of "lane splitting"—that is, passing cars within the lane—the author writes:

Example 5

The debate rages on concerning the safety of lane splitting, but for me the question has been answered many times. As long as it is approached in an intelligent manner, it is no less safe than staying in the lane, and in many circumstances it is actually safer. For example, if I am sitting in traffic between two cars, someone in the next lane can (and frequently does) change lanes into what appears to be a gap between those cars only to find an outraged motorcyclist already occupying said gap. The various responses to this situation can be imagined, and none of them is pretty.

The writer is arguing that lane splitting may be done safely and may in fact serve to avoid unsafe situations. He then offers an example. Should the example (called out in underlining) be omitted or does it support the author's conclusion? A reasonable answer, it seems, is that it does not merely clarify or illustrate; it provides evidential support for this claim. In this case providing an example is tantamount to providing an assertion that the described situation is unsafe. We can interpret the author to be reasoning as follows:

It is an unsafe situation when a car driver changes into a lane that appears to be unoc-cupied only to find a motorcycle sitting there.

Therefore, it may in fact be safer for motorcyclists to practice lane splitting.

We need some guidelines for deciding whether a sentence or passage serves no inferential purpose and, thus, may be omitted. Let us take a conservative approach.

A rule for omitting sentences: *When in doubt, in-clude the sentence.*

We will omit sentences only in those cases where is it *obvious* that no inferential pur-pose is served. Otherwise, we will include them, rewriting them if necessary for the argument's exposition.

Rewriting Sentences

Recall from Chapter 1 that we defined a statement as any sentence or part of a sentence that makes an assertion that something is or is not the case. Not all sen-tences, we noted, make assertions; thus, not all sentences are statements. When nec-essary, we may rewrite sentences or sentence parts as statements.

For our purposes, rewriting a sentence is done in order to make explicit a state-ment that functions as a premise or conclusion. Relatedly, paraphrasing is restating a text or passage. The usual purpose of paraphrasing is to simplify a lengthy passage, that is, to capture in a few sentences the meaning of a passage consisting of many sentences. In relation to exposing an argument, the purpose of both rewriting and paraphrasing is the same: to make clear what is said or written.

We need to approach the task of rewriting and paraphrasing with caution be-cause restating a person's words runs the risk of misinterpreting them. How do we avoid misinterpreting what someone has written or said? (1) Ask the person to clarify. A lot of fuss and bother is saved by this simple courtesy; but, of course, how often is the person there when you need him or her? Almost always we have to fall back on our best efforts. Thus, (2) stay as close as possible to the very words the person uses. If certain phrases are crucial, try to leave them intact. Be aware of key logical terms such as the categorical quantifiers and the logical operators. And last, (3) apply the principle of charity. Carefully choose those words that pro-vide the most plausible interpretation. (For review, see page 4 on the principle of charity.)

Keeping in mind the sensitive nature of interpreting people's words, let's move directly to the task of rewriting sentences and then paraphrasing passages.

As we saw in Chapter 1, common types of sentences that are not statements are questions, exclamations, commands, and requests. Nevertheless, we noted that, given information about the context, statements may be inferred from such sen-tences. So, for example, the following sentences may, in a suitable context, be con-strued as making statements:

Example 6

sentence: Why should I have to tell them?
statement: I should not have to tell them.

Example 7

sentence: Make your own decision!
statement: You should decide for yourself.
               I should not decide for you.

Example 8

sentence: Eureka!
statement: I have found it.
       or This is what I have been looking for.

Relatedly, consider these examples of exchanges in which one person takes another person's sentence to be or to imply a statement.

Example 9

Student: Did I miss anything important in class today, Professor?
Professor: Everything in class is important!

The professor's response, perhaps an attempt at humor, takes the student's question to imply this statement:

*"Some days nothing of importance happens in class.
Was today one of those days?"*

Example 10

Patient: Am I going to be okay, Doc?
Doctor: Stop worrying so much!
Patient: Well, that's a relief.

Neither patient nor doctor speaks directly through statements, yet statements are implied. The doctor, as interpreted by the patient, is asserting that the patient will be okay. The patient acknowledges and expresses relief. If it were important to do so, we might rewrite the dialogue as follows:

Patient: Am I going to be okay, Doc?
Doctor: You are going to be okay.
Patient: I understand you said that I am going to be okay and I am relieved to hear that.

The examples above illustrate briefly that sentences that are not themselves statements may, with caution, be rewritten as statements. Let's consider two particularly common practices: using rhetorical questions and following a question with an answer. The examples come directly from newspaper editorials or letters to the editor. The relevant sentences are numbered.

A *rhetorical question* is really a statement that, for effect, is put in the form of a question. For example, arguing that we should not go to war in the Middle East, the writer below asks the following rhetorical question:

Example 11

① *If you think we have problems now, what do you think will happen if we go to war?*

The writer is making the statement: *If we go to war, matters will be much worse.*
Now consider this letter to the editor.

Example 12

① *When will our leaders learn that "two wrongs don't make a right; that might is not right; that when our enemy hungers we should feed him, not starve him?"*
    Our poor old earth is suffering from our mistreatment of her for too many years. ② *Shall we burn and bomb and kill and maim to "preserve our way of life," i.e., go on polluting the air, wasting our natural resources . . . and refusing to face up to our real problems, the obscenely rich, the hopelessly poor, the neglected children. Wake up America!*

A reasonable interpretation of sentence ① seems to be:

> *Our leaders should know that two wrongs don't make a right, that might is not right and that when our enemy hungers, we should feed him, not starve him.*

Sentence ② is complex. Here is a reasonable restatement.

> *We should not go to war (burn, bomb, kill, and maim) to preserve our way of life.*
>
> *We should not go on polluting and wasting our natural resources.*
>
> *We should face up to our real problems: the obscenely rich, the hopelessly poor, and the neglected children.*

Here is another example, an excerpt from a tongue-in-cheek newspaper editorial entitled "Who Are the Rich?"

Example 13

Suppose you know a major league baseball player who has just signed a contract that is supposed to supply him with $1 million a year for the next seven years. ① Is he sitting back smiling contentedly? Not a bit. You see him on television with a frown creasing his face, complaining about his teammates, his team manager, his lawyer, or the umpire—and sometimes all at once. ② And is such a person, beset with such woes, someone you want to nail hard with a soak-the-rich tax scheme? ③ Who among us would be so pitiless and brutally callous as to contemplate such a thing?

Focusing just on the numbered questions in the passage, we can restate them as follows:

① *The million-dollar-a-year baseball player is not feeling content.*

② *You shouldn't want to further burden with taxes a person who is already beset with woes.*

③ *No one among us is so pitiless and brutally callous as to contemplate raising the taxes of people such as the million-dollar-a-year baseball player.*

Following a question with an answer is a common stylistic device by which writers try to engage their readers. The question serves to introduce a subject and make the reader think, at least momentarily. For example, in a *Newsweek* essay, "The Necessity of Dissent," Jonathan Alter argues that in a democracy it is essential to raise critical questions about the wisdom of going to war. During the course of his argument, he asks:

Example 14

① *Why should American soldiers die in the name of cut-rate oil? It's immoral to shed so much blood just to make the world safe for rich sheiks and gas guzzlers.*

It's not clear that the question in sentence ① is rhetorical but it is clear in the context of the paragraph that Alter argues that American soldiers should not die in the name of cut-rate oil. The statement after his question provides a premise for that conclusion.

Later in the essay Alter asks this question:

Example 15

① *How scarce is mainstream dissent? Last week the
father of a U.S. Marine wrote a critical piece in the*
New York Times. . . . *The author, Alex Molnar,
was besieged by requests for TV appearances to explain his novel views. No one had heard them before.*
    *There's some token antiwar sentiment showing
up in newspapers in the Midwest. . . . And polls
show that black Americans . . . are less supportive
than the population as a whole. But that still leaves
a deafening silence.*

Sentence ① introduces the subject of the extent of public dissent among mainstream Americans by means of a question. The rest of the passage proceeds to answer that question. In effect, Alter is asserting the statement:

Mainstream dissent is almost nonexistent

which he then supports by statements in the rest of the passage.

Paraphrasing

Example 15 presents a good example for *paraphrasing*. If our aim were to simplify Alter's essay as much as possible, then we could take that passage simply to be stating the premise:

Mainstream dissent is almost nonexistent.

The rest of his argument, not presented here, could then be constructed from other paragraphs of his essay. On the other hand, we might want to provide more of the information contained in the passage quoted. For example, we could paraphrase the first paragraph as follows:

② *Public dissent is so scarce that one person's critical
   letter to the* New York Times *caused excitement.*
③ *There is some token dissent in Midwest
   newspapers.*
④ *A poll showed some dissent among black
   Americans.*

---

① *Therefore, mainstream dissent is almost
   nonexistent.*

To illustrate both paraphrasing and exposing extended arguments, let's work through a letter to the editor from the newspaper. We will begin with a *first pass* through the example, identifying and numbering sentences or sentence parts as shown below. Then we will paraphrase the argument. Last, we will diagram the complete argument. In the process we will see that paraphrasing can be a useful step in exposing an extended argument.

Example 16

① *I think it is very unfair that the government is once again trying to raise the federal excise tax on cigarettes.* ② *Smokers already pay more than $11 billion in cigarette taxes every year. Considering that* ③ *an estimated $100 billion in taxes owed to the government will not be paid this year,* ④ *I propose that Congress try to collect those funds rather than impose new taxes on cigarettes.*

After all, ⑤ *why should smokers,* ⑥ *who contribute more than their fair share of taxes, be further financially burdened by additional taxes when* ⑦ *there are people in this country that aren't even paying what they rightfully owe?*

⑧ *All citizens should be taxed equally, even those of us who choose to smoke.* ⑨ *It is extremely unfair to target a specific consumer group time after time.* ⑩ *Smokers should not be penalized every time the government feels the need for additional revenue.*

⑪ *It is my hope that all fair-minded people will realize the unfairness of this particular tax and* ⑫ *write in opposition to their legislators.*

Notice that the third paragraph, consisting of sentence parts ⑤, ⑥, and ⑦, is a rhetorical question. We can rewrite that sentence as three statements:

⑤ *Smokers should not be further financially burdened by additional taxes*

⑥ *Smokers contribute more than their fair share of taxes*

⑦ *there are people in this country that aren't even paying what they rightfully owe*

Next, we can list all the statements in order as follows:

① *it is very unfair that the government is once again trying to raise the federal excise tax on cigarettes.*

② *Smokers already pay more than $11 billion in cigarette taxes every year.*

③ *an estimated $100 billion in taxes owed to the government will not be paid this year*

④ *I propose that Congress try to collect those funds rather than impose new taxes on cigarettes.*

⑤ *Smokers should not be further financially burdened by additional taxes*

⑥ *Smokers contribute more than their fair share of taxes.*

⑦ *there are people in this country that aren't even paying what they rightfully owe*

⑧ *All citizens should be taxed equally, even those of us who choose to smoke*

⑨ *It is extremely unfair to target a specific consumer group time after time*

⑩ *Smokers should not be penalized every time the government feels the need for additional revenue*

⑪ *It is my hope that all fair-minded people will realize the unfairness of this particular tax*

⑫ *All fair-minded people should write in opposition to their legislators*

At this point, it is useful to try to give a simple *paraphrase* of the argument. It is clear that the writer is arguing that we should oppose the federal excise tax on cigarettes. The conclusion is contained in statements ⑪ and ⑫. In support, the writer claims that ⑧ taxes should be fair and that ⑥ smokers already pay their fair share but ⑦ some people do not. Thus, we should oppose the tax because it is unfair. But furthermore, the writer also proposes that, rather than taxing cigarettes further, ④ Congress should collect the unpaid taxes from those who do not pay their share.

One way to organize the argument is to see it as containing two separable lines of reasoning. First, there is the argument that the cigarette tax is unfair, ①. Second, there is the argument that Congress should collect those unpaid taxes, ④. Both arguments use premise ⑧ as a general principle of fairness in taxation. And from both lines of reasoning it is concluded that ⑫ people should write to their legislators opposing the new cigarette tax. Thus, by diagraming our paraphrase we can see these two lines of argument.

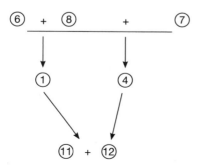

Making another pass through the argument we can begin to supply the additional inferential supports. For instance, it seems that statement ⑨ is immediately concluded from ⑧:

⑧ *All citizens should be taxed equally . . .*
↓
⑨ *It is extremely unfair to target a specific consumer group time after time*

Statement ⑨ is conjoined with ⑥ from which ⑤ and ⑩ follow:

⑨ *It is extremely unfair to target a specific consumer group time after time*

  ┌─+
  │ ⑥ *Smokers contribute more than their fair share of taxes*
  │ ⑤ *Smokers should not be further financially burdened by additional taxes*
  └─►+
   ⑩ *Smokers should not be penalized every time the government feels the need for additional revenue.*

Statement ② supports statement ⑤ as follows:

② *Smokers already pay more than $11 billion in cigarette taxes every year*
↓
⑤ *Smokers should not be further financially burdened by additional taxes*

Last, statement ③ is offered in support of statement ⑦:

③ *an estimated $100 billion in taxes owed to the government will not be paid this year*
↓
⑦ *there are people in this country that aren't even paying what they rightfully owe*

Now we can give a complete diagram of the argument.

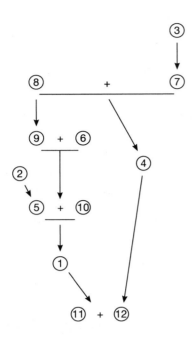

As a second example of the use of paraphrasing in exposing an extended argument, consider the following editorial from the *New York Times*.

Example 17

① *President Bush has inadvertently slighted the
U.S. Foreign Service.* ② *In his Sept. 11 speech to
Congress, Mr. Bush spoke generously and at length
about "our brave servicemen and women" in the Persian Gulf.* ③ *But he failed even to mention the brave
men and women serving as diplomats in Baghdad and
Kuwait, the hazardous cockpits of the conflict.* ④ *It
does not belittle the sacrifices of uniformed Americans
to note that Foreign Service officers are in more immediate peril.*

⑤ *More of these civilian officers have been killed
in the line of duty than all the generals and admirals
who have died in combat since World War II.* ⑥ *The
names of these diplomats are honored on plaques in the
State Department lobby.* ⑦ *In 1955 there were 75
names.* ⑧ *Since then, 90 more career diplomats have
been killed, most victims of terrorism.*

⑨ *Americans treat the Foreign Service shabbily.*
⑩ *Congress routinely slashes State Department budgets, since diplomacy has no domestic constituency.* ⑪
*Salaries are kept low and training programs starved of
funds by legislators.* ⑫ *Presidents treat ambassadorial
posts as choice booty for chums and contributors.*

⑬ *Perversely, career diplomats go unrecognized and unrewarded even as their skills are required for new problems, from narcotics and pollution to vanishing rain forests.* ⑭ *Neglect of the Foreign Service is ignominious in normal times, but incomprehensible in crisis.* ⑮ *American diplomats in Kuwait are captives in a combat zone;* ⑯ *embassy defenders rely on a swimming pool for drinking water.* ⑰ *Their courage calls for a salute;* ⑱ *at the first opportunity, Mr. Bush should make full amends.*

Let us consider how we can organize and simplify the argument. First, what is the main point of this argument? It is clear that it is a defense of the U.S. Foreign Service. Specifically, the writer argues that President Bush has insulted the Foreign Service and "should make full amends." The writer's conclusion is contained in statement ⑱ which can be rewritten as follows:

⑱ *At the first opportunity, President Bush should make amends by saluting the courage of Foreign Service officers.*

What reasons does the writer offer for that conclusion? Looking over the argument we can see these reasons:

① *President Bush has slighted the U.S. Foreign Service.*

⑰ *Their courage calls for a salute.*

⑭ *Neglect of the Foreign Service is ignominious in normal times, but incomprehensible in crisis.*

Thus, the general thrust of the argument is clear: Mr. Bush should make amends to the Foreign Service because he has slighted it, it is ignominious—indeed incomprehensible in crisis—to neglect it, and its courage should be saluted.

Thus, we can diagram the paraphrased argument as below:

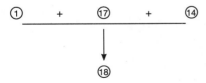

Now having paraphrased the argument we can continue to expose it by assembling statements as they bear on the major premises shown above. For example, statements ②, ③, and ④ support statement ①.

② *In his Sept. 11 speech to Congress, Mr. Bush spoke generously and at length about "our brave servicemen and women" in the Persian Gulf.*

③ *But he failed even to mention the brave men and women serving as diplomats in Baghdad and Kuwait, the hazardous cockpits of the conflict.*

④ *It does not belittle the sacrifices of uniformed Americans to note that Foreign Service officers are in more immediate peril.*

---

① *President Bush has slighted the U.S. Foreign Service.*

In support of ⑰ the writer offers two separable arguments.

⑦ *In 1955 there were 75 names [of career diplomats killed in the line of duty].*

⑧ *Since then, 90 more career diplomats have been killed, most victims of terrorism.*

---

⑤ *More of these civilian officers have been killed in the line of duty than all the generals and admirals who have died in combat since World War II.*

---

⑰ *Their courage calls for a salute.*

The second argument is:

⑮ *American diplomats in Kuwait are captives in a combat zone.*

---

⑰ *Their courage calls for a salute.*

Notice that statement ⑯ "Embassy defenders rely on a swimming pool for drinking water" seems more to illustrate their captivity in Kuwait rather than provide a reason for concluding that they are held captive. Therefore, it is reasonable to omit ⑯.

Thus, the arguments in support of ⑰ may be diagramed as shown below:

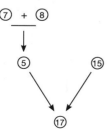

In support of ⑭ the writer offers several separable reasons as follows:

⑩ *Congress routinely slashes State Department budgets, since diplomacy has no domestic constituency.*

⑪ *Salaries are kept low and training programs starved of funds by legislators.*

⑫ *Presidents treat ambassadorial posts as choice booty for chums and contributors.*

⑬ *Perversely, career diplomats go unrecognized and unrewarded even as their skills are required for new problems, from narcotics and pollution to vanishing rain forests.*

⑨ *Americans treat the Foreign Service shabbily.*

⑭ *Neglect of the Foreign Service is ignominious in normal times, but incomprehensible in crisis.*

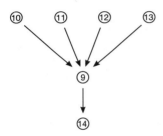

We can now assemble the various parts of the argument and complete the diagram of the whole.
Diagram of Example 17

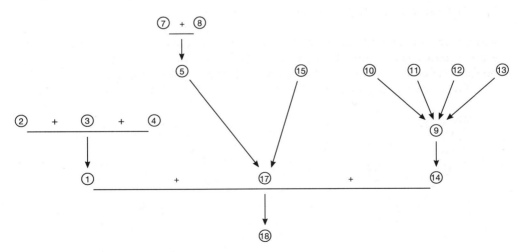

We will return to Example 17 to complete the evaluation. (See pages 319–324 below.)

Exercise 10.3   Rewriting, Paraphrasing, and Diagraming.   Expose the following extended arguments by (1) numbering sentences; (2) rewriting as statements, if necessary; and (3) drawing a diagram of the argument.

1. [Under present law] federal regulations do not require the use of anesthesia if the experimenter says it will interfere with the results of the study. In 1982, more than 130,000 painful experiments were carried out on animals without anesthesia, and drugs were commonly administered which do not relieve pain but which do paralyze the animal so that it is unable to move or cry out, permitting the experimenter to carry out an experiment involving considerable pain without having to face the animal's agony. . . . As moral beings, we have the responsibility to do everything in our power to grant the unfortunate creatures forced to submit to experimentation by humans every possible comfort in their misery. (letter to the editor)

2. To imagine that God is pleased because children pray in a classroom borders on the naive. To think that such action by pupils in a public school will inspire faith is questionable. Many pupils will have no other contact with religion and will see prayer as a kind of starting gun for the day's activities. Meanwhile, religion in which God is served by more than words is lost from sight. (newspaper article)

3. Has it ever occurred to critics what would happen with the smaller states during an election if it weren't for the Electoral College? All a candidate would have to do is work on the big states like New York, California, etc., win there and forget about the smaller states because of lower population. The Electoral College [in which each state gets one vote for each representative and senator] gives the smaller states something they need in an election—a real vote. (letter to the editor)

4. Our ears project auditory information to *both* hemispheres, not just the "contralateral" one (i.e., the one on the opposite side). Therefore, "sealing off" the right ear by using the right thumb does very little with regard to eliminating the passage of information to the left hemisphere and does not substantially enhance the flow of information to the right hemisphere. (letter to the editor)

5. There is one major problem with our society's newfound awareness of alcohol abuse and its related problems. The lunatic fringe has been proposing things like advertising bans and warning labels. Not only does this not affect the abuser but it implies that alcohol use is somehow inherently wrong. This is an unfair judgment of the millions of Americans who drink responsibly. Furthermore, when it comes to meals, a bottle of beer or a glass of wine can enhance the flavor of many dishes. Bottled water, even with the added "essences" and manufactured fizz, does nothing more than wash the food down. (letter to the editor)

6. The TWA plane hijack is another in a long line of events that show the U.S. has become the target of spies and terrorists. Unfortunately, we lack the national will to retaliate. Turning the other cheek only invites further terrorism. Our government needs more guts. (letter to the editor)

7. Parents are principally responsible for the education and upbringing of their children and are, therefore, the most qualified persons to select the formal schooling for their children. (letter to the editor)

8. As a lawyer, I often pass the New York Federal Building and view the controversial sculpture *Tilted Arc* by Richard Serra. The work is a meaningless blob, an eyesore that ruins a rare open space. Its only possible function is as a barrier against terrorists. (letter to the editor)

9. Broadcast television imposes limits, strict but self-enforced limits, on explicit sex. Why not on explicit terror? There is no reason why all the news of a terrorist event, like news of a rape, cannot be transmitted in some form. But in the interest of decency, diplomacy and our own self-respect, it need not be live melodrama. (Charles Krauthammer, essay, *Time*)

10. When, in ordinary life, we speak of *the* colour of the table, we only mean the sort of colour which it will seem to have to a normal spectator from an ordinary point of view under usual condition of light. But the other colours which appear under other conditions have just as good a right to be considered real; and therefore, to avoid favouritism, we are compelled to deny that, in itself, the table has any one particular colour. (Bertrand Russell, *The Problems of Philosophy*)

11. I am an eighteen-year-old Sikh. I strongly adhere to my religion and want to be free to practice it. I believe that if my government does not provide me with the freedom to practice my religion, and deprives me of my basic human rights, then I have the right to choose another government or have my own, which will provide the freedom that I and my kind need. (letter to the editor)

12. We have no image, no idea corresponding to [the name of God]. Hence we are forbidden to worship God in the form of an image, lest we should think we could conceive Him who is inconceivable. Hence it appears that we have no idea of God. (Thomas Hobbes, *Objections to Descartes' Meditations*)

13. Well, I should either get a job or go to college. The job market is really bad now. I don't think I have much of a chance. Besides, maybe things will be better in a couple of years. And if I go to college that should help me get a job. So, I'll go to college. That's settled!

14. I'm not against television because of the violence. I'm against television because of what it does to viewers. Watching TV hypnotizes you. It turns you into a passive, unimaginative zombie. All you do is stare. You don't think. You don't imagine. You don't even have to respond to what you see. It's all done for you and you do nothing. Think of all that time wasted! That's why I'm against television.

15. I believe that civil disobedience is sometimes the morally right thing to do. Oh, I know you hear it said that every citizen has an obligation to obey the laws of the land—and that's generally true. But do you have an obligation to

obey *every* law, even an immoral law? Some laws *are* immoral. Laws ought to protect us, but some laws actually violate people's rights. Those laws should not be obeyed. Therefore, in those cases civil disobedience *is* the right thing to do.

16. Anyone depraved enough to murder once is very likely going to harm someone again. The only sure way to prevent such a person from further crime is to put him to death. Look, we have a moral duty to protect our citizens from dangerous murderers. But, short of capital punishment, there is simply no way to protect people. The reasons are obvious. Too often murderers are out on parole in just a few years. Escape is always possible. And within the confines of prison there is the problem of protecting guards and other inmates from the dangerous murderer. It simply cannot be done. It follows, therefore, that the only way to ensure that such people do not kill again is to put them to death. So I say that capital punishment is morally just.

17. For punishment to effectively deter potential criminals several conditions must exist. First, people must believe that they will very likely be caught, convicted, and punished. Second, people must be able to control their conduct according to that belief. But most potential lawbreakers think they will not get caught and surely not punished. Furthermore, many crimes are committed impulsively by people who are temporarily so upset they are unable to discipline themselves. Thus, punishment does not work as an effective deterrent to crime.

18. Beauty, physical beauty, is not as valuable as people think. Things of real value are those which endure and which make us good people. But physical beauty neither lasts nor guarantees goodness.

19. For the past twenty years researchers have been training chimpanzees to use sign language. Just recently Washoe, the first chimp to communicate with sign language, began teaching a ten-month-old chimp named Loulis to use signs. She even went so far as to mold Loulis' hands to form signs. Thus far, Loulis has learned fifty-five words. This fact, that one chimp can teach another to use sign language, is the strongest evidence to date that animals other than humans can learn and use language.

20. Pantheism is the view that God is the universe or, put differently, that God is everything. This is not a Christian view, as can be easily seen. First, according to Christian thinking God is all-good. Second, the universe is *not* all-good. It contains both good *and* evil. Those two Christian beliefs entail that pantheism is not a Christian view.

21. Suppose a man owns a ranch and the cattle on it. If he hires another man to do all the work of raising the cattle, then when the cattle are sold the owner will pay a portion for expenses and a portion to his worker. The remainder is the owner's profit. The profit is due him, not for any work he did, but simply because he owns the cattle. This shows that the institution of private property entitles owners to value independent of their labor. But why, I ask, should a man be entitled to something without working for it? That is morally wrong. And, therefore, so also is the institution of private property.

22. Our society is heterogeneous in nature and, therefore, individuals, groups and communities have quite different ideas about the best and most desirable content of formal education. Public policy, in my opinion, should foster plu-

ralism and diversity in education rather than impose a homogeneous definition of schooling upon all. (letter to the editor)

23. Journalists are led to believe, and some may actually believe, that they only hold a mirror to life. And mirrors can hardly be accused of bad faith. Not even physicists, practitioners of a somewhat more exact science, have so arrogant a belief in the out there. For 60 years, physics has learned to live with its Uncertainty Principle: that the act of observing an event alters its nature. Journalism continues to resist the idea. And journalism, which shines lights at people, not electrons, does more than alter. It creates. First, out of the infinite flotsam of "events" out there, it makes "stories." Then, by exposing them (and their attached people, ideas, crimes), it puts them on the map. "As seen on TV" gives substance to murder as surely as it does to Ginzu knives. The parade of artifacts is varied, but the effect is the same: coverage makes them real. (Charles Krauthammer, essay in *Time*)

24. But if life has an aim, it is clear that it ought to come to an end when that aim is reached . . . if the aim of humanity is goodness, righteousness, love—call it what you will—if it is what the prophets have said, that all mankind should be united together in love, that the spears should be beaten into pruning-hooks and so forth, what is it that hinders the attainment of this aim? The passions hinder it. Of all the passions the strongest, cruellest, and most stubborn is the sex-passion, physical love; and therefore if the passions are destroyed, including the strongest of them—physical love—the prophecies will be fulfilled, mankind will be brought into unity, the aim of human existence will be attained, and there will be nothing further to live for. (Tolstoy, "The Kreutzer Sonata")

25. The idea of solidity is that of two objects, which being impell'd by the utmost force, cannot penetrate each other; but still maintain a separate and distinct existence. Solidity, therefore, is perfectly incomprehensible alone, and without the conception of some bodies, which are solid, and maintain this separate and distinct existence. (David Hume, *Treatise on Human Nature*)

26. The capacity for suffering and enjoying things is a prerequisite for having interests at all. . . . A stone does not have interests because it cannot suffer. Nothing that we can do to it could possibly make any difference to its welfare. A mouse, on the other hand, does have an interest in not being tormented, because it will suffer if it is. (Peter Singer, *Practical Ethics*)

27. If we leave selection of public art to residents of a community . . . we will end up with an aesthetic common denominator of sterile, benign and conventional art that will neither offend nor stimulate. A community, no matter how enlightened, will rarely, if ever, embrace innovation at first glance. Selection, therefore, cannot be left to a popular vote. Only a panel of recognized art experts . . . can properly choose the high caliber of public art that justifies the expenditure of public money. (Alvin S. Lane, newspaper article)

28. Because I cannot conceive God unless existing, it follows that existence is inseparable from him, and therefore that he really exists. . . . (Rene Descartes, *Meditations*)

29. As for the terms *good* and *bad,* they indicate no positive quality in things regarded in themselves, but are merely modes of thinking, or notions which we form from the comparison of things one with another. Thus one and the

same thing can be at the same time good, bad, and indifferent. For instance, music is good for him that is melancholy, bad for him that mourns; for him that is deaf, it is neither good nor bad. (Spinoza, *The Ethics*)

30. It is indeed an opinion strangely prevailing amongst men, that houses, mountains, rivers, and in a word all sensible objects, have an existence, natural or real, distinct from their being perceived by the understanding. But with how great an assurance and acquiescence soever this principle may be entertained in the world, yet whoever shall find in his heart to call it in question may, if I mistake not, perceive it to involve a manifest contradiction. For what are the aforementioned objects but the things we perceive by sense? and what do we perceive besides our own ideas or sensations? and is it not plainly repugnant that any one of *these*, or any combination of them, should exist unperceived? (George Berkeley, *Of the Principles of Human Knowledge*)

10.4 Supplying Missing Parts

In everyday conversation it is not necessary to say everything to our listeners; some ideas can be taken for granted. Very often speakers leave out what they know their listeners will "fill in." The same is true of speakers or writers giving arguments. Frequently we can find arguments in which a premise or even a conclusion is left out because it is taken for granted. Such arguments are called *enthymemes*. In logic we need to supply the missing parts to these arguments, thus making the reasoning explicit. Here is an example in which a premise is left unstated:

Example 18

All chemists are scientists, so Mrs. Merk must be a scientist.

As stated the argument is incomplete. Clearly it assumes that the premise 'Mrs. Merk is a chemist' will be understood. Supplying the missing premise (marked here with an asterisk) makes the argument explicit:

1. *All chemists are scientists.*
*2. *Mrs. Merk is a chemist.*
_____

3. *Mrs. Merk is a scientist.*

You may think of supplying missing premises as making explicit what the argument, as given, seems to assume. Consider another example of an incomplete argument:

Example 19

1. *God created the world.*
_____

3. *The world is good.*

To make explicit the reasoning of this argument, we supply a premise such as 'Whatever God creates is good'.

 1. *God created the world.*
* 2. *Whatever God creates is good.*
_____

 3. *The world is good.*

Less common are arguments with a missing conclusion. Again, a speaker may deliberately leave the conclusion unstated, relying on the listeners to complete the reasoning. So, for example, one might argue as follows:

Example 20

You're not 21 and you have to be 21 to drink in this state.

The premises point to the conclusion 'You can't drink in this state' but the speaker chooses not to express it.

As another example, consider Dr. Richard Barth's argument in defense of the purchase of a $400,000 diagnostic machine called a CT scanner, as reported in the newspaper:

Example 21

*"A hospital that's going to be in business and trying to deliver care . . . is going to have to have access to a certain degree of basic services. CT is really a basic service now." (*Rutland Herald*)*

Barth's argument leaves it to the reader to draw the conclusion that a viable hospital has to have a CT scanner.

 1. *A hospital that's going to be in business and trying to deliver care . . . is going to have to have access to a certain degree of basic services.*
 2. *The CT scanner is a basic service.*
_____

* 3. *A viable hospital has to have a CT scanner.*

One final example illustrates how we may have to rephrase an argument as well as supply missing parts. Consider this reply:

Example 22

*What? Did you ask if we were going home now? Well,
this is just the intermission and there are two more acts.*

The point the speaker is making is that "we are not going home now." Fully exposed the argument would read:

1. *We won't go home until the next two acts are over.*
2. *This is just the intermission and there are two
more acts.*

---

*3. *We are not going home now.*

As a general rule we are justified in supplying a premise if it is required to make the reasoning of the argument explicit. However, when you supply a premise you are interpreting an argument and you may be seeing in it something that the speaker does not intend. For example, suppose a person argues:

Example 23

Abortion is wrong because it is killing.

It would be natural to supply the premise 'All killing is wrong' yielding the argument:

1. *Abortion is killing.*
*2. *All killing is wrong.*

---

3. *Abortion is wrong.*

Although premise (2) completes the argument, it also renders it controversial since (2) is not obviously acceptable. If we are to practice the principle of charity (see Chapter 1, section 1.2), we should not provide missing statements that weaken an argument, unless, of course, we have some reason to think that is precisely what the speaker intends. Thus, if we were to give this speaker the benefit of the doubt, we might complete the argument as follows:

1. *Abortion is the intentional killing of a human
fetus.*
*2. *A human fetus is a person with a serious right to
life.*
*3. *It is wrong to intentionally violate the right to life
of a person.*

3a. *Abortion is wrong.*

The speaker, if he or she is available, can tell us whether this argument is intended. Otherwise we have done our best to provide a plausible argument from what we have been given.

Let's consider now an extended argument from a newspaper editorial.

Example 24

① The United States has first dibs on the letter S. ② So what's going to happen if Mikhail Gorbachev has his way and the Soviet Union gets a new name? ③ Right now it's known in English officially as the Union of Soviet Socialist Republics. ④ Gorbachev wants it renamed something that comes out in English as "Union of Sovereign Socialist States."

⑤ That will mean we can't shorten their title to "Soviets." ⑥ The initials would be U.S.S.S. and that could mean trouble. ⑦ Can you imagine a television anchorman trying to talk about a "U.S.– U.S.S.S. superpower summit"? ⑧ The tongue would be twisted completely out of shape.

⑨ And what will we call them for short? ⑩ The Sovereigns? ⑪ Sounds like an expansion team in professional basketball or hockey, or like a British soccer team.

⑫ How about "The States"? ⑬ No-no, that's us. ⑭ Perhaps "Socialist States." ⑮ But with Moscow's 500-day dash toward a market economy, the word "socialist" quickly will be outmoded. ⑯ Besides, it's a word that's not very popular among the Soviet— er, pardon, the Sovereign—people.

⑰ It was much easier back in the good old days when we called them "Reds." ⑱ Of course that word might be considered inflammatory these days, and invokes the specter of Joseph McCarthy and his ilk every time it is uttered.

⑲ But it has one important asset. ⑳ It rolls easily off the tongue. ㉑ And it fits neatly into a headline.

Example 24 is an entertaining exercise in exposing arguments. Let's take it seriously and try to expose the reasoning.

The event that provokes the editorial is described in ④ which, taken together with ③, can be rewritten as follows:

③④ Gorbachev wants to change the name of the Union of Soviet Socialist Republics to the Union of Sovereign Socialist States.

The writer opposes this change. (Notice, however, that he never says so explicitly.) He makes two major points in opposition. One is the following:

① *The United States has first dibs on the letter S.*

(To have "first dibs" means to have first choice.)

The second major point is introduced in sentence ②: "So what's going to happen if Mikhail Gorbachev has his way and the Soviet Union gets a new name?" Here we have a question that introduces a series of statements. In effect, the writer is asserting that if Gorbachev has his way and the Soviet Union gets the new name, a series of problems will occur. The writer then proceeds to list the problems this will cause us. Thus, we can rewrite sentence ② as follows:

② *If Gorbachev has his way and the Soviet Union gets the new name of Union of Sovereign Socialist States, then we will have no easy way to refer to them.*

Thus, to summarize at this point, we seem to have three major premises.

① *The United States has first dibs on the letter S.*

④ *Gorbachev wants to change the name of the Union of Soviet Socialist Republics to the Union of Sovereign Socialist States.*

② *If Gorbachev has his way and the Soviet Union gets the new name of Union of Sovereign Socialist States, then we will have no easy way to refer to them.*

Now we can see that most but not all of the rest of the passage is in support of statement ②. If Gorbachev changes the name to Union of Sovereign Socialist States, the consequences for us are as described in sentences ⑤ through ⑯. Let's assemble those points.

First, there is the claim that:

⑤ *We can't shorten their title to "Soviets."*

Second, the following premises are given:

⑥ *The initials with the new name would be U.S.S.S.*

⑦⑧ *It twists the tongue completely out of shape to refer to a summit as a U.S.–U.S.S.S. summit.*

From which we can infer as a missing conclusion:

---

*⑧ₐ *We have no convenient initials for them.*

Third, the writer lists a series of possible names we might use and then discards each.

⑪ *"The Sovereigns" sounds like an athletic team.*

---

⑨⑩ *We cannot call them "the Sovereigns" for short.*
⑬ *We are "The States."*

---

⑫ *We cannot call them "The States."*
⑮ *With Moscow's 500-yard dash toward a market economy, the word "socialist" quickly will be outmoded.*
⑯ *The word "socialist" is not popular with the people.*

---

⑭ *We cannot call them "the Socialist States."*

Finally, the writer considers the possibility of referring to the Soviets as the "Reds." He says:

⑰ *It was much easier back in the good old days when we called them "Reds."*

He offers two distinct considerations regarding that name.

⑱ *That word might be considered inflammatory and invokes the specter of Joseph McCarthy and his ilk every time it is uttered.*

On the other hand, ⑲ It has one important asset:

⑳ *It rolls easily off the tongue.*
㉑ *It fits neatly into a headline.*

But the writer reaches no *explicit* conclusion about "Reds." Does he reject that name or not? What he says can be summed up this way: It would be convenient to call them "Reds" but it would also be undesirable. Perhaps the most reasonable way to construe this set of considerations is that the writer is again suggesting a difficulty Gorbachev's name change would cause us. We can, therefore, assemble sentences ⑰ through ㉑ with a supplied missing conclusion as follows:

⑰ *It was much easier back in the good old days when we called them "Reds."*

⑲ ⑳ ㉑ *It has one important asset: It rolls easily off the tongue and fits neatly into a headline.*

⑱ *That word might be considered inflammatory and invokes the specter of Joseph McCarthy and his ilk every time it is uttered.*

---

* ㉑ₐ *It would be convenient to call them "Reds" but it would also be undesirable.*

Now let's consider how to express the conclusion of the writer's overall argument. Nowhere does the writer explicitly say that we should oppose Gorbachev's plan to change the name of the Soviet Union. What he says is that we have "first dibs" on the letter S and that we will have all kinds of problems referring to the newly named country if Gorbachev goes ahead. If we paraphrase this writer's satirical argument, we can see a reasonable statement of the missing conclusion:

① *The United States has first dibs on the letter S.*

④ *Gorbachev wants to change the name of the Union of Soviet Socialist Republics to the Union of Sovereign Socialist States.*

② *If Gorbachev has his way and the Soviet Union gets the new name of Union of Sovereign Socialist States, then we will have no easy way to refer to them.*

---

* ㉒ *Gorbachev ought to give weighty consideration to how a name change would affect us.*

Since this seems a reasonable paraphrase of the argument, we can now provide a detailed and complete exposition of the argument in argument form as follows:

① *The United States has first dibs on the letter S.*

③④ *Gorbachev wants to change the name of the Union of Soviet Socialist Republics to the Union of Sovereign Socialist States.*

⑤ *We can't shorten their title to "Soviets."*

⑥ *The initials with the new name would be U.S.S.S.*

⑦⑧ *It twists the tongue completely out of shape to refer to a summit as a U.S.–U.S.S.S. summit.*

---

*⑧ₐ *We have no convenient initials for them.*

⑪ *"The Sovereigns" sounds like an athletic team.*

---

⑨⑩ *We cannot call them "The Sovereigns" for short.*

⑬ *We are "The States."*

---

⑫ *We cannot call them "The States."*

⑮ *With Moscow's 500-yard dash toward a market economy, the word "socialist" quickly will be outmoded.*

⑯ *The word "socialist" is not popular with the people.*

---

⑭ *We cannot call them "The Socialist States."*

⑰ *It was much easier back in the good old days when we called them "Reds."*

⑲⑳㉑ *It has one important asset: It rolls easily off the tongue and fits neatly into a headline.*

⑱ *That word might be considered inflammatory and invokes the specter of Joseph McCarthy and his ilk every time it is uttered.*

---

*㉑ₐ *It would be convenient to call them "Reds" but it would also be undesirable.*

② *If Gorbachev has his way and the Soviet Union gets the new name of Union of Sovereign Socialist States, then we will have no easy way to refer to them.*

---

*㉒ *Gorbachev ought to give weighty consideration to how a name change would affect us.*

In summary, *enthymemes* are arguments that contain a missing premise or conclusion. Since in most cases what the speaker leaves out is what he or she believes is obvious and implied in the argument, it is usually not very difficult to supply those missing parts. In logic exposing an argument requires that we include those missing parts no matter how obvious they are.

Exercise 10.4 Enthymemes: Missing Premises and Conclusions.
Write out the following arguments in argument form supplying the necessary premise or conclusion. Indicate a supplied statement with an asterisk (*).

1. You haven't registered. You can't vote.

2. Vehicles that run on methanol rather than gasoline could hit the market as soon as 1995. Assuming that happens, it is certain that we won't be vulnerable to Persian Gulf politics then.

3. Most scientists are liberals, so Professor Pipes must be a liberal.

4. Vote for Congressman Smith. He's the kind of representative who cares about his people.

5. Abortion kills the fetus. It's murder.

6. Most major religions include a belief in a god. So, Confucianism must also.

7. We are certain that she feels no pain and has no sensations whatsoever because all mental life—feelings, thoughts, sensations—cease when the brain is dead.

8. John Hinckley should not be punished for his attempt to assassinate the president. He's mentally ill.

9. By the age of eighty, most people's eyes show some significant macular degeneration, a deterioration of the retina that is the leading cause of loss of vision. Hence, the problem is that we are living longer than our eyes.

10. People enjoy imitations; hence, they enjoy looking at photographs.

11. If the theory of evolution were correct, then the fossil record would show a continuous sequence of fossils connecting the simplest organisms with the higher life forms. But the fact is that there are large gaps, for example, between invertebrates and vertebrates, between reptiles and mammals, and between the apes and man. (adapted from *Science and Unreason* by Radner and Radner)

12. A minimum of 70 points is required to pass this exam, Mr. Fluke. You scored 68. You know what that means.

13. Whales must bear their young alive because all mammals do.

14. The Japanese economy is characterized by a relatively free market system and private ownership of the means of production. It is, therefore, a capitalistic economy.

15. Apes cannot reason! They don't have language.

16. If the proliferation of the bomb . . . is not stopped, safeguards for survival will become impossible. Before long a lunatic, a supreme egoist or an itchy finger will flip the switch. (letter to the editor)

17. *Animals eat each other, so why shouldn't we eat them?* The decisive point . . . is that nonhuman animals are not capable of considering the alternatives open to them or of reflecting on the ethics of their diet. Hence, it is impossible to hold the animals responsible for what they do, or to judge that because of their killing they "deserve" to be treated in a similar way. (Peter Singer, *Practical Ethics*)

18. A free man is one who lives under the guidance of reason, who is not led by fear, but who directly desires that which is good, in other words, who strives to act, to live, and to preserve his being on the basis of seeking his own true advantage; wherefore such an one thinks of nothing less than of death, but his wisdom is a meditation upon life. (Spinoza, *The Ethics*)

19. For to fear death, my friends, is only to think ourselves wise without really being wise, for it is to think that we know what we do not know. For no one knows whether death may not be the greatest good that can happen to man. But men fear it as if they knew quite well that it was the greatest of all evils. (Plato, *Apology*)

20. Nothing can ever be present to the mind but an image or perception. . . . The table, which we see, seems to diminish, as we remove farther from it: but the real table, which exists independent of us, suffers no alteration: it was, therefore, nothing but its image, which was present to the mind. (David Hume, *An Enquiry Concerning Human Understanding*)

10.5 Examining Premises

Step 3 in the procedure for evaluating arguments is to examine the premises for their truth-value. How do we know whether a statement is true or false? And if we do not know, on what grounds do we accept or reject a statement?

First, notice that in an extended argument, some premises are provided with support, some are not. In the example below, statement ③ is supported by premises ① and ②.

Example 25

① *We have evidence of an extremely large number of humans who have not lived beyond 500 years of age and no evidence of humans who have.*

② *Any living thing that ceases to live is mortal.*

③ *All humans are mortal.*

④ *Joe Montana is human.*

⑤ *Joe Montana is mortal.*

Thus, ③ might be acceptable on the grounds that ① and ② are true and provide strong inferential support. Some premises, we can say then, are accepted because we believe they are supported by good argument.

On the other hand, statements ①, ②, and ④ have no support within the argument above. On what grounds do we assess them? One possibility, as we saw with ③, is that they may also be supportable by further argument. Is it the case, then, that all premises, if acceptable, must be supported by further argument? If that is so, then the process of evaluating one argument involves evaluating every argument provided in support of each premise and the premises of those arguments, and so on. We step into what logicians call an infinite regress. In short, if the decision to accept or reject a premise must itself be supported by further argument, we will have no place to start.

The reasoning above suggests that if an argument is to be evaluated, at some point the search for further support must stop. Some statements must be taken as true. As a matter of practice, that is precisely what we do. Some premises are taken as starting points because (1) they accurately report what has been observed, (2) they are self-evidently true, or (3) they are accepted by the relevant authorities.

First, let's consider again the premises in example 25. Then we will explain the three common "starting points" above. Consider premise ④:

④ *Joe Montana is human.*

Anyone who has seen Joe Montana would accept this premise on the ground that observation is sufficient to verify it.

Premise ②, on the other hand, is not a report of observations but an assertion about the meaning of the term 'mortal'.

② *Any living thing that ceases to live is mortal.*

That premise, it is arguable, is self-evidently true.

Last, consider premise ①:

① *We have evidence of an extremely large number of humans who have not lived beyond 500 years of age and no evidence of humans who have.*

That premise reports observations and is verifiable certainly by those experts who have made the observations. We, however, who have not, are justified in accepting ① on the testimony of the experts.

Empirical and Nonempirical Statements

The above illustration of "starting points" makes use of a helpful though not uncontroversial distinction. It needs to be explained.

Let us distinguish between statements that are verifiable by experience and those that are not. The former are called *empirical statements;* the latter are called *nonempirical* or *a priori* statements.

(1) *Empirical statements are those whose truth-value is determined by observations.*

Included in the first kind are all those whose truth-value we determine by making the appropriate observations or, if impossible, by providing evidence or an hypothesis about what observations might have been made or what they might reveal. For example, consider these statements:

Example 26   *It is raining outside your window now.*

Example 27	*There is no breed of dogs with blue eyes.*
Example 28	*Abraham Lincoln fractured his leg on his fourteenth birthday.*
Example 29	*Any two bodies exert forces on each other that are proportional to the product of their masses divided by the square of the distance between them. (Newton's law of universal gravitation)*
Example 30	*The temperature of the center of the sun is 1 billion degrees Fahrenheit.*

Statements 26 and 27 describe circumstances we can check by observation. Statement 28 describes an event we might have observed had we been there. (Lincoln either did or did not observe it.) Is it true? We may never know but we do know, at least, what kind of evidence to look for: forensic evidence and reports in diaries or letters, for example. Statement 29 describes what is observable for all bodies, past, present, and future. Statement 30 could not be checked by any direct human observation but might be checked by specially designed instruments or, more likely, by estimates of the center's temperature based on knowledge of the temperatures of related bodies. All these examples illustrate statements whose truth-values are determinable by experience of the relevant sort.

(2) *Nonempirical statements are those whose truth-value is not determined by observation.*

Nonempirical statements are verifiable by means other than experience. Some nonempirical statements are said to be self-evidently true or false. That is, we see that they are true or false simply by understanding them.

Example 31	*Dermatologists are skin doctors.*
Example 32	*Dermatologists are not physicians.*

If you know what a dermatologist is, then you know that 31 is true and 32 false.

Some nonempirical statements, although hardly self-evident, nevertheless require analysis of the meanings of the terms or concepts.

Example 33	*Love is the everlasting desire for the possession of the good.*
Example 34 ·	*The human fetus is a person at the point of conception.*

Neither 33 or 34 is verifiable by observation, which does not mean that observation plays no part in their verification. But each finally stands or falls on whether we think the statement correctly captures what we mean by 'love' or by 'human fetus' and 'person'.

Some nonempirical statements are verifiable by mathematical calculation, something analogous, perhaps, to the analysis of concepts.

Example 35 $12 \times 122 = 1464$

Example 36   *A rational solution of* $x^n + y^n = a^n$
is impossible when $n > 2$.
(Fermat's last theorem)

Last, some nonempirical statements are recognizable as true or false by their logical form. *Tautologies* are those statements that are always true in virtue of their form, as for example:

		LOGICAL FORM
Example 37	*It rains or it does not rain.*	p *or not-*p
Example 38	*It can't be both raining and not raining.*	*Not both* (p *and not-*p)
Example 39	*If it rains, then it rains.*	*If* p, *then* p

Self-contradictions are the counterparts of tautologies. They are statements that, in virtue of their form, are always false.

		LOGICAL FORM
Example 40	*It is raining and it is not raining.*	p *and not-*p
Example 41	*It is not true that either it rains or not.*	*Not* (p *or not-*p)

As we saw in section 6.3 above, the truth-values of tautologies and self-contradictions—that the former are always T, the latter always F—can be demonstrated by the use of truth tables.

(3) *Statements accepted by appeal to authority.*

Some empirical statements report observations we have not personally made. Some nonempirical statements make assertions about the analyses of concepts we are not prepared to assess. In such cases, we are entitled to accept the testimony of experts, assuming we have good reasons for thinking they are experts in the appropriate matters. (See section 9.1 on fallacious appeals of authority.)

To summarize what we have seen thus far, we can say that a premise P in an argument is acceptable if P is supported by good argument or P is (1) empirically true, (2) nonempirically true, or (3) acceptable by the relevant authorities. Obversely, premise P in an argument is not acceptable if P is denied by good argument or P is (1) empirically false, (2) nonempirically false, or (3) rejected by the relevant authorities.

Below is a brief summary of the distinction between empirical and nonempirical statements.

1. Empirical statements are those whose truth value is determined by observations.

2. Nonempirical statements are those whose truth value is not determined by observation.

   (a) Some nonempirical statements are self-evidently true or false, that is, seen to be true or false by understanding the meaning of the statement.

   (b) Some nonempirical statements are true or false by analysis of the terms or concepts.

   (c) Some nonempirical statements are true or false by mathematical calculation.

   (d) Some nonempirical statements are true or false by virtue of their logical form. Tautologies, in virtue of their logical form, are always true; self-contradictions are always false.

Exercise 10.5   Empirical or Nonempirical?   Read each statement and decide whether it is better interpreted as an empirical statement or a nonempirical statement.

1. The average human brain weighs about 45.5 ounces.

2. Democrats are more likely to vote for tax increases than Republicans.

3. All people are either happy or not.

4. John's kitten has webbed toes.

5. Taoism is one of the oldest religions of China.

6. One cannot truly lie to oneself.

7. Might is right.

8. The brain of a mosquito possesses roughly 40 thousand neuron cells, and the brain of a human possesses about 1 trillion neuron cells.

9. Rules are made to be broken.

10. More women give up smoking than do men.

11. Pacifism is the doctrine that violence in all forms is morally wrong and must be avoided.

12. People cannot live the good life if they do not know themselves.

13. Happiness is contentment, good fortune, and virtue.

14. In the United States every citizen's right to privacy is guaranteed by the Constitution.

15. It is morally wrong to take advantage of a person in a business deal.

16. Materialism is the view that only matter exists.

17. The new wing of the library is a concrete monstrosity completely lacking in style and innovation.

18. Although body size varies considerably among the various species of living organisms, cell size does not vary much at all.

19. You should live according to your beliefs.

20. Every statement is either empirical or nonempirical.

10.6 Sample Evaluations

Sample Evaluation 1

Anthony Snowden, an excellent photographer himself, has argued that photography is not an art form but a craft. If this is true, then it would seem to follow that photography is not a medium for artistic creativity and should not be evaluated according to the standards of art or treated with the kind of respect and admiration appropriate to works of fine art. In short, photography should not be taken so seriously. Snowden gave the following argument during a television discussion:

> *Art requires creativity and imagination. Photography involves no such thing, for it is a mechanical process of exposing film to light. The photographer merely "opens" the camera and the resulting picture is simply what happened to be in front of it.*

Snowden's argument begins with a statement about art. It is his first premise. Then he claims that photography lacks what is required of art, he illustrates this, and he leaves the listener to draw the obvious conclusion: photography is not an art form. Here is how we may write and expose his argument.

① *Art requires creativity and imagination.*

② *Photography is a mechanical process of exposing film to light.*

③ *Mechanical processes are neither creative nor imaginative. (Missing premise)*

---

④ *Therefore, photography is neither creative nor imaginative.*

---

⑤ *Therefore, photography is not an art.*

Notice that premise ③ needs to be supplied. Why? Clearly, if Snowden believes that something lacks creativity and imagination because it is a mechanical process, then he must be assuming that mechanical processes lack creativity and imagination.

Premise ③ makes his assumption about mechanical processes explicit. Notice also that Snowden's argument consists of an argument within an argument. Is it inductive or deductive? It seems clear that the argument claims to show that photography *must* not be an art form rather than probably is not an art form. In effect, the argument defines art and then shows that photography fails to meet the definition and thus must not be art. Hence, this is a deductive argument.

First, we check validity. If we assume the premises to be true, does the conclusion have to follow? Assuming the premises, statement ④ certainly follows, and statement ⑤ must be true given premises ① and ④. Thus, this argument is deductively valid.

Are all the premises true? Premise ① claims that art must involve creativity and imagination. What type of premise is it? Is it empirical? Will observations of artworks determine whether art requires creativity and imagination? Let's think about treating this as an empirical claim. What would observations of artworks show us? Either all those artworks we observe *are* creative and imaginative or most are or most are not. We might even frame the inductive generalization from our observations that probably all artworks are creative and imaginative. But we would not have established the claim that art *must* be creative and imaginative, that, in other words, something could not be an artwork if it were neither creative nor imaginative. Thus, this premise is best understood as a nonempirical claim, a claim about the nature of art, to be exact. And it certainly seems to be true. Wouldn't our concept of art disappear or at least be radically different if we did not believe that art must involve creativity and imagination? Surely those are necessary ingredients of art. We ought, then, to accept this premise.

Premise ② says that photography is a mechanical process of exposing film to light. What kind of claim is this? It seems to be a definition, however brief, designed to tell us what photography is. Is it an accurate claim about what photography is? It is certainly true that photography *involves using* a mechanical process to make pictures. But that is not the same as saying it *is* a mechanical process. If one were to provide a more accurate partial definition of photography one should probably say that it is 'making pictures by using the mechanical process of exposing film to light'. This is a better statement of the relationship between photography and mechanical processes.

What do we say, then, about premise ②? The answer is that it is not true. Snowden overstates the connection between photography and mechanical processes, making it seem that photography is *nothing but* a mechanical process. The truth is that the camera is a tool, a machine, designed and used according to human interests. Snowden seems to overlook the elements of creativity involved in the ways cameras are designed and, more importantly, in the ways they are used by humans. Creativity and imagination are involved in the decisions to make camera lenses bend light as they do. They did not just come that way. Creativity and imagination are involved in the choices photographers make regarding subjects; composition of the image; type of film, color or black and white; degree of contrast; quality of focus; and so on. Thus, although the camera is a machine, the photographer is not.

Since premise ② is false, Snowden's argument is not good and should not be believed. He does not establish that photography is lacking in creativity and is therefore not an art form. We do not need to go any further with his argument.

Sample Evaluation 2

In his book *Animal Liberation,* Peter Singer offers an argument for the belief that plants do not feel pain. Singer says that there are

> ① *three distinct grounds for believing that nonhuman animals can feel pain: behavior, the nature of their nervous systems, and the evolutionary usefulness of pain.* ② *None of these gives us any reason to believe that plants feel pain.* ③ *In the absence of scientifically credible experimental findings, there is no observable behavior that suggests pain;* ④ *nothing resembling a central nervous system has been found in plants; and* ⑤ *it is difficult to imagine why species that are incapable of moving away from a source of pain or using the perception of pain to avoid death in any other way should have evolved the capacity to feel pain.* ⑥ *Therefore the belief that plants feel pain appears to be quite unjustified.*

If we expose Singer's argument to examine it, we have the following (notice especially the phrases I have called out with underlines):

> ① *There are three grounds for believing that nonhuman animals feel pain: (a) behavior, (b) the nature of their nervous system, and (c) the evolutionary usefulness of pain.*
>
> ③ *In the absence of scientifically credible experimental findings, there is no observable behavior in plants that suggests pain.*
>
> ④ *Nothing resembling a nervous system has been found in plants.*
>
> ⑤ *It is difficult to imagine why species that are incapable of moving away from a source of pain . . . should have evolved the capacity to feel pain.*
>
> ---
>
> * ⑤ₐ *Therefore, plants lack the three features above that in nonhuman animals are our grounds for believing pain is present. (Missing conclusion)*
>
> ---
>
> ⑥ *Therefore, the belief that plants feel pain appears to be quite unjustified.*

Singer's argument is an example of the type of inductive argument we called the argument from analogy. Notice the clues. Singer's first premise is about nonhuman animals and the features they possess that justify our belief that they feel pain. His conclusion, however, is about plants. And he reaches that conclusion on the basis of a comparison of features between nonhuman animals and plants. To be exact, he finds that plants do not appear to possess the relevant features: they lack the relevant behavior; they seem to have no nervous system; and feeling pain would seem to serve no purpose for them. Thus, the analogy that would support the belief that plants feel pain is not present. The form of reasoning certainly indicates an inductive argument. In addition, notice Singer's language. The words and phrases I have underlined indicate Singer's belief that his conclusion is very probably though not necessarily true. That is another sign, though not a decisive one, that the overall argument is inductive.

Is Singer's a good inductive argument? First, assuming the premises are true, do they provide strong support for the probable truth of the conclusion? It certainly seems so. Imagine that the premises are true but the conclusion not true. Suppose, that is, that plants do feel pain in spite of the fact that they lack those relevant similarities to animals. Plants feel pain although they have none of the physiological apparatus we correlate with pain perception, they exhibit no behavior that suggests pain, and pain would seem to serve no useful purpose for them. Now, none of that is a contradiction or a logical impossibility, but it would be highly unexpected and greatly surprising to our scientists. It runs completely counter to what our experience leads us to believe about living things. That little thought experiment shows us that the premises *do* provide strong support for the conclusion. Thus, we can say that this argument has a strongly supported inference.

Are the premises true? Premise ① is not an empirical claim because observations do not show us what the grounds for a belief are. We *can* observe whether certain features are present—behavior, nervous system, and so on—but we cannot observe whether a belief is justified because of those features. Premise ① makes a logical rather than an empirical claim. It is a claim in part about what it means to be in pain or to be a sentient creature. And it most certainly is a good claim about what justifies believing pain is present in an animal. Indeed, it describes the grounds we have for our belief that *other human beings feel pain*. If we did not accept this premise, it is hard to imagine how we would justify our belief that animals feel pain.

As for statements ③ through ⑤, each asserts an empirically verifiable claim, and each expresses what conforms to our own experience and what we have learned from scientists. Thus, it seems that the premises of Singer's argument are true. Therefore, his argument is a *good inductive argument*.

Sample Evaluation 3

As a final illustration of the procedure of evaluating an extended argument, let's complete the evaluation of example 17. The essay is reprinted below immediately followed by the diagram we completed earlier.

Example 17

① *President Bush has inadvertently slighted the U.S. Foreign Service.* ② *In his Sept. 11 speech to Congress, Mr. Bush spoke generously and at length about "our brave servicemen and women" in the Per-*

sian Gulf. ③ But he failed even to mention the brave men and women serving as diplomats in Baghdad and Kuwait, the hazardous cockpits of the conflict. ④ It does not belittle the sacrifices of uniformed Americans to note that Foreign Service officers are in more immediate peril.

⑤ More of these civilian officers have been killed in the line of duty than all the generals and admirals who have died in combat since World War II. ⑥ The names of these diplomats are honored on plaques in the State Department lobby. ⑦ In 1955 there were 75 names. ⑧ Since then, 90 more career diplomats have been killed, most victims of terrorism.

⑨ Americans treat the Foreign Service shabbily. ⑩ Congress routinely slashes State Department budgets, since diplomacy has no domestic constituency. ⑪ Salaries are kept low and training programs starved of funds by legislators. ⑫ Presidents treat ambassadorial posts as choice booty for chums and contributors.

⑬ Perversely, career diplomats go unrecognized and unrewarded even as their skills are required for new problems, from narcotics and pollution to vanishing rain forests. ⑭ Neglect of the Foreign Service is ignominious in normal times, but incomprehensible in crisis. ⑮ American diplomats in Kuwait are captives in a combat zone; ⑯ embassy defenders rely on a swimming pool for drinking water. ⑰ Their courage calls for a salute; ⑱ at the first opportunity, Mr. Bush should make full amends.

Diagram of Example 17

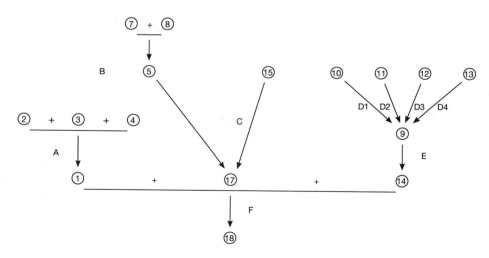

For convenience, we will label each subsidiary argument using capital letters. Let us begin by considering whether argument A supporting statement ① is good.

Argument A:

> ② *In his Sept. 11 speech to Congress, Mr. Bush spoke generously and at length about "our brave servicemen and women" in the Persian Gulf.*
> +
> ③ *But he failed even to mention the brave men and women serving as diplomats in Baghdad and Kuwait, the hazardous cockpits of the conflict.*
> +
> ④ *It does not belittle the sacrifices of uniformed Americans to note that Foreign Service officers are in more immediate peril.*
>
> ► ① *President Bush has slighted the U.S. Foreign Service.*

Given premises ②, ③, and ④ does conclusion ① follow with deductive validity? It does not seem so. We can grant that Bush fails to mention the diplomats yet deny that he has slighted them. As a counterexample, we might suppose that the sole purpose of the president's speech to Congress was to discuss the circumstances of the servicemen and women. If so, then it would have been inappropriate to mention the diplomats in Baghdad and Kuwait and, thus, no "slight" can be inferred.

Given that the inferences in A are not deductively valid, as it stands, there are two options to consider. First, we might supply missing premises to strengthen the argument. Second, we must consider whether the argument is inductively strong.

Should we supply as missing premises statements such as:

> *②a The President's recent speech to Congress was for the purpose of generally describing our U.S. commitments in the Persian Gulf.*
> +
> *②b In a general account to Congress, what the President does not mention indicates what he thinks unimportant.*

If we can reasonably assume that the writer intends premises such as *②a and *②b, then we conclude that argument A is deductively valid.

On the other hand, even if we do not include *②a and *②b, premises ②, ③, and ④ may provide inductive evidence that strongly supports the conclusion. Consider the argument to be an *argument by analogy:* the president spoke "generously and at length" about the service men and women but he did not mention the diplomats when he could have. Both servicemen and women and diplomats are in crucial and perilous positions, so the president should have referred to both groups. He did not.

Therefore, he has slighted the diplomats. Interpreted in this way, argument A is an inductively strong analogy.

Are premises ②, ③, and ④ true? Premises ② and ③ are empirical statements. It would be easy to verify them by checking the President's speech. We can accept them on the basis of authority, reasoning that the writer for the *New York Times* is likely to be a reliable authority.

Premise ④ is a nonempirical statement asserting that reporting the facts about the diplomats does not belittle the sacrifices of the servicemen and women. This is acceptable.

Thus, given that argument A is inductively strong and that the premises are acceptable, we can conclude that statement ① is probably true.

Argument B:

> ⑦ *In 1955 there were 75 names.*
> +
> ⑧ *Since then, 90 more career diplomats have been killed, most victims of terrorism.*
> ⑤ *More of these civilian officers have been killed in the line of duty than all the generals and admirals who have died in combat since World War II.*

The conclusion ⑤ does not follow deductively from ⑦ and ⑧ for the reason that we do not have information telling us that the number of generals and admirals killed since World War II is less than the sum of 75 and 90. Can we supply a missing premise here?

> *⑧ₐ *The number of generals and admirals killed in World War II is less than 165.*

The principle of charity tells us to give the arguer the benefit of the doubt. In this case it seems reasonable to supply *⑧ₐ as a missing premise. Therefore, argument B is deductively valid.

Are premises ⑦, ⑧, and *⑧ₐ true? These are all empirical statements, easily verified, and acceptable on the basis of authority.

Given that argument B is deductively valid and the premises are acceptable, we can conclude that statement ⑤ is acceptable as supported by good argument.

Argument C:

> ⑤ *More of these civilian officers have been killed in the line of duty than all the generals and admirals who have died in combat since World War II.*
> ⑮ *American diplomats in Kuwait are captives in a combat zone.*
> ⑰ *Their courage calls for a salute.*

Those premises offer deductively valid reasons for the conclusion made explicit by the addition of these two supplied premises:

> *⑮ₐ *Service to the country in life-threatening circum-*
> + *stances shows courage deserving of salute.*
>
> *⑮♭ Our foreign service officers are currently facing*
>   *life-threatening circumstances.*

Given those reasonable premises, it clearly follows that the foreign service people deserve recognition as ⑰ asserts.

Premises ⑤ and ⑮ are empirical statements, easily verified, and acceptable on the authority of the writer. Thus, ⑰ is supported by good argument.

> *Argument D:*

> ⑩ *Congress routinely slashes State Department budgets. . . .*
> ⑪ *Salaries are kept low and training programs starved of funds by legislators.*
> ⑫ *Presidents treat ambassadorial posts as choice booty for chums and contributors.*
> ⑬ *Perversely, career diplomats go unrecognized and unrewarded even as their skills are required for new problems, from narcotics and pollution to vanishing rain forests.*
> ⑨ *Americans treat the Foreign Service shabbily.*

Premises ⑩, ⑪, ⑫, and ⑬ offer independent support for conclusion ⑨. For convenience, they have been labelled inferences D1, D2, D3, and D4.

Consider first inferences D1 and D2. Notice that given premises ⑩ and ⑪, it does not deductively follow that ⑨. It may be true that the Foreign Service is underfunded and unable to meet its needs, but it does not deductively follow that it is treated shabbily. Suppose it is the case that no more funding is available considering the other priorities Congress has. The Foreign Service may not get what it needs, but it gets its fair share, and that is not shabby treatment. To accept the conclusion, we would need to be shown that Congress funds the service unfairly. The same information is needed to construe this as a strong inductive argument; thus, without that information the inference is weak.

Consider now inference D3. If it is true that presidents treat ambassadorial posts as described in ⑫, then it does follow deductively that the Foreign Service is treated shabbily. It is easy to see the strength of this inference if we supply as an acceptable missing premise a statement such as:

> *⑫ₐ Important governmental positions should not be*
>   *filled solely for reasons of political gain or reward.*

Is premise ⑫ true? It is an empirical statement, though one that is not easy to verify. Notice that it is a generalization requiring inductive evidence. It raises questions for us such as: In how many cases have presidents used ambassadorial posts to reward supporters and friends? Are those cases representative of the typical presidential ambassadorial appointment? It is true that we hear this criticism but can we accept it without further evidence? We can say at least this much: The argument in D3 would be stronger if such information were supplied.

Consider now inference D4. If it is true that diplomats go unrecognized and unrewarded, then it follows deductively that the Foreign Service is treated shabbily. However, it is arguable that the inference *begs the question*. Recall that the fallacy of begging the question occurs when an arguer assumes the conclusion in his or her premises. In this case, it seems that "shabby treatment" is assumed already in the claim that "career diplomats go unrecognized and unrewarded." If so, then conclusion ⑨ does not receive independent support from that premise.

Thus, if this discussion is persuasive, we ought to conclude that statement ⑨ is not strongly supported.

Argument E: If it is true that ⑨ Americans treat the Foreign Service shabbily, then does it deductively follow that it is ignominious to neglect the Foreign Service? Yes, it is so arguable on the ground that any shabby treatment is ignominious. However, even if deductively valid, the argument is not acceptable. We saw above that premise ⑨ is not well-supported. We might accept it on authority; however, since it is such a controversial assertion, it is perhaps better to withhold acceptance. Thus, argument E is not a good argument.

Argument F: Given that ① the president has slighted the Foreign Service, ⑰ the courage of its service people deserves salute, and ⑭ to neglect the service is ignominious, it seems to follow deductively that ⑱ the president should make amends.

Premise ①, we concluded, is acceptable as supported by good argument. Premise ⑰ is acceptable for the same reason. Premise ⑭ is not supported by good argument. However, is it acceptable on other grounds?

⑭ *Neglect of the Foreign Service is ignominious in normal times, but incomprehensible in crisis.*

Notice that it is a nonempirical statement asserting our duty to support the Foreign Service. It is not difficult to supply reasons in support, for example:

*⑭ *The Foreign Service fulfills an important role in foreign relations and a critical role in times of crisis.*

By applying the principle of charity and adding a reason that is acceptable to us, we can conclude ⑭ in the overall argument.

Thus, the premises in support of the conclusion are acceptable and, given those premises, the conclusion deductively follows. In summary, we conclude that this extended argument is a good one.

Exercise 10.6   Evaluating Extended Arguments.   Are the following arguments good? First, expose the arguments, identifying conclusions and premises. Supply missing statements as you think necessary. Indicate supplied statements with an asterisk (*). Assess the inferences for deductive validity or inductive strength. Lastly, examine the premises for truth–value. [Note to instructors: These are very challenging exercises. You may be satisfied with a paraphrased exposition of the arguments.]

1. The following is a letter to the editor.

    I must respond to the letter by Jerome Krause in the August issue of *Rider* regarding joining the AMA [American Motorcycle Association].

    ① Krause refuses to join the AMA because, in his opinion, they support an industry, hobby and sport that is polluting. ② I suggest that Krause is yet another self-righteous militant "environmental elitist" who will not be happy until we are all living in caves and eating leaves. ③ If Krause wishes to protect and ensure the survival of the sport we all love, he needs to understand that we cannot stand divided. ④ No "thinking person" wants destruction of our land and resources; however, ⑤ thinking people also know that programs such as the "California Green Sticker Program" can provide and police off-road riding areas which do not "rip up deserts" and forests, but rather, allows access by families via methods other than those sanctioned by the Sierra Club and the insanely radical Earth First! organization.

    ⑥ The AMA is probably our best hope for survival as motorcycling Americans. ⑦ I implore all of you who do not belong to the AMA to join. ⑧ If not the AMA, then some other organization which supports motorcycling and our right to keep our sport, no matter what form of our sport you may engage in.

2. The following is an excerpt from the U.S. Supreme Court decision in the case of *Cruzan v. Missouri State Supreme Court,* June 25, 1990. In this "right to die" decision the U.S. Supreme Court upheld the Missouri Supreme Court ruling that the Cruzans not be allowed to have life-sustaining treatments withdrawn from their daughter Nancy. The majority opinion below is written by Justice Rehnquist.

    (Hint: The conclusion of the argument is expressed in statements ⑤ and ㊻. Why? Notice the writer tells us in statement ⑳ what is at issue in the case before the court.)

    ① Petitioner Nancy Beth Cruzan was rendered incompetent as a result of severe injuries sustained during an automobile accident. ② Co-petitioners Lester and Joyce Cruzan, Nancy's parents and co-guardians, sought a court order directing the withdrawal of their daughter's artificial feeding and hydration equipment after it became apparent that she had virtually no chance of recovering her cognitive faculties. ③ The Supreme Court of Missouri held that there was no clear and convincing evidence of Nancy's desire to have life-sustaining treatment withdrawn under such circumstances, her parents lacked authority to effectuate such a request. ④ We granted *certiorari,* (1989), and ⑤ now affirm.

⑥ After it had become apparent that Nancy Cruzan had virtually no chance of regaining her mental faculties her parents asked hospital employees to terminate the artificial nutrition and hydration procedures. ⑦ All agree that such removal would cause her death. ⑧ The employees refused to honor the request without court approval. ⑨ The parents then sought and received authorization from the state trial court for termination. ⑩ The court found that a person in Nancy's condition had a fundamental right under the State and Federal Constitutions to refuse or direct the withdrawal of "death pro-longing procedures." ⑪ The court also found that Nancy's "expressed thoughts at age 25 in somewhat serious conversation with a housemate friend that if sick or injured she would not wish to continue her life unless she could live at least halfway normally suggests that given her present condition she would not wish to continue on with her nutrition and hydration."

⑫ The Supreme Court of Missouri reversed by a divided vote. ⑬ The court recognized a right to refuse treatment embodied in the common-law doctrine of informed consent, but ⑭ expressed skepticism about the applica-tion of that doctrine in the circumstances of the case. . . . ⑮ The court also declined to read a broad right of privacy into the State Constitution which would "support the right of a person to refuse medical treatment in every circumstance," and ⑯ expressed doubt as to whether such a right existed under the United States Constitution. ⑰ It then decided that the Missouri Living Will statute, *Mo. Rev. Stat.* embodied a state policy strongly favoring the preservation of life. ⑱ The court found that Cruzan's statements to her roommate regarding her desire to live or die under certain conditions were "unreliable for the purpose of determining her intent," "and thus ⑲ insuffi-cient to support the co-guardians' claim to exercise substituted judgment on Nancy's behalf."

⑳ In this Court, the question is simply and starkly whether the United States Constitution prohibits Missouri from choosing the rule of decision it did. ㉑ This is the first case in which we have been squarely presented with the issue of whether the United States Constitution grants what is in com-mon parlance referred to as a "right to die." ㉒ We follow the judicious coun-sel of our decision in Twin City Bank v. Nebraska, (1897), where we said that in deciding "a question of such magnitude and importance . . . it is the [better] part of wisdom not to attempt, by any general statement, to cover every possible phase of the subject."

㉓ The 14th Amendment provides that no state shall "deprive any per-son of life, liberty, or property, without due process of law." ㉔ The prin-ciple that a competent person has a constitutionally protected liberty interest in refusing unwanted medical treatment may be inferred from our prior decisions. . . .

㉕ But determining that a person has a "liberty interest" under the Due Process Clause does not end the enquiry; ㉖ ". . . whether respondent's con-stitutional rights have been violated must be determined by balancing liberty interests against the relevant state interests."

㉗ Missouri requires that evidence of the incompetent's wishes as to the withdrawal of treatment be proved by clear and convincing evidence. The question, then, is ㉘ whether the United States Constitution forbids the es-tablishment of this procedural requirement by the state. ㉙ We hold that it does not.

㉚ Whether or not Missouri's clear and convincing evidence requirement comports with the United States Constitution depends in part on what interests the state may properly seek to protect in this situation. ㉛ Missouri relies on its interest in the protection and preservation of human life, and ㉜ there can be no gainsaying this interest. . . . ㉝ We do not think a state is required to remain neutral in the face of an informed and voluntary decision by a physically able adult to starve to death.

㉞ But in the context presented here, a state has more particular interests at stake. ㉟ The choice between life and death is a deeply personal decision of obvious and overwhelming finality. ㊱ We believe Missouri may legitimately seek to safeguard the personal element of this choice through the imposition of heightened evidentiary requirements. ㊲ It cannot be disputed that the Due Process Clause protects interest in life as well as an interest in refusing life-sustaining medical treatment. ㊳ Not all incompetent patients will have loved ones available to serve as surrogate decision makers. . . .

㊴ In our view, Missouri has permissibly sought to advance these interests through the adoption of a "clear and convincing" standard of proof to govern such proceedings.

㊵ The Supreme Court of Missouri held that in this case the testimony adduced at trial did not amount to clear and convincing proof of the patient's desire to have hydration and nutrition withdrawn. . . .

㊶ No doubt is engendered by anything in this record but that Nancy Cruzan's mother and father are loving and caring parents. ㊷ If the state were required by the United States Constitution to repose a right of "substituted judgment" with anyone, the Cruzans would qualify. ㊸ But we do not think the Due Process Clause requires the state to repose judgment on these matters with anyone but the patient herself. ㊹ Close family members may have a strong feeling—a feeling not at all ignoble or unworthy, but not entirely disinterested either—that they do not wish to witness the continuation of the life of a loved one which they regard as hopeless, meaningless and even degrading. ㊺ But there is no automatic assurance that the view of close family members will necessarily be the same as the patient's would have been had she been confronted with the prospect of her situation while competent. ㊻ All of the reasons previously discussed for allowing Missouri to require clear and convincing evidence of the patient's wishes lead us to conclude that the state may choose to defer only to those wishes, rather than confide the decision to close family members.

3. The following excerpt is taken from the dissenting opinion written by Justice Stevens in the U.S. Supreme Court case of *Cruzan v. Missouri State Supreme Court*.

① Our Constitution is born of the proposition that all legitimate governments must secure the equal right of every person to "life, liberty, and the pursuit of happiness." ② In the ordinary case we quite naturally assume that these three ends are compatible, mutually enhancing and perhaps even coincident.

③ The Court would make an exception here. ④ It permits the state's abstract, undifferentiated interest in the preservation of life to overwhelm the best interests of Nancy Beth Cruzan, interests which would, according to an undisputed finding, be served by allowing her guardians to exercise her constitutional right to discontinue medical treatment.

⑤ Ironically, the Court reaches this conclusion despite endorsing three significant propositions which should save it from any such dilemma. ⑥ First, a competent individual's decision to refuse life-sustaining medical procedures is an aspect of liberty protected by the Due Process Clause of the 14th Amendment. ⑦ Second, upon a proper evidentiary showing, a qualified guardian may make that decision on behalf of an incompetent ward. ⑧ Third, in answering the important question presented by this tragic case, it is wise "not to attempt by any general statement, to cover every possible phase of the subject." ⑨ Together, these considerations suggest that Nancy Cruzan's liberty to be free from medical treatment must be understood in light of the facts and circumstances particular to her.

⑩ I would so hold: in my view, the Constitution requires the state to care for Nancy Cruzan's life in a way that gives appropriate respect to her own best interests.

⑪ This case is the first in which we consider whether, and how, the Consitution protects the liberty of seriously ill patients to be free from life-sustaining medical treatment. ⑫ So put, the question is both general and profound. ⑬ We need not, however, resolve the question in the abstract. ⑭ Our responsibility as judges both enables and compels us to treat the problem as it is illuminated by the facts of the controversy before us.

⑮ The portion of this Court's opinion that considers the merits of the case is similarly unsatisfactory. ⑯ It, too, fails to respect the best interests of the patient. ⑰ It, too, relies on what is tantamount to a waiver rationale: the dying patient's best interests are put to one side and the entire inquiry is focused on her prior expression of intent.

⑱ An innocent person's constitutional right to be free from unwanted medical treatment is thereby categorically limited to those patients who had the foresight to make the unambiguous statement of their wishes while competent. ⑲ The Court's decision affords no protection to children, ⑳ to young people who are victims of unexpected accidents or illnesses, or ㉑ to the countless thousands of elderly persons who either fail to decide, or fail to explain, how they want to be treated if they should experience a similar fate.

㉒ Because Nancy Beth Cruzan did not have the foresight to preserve her constitutional right in a living will, or some comparable "clear and convincing" alternative, her right is gone forever and her fate is in the hands of the state Legislature instead of in those of her family, her independent neutral guardian ad litem, and an impartial judge—all of whom agree on the course of action that is in her best interests. ㉓ The Court's willingness to find a waiver of this constitutional right reveals a distressing misunderstanding of the importance of individual liberty.

㉔ Only because Missouri has arrogated to itself the power to define life, and only because the Court permits this usurpation, are Nancy Cruzan's life and liberty put into disquieting conflict. ㉕ If Nancy Cruzan's life were defined by reference to her own interests, so that her life expired when her biological existence ceased serving any of her own interests, then her constitutionally protected interest in freedom from unwanted treatment would not come into conflict with her constitutionally protected interest in life.

㉖ Conversely, if there were any evidence that Nancy Cruzan herself defined life to encompass every form of biological persistence by a human being, so that the continuation of treatment would serve Nancy's own liberty, then once again there would be no conflict between life and liberty. ㉗ The opposition of life and liberty in this case are thus not the result of Nancy Cruzan's tragic accident, but are instead the artificial consequences of Missouri's effort, and this Court's willingness, to abstract Nancy Cruzan's life from Nancy Cruzan's person. . . .

4. The following essay, "Why War is Ignoble," by Howard Morland appeared in *Newsweek,* and is reprinted by permission of the author.

(Hint: Morland's conclusion is expressed in statement ㊹. Assuming that you agree, what reasons does he offer and how then should many of the other statements be treated?)

① Whenever young Americans depart for overseas battlefields, older men seem to envy them the adventure. ② On the eve of the Vietnam War, my college dean told me he was sorry he had not come under fire during his wartime service in the Pacific. ③ He wanted to know how he might have responded to the test of combat. ④ He assumed that I would understand, and his regrets may have led me to later join the Air Force rather than seek a draft deferment.

⑤ Today, because of the crisis in the Mideast, a new generation of young people hears of the salutary effects of the battlefield from their Vietnam-era elders. ⑥ In September, liberal essayist Roger Rosenblatt told a national television audience that he now wishes he had fought in Vietnam. ⑦ He said that even though he "disapproved of our being in Vietnam," he feels "deep regret" that he never experienced the "dependent connection to one another" of soldiers "thrown into an incomprehensible horror." ⑧ Watching him on the McNeil/Lehrer NewsHour sent me searching through my own Vietnam experiences for a clue to this curious longing for memories of combat.

⑨ My job in 1968 was to pilot C-141 transport planes of the type now hauling U.S. soldiers and gear to Saudi Arabia. ⑩ Except for one close call when a battle-damaged Phantom jet crashed and exploded near my plane at Da Nang Air Base, I never came in harm's way. ⑪ My own knowledge of combat comes from the stories soldiers told as I airlifted them from the battlefield zone. ⑫ One night, on a flight from Cam Ranh Bay to California, a young veteran the age of today's tennis champion Pete Sampras sat between the pilot seats and told the flight crew about his year in Vietnam. ⑬ He described a photograph in his duffel bag, of an American GI holding the severed heads of two Viet Cong prisoners. ⑭ The hapless prisoners were grabbed and beheaded as revenge for the death of an American, killed when another Viet Cong prisoner turned himself into a human bomb by detonating a concealed grenade in his own armpit. ⑮ In the eerie darkness seven miles above the Pacific, our narrator described the sound a bullet made as it plowed through a friend's body two feet away. ⑯ He thought it wise not to make close friends in combat. ⑰ His homecoming plan: lock himself in the bathroom, sit on the john, smoke cigarettes and shake for several hours.

⑱ Pondering this survivor's tale, I entered the cargo bay and sat with the coffins of a dozen veterans who had undergone the ultimate combat experience. ⑲ The young soldier on the flight deck may have embellished his war stories, I thought, but the boys in the boxes were testament to the truth. ⑳ I was struck by how lonely one feels in the company of the dead.

㉑ Two years later in Thailand, a Thai veteran made a point of showing me snapshots of Vietnamese bodies stretched out in a row. ㉒ He had helped kill them. ㉓ A fresh haircut on the corpse closest to the camera caught my eye; I wondered if the man with the haircut had sensed it would be his last. ㉔ My host seemed to invite me to explain the meaning of the carnage, but I was still young enough to believe people should live forever, and like the then young Mr. Rosenblatt, I saw no sufficient reason for that particular war.

"*Bloody shreds*": ㉕ Combat is unique in the way it celebrates untimely death at the hand of fellow human beings. ㉖ Mark Twain saw the horror in this, and, in a poem called "The War Prayer" wrote of a ghostly old man who disrupts a church service as the preacher delivers a patriotic war prayer. ㉗ The old man offers his own grim version. ㉘ "O Lord our God, Help us to tear their soldiers to bloody shreds with our shells . . . to drown the thunder of the guns with the shrieks of their wounded, writhing in pain . . . to lay waste their humble homes with a hurricane of fire." ㉙ Persuaded that it could be considered sacrilegious, Twain had his poem published posthumously. ㉚ In his bitter assessment, ". . . only dead men can tell the truth in this world." ㉛ But his warning, when it appeared, was widely ignored.

㉜ War is like other human activities in that people who enjoy it the most will do it the best, and be chosen to run it. ㉝ Obviously, not everyone enjoys it, but there is a common notion that all combatants should somehow love war, and benefit from it. ㉞ The premise of the typical Hollywood action movie is that real men love each other most when locked in a deeply fraternal exercise designed to demonstrate how short life can be. ㉟ If war is such an ennobling experience, why does it bring out the worst in people, not the best?

㊱ I have always believed that I might kill or die for a worthy enough cause. ㊲ It's the way boys were raised in my native South, as in most other places, and for good reason. ㊳ During much of history, a successful army was the most important institution a people could possess. ㊴ A bad day on the battlefield meant extinction for a number of ancient civilizations. ㊵ However, this country has never faced extinction in any of its wars. ㊶ Our recent wars have all been exercises in foreign policy, and ㊷ for such wars the worthiness of the cause must justify the slaughter. ㊸ Are we convinced that the war now brewing in the Persian Gulf is worthy of the bloodshed it would entail?

㊹ In my view, no American should ever be required to kill or die simply as a test of manhood—particularly if that test involves some politicians' perception of manhood. ㊺ And certainly no American should die simply because as a nation our imagination is too poverty-stricken to figure out how to live without cheap oil. ㊻ For lethal force to have any legitimate role, we must strictly and dispassionately confine it to legitimate questions about international law and homeland defense. ㊼ War is too brutal to be used as a rite of passage for a college dean, for an essayist, or even for a U.S. president.

㊽ I don't know why Roger Rosenblatt feels the way he feels, but I'm glad he didn't fight in Vietnam. ㊾ I wish nobody had.

Review Questions Chapter 10

1. According to your text, what are the steps in the procedure for evaluating an argument?
2. What two formats may be used for writing an exposition of an argument?
3. Define 'extended argument'.
4. What kinds of problems might extended arguments present for exposition?
5. What is the purpose of exposing an argument? How explicit should the exposition be?
6. What is an enthymeme?
7. Define 'empirical statement' and 'nonempirical statement'.
8. Under what circumstances are we justified in accepting a premise of an argument?
9. Why are tautologies nonempirical statements?
10. Why cannot a good argument have a false premise?

True or False?

1. Statements accepted by appeal to authority may be empirical or nonempirical statements.
2. Tautologies are nonempirically true but self-contradictions are empirically false.
3. Arguments with a missing premise are always deductive arguments.
4. If we see immediately that a premise of an argument is false, then as far as the evaluation of the argument is concerned, it is not good.
5. A premise of one argument may be the conclusion of another.
6. If the premise of one argument is supported by a good argument, then that premise is true.
7. Both tautologies and self-contradictions can be formally determined using truth tables.
8. A statement that serves no inferential purpose in an argument may be omitted without affecting the argument.
9. Causal statements—statements asserting that one event causes another—are empirical statements.
10. Given that an inductive generalization employs a premise asserting what has been observed about a sample of a larger group, it follows that such a premise is an empirical statement.

Answers to Selected Exercises

Chapter 1

Exercise 1.2
Sentences that contain statements are written out and the statement underlined. Conditional statements are identified.

1. Statement, conditional   **3.** Statement   **5.** Not a statement   **7.** Statement
9. Statement   **11.** Not a statement   **13.** Let us eat and drink; for *tomorrow we shall die*.
Statement   **15.** Statement   **17.** Statement   **19.** Statement   **21.** Neither a borrower nor a lender be; for *loan oft loses both itself and friend* . . . Statement   **23.** Statement   **25.** Statement

Exercise 1.4

1. 1. *Every literature major must take a course in Shakespeare.*
2. *John has taken the Shakespeare course.*

3. *Therefore, he must be a literature major.*

3. Not an argument.

5. 1. *If the president dies in office, then the first lady becomes the new president.*
2. *Barbara Bush is the first lady.*

3. *She will take over if President Bush dies in office.*

7. 1. *If the creationists are right, then the universe was created and has a beginning.*
2. *Now, whatever has a beginning must also have an end.*

3. *Therefore, if the creationists are right, the universe must have an end as well.*

9. 1. *A person can't be a marine and a sailor both.*
2. *Max is a sailor.*

3. *Therefore, it must be that he is not a marine.*

11. 1. *There is freedom in the sense of being able to move as one pleases . . .*
2. *There is freedom in the sense of being able to do and speak as one pleases . . .*
3. *There is freedom in the sense of being able to think for oneself.*
4. *This last type makes the others possible.*

5. *Therefore, it is our most important freedom.*

13. Not an argument.

15. *1. Only living things can have feelings.*
2. Computers are not living things.
___
3. Therefore, computers do not have feelings.

17. *1. You cannot hold a person liable for something he or she did not know about.*
2. You have not shown that your client did not know about the faulty wiring in the house he sold.
___
3. Therefore, we can conclude that your client cannot be excused for damages.

19. *1. The workday is often more than eight hours long;*
2. There is heavy lifting to do;
3. There is the possibility of injury;
4. There are cranky supervisors;
5. The weather does not always cooperate;
___
6. Therefore, house builders work awfully hard.

21. *1. The mind directly perceives only ideas.*
2. Material objects are not ideas.
___
3. Therefore, the mind does not directly perceive material objects.

23. *1. Being in jail is frightening enough for kids.*
2. Locking them up with adults is inviting tragedy.
___
3. Therefore, kids should not be put behind bars with adults.

25. *1. Mice are just smallish rats.*
___
2. Therefore, housecats are just smallish tigers.

27. *1. If there is no afterlife, then at the moment of death we are nothing.*
2. If there is an afterlife, then at the moment of death we are born into a new life.
___
3. Therefore, death is not to be feared.

29. *1. The most common large woodpecker in our area is the Red-headed Woodpecker.*
2. What I saw was a large woodpecker.
___
3. So, even though I did not see its head, it probably was a Red-headed Woodpecker.

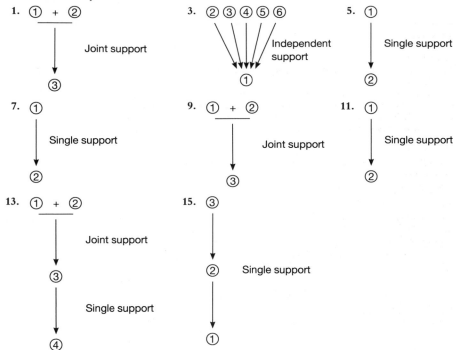

1. ① + ② → ③ Joint support

3. ② ③ ④ ⑤ ⑥ → ① Independent support

5. ① → ② Single support

7. ① → ② Single support

9. ① + ② → ③ Joint support

11. ① → ② Single support

13. ① + ② → ③ Joint support → ④ Single support

15. ③ → ② Single support → ①

Chapter 2

Exercise 2.2

1. Invalid. Counterexample: Every chemistry major must take one year of organic chemistry and Max took one year of organic chem. but he is not a chemistry major; he is a biology major.
3. Valid. Since there are at most 365 days in a year and 367 students in the class, it is inconceivable that no two students have birthdays on the same day. After each day of the year has been correlated with a student's birthday, the very next student must have a birthday on one of those days already mentioned.
5. Valid. Given that all movie stars live in Hollywood and that Robert Redford is a movie star, then it must follow that he lives in Hollywood. If he does not live in Hollywood, then either it is not true that all movie stars live in Hollywood or not true that he is a movie star.
7. Invalid. Counterexample: A sound argument is one that is valid and has all true premises. Argument (2) has all true premises, but argument (2), it can be imagined, is not valid.
9. Valid. We cannot simultaneously conceive that a person with a right to life does not have a right to whatever he or she needs in order to live and, contrary to the conclusion, that such a person thereby has a right to use another's kidneys.
11. Valid. We cannot maintain the premises that society has a right to protect itself including a right to protect its common moral view from threatening acts, that the mentioned acts of personal morality threatened a common moral view, yet deny the conclusion that society has a right to prohibit such acts.
13. Valid. If the superior forms of art are those that capture reality and film is an art that does that, then film art cannot fail to be a superior art form.
15. Valid. If many families contain tens or hundreds of species and a family is not gone until all its species are gone, then it must follow that a removal of half the families requires the death of a much greater percentage of species. To maintain the premises and deny the conclusion results in a contradiction.
17. Valid. Given that Serra's *Tilted Arc* is a site-specific structure—that is, part of and built into the structure of its site—and that a site-specific sculpture is conceived and created in relation to the particular conditions of a specific site, then we cannot deny that to remove the sculpture from the site is to destroy it.

Exercise 2.3

1. *Modus ponens.* Valid.   3. Barbara. Valid.   5. Fallacy of undistributed middle. Invalid.
7. Fallacy of denying the antecedent. Invalid.   9. *Modus ponens.* Valid.   11. Fallacy of affirming the consequent. Invalid.   13. Fallacy of denying the antecedent. Invalid.   15. *Modus ponens.* Valid.

Chapter 3

Exercise 3.3A

1. Subject: astronomers
   predicate: trained in mathematics
   form: A
   quality: affirmative
   quantity: universal

3. Subject: past presidents
   predicate: invited to a luncheon on Friday
   form: A
   quality: affirmative
   quantity: universal

5. Subject: traffic monitors
   predicate: well-trained people
   form: O
   quality: negative
   quantity: particular

7. Subject: football fans
   predicate: fanatics
   form: A
   quality: affirmative
   quantity: universal

9. Subject: members of the Kiwanis Club
   predicate: active supporters of the right-to-life movement
   form: I
   quality: affirmative
   quantity: particular

Exercise 3.3B
1. No piranhas are vicious fish.
3. Some sailboats are not equipped with out-board motors.
5. No good investments are tax-free investments.
7. No bartenders are licensed in this state.
9. Some wheelwrights are not still in business.

Exercise 3.3C
1. Some happy people are happy in the same way.
3. Some specimens from the site are not ready for examination.
5. All vicious fish are piranhas.
7. Some bartenders are not licensed in this state.
9. No chess players are grand masters.

Exercise 3.4A
1. Form E; negative; universal

eucalyptus trees   natives of Cal.

3. Form A; affirmative; universal

machines   products of intelligence

5. Form I; affirmative; particular

followers of "Reaganomics"   people whom we can respect

7. Form E; negative; universal

persons   persons wanting to be harmed

9. Form A; affirmative; universal

logicians   lovers of Venn diagrams

11. Form E; negative; universal

male vocalists   sopranos at Met

13. Form A; affirmative; universal

members of student council   persons who must maintain a 3.0 average

15. Form E; negative; universal

computers   things capable of thought

17. Form A; affirmative; universal

animal lovers   persons who will appreciate

19. Form I; affirmative; particular

teas   things containing caffeine

Exercise 3.4B
1. Some congresspersons are not muskrats.
dancers.   5. All plants are living things.
3. Some singers are not dancers. Some singers are

Exercise 3.6A
1. Valid

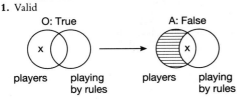

O: True   A: False

players   playing by rules   players   playing by rules

3. Valid

I: True   E: False

senators   voters   senators   voters

5. Valid

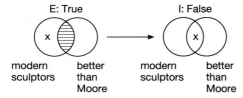

E: True   I: False

modern   better   modern   better
sculptors   than   sculptors   than
          Moore   Moore

7. Valid

A: True   O: False

philanthropists   benefactors   philanthropists   benefactors

9. Invalid

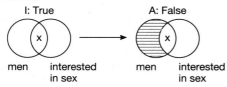

I: True   A: False

men   interested   men   interested
       in sex   in sex

Exercise 3.6B

1. If E is true, then

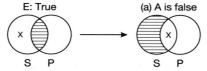 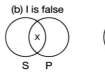

E: True   (a) A is false   (b) I is false   (c) O is true

   S   P   S   P   S   P   S   P

3. If some bats are deaf, then no inference can be drawn about the truth value of 'all bats are deaf'.

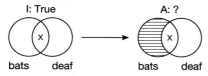

I: True   A: ?

bats   deaf   bats   deaf

no valid inference

5. If some people are not afraid of heights, nothing can be inferred about the claim that some people are afraid of heights.

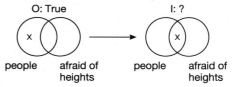

O: True   I: ?

people   afraid of   people   afraid of
       heights   heights

no valid inference

7. Given that some humans are mortal, nothing can be inferred about the claim that some humans are not mortal.

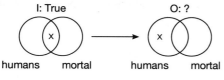

I: True   O: ?

humans   mortal   humans   mortal

no valid inference

9. Given that it is false that some Latin Americans do not speak Spanish, then 'All Latin Americans speak Spanish' is true.

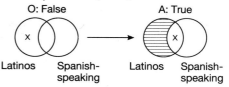

O: False   A: True

Latinos   Spanish-   Latinos   Spanish-
       speaking   speaking

Exercise 3.6C

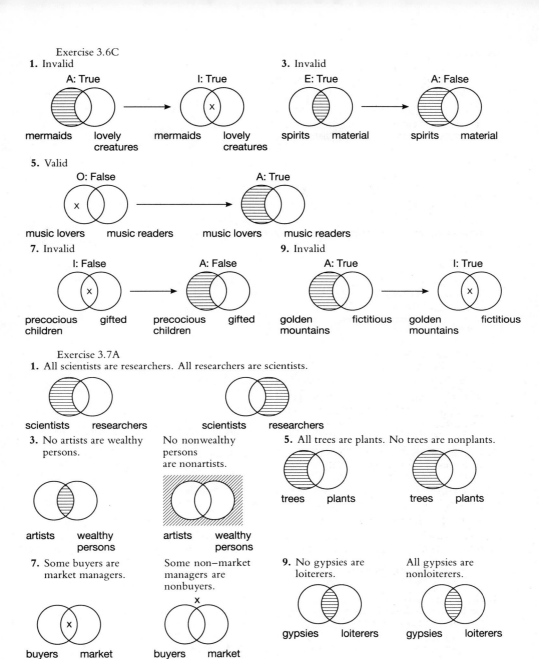

1. Invalid

A: True

mermaids   lovely creatures

I: True

mermaids   lovely creatures

3. Invalid

E: True

spirits   material

A: False

spirits   material

5. Valid

O: False

music lovers   music readers

A: True

music lovers   music readers

7. Invalid

I: False

precocious children   gifted

A: False

precocious children   gifted

9. Invalid

A: True

golden mountains   fictitious

I: True

golden mountains   fictitious

Exercise 3.7A

1. All scientists are researchers. All researchers are scientists.

scientists   researchers

scientists   researchers

3. No artists are wealthy persons.

No nonwealthy persons are nonartists.

artists   wealthy persons

artists   wealthy persons

5. All trees are plants. No trees are nonplants.

trees   plants

trees   plants

7. Some buyers are market managers.

Some non–market managers are nonbuyers.

buyers   market managers

buyers   market managers

9. No gypsies are loiterers.

All gypsies are nonloiterers.

gypsies   loiterers

gypsies   loiterers

11. Some citrus growers are not nonunion supporters. Some citrus growers are union supporters.

citrus   nonunion   citrus   nonunion
growers   supporters   growers   supporters

13. Some retired servicepeople are nonbeneficiaries. Some nonbeneficiaries are retired servicepeople.

retired   nonbeneficiaries   retired   nonbeneficiaries
service   service
people   people

15. Some sociopaths are not nonmoral people. Some sociopaths are moral people.

sociopaths   nonmoral   sociopaths   nonmoral
           people   people

      Exercise 3.7B

1. No patriots are traitors. Therefore, all patriots are nontraitors.

patriots   traitors   patriots   traitors
               Obverse; valid

3. All revolutionaries are radicals. So no revolutionaries are nonradicals.

revolutionaries   radicals   revolutionaries   radicals
                  Obverse; valid

5. Some people are not friendly, so some people are unfriendly.

people   friendly   people   friendly
            Obverse; valid

7. Some metals are liquids. Therfore, some liquids are not nonmetals. Some liquids are metals.

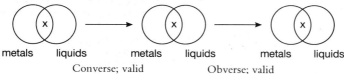

metals   liquids   metals   liquids   metals   liquids
        Converse; valid   Obverse; valid

9. No senators are infants. Therefore, no noninfants are nonsenators.

senators   infants   senators   infants

Contrapositive; invalid

Chapter 4

Exercise 4.2A
1. Some phones are things off the hook.
3. All times we have a picnic are times it rains.
5. Some historians are good writers. Some historians are not good writers.
7. All persons who go to war are young persons.
9. No faculty members are persons permitted to cancel classes.
11. All things logic develops are things identical to the mind.
13. All places where there is smoke are places where there is fire.
15. All persons identical to Aristotle are persons who developed the doctrine of the golden mean.
17. All major African religions are religions that contain the idea of a supreme god.
19. All cases in which consumer spending increases are cases in which interest rates will decline.
21. All persons are persons who need regular exercise.
23. All things identical to the whole of science are things that are nothing more than a refinement of everyday thinking.
25. All things identical to religion are things that are an illusion.

Exercise 4.2B
1. All sound arguments are good arguments.
All good arguments are sound arguments.

sound arguments   good arguments

3. Some singers are successful singers.
Some singers are not successful singers.

singers   successful singers

5. All medical doctors are persons who have earned an M.D. degree. All persons who have earned an M.D. degree are medical doctors.

medical doctors   earned M.D. degree

7. No Emperor–North American geese are regular visitors to Missouri. All non–Emperor–North American geese are regular visitors to Missouri.

Emperor-North   regular visitors
American geese

Note: Next is a solution using three categories. The advantage of this solution is that it makes

explicit the assertion that all North American Geese that are not Emperor Geese are visitors. All Emperor Geese are North American geese. No Emperor Geese are regular visitors to Missouri. All non–Emperor–North American geese are regular visitors to Missouri.

North American geese

Emperor geese   regular visitors

9. All persons who can order a drink here are persons who are twenty-one.

persons who can order   person who are 21

Exercise 4.4A

1.   members

athletes   professionals

3.   arguments with four premises

valid syllogisms   arguments unprovable

5.   reptiles

cold-blooded creatures   good pets

7.   chess players

grand masters   checkers players

9.   elected officials

Palestinians   freedom fighters

Exercise 4.4B

1. yes   **3.** yes   **5.** yes   **7.** no   **9.** no

Exercise 4.4C

1. *1. All dancers are vegetarians.*
2. No dentists are dancers.

3. No dentists are vegetarians.

dancers

Invalid

dentists   vegetarians

3. *1. No conservationists are advocates of nuclear energy.*
2. All farmers are conservationists.

3. No farmers are advocates of nuclear energy.

conservationists

Valid

farmers   advocates

5. *1. All books are books worth reading.*
2. Some books are novels.

3. Some novels are books worth reading.

books

Valid

novels   books worth reading

7. *1. Some females are not women.*
2. All mothers are females.

3. Some mothers are not women.

females

Invalid

mothers   women

9. *1. All Egyptians are North Africans.*
2. No Egyptians are Asians.

3. Some North Africans are not Asians.
Note: *Valid only by existential assumption of premise (1).*

Egyptians

North Africans   Asians

13. *1. All cameramen are photographers.*
2. Some photographers are not artists.

3. Some cameramen are not artists.

photographers

Invalid

cameramen   artists

11. *1. Some emotions are sensations caused by thought.*
2. Some sensations caused by thought are neurotic states.

3. Some emotions are neurotic states.

sensations caused

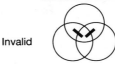

Invalid

emotions   neurotic states

15. *1. Some Japanese watches are digital watches.*
2. No analog watches are digital watches.

3. Some analog watches are not Japanese watches.

digital watches

Invalid

analog watches   Japanese watches

Exercise 4.5A

1. *1. Some bankers are voters for the new tax structure.*
2. Some bankers are not voters for the new tax structure.
3. All voters for the new tax structure are capitalists.

4. Some bankers are not capitalists.

voters

Invalid

bankers   capitalists

3. *1. All forecasters who can predict the heat wave are good weather reporters.*
2. All good weather reporters are persons trained in meteorology.

3. All forecasters who can predict the heat wave are persons trained in meteorology.

good weather reporters

Valid

forecasters   persons trained in . . .

5. *1. All things capable of thought are things capable of meaningful speech.*
2. All humans are things capable of meaningful speech.

3. All humans are things capable of thought.

capable of meaningful speech

Invalid

humans   capable of thought

9. *1. All Iranians are Persians.*
2. All Persians are Iranians.
3. No Iraqis are Persians.

4. No Iranians are Iraqis.

Persians

Valid

Iranians   Iraqis

Exercise 4.5B

1. All X are Y
All Y are Z

X

Therefore, * all X are Z
* All X are Z
All Z are T

D

A   B

Therefore, all X are T.

5. Some humans are mortals.
Some mortals are Romans.

humans

mortals   Romans

Invalid

7. *1. All poisonous snakes are things to avoid.*
2. Some snakes are nonpoisonous. = Some snakes are not poisonous snakes. (Obversion)

3. Some snakes are not things to avoid.

poisonous snakes

Invalid

snakes   things to avoid

3. No A are nonD = All A are D (Obversion)
Some A are B

X

Valid

Z   T

Therefore, * some B are D.
* Some B are D
All B are C

D

Valid

B   C

Therefore, some C are D

7. All sailors are recruits.
No volunteers are recruits.

sailors

volunteers   recruits

Therefore, * no sailors are volunteers.
* No sailors are volunteers.
All officers are volunteers.

sailors

officers   volunteers

Therefore, * no sailors are officers.
* No sailors are officers.
All veterans are officers.

sailors

veterans   officers

Valid

Therefore, no sailors are veterans.

9. All computer programmers are people proficient in BASIC.
No people proficient in BASIC are computer illiterates.

programmers

proficient in BASIC   illiterates

Therefore, * no computer programmers are computer illiterates.
* No computer programmers are computer illiterates.
No computer illiterates are mathematicians.

programmers

    Invalid

illiterates   mathematicians

11. All artisans are woodworkers.
All carpenters are artisans.

woodworkers

carpenters   artisans

Therefore, * all carpenters are woodworkers.
* All carpenters are woodworkers.
Some carpenters are journeymen.

woodworkers

carpenters   journeymen

Valid

Therefore, some journeymen are woodworkers.

Chapter 5

Exercise 5.4
1. R ⊃ C conditional   **3.** J ⊃ I conditional   **5.** −A negation   **7.** T-F symbolization permits two possible interpretations: "It is not the case that pizza and beer are recommended for people with ulcers." − (P + B) negation "Pizza is not recommended for people with ulcers and beer is not recommended for people with ulcers." −P + −B conjunction   **9.** T + −O conjunction
11. P + A conjunction   **13.** M ≡ V biconditional   **15.** −L ∨ S disjunction

Exercise 5.5

1. − (M ⊃ H)   negation   **3.** −T ∨ I   disjunction   **5.** (J ⊃ T) + R   conjunction
7. (B + A) + −S or B + (A + −S)   conjunction   **9.** L ⊃ (T + P)   conditional
11. (L ∨ T) ⊃ P   conditional   **13.** (L ∨ T) ⊃ P   conditional   **15.** T ∨ (C ⊃ −S)   disjunction
17. −(P ⊃ F) ⊃ −(B ⊃ G)   conditional   **19.** [(T + D) ∨ I] ⊃ B   conditional
20. Let statements be symbolized as follows, for example:

T = Each taxpayer must file an income tax report
C = Each taxpayer must complete a statement of earnings
A = An authorized tax preparer must file an income tax report
S = An authorized tax preparer must complete a statement of earnings

Then T-F symbolization permits two interpretations:

(T + C) ∨ (A + S)   disjunction

According to this interpretation either the taxpayer files the tax report and completes the statement of earnings or the authorized tax preparer does both.

(T ∨ A) + (C ∨ S)   conjunction

According to this interpretation either the taxpayer or the tax preparer must file the income tax report and either the taxpayer or the tax preparer must complete the statement of earnings.

Notice that according to T-F logic either interpretation correctly symbolizes the given compound statement. If one interpretation is preferable to the other, then it must be so for non–truth-functional considerations. For example, perhaps you might argue that, given the way tax preparation typically works—tax preparers usually do both tasks—the more plausible interpretation is the first.

Exercise 5.6

1. −(S + M)   **3.** C ⊃ D   **5.** S ⊃ D   **7.** H ∨ −F   **9.** H ∨ C   **11.** P ⊃ C
13. −(C ∨ P)   or   −C + −P   **15.** (a) (M ∨ F) + −(M + F)   (b) −(M + F)
17. (L + J) ⊃ U   **19.** −(C ∨ R)   or   −C + −R   **21.** −(D ∨ R)   or   −D + −R
23. (−S + −I) ⊃ B   **25.** H + (−S + −Y)   or   H + −(S ∨ Y)   **27.** (S + T) ⊃ C
29. N ⊃ C

Exercise 5.8A

1. − p

−	p
F	T
T	F

3. p ∨ q

p	∨	q
T	T	T
F	T	T
T	T	F
F	F	F

5. p ≡ q

p	≡	q
T	T	T
F	F	T
T	F	F
F	T	T

Exercise 5.8B

1. R + −S

R	+	−S
T	F	FT
F	F	FT
T	T	TF
F	F	TF

3. P ∨ (Q ⊃ R)

P	∨	(Q	⊃	R)
T	T	T	T	T
F	T	T	T	T
T	T	F	T	T
F	T	F	T	T
T	T	T	F	F
F	F	T	F	F
T	T	F	T	F
F	T	F	T	F

5. Q ⊃ (P + Q)

Q	⊃	(P	+	Q)
T	T	T	T	T
F	T	T	F	F
T	F	F	F	T
F	T	F	F	F

7. − (P + R)

−	(P	+	R)
F	T	T	T
T	F	F	T
T	T	F	F
T	F	F	F

9. − (P ∨ Q)

−	(P	∨	Q)
F	T	T	T
F	F	T	T
F	T	T	F
T	F	F	F

11. R ≡ (S ⊃ T)

R	≡	(S	⊃	T)
T	T	T	T	T
F	F	T	T	T
T	T	F	T	T
F	F	F	T	T
T	T	T	F	F
F	T	T	F	F
T	T	F	T	F
F	F	F	T	F

Exercise 5.8C

1. S ⊃ −R

```
T  F  FT
F  T  FT
T  T  TF
F  T  TF
```

3. (−T + S) ⊃ (M v C)

```
FT  F  T   T  T  T  T
TF  T  T   T  T  T  T
FT  F  F   T  T  T  T
TF  F  F   T  T  T  T
FT  F  T   T  F  T  T
TF  T  T   T  F  T  T
FT  F  F   T  F  T  T
TF  F  F   T  F  T  T
FT  F  T   T  T  T  F
TF  T  T   T  T  T  F
FT  F  F   T  T  T  F
TF  F  F   T  T  T  F
FT  F  T   T  F  F  F
TF  T  T   F  F  F  F
FT  F  F   T  F  F  F
TF  F  F   T  F  F  F
```

5. I ⊃ L

```
T  T  T
F  T  T
T  F  F
F  T  F
```

7. L + (J ⊃ B)

```
T  T  T  T  T
F  F  T  T  T
T  T  F  T  T
F  F  F  T  T
T  F  T  F  F
F  F  T  F  F
T  T  F  T  F
F  F  F  T  F
```

9. − (S v G)

```
F  T  T  T
F  F  T  T
F  T  T  F
T  F  F  F
```

11. O ≡ (S + M)

```
T  T  T  T  T
F  F  T  T  T
T  F  F  F  T
F  T  F  F  T
T  F  T  F  F
F  T  T  F  F
T  F  F  F  F
F  T  F  F  F
```

13. (S v −S) + −(S + −S)

```
T  T  FT  T  T  TT  F  FT
F  T  TF  T  T  TF  F  TF
```

15. S ⊃ (−N + −W)

```
T  F  FT  F  FT
F  T  FT  F  FT
T  F  TF  F  FT
F  T  TF  F  FT
T  F  FT  F  TF
F  T  FT  F  TF
T  T  TF  T  TF
F  T  TF  T  TF
```

17. I ⊃ (L v D)

```
T  T  T  T  T
F  T  T  T  T
T  T  F  T  T
F  T  F  T  T
T  T  T  T  F
F  T  T  T  F
T  F  F  F  F
F  T  F  F  F
```

19. (R + M) v (−L ⊃ C)

```
T  T  T  T  FT  T  T
F  F  T  T  FT  T  T
T  F  F  T  FT  T  T
F  F  F  T  FT  T  T
T  T  T  T  TF  T  T
F  F  T  T  TF  T  T
T  F  F  T  TF  T  T
F  F  F  T  TF  T  T
T  T  T  T  FT  T  F
F  F  T  T  FT  T  F
T  F  F  T  FT  T  F
F  F  F  T  FT  T  F
T  T  T  T  TF  F  F
F  F  T  F  TF  F  F
T  F  F  F  TF  F  F
F  F  F  F  TF  F  F
```

21. −C + −P

```
FT  F  FT
TF  F  FT
FT  F  TF
TF  T  TF
```

23. − D v (M + E)

```
F  T  T  T  T  T
T  F  T  T  T  T
F  T  F  F  F  T
T  F  T  F  F  T
F  T  F  T  F  F
T  F  T  T  F  F
F  T  F  F  F  F
T  F  T  F  F  F
```

25.

```
[(P v T) + V] ⊃ (W + L)          [(P v T) + V] ⊃ (W + L)
  T  T T T T  T  T T T              T  T T T T  F  T F F
  F  T T T T  T  T T T              F  T T T T  F  T F F
  T  T F T T  T  T T T              T  T F T T  F  T F F
  F  F F F T  T  T T T     row 20   F  F F F T  T  T F F
  T  T T F F  T  T T T              T  T T F F  T  T F F
  F  T T F F  T  T T T              F  T T F F  T  T F F
  T  T F F F  T  T T T              T  T F F F  T  T F F
  F  F F F F  T  T T T              F  F F F F  T  T F F
  T  T T T T  F  F F T              T  T T T T  F  F F F
row 10  F  T T T T  F  F F T         F  T T T T  F  F F F
  T  T F T T  F  F F T              T  T F T T  F  F F F
  F  F F F T  T  F F T              F  F F F T  T  F F F
  T  T T F F  T  F F T              T  T T F F  T  F F F
  F  T T F F  T  F F T     row 30   F  T T F F  T  F F F
  T  T F F F  T  F F T              T  T F F F  T  F F F
  F  F F F F  T  F F T              F  F F F F  T  F F F
```

Exercise 5.8D

1. It snows or it rains.

3. If the temperature is above freezing and there is precipitation, then it rains.

5. If it rains and the temperature is not above freezing, then the maintenance crews are salting the roads.

7. The maintenance crews are salting the roads or, if the temperature is above freezing, then classes must be canceled.

Chapter 6

Exercise 6.1

1.
```
K ⊃ D      −K   ∴   −D
T T T      FT       FT
F (T) T    (T)F     (F)T
T F F      FT       TF
F T F      TF       TF     Invalid
```

3.
```
− (G + E)      −E   ∴   G
F  T T T       FT       T
T  F F T       FT       F
T  T F F       TF       T
(T) F F F      (T)F     (F)    Invalid
```

5.
```
C ⊃ (S v M)    −M   ∴   C ⊃ S
T T  T T T     FT       T T T
F T  T T T     FT       F T T
T T  F T T     FT       T F F
F T  F T T     FT       F T F
T T  T T F     TF       T T T
F T  T T F     TF       F T T
T F  F F F     TF       T F F
F T  F F F     TF       F T F     Valid
```

7.
```
S ⊃ [E v (D + H)]     −S   ∴   −E
T T  T T T T T        FT        FT
F (T) T T T T T       (T)F      (F)T
T T  F T T T T        FT        TF
F T  F T T T T        TF        TF
T T  T T F F T        FT        FT
F T  T T F F T        TF        FT
T F  F F F F T        FT        TF
F T  F F F F T        TF        TF
T T  T T T F F        FT        FT
F T  T T T F F        TF        FT
T F  F F T F F        FT        TF
F T  F F T F F        TF        TF
T T  T T F F F        FT        FT
F T  T T F F F        TF        FT
T F  F F F F F        FT        TF
F T  F F F F F        TF        TF     Invalid
```

9.

```
M ⊃ P      P ⊃ S      −P   ∴   −M +  −S
T T T      T T T       FT       FT  F  FT
F T T      T T T       FT       TF  F  FT
T F F      F T T       TF       FT  F  FT
F Ⓣ F      F Ⓣ T      Ⓞ F      TF  Ⓕ  FT
T T T      T F F       FT       FT  F  TF
F T T      T F F       FT       TF  T  TF
T F F      F T F       TF       FT  F  TF
F T F      F T F       TF       TF  T  TF        Invalid
```

11.

```
V ⊃ −M      − −M   ∴   −V
T F FT      TFT        FT
F T FT      TFT        TF
T T TF      FTF        FT
F T TF      FTF        TF      Valid
```

13.

```
L ⊃ M   ∴   −L ⊃ −M
T T T       FT T FT
F Ⓣ T       TF Ⓕ FT
T F F       FT T TF
F T F       TF T TF      Invalid
```

15.

```
S ⊃ M      M ⊃ J   ∴   S ⊃ J
T T T      T T T       T T T
F T T      T T T       F T T
T F F      F T T       T T T
F T F      F T T       F T T
T T T      T F F       T F F
F T T      T F F       F T F
T F F      F T F       T F F
F T F      F T F       F T F      Valid
```

17.

```
P ⊃ C      −C   ∴   −P
T T T      FT       FT
F T T      FT       TF
T F F      TF       FT
F T F      TF       TF      Valid
```

19.

```
       (T + −U) ⊃ F        (T + L) ⊃ [G + (W + K)]      −K   ∴   −T v −L
        T F FT  T T         T T T T T T T T T            FT       FT F FT
        F F FT  T T         F F T T T T T T T            FT       TF T FT
        T T TF  T T         T T T T T T T T T            FT       FT F FT
        F F TF  T T         F F T T T T T T T            FT       TF T FT
        T F FT  T F         T T T T T T T T T            FT       FT F FT
        F F FT  T F         F F T T T T T T T            FT       TF T FT
        T T TF  F F         T T T T T T T T T            FT       FT F FT
        F F TF  T F         F F T T T T T T T            FT       TF T FT
        T F FT  T T         T F F T T T T T T            FT       FT T TF
row 10  F F FT  T T         F F F T T T T T T            FT       TF T TF
        T T TF  T T         T F F T T T T T T            FT       FT T TF
        F F TF  T T         F F F T T T T T T            FT       TF T TF
        T F FT  T F         T F F T T T T T T            FT       FT T TF
        F F FT  T F         F F F T T T T T T            FT       TF T TF
        T T TF  F F         T F F T T T T T T            FT       FT T TF
        F F TF  T F         F F F T T T T T T            FT       TF T TF
        T F FT  T T         T T T F F F T T T            FT       FT F FT
        F F FT  T T         F F T T F F T T T            FT       TF T FT
        T T TF  T T         T T T F F F T T T            FT       FT F FT
row 20  F F TF  T T         F F T T F F T T T            FT       TF T FT
        T F FT  T F         T T T F F F T T T            FT       FT F FT
        F F FT  T F         F F T T F F T T T            FT       TF T FT
        T T TF  F F         T T T F F F T T T            FT       FT F FT
        F F TF  T F         F F T T F F T T T            FT       TF T FT
        T F FT  T T         T F F T F F T T T            FT       FT T TF
        F F FT  T T         F F F T F F T T T            FT       TF T TF
        T T TF  T T         T F F T F F T T T            FT       FT T' TF
        F F TF  T T         F F F T F F T T T            FT       TF T TF
        T F FT  T F         T F F T F F T T T            FT       FT T TF
```

```
row 30   F  F  FT  T  F      F  F  F  T  F  F  T  T  T      FT      TF  T  TF
         T  T  TF  F  F      T  F  F  T  F  F  T  T  T      FT      FT  T  TF
         F  F  TF  T  F      F  F  F  T  F  F  T  T  T      FT      TF  T  TF
         T  F  FT  T  T      T  T  T  F  T  F  F  F  T      FT      FT  F  FT
         F  F  FT  T  T      F  F  T  T  T  F  F  F  T      FT      TF  T  FT
         T  T  TF  T  T      T  T  T  F  T  F  F  F  T      FT      FT  F  FT
         F  F  TF  T  T      F  F  T  T  T  F  F  F  T      FT      TF  T  FT
         T  F  FT  T  F      T  T  T  F  T  F  F  F  T      FT      FT  F  FT
         F  F  TF  T  F      F  F  T  T  T  F  F  F  T      FT      TF  T  FT
         T  T  TF  F  F      T  T  T  F  T  F  F  F  T      FT      FT  F  FT
row 40   F  F  TF  T  F      F  F  T  T  T  F  F  F  T      FT      TF  T  FT
         T  F  FT  T  T      T  F  F  T  T  F  F  F  T      FT      FT  T  TF
         F  F  FT  T  T      F  F  F  T  T  F  F  F  T      FT      TF  T  TF
         T  T  TF  T  T      T  F  F  T  T  F  F  F  T      FT      FT  T  TF
         F  F  TF  T  T      F  F  F  T  T  F  F  F  T      FT      TF  T  TF
         T  F  FT  T  F      T  F  F  T  T  F  F  F  T      FT      FT  T  TF
         F  F  FT  T  F      F  F  F  T  T  F  F  F  T      FT      TF  T  TF
         T  T  TF  F  F      T  F  F  T  T  F  F  F  T      FT      FT  T  TF
         F  F  TF  T  F      F  F  F  T  T  F  F  F  T      FT      TF  T  TF
         T  T  FT  T  T      T  T  T  F  F  F  F  F  T      FT      FT  F  FT
row 50   F  F  FT  T  T      F  F  T  T  F  F  F  F  T      FT      TF  T  FT
         T  T  TF  T  T      T  T  T  F  F  F  F  F  T      FT      FT  F  FT
         F  F  TF  T  T      F  F  T  T  F  F  F  F  T      FT      TF  T  FT
         T  F  FT  T  F      T  T  T  F  F  F  F  F  T      FT      FT  F  FT
         F  F  FT  T  F      F  F  T  T  F  F  F  F  T      FT      TF  T  FT
         T  T  TF  F  F      T  T  T  F  F  F  F  F  T      FT      FT  F  FT
         F  F  TF  T  F      F  F  T  T  F  F  F  F  T      FT      TF  T  FT
         T  F  FT  T  T      T  F  F  T  F  F  F  F  T      FT      FT  T  TF
         F  F  FT  T  T      F  F  F  T  F  F  F  F  T      FT      TF  T  TF
         T  T  TF  T  T      T  F  F  T  F  F  F  F  T      FT      FT  T  TF
row 60   F  F  TF  T  T      F  F  F  T  F  F  F  F  T      FT      TF  T  TF
         T  F  FT  T  F      T  F  F  T  F  F  F  F  T      FT      FT  T  TF
         F  F  FT  T  F      F  F  F  T  F  F  F  F  T      FT      TF  T  TF
         T  T  TF  F  F      T  F  F  T  T  F  F  F  T      FT      FT  T  TF
         F  F  TF  T  F      F  F  F  T  T  F  F  F  T      FT      TF  T  TF
         T  F  FT  T  T      T  T  T  F  T  F  T  F  F      TF      FT  F  FT
         F  F  FT  T  T      F  F  T  T  T  F  T  F  F      TF      TF  T  FT
         T  T  TF  T  T      T  T  T  F  T  F  T  F  F      TF      FT  F  FT
         F  F  TF  T  T      F  F  T  T  T  F  T  F  F      TF      TF  T  FT
         T  F  FT  T  F      T  T  T  F  T  F  T  F  F      TF      FT  F  FT
row 70   F  F  FT  T  F      F  F  T  T  T  F  T  F  F      TF      TF  T  FT
         T  T  TF  F  F      T  T  T  F  T  F  T  F  F      TF      FT  F  FT
         F  F  TF  T  F      F  F  T  T  T  F  T  F  F      TF      TF  T  FT
         T  F  FT  T  T      T  F  F  T  T  F  T  F  F      TF      FT  T  TF
         F  F  FT  T  T      F  F  F  T  T  F  T  F  F      TF      TF  T  TF
         T  T  TF  T  T      T  F  F  T  T  F  T  F  F      TF      FT  T  TF
         F  F  TF  T  T      F  F  F  T  T  F  T  F  F      TF      TF  T  TF
         T  F  FT  T  F      T  F  F  T  T  F  T  F  F      TF      FT  T  TF
         F  F  FT  T  F      F  F  F  T  T  F  T  F  F      TF      TF  T  TF
         T  T  TF  F  F      T  F  F  T  T  F  T  F  F      TF      FT  T  TF
row 80   F  F  TF  T  F      F  F  F  T  T  F  T  F  F      TF      TF  T  TF
         T  F  FT  T  T      T  T  T  F  F  F  T  F  F      TF      FT  F  FT
         F  F  FT  T  T      F  F  T  T  F  F  T  F  F      TF      TF  T  FT
         T  T  TF  T  T      T  T  T  F  F  F  T  F  F      TF      FT  F  FT
         F  F  TF  T  T      F  F  T  T  F  F  T  F  F      TF      TF  T  FT
         T  F  FT  T  F      T  T  T  F  F  F  T  F  F      TF      FT  F  FT
         F  F  FT  T  F      F  F  T  T  F  F  T  F  F      TF      TF  T  FT
         T  T  TF  F  F      T  T  T  F  F  F  T  F  F      TF      FT  F  FT
         F  F  TF  T  F      F  F  T  T  F  F  T  F  F      TF      TF  T  FT
         T  F  FT  T  T      T  F  F  T  F  F  T  F  F      TF      FT  T  TF
```

```
row 90    F  F  FT  T  T      F  F  F  T  F  F  T  F  F      TF      TF  T  TF
          T  F  TF  T  T      T  F  F  T  F  F  T  F  F      TF      FT  T  TF
          F  F  TF  T  T      F  F  F  T  F  F  T  F  F      TF      TF  T  TF
          T  F  FT  T  F      F  F  F  T  F  F  T  F  F      TF      FT  T  TF
          F  F  FT  T  F      F  F  F  T  F  F  T  F  F      TF      TF  T  TF
          T  T  TF  F  F      T  F  F  T  F  F  T  F  F      TF      FT  T  TF
          F  F  TF  T  F      F  F  F  T  F  F  F  F  F      TF      TF  T  TF
          T  F  FT  T  T      T  T  T  F  T  F  F  F  F      TF      FT  F  FT
          F  F  FT  T  T      F  F  T  T  T  F  F  F  F      TF      TF  T  FT
          T  T  TF  T  T      T  T  T  F  T  F  F  F  F      TF      FT  T  FT
row 100   F  F  TF  T  T      F  F  T  T  T  F  F  F  F      TF      TF  T  FT
          T  F  FT  T  F      T  T  T  F  T  F  F  F  F      TF      FT  F  FT
          F  F  FT  T  F      F  F  T  T  T  F  F  F  F      TF      TF  T  FT
          T  T  TF  F  F      T  T  T  F  T  F  F  F  F      TF      FT  F  FT
          F  F  FT  T  F      F  F  T  T  T  F  F  F  F      TF      TF  T  FT
          T  F  FT  T  T      T  F  F  T  T  F  F  F  F      TF      FT  T  TF
          F  F  FT  T  T      F  F  F  T  T  F  F  F  F      TF      TF  T  TF
          T  T  TF  T  T      T  F  F  T  T  F  F  F  F      TF      FT  T  TF
          F  F  TF  T  T      F  F  F  T  T  F  F  F  F      TF      TF  T  TF
          T  F  FT  T  F      T  F  F  T  T  F  F  F  F      TF      FT  T  TF
row 110   F  F  FT  T  F      F  F  F  T  T  F  F  F  F      TF      TF  T  TF
          T  T  TF  F  F      T  F  F  T  T  F  F  F  F      TF      FT  T  TF
          F  F  TF  T  F      F  F  F  T  T  F  F  F  F      TF      TF  T  TF
          T  F  FT  T  T      T  T  T  F  F  F  F  F  F      TF      FT  F  FT
          F  F  FT  T  T      F  F  T  T  F  F  F  F  F      TF      TF  T  FT
          T  T  TF  T  T      T  T  T  F  F  F  F  F  F      TF      FT  F  FT
          F  F  TF  T  T      F  F  T  T  F  F  F  F  F      TF      TF  T  FT
          T  F  FT  T  F      T  T  T  F  F  F  F  F  F      TF      FT  F  FT
          F  F  FT  T  F      F  F  T  T  F  F  F  F  F      TF      TF  T  FT
          T  T  TF  F  F      T  T  T  F  F  F  F  F  F      TF      FT  F  FT
row 120   F  F  FT  T  F      F  F  T  T  F  F  F  F  F      TF      TF  T  FT
          T  F  FT  T  T      T  F  F  T  F  F  F  F  F      TF      FT  T  TF
          F  F  FT  T  T      F  F  F  T  F  F  F  F  F      TF      TF  T  TF
          T  T  TF  T  T      T  F  F  T  F  F  F  F  F      TF      FT  T  TF
          F  F  TF  T  T      F  F  F  T  F  F  F  F  F      TF      TF  T  TF
          T  F  FT  T  F      T  F  F  T  F  F  F  F  F      TF      FT  T  TF
          F  F  FT  T  F      F  F  F  T  F  F  F  F  F      TF      TF  T  TF
          T  T  TF  F  F      T  F  F  T  F  F  F  F  F      TF      FT  T  TF
row 128   F  F  TF  T  F      F  F  F  T  F  F  F  F  F      TF      TF  T  TF      Valid
```

21. −(A v B) ⊃ D   C + −D ∴ A v B

```
F  T  T  T  T  T      T  F  FT      T  T  T
F  F  T  T  T  T      T  F  FT      F  T  T
F  T  T  F  T  T      T  F  FT      T  T  F
T  F  F  F  T  T      T  F  FT      F  F  F
F  T  T  T  T  F      T  T  TF      T  T  T
F  F  T  T  T  F      T  T  TF      F  T  T
F  T  T  F  T  F      T  T  TF      T  T  F
T  F  F  F  F  F      T  T  TF      F  F  F
F  T  T  T  T  T      F  F  FT      T  T  T
F  F  T  T  T  T      F  F  FT      F  T  T
F  T  T  F  T  T      F  F  FT      T  T  F
T  F  F  F  T  T      F  F  FT      F  F  F
F  T  T  T  T  F      F  F  TF      T  T  T
F  F  T  T  T  F      F  F  TF      F  T  T
F  T  T  F  T  F      F  F  TF      T  T  F
T  F  F  F  F  F      F  F  TF      F  F  F      Valid
```

23. −(P + Q)   P ∴ −Q

```
F  T  T  T      T      FT
T  F  F  T      F      FT
T  T  F  F      T      TF
T  F  F  F      F      TF      Valid
```

25. T ⊃ W   −W ∴ −T

```
T  T  T      FT      FT
F  T  T      FT      TF
T  F  F      TF      FT
F  T  F      TF      TF      Valid
```

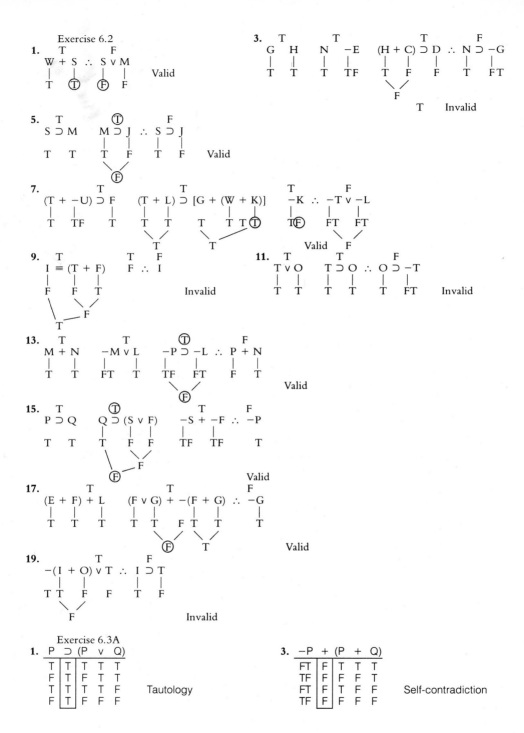

Exercise 6.2

1.
$$\begin{array}{ccc} T & & F \\ W + S & \therefore & S \vee M \\ | & | & | & | \\ T & \textcircled{T} & \textcircled{F} & F \end{array}$$
Valid

3.
$$\begin{array}{cccccc} T & & T & & T & F \\ G & H & N & -E & (H + C) \supset D & \therefore & N \supset -G \\ | & | & | & | & | & | & | & | \\ T & T & T & TF & T & F & F & T & FT \\ & & & & & \searrow & & & \\ & & & & F & & & \\ & & & T & Invalid \end{array}$$

5.
$$\begin{array}{cccc} T & & \textcircled{T} & & F \\ S \supset M & & M \supset J & \therefore & S \supset J \\ | & | & | & | & | & | \\ T & T & T & F & T & F \\ & & \searrow & \swarrow & & \\ & & \textcircled{F} & & \end{array}$$
Valid

7.
$$\begin{array}{ccccccc} T & & T & & T & F \\ (T + -U) \supset F & (T + L) \supset [G + (W + K)] & -K & \therefore & -T \vee -L \\ | & | & | & | & | & | & | & | & | \\ T & TF & T & T & T & T & T & T\textcircled{T} & T\textcircled{F} & FT & FT \\ & \searrow & \swarrow & & \searrow & \searrow & & & \searrow & \swarrow \\ & T & & T & & & Valid & F \end{array}$$

9.
$$\begin{array}{cccc} T & & T & F \\ I \equiv (T + F) & F & \therefore & I \\ | & | & | & | \\ F & F & T & \\ \searrow & & \swarrow & \\ & \searrow & F & \\ T & & \end{array}$$
Invalid

11.
$$\begin{array}{cccccc} T & & T & & F \\ T \vee O & T \supset O & \therefore & O \supset -T \\ | & | & | & | & | & | \\ T & T & T & T & T & FT \end{array}$$
Invalid

13.
$$\begin{array}{cccccccc} T & & T & & \textcircled{T} & & F \\ M + N & -M \vee L & -P \supset -L & \therefore & P + N \\ | & | & | & | & | & | & | & | \\ T & T & FT & T & TF & FT & F & T \\ & & \searrow & & \swarrow & & \\ & & & \textcircled{F} & & & \end{array}$$
Valid

15.
$$\begin{array}{ccccccc} T & & \textcircled{T} & & T & F \\ P \supset Q & Q \supset (S \vee F) & -S + -F & \therefore & -P \\ | & | & | & | & | & | & | \\ T & T & T & F & F & TF & TF & T \\ & & \searbow & \swarrow & F & & \\ & & & \textcircled{F} & & & \end{array}$$
Valid

17.
$$\begin{array}{ccccccc} T & & T & F \\ (E + F) + L & (F \vee G) + -(F + G) & \therefore & -G \\ | & | & | & | & | & | & | & | \\ T & T & T & T & T & F & T & T & T \\ & & & & \searrow & & \swarrow & \\ & & & \textcircled{F} & & T & \end{array}$$
Valid

19.
$$\begin{array}{ccccc} T & & F \\ -(I + O) \vee T & \therefore & I \supset T \\ | & | & | & | & | & | \\ T & T & F & F & T & F \\ & \searrow & \swarrow & & \\ & F & & Invalid \end{array}$$

Exercise 6.3A

1.

P	⊃	(P	∨	Q)
T	T	T	T	T
F	T	F	T	T
T	T	T	T	F
F	T	F	F	F

Tautology

3.

−P	+	(P	+	Q)
FT	F	T	T	T
TF	F	F	F	T
FT	F	T	F	F
TF	F	F	F	F

Self-contradiction

5. (P ⊃ −Q) ≡ (P + Q)

T	F	FT	F	T	T	T	
F	T	FT	F	F	F	T	
T	T	TF	F	T	F	F	Self-contradiction
F	T	TF	F	F	F	F	

7. (P v Q) v −Q

T	T	T	T	FT	
T	T	T	T	FT	
T	T	F	T	TF	Tautology
F	F	F	T	TF	

Exercise 6.3B

1. P ⊃ Q   − (P + −Q)

T	T	T		T	T	F	FT	
F	T	T		T	F	F	FT	
T	F	F		F	T	T	TF	Equivalences
F	T	F		T	F	F	TF	

3. − (P + −Q) v S   (−P v Q) v S

T	T	F	FT	T	T		FT	T	T	T	T	T	
T	F	F	FT	T	T		TF	T	T	T	T	T	
F	T	T	TF	T	T		FT	F	F	T	T	T	
T	F	F	TF	T	T		TF	T	F	T	T	T	
T	T	F	FT	T	F		FT	T	T	T	T	F	
T	F	F	FT	T	F		TF	T	T	T	T	F	Equivalences
F	T	T	TF	F	F		FT	F	F	F	F	F	
T	F	F	TF	T	F		TF	T	F	T	T	F	

5. P ≡ Q   (P ⊃ Q) + (Q ⊃ P)

T	T	T	T	T	T	T	T	T	T	
F	F	T	F	T	T	F	T	F	F	
T	F	F	T	F	F	F	F	T	T	Equivalences
F	T	F	F	T	F	T	F	T	F	

7. − (P + Q)   −P v −Q

F	T	T	T	FT	F	FT	Equivalences
T	F	F	T	TF	T	FT	
T	T	F	F	FT	T	TF	
T	F	F	F	TF	T	TF	

9. −P ⊃ Q   P v Q

FT	T	T	T	T	T	
TF	T	T	F	T	T	
FT	T	F	T	T	F	Equivalences
TF	F	F	F	F	F	

11. P ⊃ Q   Q ⊃ P

T	T	T	T	T	T	
F	T	T	T	F	F	
T	F	F	F	T	T	Neither
F	T	F	F	T	F	

Chapter 7

Exercise 7.2A

1. Simplification

p + q   ∴   p   p + q   ∴   q

T	T	T		T
F	F	T		F
T	F	F		T
F	F	F		F

T	T	T		T
F	F	T		T
T	F	F		F
F	F	F		F

3. *Modus tollens*

p ⊃ q   −q   ∴   −p

T	T	T	FT	FT
F	T	T	FT	TF
T	F	F	TF	FT
F	T	F	TF	TF

Exercise 7.2B

1. 1. F + G   premise / ∴ G
    2. G   1, Simp

3. 1. Z v T   premise
    2. −T   premise / ∴ Z
    3. Z   1,2, DS

5. 1. A ⊃ S   premise
    2. −S   premise / ∴ −A
    3. −A   1,2, MT

7. 1. G ⊃ P   premise
    2. S + −P   premise / ∴ −G
    3. −P   2, Simp
    4. −G   1,3, MT

9. 1. K v N   premise
    2. −K + O   premise / ∴ N
    3. −K   2, Simp
    4. N   1,3, DS

Exercise 7.3A

1. Hypothetical syllogism

p ⊃ Q	q ⊃ r	∴ p ⊃ r
T T T	T T T	T T T
F T T	T T T	F T T
T F F	F T T	T T T
F T F	F T T	F T T
T T T	T F F	T F F
F T T	T F F	F T F
T F F	F T F	T F F
F T F	F T F	F T F

3. Conjunction

p	q	∴ p + q
T	T	T T T
F	T	F F T
T	F	T F F
F	F	F F F

Exercise 7.3B

1. DS	**3.** MT	**5.** MP	**7.** MP	**9.** MT
11. Simp	**13.** DS	**15.** Simp	**17.** Con	**19.** DS
Simp	MT	DS	MP	MP

Exercise 7.3C

1.
1. K ⊃ P   premise
2. −P ∨ D   premise
3. −D   premise / ∴ −K
4. −P   2,3, DS
5. −K   1,4, MT

5.
1. H + −T   premise
2. T ∨ (A + J)   premise / ∴ J
3. −T   1, Simp
4. A + J   2,3, DS
5. J   4, Simp

7.
1. [(A ∨ B) + C] ⊃ (T ∨ A)   premise
2. −(T ∨ A)   premise / ∴ −[(A ∨ B) + C]
3. −[(A ∨ B) + C]   1,2, MT

9.
1. −L   premise
2. −L ⊃ (T + A)   premise / ∴ T
3. T + A   1,2, MP
4. T   3, Simp

13.
1. (S + A) ∨ (P + M)   premise
2. (S + A) ⊃ R   premise
3. −R   premise / ∴ P + M
4. −(S + A)   2,3, MT
5. P + M   1,4, DS

17.
1. T   premise
2. (T + R) ⊃ S   premise
3. R   premise / ∴ S
4. T + R   1,3, Con
5. S   2,4, MP

3.
1. S ⊃ P   premise
2. −P + −A   premise / ∴ −S
3. −P   2, Simp
4. −S   1,3, MT

11.
1. (R ∨ T) ⊃ (T ⊃ L)   premise
2. (T ⊃ L) ⊃ S   premise / ∴ (R ∨ T) ⊃ S
3. (R ∨ T) ⊃ S   1,2, HS

15.
1. (T ⊃ Q) + (S ⊃ P)   premise
2. T   premise / ∴ Q ∨ P
3. T ∨ S   2, Add
4. Q ∨ P   1,3, CD

Exercise 7.4A

1.
1. A ⊃ B   premise / ∴ −A ∨ B
2. −A ∨ B   1, Impl

5.
1. −A   premise / ∴ A ⊃ B
2. −A ∨ B   1, Add
3. A ⊃ B   2, Impl

9.
1. P ∨ −Q   premise / ∴ −P ⊃ −Q
2. −−P ∨ −Q   1, DN
3. −P ⊃ −Q   2, Impl

13.
1. A ∨ C   premise / ∴ −A ⊃ C
2. −−A ∨ C   1, DN
3. −A ⊃ C   2, Impl

3.
1. −E   premise / ∴ −(E + D)
2. −E ∨ −D   1, Add
3. −(E + D)   2, DeM

7.
1. −(A ∨ B)   premise / ∴ −B
2. −A + −B   1, DeM
3. −B   2, Simp

11.
1. −P ∨ (−R ∨ S)   premise / ∴ P ⊃ (R ⊃ S)
2. −P ∨ (R ⊃ S)   1, Impl
3. P ⊃ (R ⊃ S)   2, Impl

15.
1. −S ∨ (−R + P)   premise / ∴ S ⊃ −(R + P)
2. S ⊃ (−R + P)   1, Impl

17.
1. $-(R + S) \vee T$ premise / $\therefore (R \supset -S) \vee T$
2. $(-R \vee -S) \vee T$ 1, DeM
3. $(R \supset -S) \vee T$ 2, Impl

21.
1. A   premise
2. B   premise / $\therefore A + (B \vee C)$
3. $B \vee C$ 2, Add
4. $A + (B \vee C)$ 1,3, Con

19.
1. $-(S + R)$ premise / $\therefore S \supset -R$
2. $-S \vee -R$ 1, DeM
3. $S \supset -R$ 2, Impl

23.
1. $A \supset B$ premise
2. $S + A$ premise / $\therefore B + S$
3. A   2, Simp
4. B   1,3, MP
5. S   2, Simp
6. $B + S$ 4,5, Con

Exercise 7.4B

1.
1. $-P \vee Q$ premise
2. $(P \supset Q) \supset R$ premise / $\therefore R$
3. $P \supset Q$ 1, Impl
4. R   2,3, MP

5.
1. $(L + P) \supset Q$ premise
2. $-Q$ premise / $\therefore -L \vee -P$
3. $-(L + P)$ 1,2, MT
4. $-L \vee -P$ 3, DeM

9.
1. $R \vee (P + S)$ premise / $\therefore R \vee S$
2. $(R \vee P) + (R \vee S)$ 1, Dist
3. $R \vee S$ 2, Simp

13.
1. $A \equiv -C$ premise
2. $-A$ premise / $\therefore C$
3. $(A \supset -C) + (-C \supset A)$ 1, Equiv
4. $-C \supset A$ 3, Simp
5. $--C$ 2,4, MT
6. C   5, DN

17.
1. $C \supset D$ premise
2. $D \supset G$ premise
3. $F \supset N$ premise
4. $C \vee F$ premise / $\therefore G \vee N$
5. $C \supset G$ 1,2, HS
6. $(C \supset G) + (F \supset N)$ 3,5, Con
7. $G \vee N$ 4,6, CD

3.
1. $-P$ premise
2. $(P + R) \vee S$ premise / $\therefore S$
3. $S \vee (P + R)$ 2, Com
4. $(S \vee P) + (S \vee R)$ 3, Dist
5. $S \vee P$ 4, Simp
6. S   1,5, DS

7.
1. $-(P + Q)$ premise
2. Q   premise / $\therefore -P$
3. $-P \vee -Q$ 1, DeM
4. $--Q$ 2, DN
5. $-P$ 3,4, DS

11.
1. $-(P \vee T)$ premise / $\therefore -T$
2. $-P + -T$ 1, DeM
3. $-T$ 2, Simp

15.
1. $-(A + B)$ premise
2. B   premise
3. $D \supset A$ premise / $\therefore -D$
4. $-A \vee -B$ 1, DeM
5. $--B$ 2, DN
6. $-A$ 4,5, DS
7. $-D$ 3,6, MT

19.
1. $(A \supset B) + (C \supset D)$ premise
2. $A \vee C$ premise
3. $D \supset -S$ premise
4. $A + S$ premise / $\therefore F \supset B$
5. $A \supset B$ 1, Simp
6. A   4, Simp
7. B   5,6, MP
8. $B \vee -F$ 7, Add
9. $-F \vee B$ 8, Com
10. $F \supset B$ 9, Impl

21.
1. $P \supset (A \supset B)$ premise
2. $D \vee -B$ premise
3. $-D + A$ premise / $\therefore -P$
4. $-D$ 3, Simp
5. $-B$ 2,4, DS
6. A   3, Simp
7. $A + -B$ 5,6, Con
8. $--A + -B$ 7, DN
9. $-(-A \vee B)$ 8, DeM
10. $-(A \supset B)$ 9, Impl
11. $-P$ 1,10, MT

Exercise 7.4C

1. 1. J ⊃ (C v N)   premise
2. P ⊃ J   premise
3. P + −C   premise / ∴ N
4. P   3, Simp
5. J   2,4, MP
6. C v N   1,5, MP
7. −C   3, Simp
8. N   6,7, DS

5. 1. −F ⊃ S   premise
2. −S   premise
3. F ⊃ (−G + −K)   premise / ∴ −G
4. −−F   1,2, MT
5. F   4, DN
6. −G + −K   3,5, MP
7. −G   6, Simp

9. 1. (P ⊃ F) + P   premise / ∴ −−F
2. P   1, Simp
3. P ⊃ F   1, Simp
4. F   2,3, MP
5. −−F   4, DN

13. 1. M ⊃ P   premise
2. −P + −A   premise / ∴ −M
3. −P   2, Simp
4. −M   1,3, MT

3. 1. C ⊃ L   premise
2. L ⊃ (−S + −M)   premise
3. −M ⊃ E   premise
4. −E   premise / ∴ −C
5. −−M   3,4, MT
6. M   5, DN
7. S v M   6, Add
8. −−S v −−M   7, DN
9. −(−S + −M)   8, DeM
10. −L   2,9, MT
11. −C   1,10, MT

7. 1. (P + E) ⊃ (M + L)   premise
2. (M + L) ⊃ T   premise / ∴ −P v (E ⊃ T)
3. (P + E) ⊃ T   1,2, HS
4. −(P + E) v T   3, Impl
5. (−P v −E) v T   4, DeM
6. −P v (−E v T)   5, Assoc
7. −P v (E ⊃ T)   6, Impl

11. 1. (D v I) + −(D + I)   premise
2. D   premise / ∴ −I
3. −(D + I)   1, Simp
4. −D v −I   3, DeM
5. −−D   2, DN
6. −I   4,5, DS

15. 1. I   premise
2. N   premise / ∴ I + (N v C)
3. N v C   2, Add
4. I + (N v C)   1,3, Con

Chapter 8

Exercise 8.2

1. (a) sample: the families Pat has counselled over a ten-year period.
(b) population: presumably all U.S. families.
(c) target characteristic: dysfunctionality in families.
(d) representativeness of sample: From what we are given we can say only that the sample is composed of families with these characteristics in common: they have come in for counselling, they have come to Pat, they have come to Pat sometime during a ten-year period. We cannot say that such a sample is randomly selected; that is, that every U.S. family has an equal chance of being a member of the sample. In fact, it is a self-selected sample. Neither can we say it is a stratified random sample for there is no reason to think that the sample reflects the diversity of U.S. families. Thus, in the absence of more information about the families Pat has counselled, it does not appear to be a representative sample.
(e) The inductive generalization of this argument is, as it stands, inductively weak. Although it might be replied that over a ten-year period of counselling one ought to see at least one functional family, it should be remembered that families seek counselling precisely because they are experiencing difficulties. Thus, perhaps one ought not to expect a functional family among those seeking counselling.

3. (a) sample: one member, Lauren.
(b) population: all six-year-old children.
(c) target characteristic: 30 minutes of happiness from a Barbie doll.
(d) representativeness of sample: One little girl, presumably six years of age, is not representative of all six-year-old boys and girls as regards what they will derive a little happiness from.
(e) Inductively weak on the grounds that the sample is not representative.

5. (a) sample: an unspecified number of observations of at least one reckless skier per visit to a particular area over a five-year period.
(b) population: skiers in the particular area of observation.
(c) target characteristic: reckless behavior.

(d) representativeness of sample: From what we are given we do not know how many times Don has skied the terrain, nor how many skiers generally Don has seen during his observations. We could count his observations as representative if we make some assumptions. Suppose we assume that Don is an above average enthusiast who goes skiing once a week during the season and that the slopes are active but not crowded. Then, given weekly observations, the sample seems to be representative for an imprecise generalization.

(e) Given the assumptions made about Don's sample, one could say that this is a strong inductive generalization. But it is not a precise generalization.

7. (a) sample: 326 pension-fund actuaries.
   (b) population: 7,854 pension-fund actuaries.
   (c) target characteristic: belief that half of the nation's baby boomers will not financially be able to retire at age 65.
   (d) representativeness of sample: The sample is constructed from an American Academy of Actuaries survey. We are not given information about the sample selection method but we can reasonably assume that the academy would follow good survey practices. Therefore, on the basis of the authority of the academy, we can accept this as a representative sample.
   (e) Since the sample is accepted as representative and it shows that 72 percent predict the financial inability of baby boomers to retire, generalizing that over half of all actuaries would so predict is a strongly supported inductive generalization.

9. (a) sample: law students polled at 100 law schools.
   (b) population: 129,000 law students throughout the country.
   (c) target characteristic: percentage of law students favoring mandatory public service as part of their education.
   (d) representativeness of sample: We are not given the exact number of students interviewed for the sample, nor how the 100 law schools compare with the remaining 75. However, interviewing students at 100 out of 175 law schools appears to be a particularly large sample. Therefore, we can accept the sample as representative.
   (e) The generalization is that slightly over half of all students favor mandatory public service. Given the apparent large size of the sample, there is strong evidence for the generalization.

11. (a) sample: six household interviews of over 40,000 individuals over an 18-month period between 1977 and 1978.
   (b) population: all Americans during the study period.
   (c) target characteristic: Americans without health insurance during all or part of the study period.
   (d) sample representativeness: One should expect a stratified random sample for this study, one reflecting different income groups, different age groups, both sexes, different geographical locations, and so on. We are given no information about the diversity of the sample used, though we may assume that the NMCES can provide that information. We can accept this as a representative sample on the basis of authority keeping in mind the information we would need to make a firmer judgment.
   (e) On the assumption that the sample is representative, it is an inductively strong generalization.

13. (a) sample: 8,000 drivers over a 24-hour period.
   (b) population: all Alameda County drivers.
   (c) target characteristic: drivers wearing seat belts.
   (d) representativeness of sample: To determine whether the sample is representative, we need to know how many drivers there are in Alameda County and how "Alameda County driver" is defined. Furthermore, the sample results are likely to be affected by the day of the week and the time of year in which the survey was conducted and by the location of the survey. Are the seat belt–wearing habits of drivers affected by the distance they travel? Are drivers crossing the bridge likely to be travelling far? Is it possible that drivers unfasten their seat belts when approaching a toll booth? A more representative sample is one consisting of observations of drivers on different days in different settings.
   (e) Given the above questions about the nature of the sample, we might be skeptical of this argument's results. Let us say that it is weakly supported.

15. (a) sample: interviews of 500 rural residents of Franklin County during the month of January.
   (b) population: 70,000 residents of Franklin County.
   (c) target characteristic: most commonly purchase commodities.
   (d) representativeness of sample: The sample is clearly not representative since it does not include members from the much larger urban population.
   (e) The generalization is inductively weak.

Exercise 8.3A

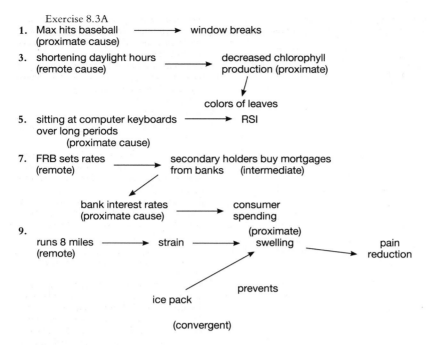

1. Max hits baseball ——————→ window breaks
   (proximate cause)

3. shortening daylight hours ——————→ decreased chlorophyll
   (remote cause)   production (proximate)
                                              ↓
                                   colors of leaves

5. sitting at computer keyboards ——————→ RSI
   over long periods
       (proximate cause)

7. FRB sets rates ————————→ secondary holders buy mortgages
   (remote)   from banks   (intermediate)

       bank interest rates ————————→ consumer
       (proximate cause)   spending

9.   (proximate)
   runs 8 miles ——————→ strain ——————→ swelling ——————→ pain
   (remote)   reduction

                             prevents
           ice pack

                    (convergent)

Exercise 8.3B

5. Sitting at a computer keyboard can produce but does not necessarily produce repetitive strain injury (RSI). Furthermore, RSI may occur in the absence of long periods at the keyboard. Thus, prolonged sitting at a computer keyboard is neither a necessary nor a sufficient condition of RSI. Prolonged sitting is best described as a partial cause, a factor that increases the likelihood of RSI.

7. The causal claims are that if the FRB lowers interest rates for preferred customers, then secondary holders will buy mortgages. And if secondary holders buy mortgages, then banks will decrease interest rates on borrowing and, if so, then consumer spending increases. It is arguable that the antecedents in each conditional are causally sufficient conditions. That is, if the FRB lowers rates, then buying increases. However, since buying may increase for other reasons as well, lowering of interest rates is not a causally necessary condition.

9. Running eight miles is neither a necessary nor sufficient condition for strained tendons; others do it and are not injured. Nevertheless, the run and Evelyn's particular conditioning are jointly sufficient. The run itself is a partial cause. Packing her ankle in ice is causally sufficient for reducing swelling but not necessary, since swelling is reducible in other ways. Reducing swelling is sufficient for reducing the pain but pain can be decreased without reducing swelling, by pain killers, for example. Thus, reducing swelling is not a necessary condition for reduction of the pain of swelling.

Exercise 8.3C

1. *1. Improper cabin pressure in an airplane causes earache. (causal statement)*
   2. Several passengers have complained of earache.

   3. Thus, there is probably a problem with cabin pressure.
   causal explanation

3. *1. Whenever an orange female cat is mated with a black male, the resulting male kittens will be orange and the resulting female kittens will be tortoiseshell. (causal statement)*
   *2. We are mating your black male and my orange female. (missing premise)

   3. Thus, they will probably produce no black kittens.
   causal prediction

5. 1. The absorbent in disposable diapers draws moisture from the skin and reduces diaper rash. *(causal statement)*

2. Therefore, if you are interested in protecting your infant from diaper rash, you'd be wise to use disposable diapers.
causal prescription

9. 1. Shaking a bottle filled with carbonated liquid releases the gas and increases the pressure inside the bottle. *(causal statement)*
2. The soda bubbled out and all over when you opened it.

3. Therefore, you shook the bottle filled with carbonated liquid. *(missing conclusion)*
causal explanation

11. 1. Measurable levels of stress are not correlated with complications in pregnancy.

2. Measurable levels of stress do not increase the likelihood of complications in pregnancy. *(causal statement)*
causal conclusion

7. 1. The mammalian eye may exhibit two types of nerve receptors, cone-shaped receptors for color vision and rod-shaped receptors for low-intensity light.
*2. Color vision is caused by having cone-shaped receptors and night vision is caused by having rod-shaped receptors. *(missing premise)* *(causal statement)*
3. Owls have only rods.

4. Therefore, owls can hardly see in daylight.
causal explanation

1. The mammalian eye may exhibit two types of nerve receptors, cone-shaped receptors for color vision and rod-shaped receptors for low-intensity light.
*2. Color vision is caused by having cone-shaped receptors and night vision is caused by having rod-shaped receptors. *(missing premise)* *(causal statement)*
3. Hens have only cones.

4. Therefore, hens can hardly see at night.
causal explanation

13. 1. Shortly after the arrival of Cortez and his Conquistadores, smallpox spread like wild-fire through the Indian population.
2. As smallpox was then prevalent in Europe, the Spaniards had probably developed immunity to it through early exposure, whereas the Indians, who had no racial experience with it, proved very susceptible.
*3. Exposure to smallpox, without having developed immunity, causes death. *(missing premise)* *(causal statement)*

4. By killing at least half the Indians and demoralizing them at a critical time, the epidemic certainly played a part as important as Spanish arms and valor in bringing about the conquest of the South American continent.
causal explanation

15. 1. Of 838 subjects, who had survived a previous heart attack and had cholesterol levels above 220, half modified their diets, some were given drugs, while the other half underwent a surgical procedure that reduced absorption of cholesterol.
2. In the surgery group, cholesterol levels dropped to an average of 96 compared with 241 in the control (nonsurgery) group.
3. Over a 10-year period the combined rate of second heart attacks or death from heart disease was 35 percent lower in the treated patients—and they required less than half as many cardiac operations as the controls.

4. Therefore, cholesterol does contribute to heart disease. *(causal statement)*
causal conclusion

Exercise 8.3D
1. (1) The causal assertion is that the addition of white is what causes purple to change to lavender.
(2) The method of residue is employed. Smith believes that lavender is caused by the combination of red, blue, and white. He knows that red and blue make purple, so the remaining color, white, must account for the change of purple to lavender.

3. (1) The causal assertion is that Bud's cat is the cause of her allergic reaction. (2) The methods of agreement and difference are employed. By agreement she knows that her allergic reaction occurs whenever the cat is present; and by difference she knows that whenever the cat is not present, she does not have an allergic reaction. By these methods, she seems to have good evidence for her causal assertion.

5. (1) The causal assertion is that turning the knob causes the music to change volume. (2) The method of concomitant variation is employed. Kay-kay notices that loudness and softness vary proportionately to turning the knob one way or the other.

7. (1) The causal assertion is that social interaction reduces the incidence of chronic ailment. (2) The methods of agreement and difference are employed. By agreement, it is implied that jobs with a high degree of social interaction are correlated with reduced chronic ailment; whereas, by difference, jobs without a high degree of social interaction are correlated with no reduction in chronic ailment.

9. (1) The causal assertion is that caffeine does not increase the risk of heart disease. There is also a suggestion, but not an assertion, that using decaffeinated products contributes slightly to heart disease. (2) The methods of agreement and difference are employed. If caffeine increases the risk of heart disease, then by the method of agreement caffeine users should exhibit higher risk of heart disease and by the method of difference, nonusers should show lower risk. However, a comparison between caffeine users and those who use neither caffeinated nor decaffeinated products showed no difference. In addition, the facts that slightly higher risk was present with users of decaffeinated products (agreement) and absent with nonusers (difference) suggests a possible causal relation between the use of decaffeinated products and heart disease.

11. (1) The causal assertion is that the bumps in the road are causing the misfiring of the engine. (2) The methods of agreement and difference are employed. By agreement, it is noticed that misfiring is present whenever there is a bump. By difference, it is noticed that whenever there is no bump, there is no misfiring.

13. (1) The causal assertion is that seeing the movement of celestial objects across the sky causes birds to calibrate their innate sense of magnetic north. (2) The study employs the methods of difference and concomitant variation. By concomitant variation, the study shows that whenever birds are shown a rotating disk of artificial stars—whether rotating on an axis at true north, east, south, or west—they calculated for what they believed would be south accordingly. On the other hand, by the method of difference, when birds were shown no disk of stars at all, there was no calculation, no adjustment, for south. They followed their innate sense of magnetic north.

15. The causal assertion is that heavy rains in West Africa are causally connected to hurricane patterns in the eastern U.S. On the basis of this and the fact that rainstorms are expected in Africa, Gray makes the prediction that there will be hurricanes on the east coast of the U.S. (2) The study uses the methods of agreement and difference. By agreement, Gray reports, strong hurricanes are present when rain in the western Sahel region of Africa is plentiful. By difference, he reports, drought in the Sahel is correlated with fewer hurricanes on the east coast.

Exercise 8.4

1. Subject: the case of police officers using their revolvers in actual situations.
Analogue: the case of police officers using their revolvers in practice.
    The argument is that, since using a revolver in practice is like using it in actual situations, if an officer does well in practice, he or she will do well in actual situations.
    Relevant analogy? Is target practice sufficiently similar to using a gun in actual situations to support the claim that officers who shoot well in practice will shoot well in actual situations? There are relevant similarities: good marksmanship is essential for good performance in actual situations. Without it, an officer cannot be expected to shoot well. On the other hand, there are dissimilarities. Compare target practice with actual situations. There are likely to be differences in lighting and setting. There are psychological differences, for example, the element of surprise, an officer's anxiety and fear about killing and being killed, little or no information about the assailant(s), the officer's reaction to seeing injury, and so on. The features likely in an actual situation—dissimilar to the practice setting—are likely to bear negatively on the officer's performance. Thus, there are relevant dissimilarities that weaken the analogy. This argument is inductively weak.

3. Subject: the universe.
Analogue: organisms.
    The argument, a causal analogy, is that the universe is probably a product of natural processes because it is analogous to organisms in its organization of parts and organisms are products of natural processes. In short, since the two things are similar in their organization, they are probably similar in their origin.

Relevant analogy? It does seem true that the universe is a highly organized system composed of dependent parts, working together, whose activities are irreversible. Are there dissimilarities between organisms and the universe? Organisms are living things; the universe is not a living thing. Most organisms generate through some form of sexual reproduction; the universe does not. Organisms die; the universe does not die because it is not an animate thing. There may be other differences as well but are these *relevant* dissimilarities? Do these differences bear negatively on the likelihood of a similar origin? The features possessed by the universe and not by organisms do not seem to bear negatively on whether the universe is also a product of natural processes. Thus, it seems reasonable to conclude that the analogy is inductively strong.

5. Subject: what Dad thinks is appropriate as a tie for the wedding.
Analogue: what Dad thinks is pretty as a TV performer.

The argument, an aesthetic analogy, reasons that Dad will like the tie because he liked Madonna on TV.

Relevant analogy? Both the TV program and the tie feature a picture of Madonna, and Dad thinks Madonna is pretty. That similarity is not relevant to what Dad thinks is pretty and appropriate for a tie at the wedding. Thus, the argument is inductively weak.

7. Subject: other people.
Analogue: my own case.

The argument is that, since people are like me and I feel pain when fire touches me, so when fire touches them, they feel pain, too.

Relevant analogy? Other people are like me in behavior and physiology. The dissimilarities between me and other people such as my particular body, personality, and locations in space and time do not seem to be relevant dissimilarities. Thus, the argument is arguably inductively strong.

9. Subject: cats.
Analogue: humans.

The argument is that cats do not see in color because they are like us in so many other ways, yet lack the nerve cells we know are required for color vision in humans.

Relevant analogy? The argument implies but does not assert that there are a number of physiologically relevant similarities. Most of the obvious dissimilarities between cats and humans are irrelevant to the issue of how the eyes work. But similarity in structure of the eye and brain is relevant. Thus, if their nervous system is, by assumption, like ours in many ways, yet unlike ours in the presence of cells responsible for color vision, then the analogy is inductively strong.

11. Subject: a football player's ability to tackle another player.
Analogue: a football player's ability to tackle a tackling dummy.

The argument is that, since the dummy is like a real player in inertia—size, weight, and shape offering resistance—a player who cannot hold onto the dummy probably cannot hold onto the real player.

Relevant analogy? The similarity in inertia between the dummy and the real player are relevant to predicting a player's ability to hold on. The typical dissimilarities between a tackling dummy—inanimate, faceless, no grasping hands—and a real player seem not to bear negatively on whether a player has the strength to hold on. Thus, the argument is inductively strong.

13. Subject: animals.
Analogue: humans.

The argument is that the similarity in basic nervous systems between animals and humans is a basis for concluding that animals feel pain as we do.

Relevant analogy? Our evidence about pain perception is that it is dependent on the nervous system. We have no evidence of pain perception in creatures lacking a nervous system. Thus, the similarity in nervous system between humans and animals is relevant. The dissimilarities between humans and all other animals—size, shape, appearance, and so on—probably do not bear negatively on the capacity to feel pain. Therefore, it is an inductively strong argument.

15. Subject: MacDonald's sweepstakes.
Analogue: national clearinghouse sweepstakes.

The argument is that since both sweepstakes are national games with prizes of one million dollars and the clearinghouse sweepstakes have a winning ratio of 1 in 70,000, probably so does the MacDonald's sweepstake.

Relevant analogy? The facts that the MacDonald's sweepstakes is like the other sweepstakes in having the same prize and being national do not make it more likely that the winning ratio is the same. Thus, from what we are given, the argument seems weak.

If, on the other hand, we were told that all national lotteries with large prizes must meet certain regulations, then we could expect winning ratios to be regulated, too. Can we assume that large games are constructed similarly? If so, that is background information that strengthens the argument.

Chapter 9

Exercise 9.1A

1. Appeal to force. The arguer threatens loss of job to win listeners' acceptance of the arguer's position, namely, that they should keep quiet about the funding.
3. *Ad hominem,* abusive. The argument is that since Tolstoy was unable to live as he preached, then his prescription is not worth our attention.
5. Appeal to pity. The argument is that feeling sorry for the speaker is a good reason for agreeing to go out with him.
7. Equivocation, between use and mention. The word 'love' is first used to refer to the phenomenon of love. Then it is "mentioned," that is, used to refer to the word 'love' which consists of four letters.
9. Hasty generalization. A three-day visit to Los Angeles does not provide a representative sample of the general aesthetic character of California.
11. Slippery slope. Studying philosophy, it is argued, ultimately leads by a series of steps to damnation. Becoming critical does not necessarily or even probably lead to giving up one's religion. Neither does atheism lead to immorality. Further, *some* would argue that a life of immorality does not result in damnation on the grounds that there is no such thing as damnation.
13. Red herring. Rather than addressing the issue of working conditions, the speaker diverts attention to the character of those employees who complain. The speaker, it can be said, also commits the fallacy of appeal to force.
15. Appeal to pity. It is argued that feeling sorry for the speaker is a good reason for accepting the paper late.
17. Appeal to authority. This is a fallacious appeal to authority because expertise in American literature does not make one an authority about matters of nuclear energy.
19. Appeal to force. The speaker offers a threat as a reason for accepting belief in Christ.
21. Equivocation. In the first occurrence the word 'see' normally means "understand." In the second occurrence the word 'see' refers to visual perception. To see what a person is saying is to understand what is said. Thus, the premise—we can only see what is visible—is not true. We can also see, in the first sense, what a person means.
23. Fallacy of composition. The argument employs the assumption that what is true of the parts (no team member can lift over 250 pounds) is true of the whole (the team cannot lift over 250 pounds). In this case we know that the lifting ability of one individual is not the same as the lifting ability of a group of individuals.
25. *Ad hominem, tu quoque.* The speaker defends his action by charging his opponent with having done the same action. In fact, the police officer's speeding is not the same kind of action as a citizen's speeding. Police officers are authorized to exceed speed limits when engaged in their duties. In such circumstances police officers do not speed unlawfully.
27. Equivocation. The phrase "controlling his pupils" is ambiguous between controlling his students and controlling his eyeballs. A cross-eyed teacher can do the former while, perhaps, not being able to do the latter.
29. Not a fallacy. This is a legitimate appeal to authority.
31. Straw man. The arguer interprets the claims of Plato and Aristotle as meaning that all humans are rational and all humans are two-legged, respectively. The arguer claims, rightly, that neither universal statement is true and, thus, concludes that the two philosophers are wrong. However, Plato's and Aristotle's claims should not be interpreted as universal statements but rather as generalizations of the form "In general, all humans are . . ."
33. Equivocation. The phrase "making discriminations on the basis of color" is ambiguous between discriminating between colors and discriminating between people in terms of their color. The latter is racial discrimination; the former is not. The former is a legitimate part of art instruction.
35. Appeal to authority. The *National Enquirer* is not recognized as an authoritative publication regarding UFOs and extraterrestrials. Thus, this is a fallacious appeal to authority.
37. Appeal to the people. The arguer bases his disapproval of the son's actions on what he believes is commonly disapproved. The fact, if it is one, that people generally disapprove of living together is not a good reason for disapproving of the practice.
39. Equivocation. Here the phrase "we are all brothers" is ambiguous between meaning that we are all human and we are all siblings of the same parents. Only the latter meaning justifies a claim to part of the millionaire's money.

Exercise 9.1B

1. *Ad hominem,* abusive. The lawyer Swasey commits this fallacy by implying that, since Justice Stephen was committed as feeble-minded, his position on the importance of a speedy trial is not a good reason for denying the continuance. Justice Holmes should have replied that even the feeble-minded can say what is true.

3. Appeal to pity. The arguer attempts to win sympathy for the tobacco industry by claiming, first, that "the case against cigarette smoking has by no means been proven" and then describing a number of actions he calls "harassment."

5. Straw man. Schlafly interprets the pro-abortion position unfairly as seeking to protect the right to kill babies. She rejects this on the ground that women do not want to kill their babies. In that, she is correct. However, abortion proponents do not seek the right to kill babies; they seek the right to abortion. Abortion, proponents claim, is not the act of killing a baby.

7. Equivocation. The arguer is objecting to the claim that religion is not taught in the public schools. The arguer states that "secular humanism" is being taught in the schools and since, so he or she claims, that is a religion, it follows that religion *is* being taught in the schools. The word 'religion' is used in two different senses: (1) an organization centered around a body of beliefs involving some notion of the divine or supernatural as, for example, Christianity, Islam, or any of the world's major religions; and (2) a body of beliefs or theories that addresses major questions about human existence. The argument is as follows:

   1. *Secular humanism is being taught in the schools.*
   2. *Secular humanism is a body of beliefs or theories that addresses major questions.*
   3. *A body of beliefs or theories that addresses major questions is a religion.*

   4. *Therefore, an organization centered around a body of beliefs involving some notion of the divine is being taught in the schools.*

   The laws that prohibit the endorsement of any particular religion in the public schools are aimed at religions in the proper sense, that is, (1) above. They are not aimed at the teaching of beliefs or theories that address major questions, no doubt in part because such beliefs or theories do not constitute religious views even in some stretched sense of the word as in (2) above.

9. *Ad hominem,* circumstantial. The arguer accuses government leaders of self-serving motives in their decisions. They "put profit above freedoms and life." The argument then is that the public should not believe them because they have ulterior motives for their actions.

11. Appeal to authority. Is Willie Nelson, or someone of his caliber, an authority on the plight of the American farmer? If not, then this is a fallacious appeal to authority. We know that Nelson is knowledgeable and talented as an entertainer but that does not give one expertise in agriculture. Whatever expertise Nelson has about the problems of farming, he would seem to have second-hand. Thus, it is peculiar, to say the least, that only a person with second-hand knowledge can understand the plight of the American farmer.

13. Either/or fallacy; begging the question. The survey and, particularly, Landers's conclusion commits the either/or fallacy. The alternatives are affection or sex, either "tender words and loving embraces" or "an orgasm produced by a silent, mechanical, self-involved male." Furthermore, it begs the question to so describe the alternatives. Who, after all, would choose sex with a mechanical, self-involved male? Suppose respondents were asked to choose among sex without affection, affection only, or sex with affection. The results might be the same but at least it would be clear that respondents were not being forced to choose between two lesser alternatives.

15. Inconsistency. The doctor seems to give conflicting advice. Have the surgical removal right away, don't wait; and, on the other hand, delay surgery, you can always choose it later. A listener would not know which to accept.

17. Slippery slope. The arguer describes a series of events that will take place if we do not solve the farm crisis. It is not generally true that farms are being taken over by large conglomerates. There is no reason to believe that our "food will be controlled by a select few" and no reason to believe that "some catastrophe will send bread to $3 a loaf."

19. False analogy, it can be argued. If the fetus is not a person with a right to life equivalent to children and adults, then the argument commits the fallacy of false analogy. The argument, based on an analogy between fetuses and persons, assumes what needs to be supported, namely, that fetuses are analogous to persons. Thus, it is arguable that this argument commits the fallacy of begging the question as well. To determine whether this argument is a good one, we will have to look at the complex question of the moral status of the fetus.

21. *Ad hominem,* circumstantial. The implication of this passage is that the Democratic Party chooses candidates in terms of imagery, not in terms of political ability.

23. Equivocation. George Schultz and the writer of this argument do not use the phrase "escape from justice" in the same sense. Schultz means civil justice, whereas the writer probably is referring to divine justice. In light of that ambiguity the arguer should not conclude that Schultz is a nonbeliever.

25. *Ad hominem,* circumstantial. The arguer urges us to ignore entertainment industry benefits on the grounds that the fundraisers have selfish motives: to corrupt the young, exploit, and make themselves appear good when they are in fact bad. The arguer commits abusive *ad hominem* as well in the emotion-laden language used to describe the industry: cold-hearted, contemptibly exploitative, squalid role as corrupter, and so on.

27. Begging the question. Rather than asking respondents how they would characterize television programming, the survey presents choices that no reasonable person would accept. Who favors obnoxious, gratuitously violent, pornographic programming? Another possible analysis is the either/or fallacy.

29. Either/or fallacy. The arguer presents only two alternatives: kill the suspect or "let this criminal be released after a prison term—to kill again." The latter is clearly unacceptable, therefore, the arguer concludes that it is justified to kill the suspect. The arguer overlooks other outcomes such as life imprisonment or rehabilitation.

31. Inconsistency. Younger argues that life imprisonment without the possibility of parole is not an acceptable alternative to capital punishment because, he says, there must always be "a safety valve," the right of the governor to commute a sentence. However, by the same reasoning capital punishment should be unacceptable since by putting a person to death we eliminate the "safety valve" making it impossible for the governor to exercise the right to commute a sentence. Thus, Younger implies that (1) the option to commute must always exist, yet by endorsing capital punishment he implies that (2) the option to commute need not always exist.

33. *Ad hominem,* circumstantial. Stare's position on the dietary value of sugar is not to be accepted, it is argued, because Stare is a biased authority. The arguer claims that Stare's research department is financially supported by the sugar industry.

35. Is a fallacy committed? The argument is that spanking or physically punishing children causes a violent society, which, in turn, leads to child abuse and creates a vicious cycle. Two questions should be considered about this argument: (1) Do we clearly understand the causal connection between physical discipline and violent behavior in adult life? (2) Does it not beg the question to blur the distinctions between "child abuse," "striking a child," "violence to the body," and, on the other hand, spanking? Is this an argument against spanking as well as child abuse?

37. Straw man; false analogy. The argument is that regulation of smoking is unacceptable because, to be consistent, we must then regulate and, perhaps, prohibit *all other* potential health hazards, too: cough syrup, pecan pies, footballs, aspirin, automobiles, sunbathing, and so on. This argument misrepresents the requirements for consistency. Consistency does not require proponents of smoking regulation to endorse regulating all possible health hazards no matter how remotely hazardous. It requires only that they endorse regulating *similarly* hazardous products. This misrepresentation suggests the fallacy of straw man but it also suggests false analogy; namely, the disanalogy between the harmful effects of smoking and such things as playing football, driving a car, sunbathing, etc.

39. Inconsistency. The writer's position on abortion is inconsistent. One cannot say, on the one hand, that abortion is wrong and, on the other, that women have a right to choose abortion. If one believes an act is wrong, then one believes no one has a right to do it, and the obverse.

41. Inconsistency. It seems to be inconsistent, the cartoonist implies, to censor one rock video and not the other when both depict socially deviant behavior.

43. False analogy. Searching for killer bees does not involve potential invasions of privacy, whereas searching homes for missing children does.

45. Straw man; equivocation. The argument is that if opponents would acknowledge that all laws limit individual liberty for the collective good, then Fundamentalism's influence on passing liberty-limiting laws is unobjectionable, at least on grounds of oppressing freedom. However, opponents might argue that this misrepresents their concerns. They do not object, they might say, to laws that limit freedom for the collective good as such, but they do object to laws that do not reflect a proper balance between the goals of promoting the collective good and preserving individual freedom. Thus, the arguer strikes at a straw man.

It is also arguable that this argument equivocates in its use of the phrase "collective good." Defenders of personal liberty may acknowledge that laws should limit freedom for the collective good in the sense that "collective good" refers to protection from harm. But they may not accept that laws should limit freedom for the collective good when that means telling people what values they should hold.

Chapter 10

Exercise 10.3
Note: For convenience statements are abbreviated by using '. . .' (ellipsis). These answers represent reasonable analyses of the passages in the exercises. Yours might differ. Compare yours and be prepared to discuss and defend your analysis.

1. ① Federal regulations . . . study.
   ② In 1982, . . . agony.
   ③ As moral beings, . . . misery.

3. The first sentence, a rhetorical question, and the second sentence in the passage are rewritten as statements ① and ②.
   ① Critics should know that if it weren't for the Electoral College, then the consequences for smaller states would be unfortunate.
   ② If it weren't for the Electoral College, then all a candidate . . . population.
   ③ The Electoral . . . a real vote.

5. ① There is . . . its related problems.
   ② The lunatic . . . warning labels.
   ③ Not only . . . affect the abuser.
   ④ It implies . . . inherently wrong.
   ⑤ This is . . . responsibly.
   ⑥ Furthermore, . . . dishes.
   ⑦ Bottled water, . . . food down.

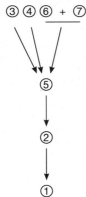

7. ① Parents are . . . upbringing of their children.
   ② [Parents] are the most qualified . . . schooling for their children.

9. The second sentence, a rhetorical question, is rewritten as statement ②.
   ① Broadcast . . . explicit sex.
   ② Broadcast should impose limits . . . on explicit terror.
   ③ There is no . . . some form.
   ④ But . . . live melodrama.

11. The first sentence does not figure in the argument and may, therefore, be omitted. The second sentence contains as a premise the statement "I want to be free to practice my religion."

① I want to be free . . . my religion.
② I believe that if my government . . . and my kind need.

13. ① I should either . . . college.
② The job market . . . bad now.
③ I don't think . . . chance.
④ Besides, . . . years.
⑤ If I go . . . get a job.
⑥ I'll go to college.

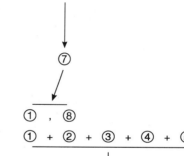

15. The third sentence, a rhetorical question, is rewritten as statement ③.
① I believe . . . to do.
② I know . . . true.
③ You have no obligation to obey every law, particularly not an immoral law.
④ Some laws are immoral.
⑤ Laws ought to protect us.
⑥ Some laws actually violate people's rights.
⑦ Those laws should not be obeyed.
⑧ In those cases . . . thing to do.

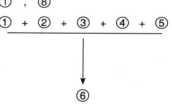

17. ① For punishment . . . conditions must exist.
② First, people . . . punished.
③ Second, people . . . belief.
④ Most potential lawbreakers . . . not punished.
⑤ Many crimes . . . themselves.
⑥ Punishment . . . to crime.

① + ② + ③ + ④ + ⑤
‾‾‾‾‾‾‾‾‾‾‾‾‾‾‾‾‾‾

⑥

19. The last sentence in the passage is rewritten as two statements: ⑤, a premise and ⑥, a conclusion.
① For the . . . sign language.
② Just recently, Washoe . . . signs.
③ She even . . . signs.
④ Thus far, . . . words.
⑤ One chimp can . . . to use sign language.
⑥ Animals other than humans . . . language.

① + ② + ③ + ④ + ⑤
‾‾‾‾‾‾‾‾‾‾‾‾‾‾‾‾‾‾

⑥

21. The first four sentences of this passage are best construed as a conditional: as the assertion that if a man does own a ranch and the cattle on it, then . . . etc. In addition, sentences ⑥ and ⑦ are combined as statement ③ in the argument.

① If a man owns a ranch and the cattle on it and if he hires another . . . , then . . . a portion to his worker and the remainder is the owner's profit, then the profit is due him, not for any work he did, but simply because he owns the cattle.

② This shows that the institution of private property entitles owners to value independent of their labor.

③ It is morally wrong that a man be entitled to something without working for it.

④ The institution of private property is morally wrong.

```
        ①
        │
        ▼
  ②  +  ③
  ─────────
        │
        ▼
        ④
```

23. The passage asserts a belief held by, at least, some journalists and offers an argument as to why that belief is not true. Thus, statement ① is written as the denial of the belief ascribed to journalists in the opening sentence. Secondly, the sentence beginning "As seen on TV" can be taken as an illustration, not a statement providing inferential support; thus it can be omitted.

① It is not true as journalists are led to believe, and some may actually believe, that they only hold a mirror to life and that they can hardly be accused of bad faith.

② Not even physicists . . . have so arrogant a belief in the out there.

③ For 60 years . . . alters its nature.

④ Journalism . . . the idea.

⑤ Journalism, which . . . does more than alter.

⑥ Journalism creates.

⑦ First, out of the . . . makes "stories."

⑧ Then, by . . . on the map.

⑨ The parade of artifacts . . . them real.

25. ① The idea of solidity is . . . and distinct existence.

② Solidity, . . . this separate and distinct existence.

```
①
│
▼
②
```

27. ① If we leave . . . stimulate.

② A community . . . at first glance.

③ Selection . . . vote.

④ Only a panel . . . public money.

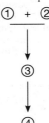

29. The last sentence offers an example, not evidential support.

① As for the terms . . . in themselves.

② The terms good and bad are merely modes . . . one with another.

③ One and the same . . . and indifferent.

Exercise 10.4
1. Supplied premise: You can vote only if you have registered.
3. Supplied premise: Professor Pipes is a scientist.
5. Supplied premises: A fetus is an innocent human being. Killing an innocent human being is murder.
7. Supplied premise: Her brain is dead.
9. Supplied premise: We are living longer than the age of 80.
11. Supplied conclusion: The theory of evolution is not correct.
13. Supplied premise: Whales are mammals.
15. Supplied premise: Having language is necessary for reasoning.
17. Supplied premise: Animals can only be held responsible for what they do if they are capable of considering the alternatives open to them or of reflecting on the ethics of their actions.
19. Supplied conclusion: We do not know that death is not the greatest good that can happen to us.

Exercise 10.5
1. empirical   3. nonempirical   5. empirical   7. nonempirical   9. nonempirical
11. nonempirical   13. nonempirical   15. nonempirical   17. nonempirical   19. nonempirical

Exercise 10.6
1. The writer of this letter to the editor urges readers to reject Jerome Krause's argument and join the AMA or, at least, some other motorcycle organization. Presumably, Krause's argument against joining the AMA is like this:
Krause's argument
① *The AMA supports a sport that is environmentally harmful.*

⑩ *Therefore, you should not join the AMA.*
The purpose of this letter to the editor is to rebut that argument. The writer explicitly argues against ⑩ and implicitly argues against ①. As we see, the overall conclusion of the writer's argument is:
⑦ I implore all of you to join the AMA.
⑧ If you do not join the AMA, then join some other organization which supports motorcycling and our right to keep our sport, no matter what form of our sport you may engage in.
    The writer offers two major reasons in support of the conclusion above. They are:
⑥ The AMA is probably our best hope for survival as motorcycling Americans.
and a supplied statement:
*⑩ The AMA does not support a sport that is environmentally harmful.
Each major premise is supported by subsidiary arguments.
    First, in support of ⑥ the writer provides premise ③. The AMA is our best hope, it is argued, because:
③ If Krause wishes to protect and ensure the survival of the sport we all love, he needs to understand that we cannot stand divided.
That premise can be rewritten as stating that
*③ If we wish to protect and ensure the survival of the sport we all love, then we cannot stand divided.
In other words, the writer claims that the survival of the sport requires that motorcyclists be united. Now it does not necessarily follow from *③ that the AMA is the best hope for survival. It must be added that the AMA provides the kind of union required for survival. Thus, the argument needs a supplied premise: *③ₐ The AMA provides the kind of union required for survival.
    Thus, the argument in support of ⑥ is as follows:
*③ *If we wish to protect and ensure the survival of the sport we all love, then we cannot stand divided.*
*③ₐ *The AMA provides the kind of union required for survival.*

⑥ *The AMA is probably our best hope for survival as motorcycling Americans.*

    The opening sentence of this letter to the editor contains the charge Krause levels against the AMA. Sentence ① can be rewritten, making that explicit, as ① "Krause claims that the AMA supports an environmentally harmful sport." To rebut Krause's charge, the writer offers the following arguments.

① *Krause claims that the AMA supports an environmentally harmful sport.*

② *Krause is yet another self-righteous militant "environmental elitist" who will not be happy until we are all living in caves and eating leaves.*

*⑨ *Krause's claim that the AMA supports an environmentally harmful sport is false. (Supplied statement)*

Second, *⑨ is also supported by this argument.

④ *No "thinking person" wants destruction of our land and resources.*

⑤ *Thinking people also know that programs such as the "California Green Sticker Program" can provide and police off-road riding areas which do not "rip up deserts" and forests, but rather, allow access by families via methods other than those sanctioned by the Sierra Club and the insanely radical Earth First! organization.*

*⑪ *The AMA supports environmentally safe programs like the California Green Sticker Program. (Supplied statement)*

*⑨ *Krause's claim that the AMA supports an environmentally harmful sport is false. (Supplied statement)*

*⑩ *The AMA does not support an environmentally harmful sport. (Supplied statement)*

Below the argument is diagramed and inferences are labeled.

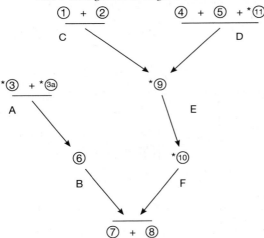

Evaluation of inferences:

Argument A [Given *③ + *③a, therefore ⑥]. The argument is deductively valid. Are the premises true or acceptable? Premise *③ seems a reasonable statement to grant since there is strength in numbers. However, there is no support offered for the claim that the AMA provides what is needed. It is an empirical claim and could be decided by more information but none is provided. Therefore, we cannot say that *③a is true. Furthermore, we should not accept *③a merely for the sake of the argument precisely because the worthiness of the AMA is the issue debated in the overall argument. It begs the question to accept without argument that the AMA provides the necessary kind of union for motorcyclists. Thus, Argument A is not good.

Argument B [Given ⑥, therefore ⑦ + ⑧]. If premise ⑥ is true, then it follows with a high degree of inductive probability that one should join the AMA. However, we saw above that the argument in support of ⑥ is not acceptable because no support is provided for the claim that the AMA provides the kind of organization that motorcyclists need. Therefore, premise ⑥ is not acceptable in Argument B and, thus, Argument B fails.

Argument C [Given ① + ②, therefore *⑨]. This is not a good argument. It commits the *ad hominem,* abusive fallacy. Even granting the premises, it does not follow that Krause's claim is false. Furthermore, the description of Krause in premise ② is highly emotional, abusive, and unsupported. This argument must be rejected as fallacious.

Argument D [Given ④ + ⑤ + *⑪, therefore *⑨].

④ No "thinking person" wants destruction of our land and resources.

⑤ Thinking people also know that programs such as the "California Green Sticker Program" can provide and police off-road riding areas which do not "rip up deserts" and forests, but rather, allow access by families via methods other than those sanctioned by the Sierra Club and the insanely radical Earth First! organization.

*⑪ The AMA supports environmentally safe programs like the California Green Sticker Program. From those premises the conclusion, *⑨, does not deductively follow, since it is possible that, although the AMA supports environmentally safe programs, despite those efforts, it still encourages a sport that is polluting the environment. On the other hand, is the argument inductively strong? It appears to be an analogical argument to the effect that the AMA, in virtue of supporting California's program, is like those groups of "thinking people" who do not want destruction of the environment. Construed as an inductive analogy, there is good evidence for the conclusion. We may consider it a strong inductive argument.

Are the premises true? Premise ④ is certainly acceptable. Premises ⑤ and *⑪ are problematic. Both are empirical statements; neither is provided any support within the argument. Do thinking people know about the California program? Does the California program protect the environment while allowing motorcycling? Does the AMA support environmentally safe programs like the California program? Perhaps we can accept these premises on the basis of the writer's authority; however, the writer's failure to provide any evidence in support and particularly failing to make explicit and offer support for *⑪ weakens the reliability of this argument. It is reasonable that we not accept this argument without further evidence. Thus, the argument is not good; it does not persuade.

Argument E [Given *⑨, therefore, *⑩]. If it is true that Krause's charge is false, then it necessarily follows that the AMA does not support an environmentally harmful sport.

As regards the acceptability of premise *⑨, however, we saw above that *⑨ is not well supported. The writer has not adequately supported his claim that Krause is mistaken because the writer fails to make explicit the AMA's history regarding respect for the environment. Thus, Argument E is not good.

Argument F [Given *⑩, therefore, ⑦ + ⑧]. Given premise *⑩, it does not deductively follow that one should join the AMA since it is consistent with *⑩ that there are other objections to joining the AMA or other groups. However, *⑩ offers reasonable inductive support for joining. The inference from *⑩ to ⑦ + ⑧ can be construed as an inductively strong moral analogy. Given that the only groups one should join are those that are environmentally safe and *⑩ the AMA does not support harm to the environment, then by analogy to such groups, there is good reason for joining the AMA. The problem with this argument, however, is that premise *⑩ is not known to be true, neither is it given sufficient support in Argument E. Therefore, Argument F should not be accepted.

Conclusion. According to the analysis given, the writer's argument in support of joining the AMA is not acceptable. It would have been a stronger argument had the writer made explicit and offered evidence in support of statement *⑪.

3. In this excerpt Supreme Court Justice Stevens writes the dissenting opinion in the U.S. Supreme Court case of *Cruzan v. Missouri State Supreme Court.* Since this exercise presents a rebuttal to the majority opinion, it will help to review what that majority opinion maintained. (See Exercise 2 above.) The majority opinion can be summarized as follows:

The standard for discontinuation of life-sustaining treatment required by the state of Missouri is constitutionally sound.

The state ruled that the standard was not met in the case of Nancy Cruzan.

Therefore, the U.S. Supreme Court finds that the state of Missouri is entitled to refuse the Cruzan parents' request to have life-sustaining treatment discontinued for their daughter Nancy.

Justice Stevens rejects the conclusion on the grounds that the first premise is false. In brief, Stevens' argument in opposition to the Court's decision is the following:

④ It [the Court's decision] permits the state's abstract, undifferentiated interest in the preservation of life to overwhelm the best interests of Nancy Beth Cruzan, interest which would, accord-

ing to an undisputed finding, be served by allowing her guardians to exercise her constitutional right to discontinue medical treatment.

Supplied premise

* ④ₐ *It is wrong to permit the state's interest in the preservation of life to overwhelm the best interests of Nancy Cruzan.*

Supplied conclusion

* ④ᵦ *The Court's decision should be reversed; that is, the Court should reject Missouri's standard for the discontinuation of life-sustaining treatment and authority to discontinue treatment should be granted to the Cruzan parents.*

The salient reasons Stevens offers for his claim * ④ₐ that the state's interest in the protection of life should not be permitted to overwhelm Cruzan's best interests are these:

⑩ The Constitution requires the state to care for Nancy Cruzan's life in a way that gives appropriate respect to her own best interests.

⑯ [The portion of this Court's opinion that considers the merits of the case] fails to respect the best interests of the patient.

㉒ Because Nancy Beth Cruzan did not have the foresight to preserve her constitutional right in a living will, or some comparable "clear and convincing" alternative, her right is gone forever and her fate is in the hands of the state Legislature instead of in those of her family, her independent neutral guardian ad litem, and an impartial judge—all of whom agree on the course of action that is in her best interests.

㉗ The opposition of life and liberty in this case are not the result of Nancy Cruzan's tragic accident, but are instead the artificial consequence of Missouri's effort, and this Court's willingness, to abstract Nancy Cruzan's life from Nancy Cruzan's person. . . .

An initial diagram of the argument on this analysis is this:

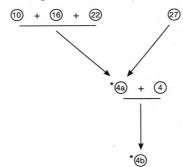

Now we can begin to assemble the subsidiary arguments in support of the premises above.

First, Stevens offers argument in support of ⑩ that the Constitution requires the state to care for Cruzan's life while respecting her best interests. He argues this on the grounds that the Constitution is committed to the protection of life, liberty, and the pursuit of happiness and that these are *usually* considered compatible or mutually enhancing ends.

① Our Constitution is born of the proposition that all legitimate governments must secure the equal right of every person to "life, liberty, and the pursuit of happiness."

② In the ordinary case we quite naturally assume that these three ends are compatible, mutually enhancing and perhaps even coincident.

Further, he states that ③ "The Court would make an exception here," that is, the Court makes an exception in the Cruzan case to the usual compatibility of the rights of life, liberty, and the pursuit of happiness. Since Stevens argues next that the Court should not regard the Cruzan case as an exception to the usual assumption of compatibility, let us rewrite ③ to make explicit his claim:

* ③ₐ [Rewritten ③] The Court should not make an exception in the Cruzan case. (That is, it should not make an exception here to the usual compatibility of the rights of life, liberty, and the pursuit of happiness.)

Now in support of * ③ₐ Stevens claims that the Court endorsed three propositions, according to which those ends are compatible and, therefore, ⑨. The arguments are:

⑥ First, a competent individual's decision to refuse life-sustaining medical procedures is an aspect of liberty protected by the Due Process Clause of the 14th Amendment.

⑦ Second, upon a proper evidentiary showing, a qualified guardian may make that decision on behalf of an incompetent ward.

⑧ Third, in answering the important question presented by this tragic case, it is wise "not to attempt by any general statement, to cover every possible phase of the subject."

Therefore:

⑨ Together, these considerations suggest that Nancy Cruzan's liberty to be free from medical treatment must be understood in light of the facts and circumstances particular to her.

Therefore:

*③ₐ The court should not make an exception in the Cruzan case.

Thus, the support for ⑩ is diagramed as follows:

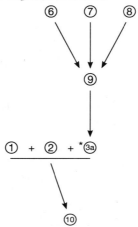

In support of ⑯ + ㉒ Stevens offers a chain of arguments. Here is an analysis of that reasoning.

⑰ [The portion of this Court's opinion that considers the merits of the case] relies on what is tantamount to a waiver rationale: the dying patient's best interests are put to one side and the entire inquiry is focused on her prior expressions of intent.

⑱ An innocent person's constitutional right to be free from unwanted medical treatment is thereby categorically limited to those patients who had the foresight to make the unambiguous statement of their wishes while competent.

From which a number of implications are drawn:

⑲ The Court's decision affords no protection to children,

+

⑳ The Court's decision affords no protection to young people who are victims of unexpected accidents or illnesses.

+

㉑ The Court's decision affords no protection to the countless thousands of elderly persons who either fail to decide, or fail to explain, how they want to be treated if they should experience a similar fate.

Therefore:

⑯ [The portion of this Court's opinion that considers the merits of the case] fails to respect the best interests of the patient.

+

㉒ Because Nancy Beth Cruzan did not have the foresight to preserve her constitutional right in a living will, or some comparable "clear and convincing" alternative, her right is gone forever and her fate is in the hands of the state Legislature instead of in those of her family, her independent neutral guardian ad litem, and an impartial judge—all of whom agree on the course of action that is in her best interests.

Last, we have the argument in support of ㉗ provided by statements ㉔, ㉕, and ㉖. Here Stevens asserts that the Court permits the state of Missouri to "define" life, whereas it might have considered the argument implied by statements ㉕ and ㉖ below. If so, he suggests, the right to refuse treatment and the right to protection of life are seen to be compatible.

㉔ Only because Missouri has arrogated to itself the power to define life, and only because the Court permits this usurpation, are Nancy Cruzan's life and liberty put into disquieting conflict.

㉕ If Nancy Cruzan's life were defined by reference to her own interests, so that her life expired when her biological existence ceased serving any of her own interests, then her constitutionally protected interest in freedom from unwanted treatment would not come into conflict with her constitutionally protected interest in life.

㉖ Conversely, if there were any evidence that Nancy Cruzan herself defined life to encompass every form of biological persistence by a human being, so that the continuation of treatment would serve Nancy's own liberty, then once again there would be no conflict between life and liberty.

A complete diagram of the argument on this analysis can now be presented.

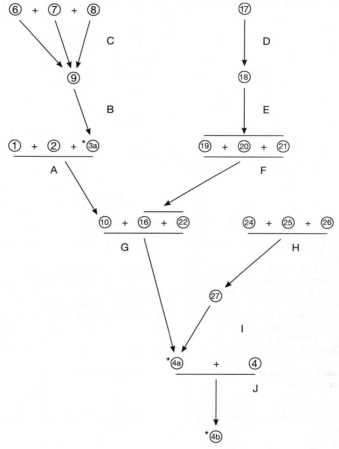

Having exposed the overall argument and labeled each subsidiary argument, we can determine whether each argument is a good one by assessing the inferences and checking the acceptability of premises. Let's begin with the arguments in support of statement ⑩.

Argument A [Given ① + ② + *㉚, therefore ⑩]. Given that our Constitution is committed to the protection of the rights of life, liberty, and the pursuit of happiness, that *ordinarily* these three ends are compatible, and that no exception should be made in this case, ⑩ deductively follows.

Are the premises acceptable? No support is offered for premises ① and ②; however, they can be accepted as relevant appeals to authority. Premise *㉚ is the conclusion of arguments B and C; we shall have to evaluate them to determine whether *㉚ is acceptable and argument A is good.

Arguments B and C [Given ⑥, ⑦, ⑧, therefore ⑨, and therefore *㉚]. The reasoning is that *㉚ The court should not make an exception in this case (to the usual compatibility of the rights of life, liberty, and the pursuit of happiness) because ⑨ Nancy Cruzan's liberty to be free from medical treatment must be understood in light of the facts and circumstances particular to her.

In other words, no exception to the general compatibility of life, liberty, and the pursuit of happiness should be made because her case should be decided relative to her only.

The case should be decided relative to her circumstances only because, Stevens says:

⑥ First, a competent individual's decision to refuse life-sustaining medical procedures is an aspect of liberty protected by the Due Process Clause of the 14th Amendment.

⑦ Second, upon a proper evidentiary showing, a qualified guardian may make that decision on behalf of an incompetent ward.

⑧ Third, in answering the important question presented by this tragic case, it is wise "not to attempt by any general statement, to cover every possible phase of the subject."

Premise ⑧ provides a deductively valid reason for ⑨. That is, given that it is wise not to attempt to cover every possible phase of the subject, then it follows necessarily that Cruzan's case should be decided without implications for general principles such as the compatibility of life, liberty, and the pursuit of happiness.

Stevens claims that premise ⑧ is endorsed by the writers of the majority opinion, thus, as he argues, they ought to accept the conclusion. Let us also accept ⑧ as true, noting, however, that it is not supported within this argument and might be rejected by those who believe that the Court should indeed tackle the general problem of the right of incompetents to have treatment withdrawn on their behalf.

Premise ⑥ does not deductively entail ⑨ for the simple reason that ⑥ applies to competent individuals and Cruzan is not competent. Premise ⑦, on the other hand, applies to cases in which a guardian has *shown proper evidence* of entitlement to decide on an incompetent's behalf. Given ⑦ and a supplied premise stating that *the Cruzan parents have shown proper evidence,* then ⑨ follows deductively. However, whether ⑦ applies to the case of Nancy's parents is precisely the issue before the court. Thus, supplying that missing premise begs the question; whereas, without it, the conclusion ⑨ does not deductively follow.

Perhaps ⑥ and ⑦ provide inductive evidence for ⑨. According to ⑥ and ⑦ there are lawful guidelines protecting the rights of competent individuals and incompetent wards from unwanted medical treatment. Although Nancy Cruzan's case does not strictly fall under either provision, hers is at least analogous to those cases. Therefore, by analogy it is at least reasonable to conclude that her liberty interests should be respected as well. In short, ⑥ and ⑦ are evidence that the law seeks to protect the interests of incompetents and Cruzan's case is sufficiently similar to those other cases. Thus, the inference is inductively strong. The premises are empirically true. Thus, the arguments in support of ⑨ are acceptable.

Given that ⑨ is acceptable and ⑨ entails *③a, the argument in support of *③a is acceptable.

Argument D [Given ⑰, therefore, ⑱]. Given ⑰, that "the entire inquiry is focused on . . ." prior expressions of intent," then the inference to ⑱ is arguably valid. Is ⑰ true? It is an empirical statement verifiable by checking the reasoning of the majority decision. And that reasoning is that the Cruzans' case failed to meet the state's standard for "prior expressions of intent." So ⑰ is true. Argument D is good.

Argument E [Given ⑱, therefore ⑲ + ⑳ + ㉑]. Statements ⑲ and ⑳ deductively follow from ⑱ given a supplied premise stating that children and young people are not considered competent to make unambiguous statements of their wishes. Statement ㉑ follows deductively for, if the right to refuse treatment is limited to those who have made advanced directives, then no such right can be exercised on behalf of those who have not. Premise ⑱ is acceptable as a strongly supported statement from the previous argument.

Argument F [Given Arguments D and E and ⑲ + ⑳ + ㉑, therefore ⑯ + ㉒]. The argument has been that the Court's decision "affords no protection" to specific classes of individuals because, given ⑰ and ⑱, "the dying patient's best interests are put to one side" while the issue focuses on evidence of prior intent. It follows deductively that ⑯ the decision "fails to respect the best interests of the patient" and that ㉒ Nancy Cruzan's "right is gone forever." The arguments in support of ⑯ and ㉒ are strongly supported and based on acceptable premises.

Argument G [Given ⑩ + ⑯ + ㉒, therefore *㊽]. Premise ㉒ asserts, among other things, that the course of action in Nancy's best interests is to have medical treatment withdrawn. The argument paraphrased, therefore, is:

⑩ *The Constitution requires the state to care for Nancy Cruzan's life in a way that gives appropriate respect to her own best interests.*

⑯ *[The Court's decision] fails to respect the best interests of the patient.*

㉒ *[The course of action in Nancy's best interests is to have medical treatment withdrawn.]*

㊽ It is wrong to permit the state's interest in the preservation of life to overwhelm the best interests of Nancy Cruzan.

Given that ⑩ the Constitution requires the state to care for Cruzan's life in a way that respects her best interests, that ⑯ the decision fails to respect her best interests, and that, as ㉒ asserts, exercising the right to discontinue treatment is in her best interests, it follows deductively that *㊽ it is wrong for the Court to allow the state to override her best interests.

The premises are acceptable as supported by good arguments. Therefore, the conclusion is acceptable.

Argument H [Given ㉔ + ㉕ + ㉖, therefore ㉗]. Here Stevens argues that the Court should not juxtapose life and liberty but should view them as compatible. His argument is that if life is defined in terms of interests as expressed by the individual, then the protection of the rights to life and liberty are not opposed. Stevens would have it that, unless we have evidence to the contrary (premise ㉖), a person's interests in life cease "when her biological existence ceased serving any of her own interests." Given these premises, ㉗ deductively follows. Are the premises true? Premise ㉔ contains words that beg the question: "has arrogated to itself the power to define life" and "usurpation." This premise should not be accepted without argument supporting the use of those terms. Premises ㉕ and ㉖ are conditionals and seem to be nonempirically true. Therefore, argument H is good, although not because of premise ㉔.

Argument I [Given ㉗, therefore *㊽]. Presumably Stevens means by the phrase "abstracting Cruzan's life from Cruzan's person" to refer to a distinction between Cruzan's biological existence and her existence as a person, a being with some awareness of life. Since the Court, he says, is willing to distinguish between the duties the state has to her biological existence and the duties the state has to act in the best interests of persons, it places life and liberty in opposition. And since, as Stevens implies, the Court should not treat life and liberty as incompatible in this case, it follows deductively that the Court should not permit the state of Missouri to override Cruzan's best interests.

Furthermore, premise ㉗ is acceptable as a statement supported by a good argument. Therefore, argument I is acceptable.

Argument J [Given ④ + *㊽, therefore *㊾]. Given that ④ the Court's decision permits the state to override the patient's best interests and that *㊽ it is wrong to do so, it follows deductively that *㊾ the Court's decision should be reversed.

This argument is a good one if premises ④ and *㊽ are acceptable. On this analysis both premises are acceptable as statements supported by good argument.

Conclusion

According to this analysis of Stevens' minority opinion, it is a good argument. If one disagrees with this analysis, then one must show either that major inferences, in particular the inferences of G and H, are neither strong nor valid, or that they rest on false premises.

Suggestions for Further Study

Beardsley, Monroe. *Thinking Straight*. 3d ed. Englewood Cliffs, N.J.: Prentice-Hall, 1966.
Cedarbloom, Jerry, and David W. Paulsen. *Critical Reasoning: Understanding and Criticizing Arguments and Theories*. 2d ed. Belmont, Calif.: Wadsworth, 1986.
Conway, David A., and Ronald Munson. *The Elements of Reasoning*. Belmont, Calif.: Wadsworth, 1990.
Copi, Irving M., and Carl Cohen. *Introduction to Logic*. 8th ed. New York: Macmillan, 1990.
Dauer, Francis Watanabe. *Critical Thinking: An Introduction to Reasoning*. Oxford: Oxford University Press, 1989.
Fisher, Alec. *The Logic of Real Arguments*. Cambridge: Cambridge University Press, 1988.
Fogelin, Robert J., and Walter Sinnott-Armstrong. *Understanding Arguments: An Introduction to Informal Logic*. 4th ed. San Diego, Calif.: Harcourt Brace Jovanovich, 1991.
Hurley, Patrick J. *A Concise Introduction to Logic*. 4th ed. Belmont, Calif.: Wadsworth, 1991.
Kahane, Howard. *Logic and Contemporary Rhetoric: The Use of Reason in Everyday Life*. 5th ed. Belmont, Calif.: Wadsworth, 1989.
Kneale, William K., and Martha Kneale. *The Development of Logic*. Oxford: Clarendon Press, 1964.
Mates, Benson. *Elementary Logic*. 2d ed. New York: Oxford University Press, 1972.
Skyrms, Brian. *Choice and Chance: An Introduction to Inductive Logic*. 3d ed. Belmont, Calif.: Wadsworth, 1986.
Walton, Douglas N. *Informal Logic: A Handbook for Critical Argumentation*. Cambridge: Cambridge University Press, 1989.
Wolfram, Sybil. *Philosophical Logic: An Introduction*. London: Routledge, 1989.

Index

Argument from analogy, 189, 222ff., 321
    criteria of inductive strength, 223, 231, 234
    features of, 222
    summarized, 230–231
    (*see also* analogue; common feature; false analogy; inferred feature; similarities; subject)
Aristotle, 38, 40, 50
Association, 178

Bar,
    in categorical logic, 92ff.
    "not"-sign, in truth functional logic, 115
Barbara, valid logical form, 29
Begging the question, 258–260, 266, 324
    complex question, 259, 266
Biased sample, (*see* sample)
Biconditional sign, 115
Biconditional statements, 114–115
    truth function for, 133–134
    (*see also* material equivalence)
"Both are . . . not," 123
Brackets, 119–121

Categorical form, 38
    (*see also* categorical statement)
Categorical logic, 38ff.
Categorical statement, 38
    four forms, 42–43
    standard form of, 75–76
    (*see also* Venn diagram)
Categorical syllogism, 38, 88–89
    special cases for, 96–105
    standard form of, 88
    testing validity for, 89–94
    (*see also* Venn diagrams)
Category, 39–40
    (*see also* predicate term; subject term)
Causal argument, 189, 197–219, 234
    (*see* causal conclusion; Mill's methods)
Causal conclusion, 207, 219, 234
    criteria of inductive strength, 219, 234
Causal explanation, 205–207
Causal prediction, 205–207
Causal prescription, 205–207
Causal statement, 198–199
Causally necessary condition, 199–201
Causally sufficient condition, 199–201

Cause, 197ff.
    convergent, 201
    false, (*see* false cause)
    intermediate, 202
    partial, 200
    proximate, 202
    remote, 202
    senses of the word, 199–201
Charity, (*see* principle of)
Circular reasoning, (*see* begging the question)
Common feature, in argument from analogy, 222
Commutation, 178
Complex question, (*see* begging the question)
Composition, fallacy of, 253–254, 266
Compound statement, 111–112
Conclusion, 9, 21
    clue words, 10
    follows necessarily, 19, 24–25
    follows probably, 19
    missing, (*see* supplying missing parts)
    of a valid argument, 34–35
Concomitant variation, (*see* method of)
Conditional sign, 115
Conditional statement, 6
    antecedent, 30
    consequent, 30
    translating into categorical form, 82ff.
    translating into truth functional form, 115, 125–129
    truth function for, 133–134
    truth functional, 114–115
    variations on, 125ff.
    (*see also* Modus ponens; Modus tollens)
Conjunct, (*see* conjunction)
Conjunction,
    truth function for, 132, 134
    truth functional, 112–113, 123
    valid rule of inference, 168, 178
    variations on, 123–24
Conjunction sign, 115
Conjunctive statement, (*see* conjunction)
Consequent, 31, 114
Constructive dilemma, 169, 178
Contingent statement, 151, 154
Contradiction, (*see* self-contradiction; contradictory statements)

Generalization, (*see* inductive gener-
    alization; hasty generalization)
Good argument, 18–21, 23, 33, 186,
    280–281
    defined, 19
    (*see also* deductive validity; induc-
        tive strength; premise)
Grouping and the scope of operators,
    118–121

Hasty generalization, fallacy of, 193,
    252–253, 266
Horseshoe, 115, 117
Hypothetical syllogism, 167, 178

I-form statement, 42
    Venn diagram for, 47
"If," 125, 128
"If and only if," 82–83, 112, 115
    categorical translation, 82–83
    truth functional translation,
        114–115, 128
    (*see also* biconditional)
"If . . . then," 82, 112, 115, 128
    categorical translation, 82–83
    truth functional translation,
        125–129
    (*see also* conditional; "only"; "only
        if"; "The only")
"Implies," 128
Inclusive "or," (*see* disjunction)
Inconsistency, fallacy of, 263–265,
    267
Independent support, 15
Indirect truth table, 147–150
Induction, (*see* inductive strength)
Inductive argument, (*see* inductive
    strength)
Inductive generalization, 189–195
    criteria of inductive strength,
        191–194
    features of, 190
    (*see also* population; sample; statis-
        tical generalization; target
        characteristic)
Inductive logic, 185ff.
Inductive strength, 19–21, 186–189,
    234, 280–281
    criteria, summarized, 234
    deductive validity and, 19–21, 187,
        280–281
    defined, 187
    good argument and, 19–21, 186,
        280–281

probability, mathematically de-
    scribed, 187–188
(*see also* argument from analogy;
    causal conclusion; inductive
    generalization)
Inference,
    deductively valid, (*see* deductive
        validity)
    defined, 8
    inductively strong, (*see* inductive
        strength)
    on the modern square, 52–54
    on the traditional square, 51–52,
        55–59
    valid rules of, (*see* equivalences;
        rule of inference)
    with the operations, 62–68, 70–72
Inferred feature, in argument from
    analogy, 222
Informal fallacy, 237
    summarized, 266–267
    (*see also* specific fallacies)
Invalid deductive argument, (*see* de-
    ductive validity)
Invalid logical form, 28–32
    (*see also* fallacy of affirming the
        consequent; fallacy of denying
        the antecedent; fallacy of un-
        distributed middle)
Invalidity, (*see* deductive validity)

Joint support, 14

Logic,
    defined, 1
    inductive, (*see* inductive logic)
    psychology and, 2
    system of, (*see* logical systems)
    (*see also* categorical; truth
        functional)
Logical equivalence, 61, 159
    (*see also* equivalence)
Logical form, 28
    (*see also* invalid logical form; valid
        logical form)
Logical operator, 112ff.
    symbols for, 115
    truth functions for, (*see* specific
        operators)
Logical system,
    practical use of, 37
    purpose of, 38

"Many," 80–81
Material equivalence, 176–177